Everyman, I will go with thee,
and be thy guide

THE EVERYMAN
LIBRARY

*The Everyman Library was founded by J. M. Dent
in 1906. He chose the name Everyman because he wanted
to make available the best books ever written in every field
to the greatest number of people at the cheapest possible
price. He began with Boswell's 'Life of Johnson';
his one thousandth title was Aristotle's 'Metaphysics',
by which time sales exceeded forty million.*

*Today Everyman paperbacks remain true to
J. M. Dent's aims and high standards, with a wide range
of titles at affordable prices in editions which address
the needs of today's readers. Each new text is reset to give
a clear, elegant page and to incorporate the latest thinking
and scholarship. Each book carries the pilgrim logo,
the character in 'Everyman', a medieval morality play,
a proud link between Everyman
past and present.*

Jean-Jacques Rousseau

THE SOCIAL CONTRACT
AND DISCOURSES

Translated and introduced by
G. D. H. COLE

Revised and augmented by
J. H. BRUMFITT AND JOHN C. HALL
University of St Andrews

Updated by
P. D. JIMACK
University of Stirling

EVERYMAN
J. M. DENT · LONDON
CHARLES E. TUTTLE
VERMONT

Introduction and revisions © David Campbell Publishers, 1973

Biographical note, chronology and bibliography
© J.M. Dent, 1993

First published in Everyman 1913
New edition 1973
Reprinted 1975, 1977, 1979, 1982, 1983
Reset 1986
Reprinted 1988, 1990, 1992
This Edition 1993
Reprinted 1995, 1996 (twice), 1997, 1998, 1999 (twice)

J.M. Dent
Orion Publishing Group,
Orion House, 5 Upper St Martin's Lane,
London WC2H 9EA
and
Charles E. Tuttle Co. Inc.
28 South Main Street,
Rutland, Vermont
05701, USA

Printed in Great Britain by
The Guernsey Press Co. Ltd, Guernsey, C.I.

British Library Cataloguing-in-Publication Data is available
upon request.

ISBN 0 460 87357 1

CONTENTS

Contents

Book IV
Which treats further of political laws and sets forth the means of strengthening the constitution of the State.

NOTE ON THE AUTHOR AND EDITORS

JEAN-JACQUES ROUSSEAU was born in Geneva on 28 June 1712, the son of a watchmaker. He fled his native city after a stormy childhood, finding refuge with Madame de Warens, with whom he lived for ten years. He came to Paris in 1742 and first achieved fame with the *Discourse on the Arts and the Sciences* of 1750. His hostility to contemporary society, coupled with physical and mental illness, led to his increasing withdrawal from 'the world', and his solitude was augmented by the persecution which followed his publication of *Émile* in 1762. After a period of wandering, in Switzerland, England and France, he died 2 July 1778.

G. D. H. COLE (1889–1959) was successively Fellow of University College and Nuffield College, Oxford, and Chichele Professor of Social and Political Theory at Oxford (1944–57). He was in his youth a pioneer of socialist thought in England and was the author of many books on social history and political theory.

J. H. BRUMFITT is Professor of French in the University of Saint Andrews. He was educated at Bradford Grammar School and Queen's College, Oxford. He is the author of *The French Enlightenment* (1972) and of *Voltaire Historian* (1958) and editor and translator of a number of works by Voltaire and others.

J. C. HALL is Senior Lecturer in Moral Philosophy in the University of Saint Andrews. He was educated at Kingswood School and Balliol College, Oxford. He is the author of *Rousseau: an Introduction to his Political Philosophy* (1973) and of articles on Plato, Aristotle and moral philosophy.

P. D. JIMACK is Professor of French at the University of Stirling.

CHRONOLOGY OF ROUSSEAU'S LIFE

Year	Age	Life
1712		Born Geneva, 28 June. Mother dies in childbirth
1718–19	6–7	Reads novels left by mother, then Plutarch
1725	13	Apprenticed to engraver for five years
1728	16	Runs away from Geneva, mets Mme de Warens, converts to Catholicism in Turin. Travels in Italy, meets M. Gaime, one of two models for Vicaire Savoyard in *Emile*
1729	17	Returns to Annecy to stay with Mme de Warens. Few weeks in seminary training for priesthood. meets M. Gâtier, second model for Vicaire Savoyard
1729–30	17–18	Six months at Annecy Cathedral choir school
1732	20	Music teacher in Chambéry
1736	24	Idyllic stay with Mme de Warens at Les Charmettes, near Chambéry. Period of intensive self-education
1740	28	Unsuccessful experience as tutor to two young sons of M. de Mably in Lyon

CHRONOLOGY OF HIS TIMES

Year	Cultural context	Historical Events
1715		Death of Louis XIV Regency in France (1715–23)
1717	Watteau, *L'Embarquement pour Cythère*	
1719	Defoe, *Robinson Crusoe*	
1720		French financial crash resulting from collapse of John Law's attempt to reform finances
1721	Montesquieu, *Lettres persanes* Bach, *Brandenburg Concertos*	'South Sea Bubble' crash
1722–42		Walpole in power in England
1723		Louis XV assumes full powers on his majority
1726	Swift, *Gulliver's Travels*	Fleury in power in France (1726–43)
1728	Gay, *The Beggars' Opera*	George II comes to throne
1729	Bach, *St Matthew Passion*	Treaty of Seville (between England and Spain)
1730	Marivaux, *Le Jeu de l'amour et du hasard*	
1731	Prévost, *Manon Lescaut*	
1733	Pope, *Essay on Man* (1733–4) Hogarth, *The Rake's Progress* (1733–5)	War of Polish Succession (1733–5)
1735–36	Marivaux, *Le Paysan parvenu*	
1738		3rd Treaty of Vienna
1739		England declares war on Spain (War of Jenkins's Ear)
1740–41	Richardson, *Pamela*	Frederick II (the Great) comes to throne of Prussia on death of father
1741–48		War of Austrian Succession

Year	Age	Life
1742	30	Arrives in Paris, presents Project on new system of musical notation to Académie des Sciences
1743–44	31–2	Secretary to French Ambassador in Venice
1745	33	Back in Paris, meets Thérèse Levasseur, with whom he will cohabit for the rest of his life. Finishes his opera *Les Muses Galantes*
1746	34	Birth of first of his 5 children, all placed in orphanage (at his insistence)
1749	37	Undertakes to write articles on music for *Encyclopédie*. On way to visit Diderot in prison at Vincennes, reads announcement of essay competition by Académie de Dijon, on question whether development of sciences and arts has been morally beneficial. Claims he experienced sudden inspiration on which all philosophical works were to be based
1750	38	*Discours sur les sciences et les arts* wins first prize and makes him famous
1752	40	Opera *Le Devin du village* performed before Louis XV
1753	41	*Lettre sur la Musique française*
1754	42	Visit to Geneva, reconverts to Calvinism, regaining Genevan citizenship
1755	43	*Discours sur l'inégalité*, and article 'Economie politique' in *Encyclopédie*
1756	44	Goes to live at l'Hermitage, house on estate of Mme d'Epinay

Year	Artistic Events	Historical Events
1742	Voltaire, *Mahomet* Boucher, *Diane sortant du bain* Handel, *The Messiah* Young, *Night Thoughts* (1742–5)	
1745		The Young Pretender ('Bonnie Prince Charlie') invades England
1746	Diderot, *Pensées philosophiques*	Jacobites crushed at Culloden
1747–8	Richardson, *Clarissa*	
1748	Montesquieu: *De l'Esprit des lois* Hume, *Enquiry concerning Human Understanding*	Treaty of Aix-la-Chapelle
1749	Diderot, *Letter sur les Aveugles*, leading to his imprisonment Fielding, *Tom Jones* Buffon, *Histoire naturelle* (1749–89)	Flare-up of religious persecution in France against Jansenists
1750	Johnson starts *The Rambler*	
1751	Volume I of *Encyclopédie*, edited by Diderot and d'Alembert Gray, *Elegy in a Country Churchyard*	
1752	Hume, *Political Discourses*	
1753	Tiepolo completed frescoes for palace of Prince-Bishop of Würzburg	
1754	Diderot, *Pensées sur l'interprétation de la nature* Condillac, *Traité des sensations* Hume, *History of Great-Britain* (1754–62)	
1755	Johnson, *Dictionary*	Lisbon earthquake
1756	Birth of Mozart	Seven Years War (1756–63)

Year	Age	Life
1757	45	Falls in love with Mme d'Houdetot. Beginning of quarrels with Diderot and Encyclopedists. Moves to Montmorency at invitation of Maréchal de Luxembourg
1758	46	*Lettre sur les Spectacles*, refuting d'Alembert's article 'Genève' in *Encyclopédie*
1761	49	*La nouvelle Héloïse*, immense success
1762	50	*Du Contrat Social* (April) and *Emile* (May). Both condemned, first in Paris, then in Geneva. Flees to Switzerland to escape arrest, ending up in Môtiers
1763	51	*Lettre à Christophe de Beaumont,* defending *Emile*
1764	52	*Lettres écrites de la Montagne*
1765	53	*Projet de Constitution pour la Corse*. Rousseau's house in Môtiers stoned
1766	54	Goes to England (Chiswick, then Wootton) with Hume, followed by Thérèse in company of Boswell. Quarrels with Hume.
1767	55	Returns to France under name of Renou, reported by police spy. *Dictionnaire de Musique*

Year	Artistic Events	Historical Events
1757		Damiens executed for attempted assassination of Louis XV. In India, Clive wins battle of Plassey, leading to conquest of Bengal. Pitt Prime Minister (1757–61)
1758	Helvétius, *De l'Esprit,* causing scandal leading to banning of *Encyclopédie* (1759)	British capture from French Louisburg and Fort Duquesne, renamed Pittsburg Choiseul in power in France (in various posts) (1758–70)
1759	Volaire, *Candide* Johnson, *Rasselas* Sterne, *Tristram Shandy* (1759–67) Diderot, *Salons,* accounts of exhibitions at Paris Salon (1759–81)	British capture Quebec
1760		Death of George II, succeeded by George III. British capture Montreal
1761	Greuze, *L'Accordée de Village* Diderot, *Le Neveu de Rameau* (1761–76)	Execution of Jean Calas, Toulouse Protestant accused without evidence of murdering his son
1762	Gluck, *Orfeo ed Euridice* Macpherson ('Ossian'), *Fingal*	Catherine II comes to throne. Closure of Jesuit colleges in France
1763	Voltaire, *Traité sur la tolérance,* responding to Calas affair Mozart performed in Paris (1763–4)	Treaty of Paris, giving eastern half of N. America to British
1764	Voltaire, *Dictionnaire philosophique*	Jesuits expelled from France. Bougainville founded French colony in Falkland Islands
1765		East India Company acquires Bengal. British establish fort in Falklands
1766	Publication by Diderot of remaining volumes of *Encyclopédie* Lessing, *Laokoon* Ramsay painted portraits of Hume and Rousseau	French cede Falklands possession to Spain
1767	Haydn, *Stabat Mater*	British Government imposes import duties in American colonies on tea, glass, etc.

Year	Artistic Events	Historical Events
1769–70		Financial crisis in France
1770	D'Holbach, *Système de la Nature* Gainsborough, *The Blue Boy* Raynal (and others), *Histoire des Deux Indes*, major attack on colonialism (1770–80)	American import duties, except tea, repealed. Spain attempts to drive British from Falklands. Maupeou, French Chancellor, curtails power of *Parlements*, causing storm of protest (1770–1)
1771–8	Diderot wrote *Jacques le fataliste*	
1773		Boston Tea Party
1774	Goethe, *The Sorrows of Young Werther*	Death of Louis XV, succeeded by Louis XVI. Massachusetts in revolt. Turgot attempts to reform French finances (1774–6)
1775	Beaumarchais, *Le Barbier de Séville*	
1776	A. Smith, *The Wealth of Nations*	American Declaration of Independence
1778	Death of Voltaire. Mozart in Paris, composes *Paris Symphony*	

INTRODUCTION

When a great writer comes to be known by posterity chiefly as the author of a single book, and this book expresses only one aspect of his thought, misunderstanding of his attitude is very likely indeed to arise. I am not suggesting that this is exactly Rousseau's case; for in addition to *The Social Contract* both the *Confessions* and *Émile* are still widely read, though largely by different readers. It is mainly in relation to political ideas that Rousseau, on the strength of what he says in *The Social Contract*, has been interpreted in a great many different ways, usually without much attempt to refer to his other political writings in the hope of elucidating his meaning. This is largely because he himself, before putting *The Social Contract* into final shape, abandoned his intention of writing a much more comprehensive work on *Political Institutions*, for which he had made extensive preliminary studies. In deciding to abandon this larger book, explicitly on the ground that it was 'beyond his powers' to finish it to his own satisfaction, Rousseau actually destroyed a large part of the draft he had made, leaving little more than the manuscript of that part which he had made up his mind to turn into *The Social Contract* by thorough revision. In addition, however, to the preserved part of his original draft, he kept by him a considerable number of preliminary studies for the projected larger work – some of them mere notes, but several worked up into long essays on particular subjects. These studies remained unpublished until long after his death – much of them until the present century; and the traditional interpretations of his political thought were developed without knowledge of them and, for the most part, without much attempt to relate *The Social Contract* to what he said in his other published writings. Thus it came about that whereas a great deal continued to be written about 'the great romantic' as revealed in the

Confessions and in his correspondence, and also about the great advocate of naturalistic education as revealed in *Émile*, there grew up an interpretation of Rousseau the political thinker, derived mainly from *The Social Contract*, that seemed to have little in common with what was written about him in these other aspects. *The Social Contract*, studied by itself, can be interpreted – and has been – in a number of different ways; but none of them appears to bear any clear relationship to either Romanticism or Naturalism. The social bond which it sets out explicitly to justify, and of which it attempts to provide a rational account, is represented not as 'natural' but as a work of human artifice; and the arguments used in justifying it have no element of the romantic. There is nothing at all in *The Social Contract* about the 'noble savage'; and though there is something about the corrupting influence of luxury and about the virtue of a simple way of living, the life of the citizen in a well-founded State seems to be based not on conformity with nature but on the acceptance of an essentially artificial form of community inspired by the predominance of the General Will.

No doubt Rousseau's interpreters, in the field of political thought, have taken some account of the political writings which he published before *The Social Contract* – of the two academic *Discourses* on the *Arts and Sciences* and on the *Origin of Inequality*, and of the article on *Political Economy* which appeared in the *Great Encyclopaedia* in 1755. But the tendency has been to regard the *Discourses* as early efforts which had been outgrown before *The Social Contract* took its final form and to treat the article as a relatively minor writing, though the account given in it of the 'general will' differs substantially from the treatment of that conception in *The Social Contract*. Rousseau has been described as advancing over years from a rhetorical and not very serious attack on 'civilization' to a quite opposite conclusion in which he justified the social bond; and *The Social Contract* has been regarded as the complete exposition of an amended doctrine – which, on his own showing, it certainly was not. Among his later writings his works on *The Government of Poland* and his unfinished plan for *The Constitution of Corsica* are both specialized and contribute only to a limited extent to the understanding of his general doctrine. There is much of high importance in his *Letters Written from the Mount* and in his *Dialogues*; but it is most of all to the earlier drafts of his projected work on *Political Institutions* and to the essays related to it that we must turn in order to fit *The Social Contract* into its appropriate place in the structure of Rousseau's political thought and, thus assisted, to relate it to the general body of his philosophical and social ideas.

Rousseau's two *Discourses*, both of which are included in the present volume, appeared respectively in 1750 and 1755, and were followed by the article on *Political Economy* in 1758 and by *The Social Contract* in 1762 – the same year as *Émile*. The *Letters Written from the Mount* appeared in 1764, and the *Considerations on the Government of Poland* four years after the author's death, in 1782. The other works important for the study of Rousseau's political ideas, with the exception of one section of his summary and commentary on certain writings of the Abbé de Saint-Pierre, were also published posthumously. They include *The Constitution of Corsica*, the *Dialogues: or, Rousseau Judge of Jean Jacques*, and the various essays and fragments connected with his plan for a general work on *Political Institutions*. Most of the relevant material is included in C. E. Vaughan's important collection of *The Political Writings of Jean Jacques Rousseau* (2 volumes, 1915) and much of it in the standard comparative edition of *Du Contrat Social*, edited by E. Dreyfus-Brisac in 1896. This latter gives the full text of the early version of *The Social Contract* from the Geneva manuscript.

Rousseau first conceived the notion of writing a major work on *Political Institutions* while he was living in Venice as secretary to the French ambassador in 1743–4. He soon put this task aside, but returned to it after being awarded the prize by the Academy of Dijon for his first *Discourse*. Even before this, in 1749, he had begun writing an essay on the *Origin of Languages*, intended in the first instance mainly as a contribution to the history of music, but before long developed into a general discussion of the relations between language and society, posing the conundrum 'Which came first?' It seemed impossible to believe that society could have come into being among men who had still no means of verbal communication; but, as against this, it was no less difficult to believe that language could have been developed except among men already living in a social state. From this unanswered problem Rousseau was led on to consider others – notably the question whether society should or should not be regarded as 'natural' to man – as arising out of an innate instinct of sociability – which was the view of many of his contemporaries. Rousseau argued this issue out with himself on paper, and ended by rejecting the notion of an innate 'social sense', and therewith that of a natural 'general society of mankind', as underlying the separate existences of particular societies and giving rise to an inclusive social obligation binding all men together in terms of a common natural morality. He would not accept this conception of a 'social sense' because he saw it as ambivalent – as accounting, if it existed at all, not only for the legitimate forms of society in which he was primarily interested, but also equally for all the corrupt forms which he saw around him. He was seeking for an explanation not of the mere existence of societies, for good or ill, but of the nature of the good society – that is, of a society based on a social bond which would leave men as free as they were in a state of nature. At this stage of his thought he planned to begin his contemplated great work with a refutation of the notion of a 'general society of mankind', leading up to an account of the origin of true society in a 'social contract' into which men entered directly from the 'state of nature'.

This led him to attempt to describe the supposed 'state of nature', as contrasted with the social state. In this connection he delivered a frontal attack on Hobbes's conception of the 'state of nature' as a war of all against all, waged by a number of ferocious egoists each acting against his fellow-men in pursuance of his personal appetite for possession and power. This Hobbesian inferno, he said, bore no sort of resemblance to the behaviour to be expected of primitive men in the absence of organized society. He wrote an essay on *War* in which he set out to show that war was essentially a product of society, and that nothing like it could arise among men who had not become organized into actual societies. In place of Hobbes's account he put forward his own, based on an attempt to strip away from men as they actually were every characteristic attributable to their social intercourse in organized groups. Indeed, he went even further, back to a world of 'natural men' who roamed the world alone and had at most only the most occasional and fortuitous meetings and connections. Men in this primitive condition, he argued, far from being natural enemies, could have had hardly anything to quarrel about. Far from being driven into antagonism by rampant desires, they would be moved only by the naturally limited appetites for a sufficiency of food, clothing and shelter, and for sexual satisfactions which would not go beyond the lukewarmness of natural bodily impulses. They would not form persisting families – much less classes. Children would leave and forget their mothers as soon as they were able to look after themselves: there would be no marriages or sustained household connections: men would not wish to treat their wives as their property – for no such conception as that of property would exist – nor would there be any love between the sexes transcending or outlasting the mere performance of the sexual act. Primitive, non-social man would be neither an egoist nor an altruist in any moral sense: he would be pre-moral. But he would have in him already, as essential parts of his nature, the qualities which under the influence of society would subsequently take on a moral character. In particular he would be moved by two innate and complementary sentiments, to which Rousseau gave the names of *amour de soi* and *pitié*. His *amour de soi* would lead him to seek the gratification of his narrowly limited desires, which would include no forethought for the future, at any rate beyond the shortest range; and at the same time his *pitié*, or compassion, would make it painful to him to witness the suffering of any fellow-being he could recognize as resembling himself. He would therefore avoid causing pain to other men beyond what was indispensable for satisfying his own desires; and the limited range and strength of these desires would seldom give rise to conflict and never to angry passions or to hatred lasting beyond the immediate occasion.

Rousseau thus presented a picture of a 'state of nature' which, if not idyllic, was wholly free from the ferocious misery depicted by Hobbes, and furnished in itself no sufficient reason why men should be ready in order to escape from it to give up their natural liberty and accept the absolute rule of a Sovereign. He could not, on this foundation, account for the origin of societies in simply utilitarian terms. Society could be accounted for, and justified, only as a means of enabling men to advance to a higher level of achievement than could be arrived at in its absence. It had to be regarded as a necessary means to the development of the moral potentialities of man's original nature.

This is the foundation of Rousseau's conception of the Social Contract, which he represents as an agreement among men previously in a 'state of nature' to constitute a 'corporate and collective person' through which they endow themselves with a constitution or code of laws designed to regulate both their mutual relations and their relations with other men. This freely adopted Contract thereupon becomes the standard by which they set out to govern their ways of living; and as they have made it among themselves, without handing over their natural liberty to any person other than themselves as a collectivity, they can, Rousseau argues, fairly be said 'to remain as free as before' and to have gained the service of a social instrument by use of which they can give themselves, collectively and severally, a new moral stature and can live together, not indeed 'naturally' – for the social bond is essentially artificial – but in the only way consistent with the higher development of their natural faculties and sentiments.

Much of the argument I have just outlined was set out by Rousseau in his second *Discourse*, dealing with *The Origin of Inequality*, and in the excursus which he appended to it in its published form. A good deal more was set down in his various essays and in the drafts which he made in preparation for his work on *Political Institutions*. But in proportion as he became clear in his own mind about the meaning of the Social Contract, he grew conscious of the difficulty of his original undertaking, in which he would have needed to deal not only with the nature of the social bond in any particular society, but also with the problems of the relations between one society and another, and with the whole question of moral obligations as arising for mankind as a whole and for each individual in matters affecting others than his fellow-citizens and his own State. To many of these wider problems he found himself quite unable to arrive at satisfactory answers; and he solved his personal difficulty by giving up his greater project and extracting from what he had written the part dealing with the narrower question of citizenship in a single society. This question, and this only, is discussed in the final version of *The Social Contract*.

Long before this, Rousseau had had to ask himself the question whether in his account of the 'origin' of society and of the Social Contract he was setting out to give an account of what had actually occurred as a matter of historical fact. He wrote at a time when social theorists were well accustomed to engage in the presentation of 'imaginary history' – that is, to assert what must have happened in the past to account for the situations in which men actually found themselves. He was well aware that there existed no factual evidence or testimony to show how men had actually passed from the supposed primitive 'state of nature' – which was itself conjectural –to the 'social state'; and he did not pretend, either to himself or to his readers, that he was in a position to give a factual account of the past on a basis of logical necessity. The account he did give he did not profess to regard as historically accurate. There were, he said, many possible ways and stages by which actual societies could have developed, and he did not profess to know what these had factually been. What concerned him was not the factual history, but the essential character of the development from man's primitive condition to the life of organized societies; and this, he thought, could be described accurately enough to provide a foundation for his conception of the necessary elements of social obligation.

Rousseau was not, of course, in any sense the inventor of the doctrine of the Social Contract. On the contrary he was the last in time of its great proponents; and what he did was to transform it and, in doing so, to give to subsequent political theory a new basis which transcended its limits and thus contributed to its disuse.

The Social Contract theory is as old as the sophists of Greece (see Plato, *Republic*, Book II, and the *Gorgias*), and as elusive. It has been adapted to the most opposite points of view, and used, in different forms, on both sides of every question to which it could conceivably be applied. It is frequent in medieval writers, a commonplace with the theorists of the Renaissance, and in the eighteenth century already nearing its fall before a wider conception. It would be a long, as well as a thankless, task to trace its history over again: it can still best be followed in D. G. Ritchie's admirable essay on it in *Darwin and Hegel and Other Studies*. For us, it is important only to regard it in its most general aspect, before studying the special use made of it by Rousseau. Obviously, in one form or another, it is a theory very easily arrived at. Wherever any form of government apart from the merest tyranny exists, reflection on the basis of the State cannot but lead to the notion that, in one sense or another, it is based on the consent, tacit or expressed, past or present, of its members. In this alone, the greater part of the Social Contract theory is already latent. Add the desire to find actual justification for a theory in facts, and, especially in an age possessed only of the haziest historical sense, this doctrine of consent will inevitably be given a historical setting. If, in addition, there is a tendency to regard society as something 'unnatural' to humanity, the tendency will become irresistible. By writers of almost all schools, the State will be represented as having arisen, in some remote age, out of a compact or, in more legal phrase, contract between two or more parties. The only theorists who will be able to resist this notion are those who either maintain the divine right of kings, and hold that all existing governments have been imposed on the people by the direct interposition of God, or those who are content to explain society entirely in terms of force – the 'right' of the strongest. All thinkers who are not prepared to maintain one or other of these notions will tend to be partisans of some sort of Social Contract theory.

It is, therefore, not surprising that we find among advocates of this theory writers of the most opposite points of view. Barely stated, it is a mere formula which can be filled in with any content from absolutism to pure republicanism. In the hands of some of its supporters, it turns out to be a weapon that cuts both ways. We shall be better able to judge of its usefulness when we have seen its chief varieties at work.

All Social Contract theories that are at all clearly defined fall under one or other of two heads. They represent society as based on an original contract, either between the people and the government, or between all the individuals composing the State. Historically, Social Contract theories tended to pass from the first to the second of these forms.

The doctrine that society is founded on a contract between the people and the government is of medieval origin. It was often supported by references to the Old Testament, which contains a similar view in an embryonic form. It is found in most of the great political writers of the sixteenth century; in Buchanan, and in James I: it persists into the seventeenth in the works of Grotius and Pufendorf. Grotius is sometimes held to have stated the theory so as to admit both forms of contract; but it is clear that he was thinking only of the first form as admitting democratic as well as monarchical government. We find it put very clearly by the Convention Parliament of 1688, which accuses James II of 'endeavouring to subvert the constitution of the kingdom by breaking the original contract between king and people'. While Hobbes, on the side of the royalists, was maintaining the contract theory in its second form, the Parliamentarian Algernon Sidney adhered to the idea of a contract between the people and the government.

In this form, the theory clearly admits of opposite interpretations. It may be held that the people, having given itself up once for all to its rulers, has nothing more to ask of them, and is bound to submit to any usage they may choose to inflict. This, however, is not the implication most usually drawn from it. The theory, in this form, originated with theologians who were also lawyers. Their view of a contract implied mutual obligations; they regarded the ruler as bound, by its terms, to govern constitutionally. The old idea that a king must not violate the sacred customs of the realm passes easily into the doctrine that he must not violate the terms of the original contract between himself and his people. Just as, in the days of the Norman kings, every appeal on the part of the people for more liberties was couched in the form of a demand that the customs of the 'good old times' of Edward the Confessor should be respected, so in the seventeenth century every act of popular assertion or resistance was stated as an appeal to the king not to violate the contract. The demand was a good popular cry, and it seemed to have the theorists behind it. Rousseau gives his refutation of this view, which he had, in the *Discourse on Inequality*, maintained in passing, in the sixteenth chapter of the third book of the *Social Contract*. (See also Book I, chap. 4, *init.*) His attack is really concerned also with the theory of Hobbes, which in some respects resembles, as we shall see, this first view; but, in form at least, it is directed against the form of contract theory which makes the contract one between the government and the people. We shall need to examine it more closely when the second view has been considered.

This second view, which may be called the <u>Social Contract theory</u> proper, <u>regards society as originating in, or based on, an agreement</u> <u>between the individuals composing it</u>. It seems to be found first, rather vaguely, in Richard Hooker's *Ecclesiastical Polity*, from which Locke largely borrowed: and it reappears, in varying forms, in Milton's *Tenure of Kings and Magistrates*, in Hobbes's *Leviathan*, and in Locke's *Treatises on Civil Government*. The best-known instance of its actual use is by the Pilgrim Fathers on the *Mayflower* in 1620, in whose declaration occurs the phrase: 'We do solemnly and mutually, in the presence of God and of one another, covenant and combine ourselves together into a civil body politic.' The natural implication of this view would seem to be the corollary of complete popular Sovereignty which Rousseau draws. But before Rousseau's time it had been used to support views as diverse as those which rested on the first form. We saw that, in Grotius's great work, *De Jure Belli et Pacis*, it was already possible to doubt which of the two theories was being advocated. The first theory was, historically, for the most part, a means of popular protest against royal aggression. As soon as the possibility of popular government was taken into account, the act of contract between people and government became in effect merely a contract between the individuals composing the society, and readily passed over into the second form.

The second theory, in its ordinary form, expresses only the view that the people is everywhere Sovereign, i.e. the final repository of authority, and that, in the phrase of Milton's treatise, 'the power of kings and magistrates is only derivative'. Before, however, this view had been worked up into a philosophical theory, it had already been used by Hobbes to support precisely opposite principles. Hobbes agreed that the original contract was one between all the individuals composing the State, and that the government was no party to it; but he regarded the people as agreeing, not simply to form a State, but in one and the same act to invest a certain person or certain persons with the government of it. He agreed that the people was the final source of all authority, but regarded the people as alienating its Sovereignty by the contract itself and as delegating its powers, wholly and for ever, to the government which its members agreed to set up. As soon, therefore, as the State is established, the government becomes for Hobbes the Sovereign; there is no further question of popular Sovereignty but only of passive obedience: the people is bound, by the contract, to obey its ruler, no matter whether he govern well or ill. It has alienated all its rights to the Sovereign, who is, therefore, absolute master. Hobbes, living in a time of civil wars, regarded the worst government as preferable to anarchy, and was therefore at pains to find arguments in support of any form of absolutism. It is easy to pick holes in his system, and to see into what difficulties a conscientious Hobbist might be led by a revolution. For as soon as the revolutionaries got the upper hand he would have to sacrifice one of his principles: he would have to side against either the actual or the legitimate Sovereign. On this issue, Hobbes himself felt no doubt. According to him the Soverign, by failing to govern, forfeited his Sovereignty to his *de facto* successor without any need

for a further appeal to the verdict of the people. It is easy also to see
that alienation of liberty, even if it be possible for an individual –
which Rousseau denies – cannot bind his posterity. But, with all its
faults, the view of Hobbes was on the whole ruthlessly logical; and to
it Rousseau owed a great deal.

The special shape given to the second type of Social Contract
theory by Hobbes looks, at first sight, rather like a combination, into
a single act, of both the contracts. This, however, is not the view
Hobbes took of it. The theory of a contract between government and
people had, as we have seen, been used mainly as a support for
popular liberties, a means of assertion against the government.
Hobbes, whose whole aim was to make his government Sovereign,
could do this only by leaving the government outside the contract;
for he thus avoided the necessity of submitting it to any obligation
whatsoever and left it absolute and irresponsible. He secured, in fact,
not merely a State possessed of unbounded rights against the
individual, but a determinate authority with the 'right' to enforce
these rights. His theory was not merely Statism (*étatisme*): it was
pure despotism.

It is clear that, if such a theory is to be upheld, it can stand only by
the view, which Hobbes shared with Grotius, that a man can alienate
not only his own liberty, but also that of his descendants, and that,
consequently, a people as a whole can do the same. This is the point
at which both Locke and Rousseau attacked Hobbes's theory.
Locke, whose aim was largely to justify the English Revolution of
1688, made government depend, not merely at its institution, but
always, on the consent of the governed, and regarded all rulers as
liable to be displaced if they governed tyrannically. Locke omitted,
however, to provide any machinery short of revolution for the
expression of popular opinion, and on the whole seemed to regard
the consent of the people as something essentially tacit and assumed.
He regarded every man who lived as a member of a society as
consenting by implication to its mode of government, until he
actually rebelled against it or withdrew from its territory by
emigrating. Locke regarded the State as existing mainly to protect

life and property, and was, in all his assertions of popular rights, so cautious as to reduce them to little more than a final right of rebellion against flagrant misgovernment. Not until we come to Rousseau is the second form of the contract theory developed into a thorough-going assertion of democratic rights.

Rousseau saw clearly the necessity, if popular consent to government were to be more than nominal, of giving it some effective means of continuous expression. For Locke's theory of tacit consent, Rousseau substituted that of an active agreement, periodically renewed. He looked back with admiration to the city-states of ancient Greece and, in his own day, reserved his admiration for the Swiss free cities, such as Berne and, above all, Geneva, his native place. Seeing in the Europe of his day no instance in which representative government was working at all democratically, he was unable to conceive that means might be found of giving effect to this active agreement of the people in a large nation-state; accordingly he concluded that real self-government was impossible except for a city or for a very small State such as Corsica, in which each citizen would be able to participate directly in the conduct of affairs. He would have liked, if he had deemed it practicable, to break up the nation-states of Europe, and to create instead federative leagues of independent city-states.

It matters, however, comparatively little for the appreciation of Rousseau's political theory in general that he never set out to make himself a theorist of the large modern State. The State, if it is to be compatible with human freedom, must have in essentials everywhere the same fundamental kind of Sovereignty. By taking the rightly based Sovereign State at its simplest, he was able, far better than his predecessors, to bring out the real character of the 'social tie' – an alternative phrase which he often used for the Social Contract. His doctrine of the underlying principle of political obligation is that of real popular Sovereignty which is common to the great humanist thinkers from his time. This essential quality of his doctrine has been obscured only because some of his critics have failed to put the Social Contract theory in its proper place in his system.

This theory was, we have seen, a commonplace. The amount of historical authenticity assigned to the contract which was almost universally presupposed varied enormously. Generally, the weaker a writer's rational basis, the more he appealed to history – and invented it. It was, therefore, almost inevitable that Rousseau should cast his theory into the contractual form. There were, indeed, writers of his time who laughed at the contract, but they were not writers who constructed a general system of political philosophy. From Cromwell to Montesquieu and Bentham, it was the practically minded man, impatient of unactual hypotheses, who refused to accept the idea of contract. The theories were as preponderantly in its favour as the theorists of the age of Darwin were in favour of some form of 'organic' theory. But we, criticizing them in the light of later events, are in a better position for estimating the position the Social Contract really took in their political systems. We see that Locke's doctrine of tacit consent made popular control so unreal that he was forced, if the State was to have the initial basis, to make his contract historical and actual, binding posterity for all time, and that he was also led to admit a quasi-contract between people and government, as a second vindication of popular liberties. Rousseau, on the other hand, based no vital argument on the historical nature of the contract, in which, indeed, he clearly did not believe. 'How,' he asked, 'did this change [from 'nature' to 'society'] come about?' And he answered that he did not know. Moreover, his aim was to find 'a sure and legitimate rule of administration, taking men as they are and laws as they might be'; that is to say, his Social Contract is something which will be found at work in every legitimate society but will be in abeyance in all forms of despotism. He clearly meant by it no more and no less than the fundamental principle of political association, the basis of the unity which enables men, associated in a State, to realize political liberty by giving up lawlessness and licence. The presentation of this doctrine in the quasi-historical form of the Social Contract theory was due to the accident of the time and place in which Rousseau wrote. At the same time, the importance of the conception is best to be seen in the hard death it dies. Though no one, for a hundred years or so, has thought of regarding it as historical, it has been so difficult to find any other phrase explaining as well or better the basis of political union that, to this day, the phraseology of the contract theory largely persists. A conception so vital cannot have been barren.

I have treated Rousseau, so far, as an exponent of the Social Contract doctrine in its second form – that of a contract between all the citizens. Sometimes, however, he speaks of it in a third sense – that of a contract between all the citizens individually of the one part and these same citizens collectively of the other part – i.e. of a contract between the citizens and the State. In this form of the doctrine the sovereign people in one capacity contracts with itself in another capacity, and this constitutes a valid contract because the State which the individuals set up is, or becomes, a distinct 'corporate person' capable of entering into a valid agreement with its members as moral persons distinct from itself. This, to be sure, involves a superficial illogicality, in that the State exists as a corporate person only by virtue of the Contract and can therefore hardly be a party to its making. But Rousseau might have answered that the individuals too become 'corporate persons' only when they pass from the 'State of nature' into the 'social state'. Rousseau's point is, of course, that the individuals, in entering into the Contract, are not surrendering their liberty one to another but transferring it to a new moral person in whose being they share, so that their liberty is not being given up by them but only transferred.

The Social Contract is indeed, in Rousseau's own thought, only one of the three different ways in which the basis of political union is stated, according to the preoccupation of his mind. When he is thinking quasi-historically, he describes his doctrine as that of the Social Contract. In a semi-legal aspect, using the terminology, if not the standpoint, of jurisprudence, he restates the same doctrine in the form of popular Sovereignty. This use tends continually to pass over into the more philosophical form which comes third. 'Sovereignty is the exercise of the general will.' Philosophically, Rousseau's doctrine finds its expression in the view that the State is based not on any original convention, not on any determinate power, but on the living and sustaining will of its members. We have now to examine first Sovereignty and then the General Will, which is ultimately Rousseau's guiding conception.

Sovereignty is, first and foremost, a legal term, and it has often been held that its use in political philosophy merely leads to confusion. In jurisprudence, we are told, it has the perfectly plain meaning given to it in Austin's famous definition. The Sovereign is '*a determinate* human superior, *not* in a habit of obedience to a like superior, but receiving *habitual* obedience from the *bulk* of a given society'. Where Sovereignty is placed is, on this view, a question purely of fact, and never of right. We have only to seek out the determinate human superior in a given society, and we shall find the Sovereign. In answer to this theory, it is not enough, though it is a valuable point, to show that such a determinate superior is rarely to be discovered in actual existence. Where, for example, is the Sovereign of Great Britain or of the British Commonwealth? Is it the King or Queen, who is called the Sovereign? Or is it Parliament, which is the legislature (for Austin's Sovereign is regarded as the source of law)? Or is it a consensus of the various Parliaments of the Commonwealth? Or is it the electorate, or the whole mass of the population, with or without the right of voting? Clearly all these exercise a certain influence in the making of laws. Or, finally, is it now the Cabinet? For Austin, one of these bodies would be ruled out as indeterminate (the mass of the population) and another as responsible (the Cabinet). But are we to regard the House of Commons or those who elect it as forming part of the Sovereign? The search for a determinate Sovereign may be a valuable exercise in the art of political jurisprudence; but it has evidently nothing to do with political theory as concerned with human rights.

It is, therefore, essential to distinguish between the legal Sovereign of jurisprudence, and the political Sovereign of political philosophy. Even so, it does not at once become clear what this political Sovereign may be. Is it the body or bodies of persons in whom political power in a society actually resides? Is it merely the complex of actual institutions by which the will of the society is expressed? This would leave us still in the realm of mere fact. The Sovereign, in the philosophical sense, is neither the nominal Sovereign nor the legal Sovereign, nor the political Sovereign of fact and common sense: it is the consequence of the fundamental bond of union, the embodiment of the notion of Social Contract, the foreshadowing of that of the General Will. The Sovereign is that body in a society in which formal political authority *ought* always to reside, and in which the *right* to such authority *does* always reside.

The idea at the back of the philosophical conception of Sovereignty is, therefore, essentially the same as that which we found to underlie the Social Contract theory. It is the view that the people, whether or not it can alienate its rights, is by right the ultimate director of its own destinies, the final power from which there is no appeal to any determinate superior. In a sense, this is recognized even by Hobbes, who makes the power of his absolute Sovereign – the predecessor of Austin's 'determinate human superior' – issue first of all from the Social Contract, which is a popular act of all the original citizens. The difference between Hobbes and Rousseau on this point is solely that Rousseau regards as inalienable a supreme power which Hobbes makes the people alienate in its first corporate action. That is to say, Hobbes accepts the theory of popular supremacy in name only to destroy it in fact; Rousseau asserts the theory in its only logical form, and is under no temptation to evade it by means of false historical assumptions. In Locke, a distinction is already drawn between the legal and the actual Sovereign, which Locke calls 'supreme power'; Rousseau unites the absolute Sovereignty of Hobbes and the 'popular consent' of Locke into the philosophic doctrine of popular Sovereignty which has since been the established form of the theory. His final view represents a return from the perversions of Hobbes to a doctrine already familiar to medieval and Renaissance writers; but it is not merely a return. In its passage the view has fallen into its place in a rational system of political philosophy.

In a second important respect Rousseau differentiates himself from Hobbes. For Hobbes, the Sovereign is identical with the government. Hobbes is so hot for absolutism largely because he regards revolution, the overthrow of the existing government, unless a new government immediately and effectively usurps its place, as at the same time the dissolution of the body politic, and a return to complete anarchy or to the 'state of nature'. Rousseau and, to some extent, Locke meet this view by making a sharp distinction between the supreme power and the government. For Rousseau, they are so clearly distinct that even a completely democratic government is not at the same time the Sovereign; its members are sovereign only in a different capacity and as a different corporate body, just as two different societies may exist for different purposes with exactly the same members. Pure democracy, however, meaning the government of the State by all the people in every detail, is not, as Rousseau says, a possible human institution. All governments are really *mixed* in character; and what we call democratic governments are only comparatively democratic. Government will always be to some extent in the hands of selected persons. Sovereignty, on the other hand, is in Rousseau's view absolute, unalienable, and indivisible. It cannot be limited, abandoned, or shared save among a number of equals. It is an essential part of all legitimate social existence that the right to control the destinies of the society shall belong, in the last resort, to the whole people. There must be somewhere in the society an ultimate court of appeal, which must be made up of all the citizens; but, unless Sovereignty is distinguished from government, the government, usurping the name of Sovereign, will inevitably claim to be absolute. The only way to avoid Hobbes's conclusion is, therefore, to establish a clear separation between Sovereignty and government.

Rousseau tries to do this by an adaptation of the doctrine of the 'three powers'. But instead of three independent powers sharing the supreme authority, he gives only two powers, and makes one of these wholly dependent on the other. He substitutes for the co-ordination of the legislative, the executive, and the judicial authorities a system in which the legislative power, or Sovereign, is always supreme, the executive, or government, always subordinate and derivative, and the judicial power merely a part of government. This division he makes, naturally, one of *will* and *power*. The government's function is merely to carry out the decrees, or acts of will, of the Sovereign people. Just as the human will transfers a command to the members of the body for execution, so the body politic may give its decisions force by setting up an authority which, like the brain, will transmit its commands to its members. In delegating the powers necessary for the execution of its will, it is abandoning none of its supreme authority. It remains Sovereign, and can at any moment recall the grants it has made. Government, therefore, exists only at the Sovereign's pleasure, and is always revocable by the sovereign will.

It will be seen, when we come to discuss the nature of the General Will, that this doctrine really contains the most important part of Rousseau's theory. Here, we are concerned rather with its limitations. The distinction between legislative and executive functions is in practice always hard to draw. In Rousseau's doctrine, it is drawn at a quite different point from that to which we are accustomed. Most of the enactments we ordinarily think of as 'laws' are for him in their essence executive acts.

Rousseau, when he speaks of 'legislation', means something essentially different from what is usually meant by the word in modern parlance. Governments, including representative assemblies, cannot ever make laws, in Rousseau's sense of the word. They can enact only decrees, which are applications of law to particular persons, groups, or situations. Laws, as distinct from decrees, can be enacted only by the Sovereign people, acting directly and not by way of representation. Law-making is a function of Sovereignty, not of government. The laws consist not of the whole body of regulations to which the citizens are subject but only of the fundamental declarations of principle on which the entire social order rests. The laws, in this sense, can never legitimately discriminate between persons or groups: they must always apply equally to all the citizens. Discrimination between citizens is always a matter of government and of decrees, never of Sovereignty or of law in the strict sense.

All decrees are to be made only subject to the provisions of the fundamental laws, which it is the province of the government to apply, but never to infringe. Law is general, and the government is subject to it no less than the individual citizen: laws can be made, and governments authorized, only by the direct decision of the Sovereign people.

This distinction, the full force of which can only be seen in connection with the General Will, means roughly that a matter is general when it concerns the whole community equally, and makes no mention of any particular class or group; as soon as it refers to any group or person, it becomes particular, and can no longer form the subject-matter of an act of Sovereignty. However just this distinction may seem in the abstract, it is clear that its effect is to place most of the legislative function, as we understand it, in the hands of the government and not of the Sovereign: modern 'legislation' is almost always concerned with particular classes and interests. It is not, therefore, a long step from the view of Rousseau to the modern theory of democratic government in which the people's power is mainly that of removing its rulers if they displease it. We must, however, remember that 'government' in Rousseau's sense acts under a code of laws made directly by the Sovereign people. As long as we confine our view to the city-state of which Rousseau is thinking, his distinction is capable of preserving for the people a real law-making authority superior to that of the 'government'. A city can often generalize where a nation must particularize.

It is in the third book of *The Social Contract*, where Rousseau is discussing the problem of government, that it is most essential to remember that his discussion has in view mainly the city-state and not the nation. Broadly speaking, his principle of government is that it can be democratic only in small States, whereas aristocratic government suits best those of medium extent, and monarchical government is needed to hold great States together (Book III, chap. 3). In considering this view, we have to take into account two things. First, Rousseau rejects all claims to Sovereignty on behalf of representative institutions; will – that is, freedom of individual judgment – being, in his theory, inalienable, representative Sovereignty is impossible. As he regards all general acts of legislation as functions of Sovereignty, in which every citizen is entitled to participate directly, no such act can be within the competence of a representative assembly. In judging this theory, we must take into account all the circumstances of Rousseau's time. France, Geneva, and England were the three States he had most in mind. In France, representative government was practically non-existent; in Geneva, it was only partially necessary; in England, it was a mockery, used to support an oligarchy against a debased monarchy. Rousseau may well be pardoned for not taking the ordinary modern view of it. Nor indeed is it, even in the modern world, so satisfactory an instrument of the popular will that we can afford wholly to discard his criticism.

The second factor is the immense development both of local government and of delegation to statutory functional bodies. It seemed to Rousseau that, in the nation-state, all authority must necessarily pass, as it had in France, to the central power. Devolution was hardly dreamed of; and Rousseau saw the only means of securing effective popular government in a federal system, starting from the small unit as Sovereign. The nineteenth and twentieth centuries have proved fruitful in both delegation and devolution of authority, and have thrown much fresh light on the possibilities of federal institutions. There are, however, still many shrewd comments and fruitful suggestions to be found both in the third book of *The Social Contract* and in Rousseau's commentaries on the *Polysynodie* of the Abbé de Saint-Pierre, with its proposals for the establishment of a system of functional administration in France.

The point in Rousseau's theory of Sovereignty that offers most difficulty is his view (Book II, chap. 7) that, for every State, a *Legislator* is necessary. We shall understand the section only by realizing that the legislator is, in fact, in Rousseau's system, the spirit of institutions personified; his place, in a developed society, is taken by the whole complex of social custom, organization, and tradition that has grown up with the State. This is made clearer by the fact that the legislator is not to exercise legislative power; he is merely to submit his suggestions for popular approval. Thus Rousseau recognizes that, in the case of institutions and traditions as elsewhere, will, and not force, is the basis of the State.

This may be seen in his treatment of law as a whole (Book II, chap. 6), which deserves very careful attention. He defines law as 'acts of the general will', and, agreeing with Montesquieu in making law the 'condition of civil association', goes beyond him only in tracing it more definitely to its origin in an act of will. The Social Contract renders law necessary, and at the same time makes it quite clear that valid laws can proceed only from the body of citizens who have constituted the State. 'Doubtless,' says Rousseau, 'there is a universal justice emanating from reason alone; but this justice, to be admitted among us, must be mutual. Humanly speaking, in default of natural sanctions, the laws of justice are ineffective among men.' Of the laws which set up among men this reign of mutual justice within a particular Society the General Will is the source.

We thus come at last to the General Will, the most disputed, and certainly the most fundamental, of all Rousseau's political concepts. No critic of *The Social Contract* has found it easy to say either what precisely its author meant by it, or what is its final value for political philosophy. The difficulty is increased because Rousseau himself sometimes halts in the sense which he assigns to it, and even seems to suggest by it two different ideas. Of its fundamental meaning, however, there can be no doubt. The effect of the Social Contract, according to Rousseau, is the creation of a new individual. When it has taken place, 'at once, in place of the individual personality of each contracting party, this act of association creates a corporate and collective body, composed of as many members as the assembly contains voters, and receiving from the act its unity, its common identity (*moi commun*) its life and its will' (Book I, chap. 6). The same doctrine has been stated earlier, in the *Political Economy*, without the historical setting. 'The body politic, therefore, is also a moral being, possessed of a will; and this general will, which tends always to the preservation and welfare of the whole and of every part, and is the source of the laws, constitutes for all the members of the State, in their relations to one another and to it, the rule of what is just or unjust.' It will be seen at once that the second statement, which could easily be fortified by others from *The Social Contract*, says more than the first. It is not apparent that the common will, created by the institution of society, need 'tend always to the welfare of the whole'. Is not the common will at least as fallible as the will of a single individual? May it not equally be led away from its true interests to the pursuit of pleasure or of something which is really harmful to it? And, if the whole society may vote for what conduces to the momentary pleasure of the members and at the same time to the lasting damage of the State as a whole, is it not still more likely that some of the members will try to secure their private interests in opposition to those of the whole and of others? All these questions, and others like them, have been asked by critics of the conception of the General Will.

Two main points are involved, to one of which Rousseau gives a clear and definite answer. 'There is often,' he says, 'a great deal of difference between the *will of all* and the *general will*; the latter considers only the common interest, while the former takes private interests into account, and is no more than a sum of particular wills.' 'The agreement of all interests is formed by opposition to that of each' (Book II, chap. 3). It is indeed possible for a citizen, when an issue is presented to him, to vote not for what he believes to be the good of the Society, but for his own good or for that of a section; but in such a case, his vote, from the point of view of the General Will, is merely negligible. But, Rousseau asks, 'does it follow . . . that the general will is exterminated or corrupted? Not at all: it is always constant, unalterable, and pure; but it is subordinated to other wills which encroach upon its sphere. . . . The fault [each man] commits [in detaching his interest from the common interest] is that of changing the state of the question, and answering something different from what he is asked. Instead of saying, by his vote "It is to the advantage of the State," he says: "It is of advantage to this or that man or party that this or that view should prevail." Thus the law of public order in assemblies is not so much to maintain in them the general will as to secure that the question be always put to it, and the answer always given by it' (Book IV, chap. 1). These passages, with many others that may be found in the text, make it quite clear that by the General Will Rousseau means something quite distinct from the Will of All, or of a majority. The only excuse for confusion lies in his view that when, *in a city-state* resting on popular Sovereignty, all particular associations are avoided, votes guided by individual self-interest will always tend to cancel one another out, so that majority voting will result in the General Will finding expression. This clearly need not be the case, and in this respect we may charge Rousseau with pushing the democratic argument too far. The point, however, can be better dealt with at a later stage. Rousseau makes no pretence that the mere voice of a majority is infallible; he only says, at the most, that, *given his ideal conditions*, 'it would be subject only to errors of judgment about means, and not to perversion by particular or sectional interests'.

The second main point raised by critics of the General Will is whether, in defining it as a will directed solely to the common interest, Rousseau meant to exclude acts of public immorality and short-sightedness. He answers these questions in different ways. First, an act of public immorality would be merely an instance of collective selfishness, different in no particular from similar acts prompted by group interests, and therefore forming no part of the General Will. Secondly, a mere ignorance of our own and the State's good, entirely unprompted by selfish desires, does not make our will anti-social or individual. 'The general will is upright and always tends to the public advantage; but it does not follow that the deliberations of the people always have the same rectitude. Our will is always for our own good, but we do not always see what that is; the people is never corrupted, but it is often deceived, and on such occasions only does it seem to will what is bad' (Book II, chap. 3).

The treatment of the General Will in the *Political Economy* is brief and lucid, and furnishes the best guide to Rousseau's general meaning. The definition of it in this work, which has already been quoted, is followed by a short account of the nature of *general wills* as a whole. 'Every political society is composed of other smaller societies of different kinds, each of which has its interest and its rules of conduct; but those societies which everybody perceives, because they have an external and authorized form, are not the only ones that actually exist in the State: all individuals who are united by a common interest compose as many others, either transitory or permanent, whose influence is none the less real because it is less apparent. . . . The influence of all these tacit or formal associations causes, by the influence of their will, as many different modifications of the public will. The will of these particular societies has always two relations; for the members of the association, it is a general will; for the great society, it is a particular will; and it is often right with regard to the first object . . . and wrong as to the second, the most general will is always the most just also, and . . . the voice of the people is in fact the voice of God.'

The General Will, Rousseau continues in substance, is always for the common good; but it is sometimes divided into smaller general wills, which are wrong in relation to it. The supremacy of the great General Will is 'the first principle of public economy and the fundamental rule of government'.

In this passage, which differs only in clearness and simplicity from others in *The Social Contract* itself, it is easy to see how far Rousseau had in his mind a perfectly definite idea. Every association of several persons creates a new common will; every association of a permanent character has already a 'personality' of its own, and in consequence a 'general' will; the State, the highest known form of association, is a fully developed corporate and collective being with a common will which is, in the highest sense yet known to us, general. All such wills are general only for the members of the associations which exercise them; for outsiders, or for other similar associations, they are merely particular wills. This applies even to the State; 'for, in relation to what is outside it, the State becomes a simple being, an individual' (*Social Contract,* Book I, chap. 7). In certain passages in *The Social Contract,* in his criticism of the Abbé de Saint-Pierre's *Project of Perpetual Peace,* and in the second chapter of the original draft of the *Social Contract*, Rousseau takes into account the possibility of a still higher individual, 'the federation of the world'. In the *Political Economy*, thinking of the nation-state, he affirms what in *The Social Contract* (Book II, chap. 3) he denies of the city, and recognizes that the life of a nation is made up of the whole complex of its institutions, and that the existence of lesser general wills is not necessarily a menace to the General Will of the State. In *The Social Contract*, he treats of these lesser wills only in relation to the government, which, he shows, has a will of its own, general for its members, but particular for the State as a whole (Book III, chap. 2). This governmental will he there prefers to call *corporate will*, and by this name it will be convenient to distinguish the lesser general wills from the General Will of the State that is over them all.

In *The Social Contract* Rousseau writes as if the General Will of the State is final in relation to its own citizens, though he also says that in relation to other States and to individuals who are not its citizens it is only a particular will. He leaves altogether undiscussed, in *The Social Contract*, the major issue with which he had intended to deal in his projected work on *Political Institutions* as a whole – that is to say, the problem of a greater General Will transcending that of any individual State. In the surviving part of his unpublished draft he denied that there existed any 'general society of mankind' and by implication that mankind could be regarded as possessing any General Will common to the whole species. This, however, did not mean that he regarded the General Will of each State, or of each legitimate State resting on popular Sovereignty, as final and absolute; for he unquestionably accepted as conditioning the activities of the General Will, wherever it was to be found, the overriding authority of a Natural Law binding upon all mankind. This Natural Law was to be incorporated in the fundamental code of legislation of each Sovereign State, and was to govern both relations between States and those between States and individuals. This concept finds its place in *The Social Contract* only when we come to the articles of the Civil Religion prescribed in Chapter 8 of Book IV. The articles of Civil Religion there laid down are, in effect, a brief statement of the fundamental requirements of the Natural Law. In *Émile*, these requirements are much more fully stated in the 'Profession of Faith of the Savoyard Vicar'; and for a full understanding of Rousseau's conception of Natural Law and its implications in the field of politics, it is necessary to take *Émile* and *The Social Contract* together. Undoubtedly Rousseau was conscious of a major difficulty in defining the relations that ought to subsist between States in such a way as to relate them to his concept of General Will. This, indeed, was the main reason why he abandoned his project of publishing a complete treatise on Political Institutions and limited himself to extracting from what he had written a part dealing with the special relation between Sovereign and citizens in States resting on a legitimate basis of popular Sovereignty.

So far, Rousseau's meaning is tolerably clear; he is saying that there exists in every citizen who is a party to the Social Contract a recognition of his obligation so to act as to further the good of the society into which he has entered. When he acts in accordance with this obligation, he makes his contribution to the General Will, be his judgment good or faulty. When he acts from selfish motives or on a basis of sectional interest, he fails to make any contribution to the General Will. 'When in the popular assembly a law is proposed, what the people is asked is not precisely whether it accepts or rejects the proposal, but whether it is in conformity with the general will, which is their will' (Book IV, chap. 2). Rousseau then adds these words: 'When therefore the opinion that is contrary to my own prevails, this proves neither more nor less than that I was mistaken, and that what I thought to be the general will was not so.' It proves, of course, nothing of the sort, unless the votes cast from selfish or sectional motives in fact cancel one another out, so that the voters who honestly answer the right question prevail. On Rousseau's own showing there can be no security that the view of the majority will express the General Will. All that can be said is that in a rightly based democratic society there will be a better chance of the egoisms and sectionalisms cancelling one another out than in societies where voting power is monopolized by a sectional interest, or interests, at the expense of the rest of the citizens. The case for democratic participation is not that the majority is always right, but that no minority can be trusted not to prefer its own advantage to the good of the whole. The essential is to endow the society with a set of fundamental laws and principles that will induce the citizens to cast their votes as far as possible in the spirit of the General Will.

The idea of the General Will is indeed essentially ethical: it is a principle of moral conduct applied to political behaviour. Ethically, it is one and the same as Kant's conception of moral rationality. Kant, in effect, took it from Rousseau and applied it to the entire realm of conduct. The justification for this extension is to be found in Rousseau's own attitude; for he protested more than once against attempts to treat moral and political philosophy apart, as distinct studies, and asserted their absolute unity. This is brought out clearly in *The Social Contract* (Book I, chap. 8), where he is speaking of the change brought about by the establishment of society. 'The passage from the state of nature to the civil state produces a very remarkable change in man, by substituting justice for instinct in his conduct, and giving his actions the morality they had formerly lacked. . . . What man loses by the social contract is his natural liberty and unlimited right to everything he tries to get and succeeds in getting; what he gains is civil liberty . . . which is limited by the general will. . . . We might, over and above all this, add to what man acquires in the morality they had formerly lacked . . . *the mere impulse of appetite is slavery, while obedience to a law which we prescribe to ourselves is liberty.*'

This chapter contains the gist of the Kantian moral philosophy. The morality of our acts consists in their being directed in accordance with universal law; acts in which we are guided merely by our passions or appetites are not moral acts. Further, man can only possess freedom when his whole being is unified in the pursuit of a rational end, which alone excludes contradiction: only moral acts, only men directing their lives by universal law, are free. In Kantian language, the will is autonomous (i.e. prescribes to itself its own law) only when it is directed to a universal end; when it is guided by selfish passions, or particular considerations, it is heteronomous (i.e. receives its law from something external to itself), and in bondage. Rousseau, as he says (Book I, chap. 8), was not directly concerned with the ethical sense of the word 'liberty', and Kant was, therefore, left to develop the doctrine into a system; but the phrases of this chapter prove false the view that the doctrine of a Real Will arose first in connection with politics, and was only transferred thence to moral philosophy. Rousseau based his political doctrine throughout on his view of human freedom; it is because man is by nature a free agent capable of being determined by universal law prescribed by himself that the State is in like manner capable of realizing the General Will – that is, of prescribing to itself and its members a similar universal law.

The General Will, then, is the application of human freedom to political institutions. Before the value of this conception can be determined, there is a criticism to be met. The freedom which is realized in the General Will, we are told, is the freedom of the State *as a whole*; but the State exists to secure *individual* freedom for its members. A free State may be tyrannical; a despot may allow his subjects every freedom. What guarantee is there that the State, in freeing itself, will not enslave its members? This criticism has been made with such regularity that it has to be considered in some detail.

'The problem is to find a form of association which will defend and protect with the whole common force the person and goods of each associate, and in which each, while uniting himself with all, may still obey himself alone, and remain as free as before.' 'The clauses of this contract . . . are everywhere the same and everywhere tacitly admitted and recognized. . . . These clauses, properly understood, may be reduced to one – the total alienation of each associate, together with all his rights, to the whole community . . . ; for, if the individuals retained certain rights, as there would be no common superior to decide between them and the public, each, being on one point his own judge, would ask to be so on all, and the state of nature would continue' (Book I, chap. 6).

Rousseau sees clearly the difficulty of putting any formal limits on the authority which the citizens transfer to the State; he sees that men, in accepting incorporation into a State, must agree to endow themselves collectively with an unlimited power to regulate their common affairs in the general interest. Limited Sovereignty is a contradiction in terms: unlimited moral Sovereignty of all over all is the only practicable foundation for human societies. The Sovereign people has a right to enforce whatever the general interest requires, and where this interest calls for public intervention no appeal can be made against it to individual rights. Nevertheless, Rousseau follows up his assertion of the unlimited character of Sovereignty with a discussion of 'the limits of the sovereign power' (Book II, chap. 4). He has been accused in this matter of contradicting himself; but there is no real contradiction. Wherever the State needs to intervene for the good of the whole, its right to intervene is unlimited; but it has no right to intervene except when and where this condition is satisfied. The General Will, being by definition always in the right, will declare for intervention only when the common interest requires it. 'The Sovereign', says Rousseau, '. . . cannot impose upon its subjects any fetters that are useless to the community, nor can it even wish to do so.' As, however, the infallibility of the General Will in respect of ends is not enough to make the State infallible, especially about means, there still remains an objection. Since the General Will cannot always be arrived at, who is to judge whether an act of intervention is justified? Rousseau's answer fails to satisfy many of his critics. 'Each man alienates, I admit, by the social compact, only such parts of his powers, goods, and liberty, as it is important for the community to control; but it must also be granted that the Sovereign is sole judge of what is important.' Thus we are back in the old difficulty; for the voice of the Sovereign, despite what Rousseau says, may fail to give expression to the General Will and the General Will itself may be mistaken about means. There can be, however, within a society, no higher court of appeal. If the Sovereign fails to express the General Will, or to judge aright about means, it cannot be expressed at all – or at any rate cannot be made effective; and, if it is expressed, mistakes may still occur.

Does Rousseau's conclusion that the Sovereign people must have the final word constitute him in any sense a 'totalitarian'? Clearly not, in any sense that would make him an advocate of the widest possible state interference with personal liberties, which he was, on the contrary, most anxious to preserve. He was no apostle of *Gleichschaltung*: he desired no more regulation of the citizen's personal life than the common interest imperatively demands. The most he did was to insist on the paramountcy of the general interest over all particular interests. He was, moreover, eager to incorporate in the fundamental constitution the articles of his proposed Civil Religion – which, as we saw, was in effect a formulation of the essential dictates of Natural Law – and among these he included, as an indispensable element, mutual toleration and the absolute exclusion of religious intolerance. To this precept and to the other articles of the Civil Religion the State and its citizens were under a sacred obligation to conform as a matter of common human morality, from which there could be no appeal to *raison d'état* in any form. Such an attitude is entirely remote from totalitarianism; and I feel sure Rousseau must be fully acquitted of the charge.

The answer, therefore, to the critics who hold that in securing civil liberty Rousseau has sacrificed the individual may be put after this fashion. Liberty is not a merely negative conception; it does not consist solely in the absence of restraint. The purest individualist, Herbert Spencer for example, would grant that a certain amount of State interference is necessary to *secure* liberty; but as soon as this idea of securing liberty is admitted, the whole idea has undergone profound modification. It can no longer be claimed that every interference on the part of the State lessens the liberty of the individual: the members of a State may be more free when all are restrained from doing one another mutual damage than when anyone is left 'free' to enslave another or be himself enslaved. This principle admitted, the precise amount of State interference that is necessary to secure freedom will always be a matter for particular determination; every case must be decided on its own merits, and, in right, the Sovereign will be subject only to the law of reason.

It has often been held that Rousseau cannot really have inspired the French Revolution because this view is totally inconsistent with the 'rights of man', which the revolutionaries so fervently proclaimed. If every right is alienated in the Social Contract, what sense can there be in talking of 'natural rights' afterwards? This, however, is to misrepresent Rousseau's position. The rights of man, as they are preached by the modern individualist, are not the rights of which Rousseau and the revolutionaries were thinking. We have seen that the theory of *The Social Contract* is founded on human freedom: this freedom carries with it, in Rousseau's view, the guarantee of its own permanence as a right: it is inalienable and indestructible. When, therefore, government becomes despotic, it has no more right over its subjects than the master has over his slave (Book I, chap. 4); the question is then purely one of might. In such cases, appeal may be made either to the terms of the Social Contract, or, putting the same idea another way, to the 'natural right' of human freedom. This natural right is in no sense inconsistent with the complete alienation supposed in the Contract; for the Contract itself reposes on it and guarantees its maintenance. The legitimate State must, therefore, treat all its members as equal participants in Sovereignty; but as long as this is done, its authority is final. If it leaves the general for the particular, and treats one man differently from another, it ceases to be Sovereign; for equality is presupposed in the terms of the Contract.

It is more profitable to attack Rousseau for his identification of the interests of each of the citizens with those of all; but here, too, he does not maintain that there can be no opposition between a man's particular interests and the General Will as present in him; on the contrary, he explicitly and consistently affirms the presence of such opposition (Book I, chap. 7). What he asserts is, first, that the Sovereign, as such, cannot have any interest contrary to the interest of the citizens as a whole – which is obvious; and, secondly, that it cannot have an interest contrary to that of any individual – which is not. The second point Rousseau tries to prove by showing that the omnipotence of the Sovereign is essential to the preservation of society, which in turn is necessary for the individual as the means to the good life. His argument, however, really rests on the fundamental character of the General Will. He would admit that, in actual States, the interest of the many might often conflict with that of the few; but he would contend that in a rightly founded society based on popular Sovereignty and social equality, the *real* interest of State and individual would be bound to coincide.

Thus the justification of Rousseau's theory of liberty returns to the point from which it set out – the omnipotence of the *General Will* in State and individual. It is in this sense that he speaks of man in the State as 'forced to be free' by the General Will, much as Kant might speak of a man's lower nature as forced to be free by the universal mandate of his higher, rational will. It is in this recognition of the State as a moral being, with powers of determination similar to the powers of the individual mind, that the significance of the General Will ultimately lies. Even, however, among those who have recognized its meaning, there are some who deny its value as a conception of political philosophy. If, they say, the General Will is not the Will of All, if there can be no assurance of its being arrived at by a majority vote or by any system of voting whatsoever, then it is nothing; it is a mere abstraction, neither general, nor a will. This is, of course, precisely the criticism to which Kant's conception of the 'real will' is often subjected. Clearly, it must be granted at once that the General Will does not form the whole actual content of the will of every citizen. Regarded as actual, it must always be qualified by 'in so far as' or its equivalent. This, however, is far from destroying the value of the concept. In seeking the universal basis of society, we are not seeking anything that is wholly actualized in any society, though we must be seeking something which exists, more or less perfectly, in every society that has a claim to rest on legitimate foundations.

The point of the Social Contract theory, as Rousseau states it, is that legitimate society exists by the agreement of the people, and acts by popular will. Active will, and not force or even mere consent, is the basis of the 'republican' State, which can possess this character only because individual wills are not really self-sufficient and

separate, but complementary and interdependent. The answer to the
question 'Why ought I to obey the General Will?' is that the General
Will exists in me and not outside me. I am 'obeying only myself', as
Rousseau says. The State is not a mere accident of human history, a
mere device for the protection of life and property; it responds to a
fundamental need of human nature, as soon as men have to find ways
of living in conditions which make it impracticable to maintain the
isolation characteristic of the primitive 'state of nature'. From that
point individual human nature requires the State, in a form
compatible with the retention of human freedom. The complex of
social institutions is not a *merely* artificial structure, artificial though
it be. It is a direct outcome of mutual dependence and fellowship
when the 'state of nature' is superseded. The State is, for men who
have passed beyond this condition, a necessary extension of their
individuality as well as a means of mutual protection.

The problem, however, still remains of making the General Will,
in any particular State, active and conscious. It is clear that there are
States in which visible and recognized institutions hardly answer in
any respect to its requirements. Even in such States, however, there is
a limit to tyranny; deep down, in immemorial customs with which
the despot dare not interfere, the General Will is active and
important. It does not reside merely in the outward and visible
organization of social institutions, in that complex of formal
associations which we may call the State; its roots go deeper and its
branches spread further. It is realized, in greater or less degree, in the
whole life of the community, in the entire complex of private and
public relations which, in the wildest sense, may be called Society. It
finds expression not only in Parliaments or other agencies of
government, or in churches, universities, trade unions, and all
manner of groups and associations, but also in the most intimate
personal relationships and in all the variety of customs and social
observances.

But, if all these things go to the making of the General Will in every
community, the General Will has, for politics, primarily a narrower
sense. The problem here is to secure its supremacy in the official

institutions and public councils of the nation. This is the question to which Rousseau chiefly addressed himself. Here, too, we shall find the General Will the best possible conception for the guidance of political endeavour. For the General Will is realized not whenever that is done which is best for the community, but when, in addition, the community as a whole has willed the doing of it. The notion of the General Will embraces a demand not only for good government, but also for self-government – not only for rational conduct, but for goodwill. The good State must be a State based on equality – on the equal participation of all its citizens. It must be, at bottom, a democracy, even if its 'government', in the limited sense in which Rousseau uses the word, may sometimes need to be aristocratic, or even monarchical. Rousseau said that aristocracy was the best of all *governments*, but he said also that it was the worst of all usurpers of *Sovereignty*. Nor must it be forgotten that he expressly specified elective aristocracy. *There is no General Will unless the people wills the good.* General Will may be embodied in one man willing universally; but it can be embodied in the State only when the mass of citizens so wills. The will must be 'general' in two senses: in the sense in which Rousseau used the word, it must be general in its object, i.e. universal; but it must also be generally held, i.e. common to all or to the majority.*

The General Will is, then, above a universal and, in the Kantian sense, a 'rational' will. It would be possible to find in Rousseau many more anticipations of the view of Kant; but it is better here to confine comment to an important difference between them. It is surprising to find in Kant, the originator of modern 'intellectualism', and in Rousseau, the great apostle of 'sentiment', an essentially similar view on the nature and function of the will. Their views, however, present a difference; for, whereas the moving force of Kant's moral imperative is purely 'rational', Rousseau finds the sanction of his General Will in human feeling itself. As we can see from a passage in

---

* The term 'general' will means, in Rousseau, not so much 'will held by several persons', as will having a general (universal) object. This is often misunderstood; but the mistake matters the less, because the General Will must, in fact, be both.

the original draft of *The Social Contract*, the General Will remains purely rational. 'No one will dispute that the General Will is in each individual a pure act of the understanding, which reasons while the passions are silent on what a man may demand of his neighbour and on what his neighbour has a right to demand of him.' The will remains purely rational, but Rousseau feels that it needs an external motive power. 'If natural law,' he writes, 'were written only on the tablets of human reason it would be incapable of guiding the greater part of our actions; but it is also graven on the heart of man in characters that cannot be effaced, and it is there it speaks to him more strongly than all the precepts of the philosophers' (from an unfinished essay on *The State of War*). The nature of this guiding sentiment is explained in the *Discourse on Inequality* (p. 73, footnote), where *amour-propre* is contrasted with love of self (*amour de soi*). Naturally, Rousseau holds, man does not want everything for himself, and nothing for others. 'Amour-propre' and 'altruism' are both one-sided qualities arising out of the perversion of man's natural propensities – his *amour de soi* and his *pitié*. These together constitute the fundamental characteristics of human nature, and justify speaking of man as naturally good rather than bad because they provide a basis for the acceptance of mutual justice as the rule of conduct in society. The rational precepts of the General Will, therefore, find an echo in the heart of the 'natural' man, and, if we can but secure the human being against perversion by wrongly constituted societies, the General Will can be made actual.

This is the meeting-point of Rousseau's educational with his political theory. His view as a whole can be studied only by taking together *The Social Contract* and *Émile* as explained by the *Letters Written from the Mount* and other works. The fundamental dogma of the natural goodness of man finds no place directly in *The Social Contract*; but it lurks behind the whole of Rousseau's political theory. His educational, his religious, his political and his ethical ideas are all inspired by a consistent attitude.

Indeed Rousseau is by no means the inconsistent thinker he is often made out to be. He failed, no doubt, to find the solution of many of his problems; but his approach to them all rested on a consistent belief in three things – the inalienability of human liberty, the natural propensity of man to goodness, and the necessity of basing political institutions on democratic sovereignty as the means of expression of the General Will.

G. D. H. COLE

THE DEVELOPMENT OF ROUSSEAU'S
POLITICAL PHILOSOPHY

The work commonly called the *Discourse on the Arts and Sciences* is rightly placed at the beginning of a collection of Rousseau's works of political philosophy, although itself it contains no philosophy and is only marginally concerned with politics. It was the notoriety that he won by the publication of this work that first gave him occasion to engage in public controversy, and it was the discipline and self-criticism that this controversy imposed that first led him to engage in systematic philosophical thinking about society and politics. The *Discourse* (the word in this context means 'prize essay' or 'dissertation') was written on the subject, set by the Academy of Dijon, 'Whether the restoration of the Sciences and the Arts has had a purifying effect on morals [*mœurs*]'. The advertisement containing the subject appeared in October 1749. Rousseau (so he informs us in one of the series of autobiographical letters he wrote to Malesherbes in 1762) read it while walking along the road from Paris to Vincennes to visit his friend Diderot in prison, whereupon he underwent a sudden revelation. Part of the discourse he wrote in pencil on the spot, and the rest within six months. In July 1750 it was awarded the prize, and was published in November.

At once a host of attempted refutations appeared. To five of these Rousseau wrote replies, published between June 1751 and some time in the following year. These replies do not appear in this volume, but two of them are of some length and importance, viz. the *Reply to Stanislas, King of Poland* and the *Last Reply* (or *Reply to Bordes*), the former written in answer to a defence primarily of theological learning, the latter in answer to a defence of learning in general. In these replies Rousseau for the first time backed up his assertions with arguments and clarified them with distinctions. Furthermore, although he never explicitly withdrew any part of the *Discourse*, he modified his position in a number of ways, of which the following are a selection:

(*a*) In the *Discourse* 'morals' is left undefined, and often in practice Rousseau takes over from his ancient sources a tacit equation of virtue with prowess in war, and of vice with weakness and cowardice. In the replies this probably quite unintended military bias is largely eliminated. The vice he is most concerned with is hypocrisy, and the virtues characteristic of pre-civilized peoples are listed in the *Last Reply* as 'a severity of morals that is an infallible mark of their purity, good faith, hospitality, justice, and, what is very important, a great horror of debauchery, the fertile mother of all other vices'.

(*b*) In the replies, Rousseau narrows the object of his attack. It is no longer the cultivation of the arts and sciences in itself that is condemned, but their cultivation by the people generally, who have not sufficient virtue or talent to make good use of them. The condemnation no longer covers every art and every science, but only those that are useless or sophistic, particularly the study of literary style, leading as it does to polite manners and so to hypocrisy.

(*c*) In the course of writing the replies, Rousseau comes to see the contention of the *Discourse* as being only a special case of a wider thesis, viz. that man is by nature good, and that his present vices are the result of the corruption of his nature in his social environment, not only through the misuse of the arts and sciences, but also through inequality (called in the *Reply to Stanislas* 'the first source of evil'), luxury, and the political constitution. He excuses himself at this point from discussing the last, but the seed has been sown.

Rousseau's final thoughts on the subject of the first *Discourse* are to be found in the long footnote (i) to the *Discourse on the Origin of Inequality* (pp. 118–26 of this volume). Here the transformation begun in the replies is completed. The arts and sciences (or rather their misuse) are still seen as tending to corrupt morals, but only because of the corrupt social context in which they arise, and which Rousseau describes and discusses in the main text of the second *Discourse*.

This second *Discourse* was also in form prompted by a question set (in November 1753) by the Academy of Dijon, but the scale of the work goes far beyond the limits set by the Academy (viz. that the dissertation submitted should not take more than three-quarters of an hour to read aloud). Written in June 1754 it incorporates the results of four years of thinking and reading by Rousseau on the subject of the nature of man and the causes of his corruption. The subject was treated as an historical one – Rousseau's claim (on pp. 50–1) that he was not concerned with historical fact is not to be taken too seriously; it was, in part at least, a sop to the religious authorities. He based his account of natural man on the best factual material available to him – travellers' reports of primitive peoples and of the great apes, and Buffon's *Natural History*. His account of the successive stages of human society owes much also to earlier political theorists, particularly to Grotius and Pufendorf, the leading writers of the Natural Law School, and to Locke. It is in a version similar to that put forward by these writers that the social contract first appears in Rousseau's writing (see p. 98), and he here follows the view of Pufendorf that the social contract, setting up an ordered society, was distinct from and preceded the contract of government, between people and rulers (see p. 106). Both these contracts are thought of by Rousseau at this time as stages in the history of man's corruption, not as the basis of a truly legitimate social order.

Rousseau's thinking at this time about what government ought to be, as distinct from what it was, is partly shown in the article *Political Economy* (pp. 128–68 of this volume). This was written for Volume V, published in November 1755, of the *Encyclopédie*, edited by Diderot and d'Alembert. Rousseau had been a close friend of Diderot's for some years, and had written articles on music for earlier volumes. According to his own account in Book IX of the *Confessions*, Rousseau had been working since 1750 or 1751 (i.e. since the controversy aroused by the first *Discourse*) on a work of political theory to be called *Political Institutions*, and the encyclopedia article allows us to see how this work was progressing in 1754–5. It is in this article and in an article by Diderot for the same volume (viz. that on *Droit naturel* (*moral*)) that the expression 'general will' is introduced for the first time in the sense Rousseau was to make his own.

When in 1756 Rousseau took up residence in the country, one of the tasks he set himself was to work on his *Political Institutions*. The work went slowly, competing for his time with three other projects: the novel *Julie, ou la Nouvelle Héloïse*, the educational treatise *Émile*, and the editing of the works of the Abbé de St-Pierre. In 1759, he says, 'I looked into the state of this book, and found that it still required several years' more labour on it. I had not the courage to continue with it. . . . Accordingly I abandoned it, deciding to extract from it whatever could be extracted and then to burn the rest; and pushing eagerly ahead with that task, without any interruption to *Émile*, in less than two years I put the finishing touches to the *Social Contract*' (*Confessions*, Book X).

There survives a manuscript (MS. Fr. 225 in the Geneva library catalogue), commonly called the Geneva MS, which, as I have argued elsewhere, probably represents the extract from his previous work that Rousseau made on this occasion. It is a fair copy with subsequent alterations, bears the title *Social Contract*, and has lost its final pages, breaking off in the middle of the chapter numbered, both in the MS and in the final version, Book III, Chapter 1. Much of the material to be found in Books I and II of the final version, published in April 1762, is already in the Geneva MS in almost identical words; but the order has been changed, some chapters and paragraphs of the MS have been dropped from the final version (including two passages taken over verbatim from the *Political Economy* article), and others not in the MS have been added (including the whole of Chapters 2, 3, and 5 of Book II). For the present edition the most important of the omitted chapters (Book I, Chapter 2 of the MS), in which Rousseau shows why political institutions are necessary at all, has been newly translated and is printed in its original place at the beginning of the main text. Other important variants have been printed in an appendix.

It is important, if we are to judge whether Rousseau's thought developed between the writing of the Geneva MS and that of the final version, to form some idea of the contents of the missing part of the MS. Fortunately we do not depend on guesswork to enable us to do this. Rousseau included in Book V of *Émile*, as an indication of the kind of education in political theory that his ideal pupil was to receive, a summary of the *Social Contract*, which he at that time expected would not be published until after the appearance of *Émile*. This summary is of an earlier version of the *Social Contract*, intermediate between that of the Geneva MS and that finally published, though in the parts where we have both it is closer to the latter. However, after summarizing Book III, Chapters 1 to 3, Rousseau does not go on to summarize the rest of Book III and Book IV. Instead we find in *Émile* a section on international relations, federation and war, that has no counterpart in the published text. The matter contained in Book III, Chapters 15 to 18 and in part of Chapter 12 can be found in *Émile* at an earlier point, following the summary of Book II, Chapter 6. We must assume that this reflects the order of the text Rousseau was summarizing, and that the portions unsummarized were probably largely, if not wholly, absent from that text. *A fortiori* they were probably absent from the still earlier text of the Geneva MS. In the present edition the summary of the *Social Contract* in *Émile* is reproduced in an appendix in a revised translation.

The development of Rousseau's political thinking up to the publication of the *Social Contract* can be traced if we consider in turn first the *Political Economy* article, then the text of the Geneva MS, and finally the parts of the *Social Contract* that are found only in the final version. His interest is at first in discovering what kind of activity on the part of government will make men virtuous rather than corrupt them. The general will is first introduced in this context as providing a rule of justice for all good governments. By the time he wrote the material copied in the Geneva MS his interest shifted to the formal conditions that must be fulfilled if any government is to be legitimate. He finds such a condition in the sovereignty of the general will. Finally, in the latest additions to the *Social Contract*, he is concerned with finding a specific constitution that will guarantee that the general will can always be expressed. At this stage his interest has narrowed. Whereas in the parts found in the Geneva MS he shows a concern for the legitimate government of all peoples, in the latest parts he shows interest only in city-states, particularly Geneva. The reader who is interested in Rousseau's theory of political legitimacy in general would do well to concentrate his attention on the earlier parts, in which Rousseau is considering that issue, rather than with the later parts, in which Rousseau is answering a different question. The present edition is the first in English in which the reader is given the information that will enable him to make this distinction.

J. C. H.

SUGGESTIONS FOR FURTHER READING

Rousseau's Works

The political or semi-political works published by Rousseau himself (with dates of first publication) are: *Discours sur les Sciences et les Arts* (1750); replies to the Abbé Raynal (in *Mercure*, June 1751), to Stanislas, King of Poland (*Observations*, 1751), to Gauthier (*Lettre à M. Grimm*, 1751), to Bordes (*Dernière Réponse*, 1752), and to Lecat (1752); *Discours sur l'origine et les fondements de l'inégalité parmi les hommes* (1755); *Economie Politique*, 1755 (article in vol. V of the *Encyclopédie* of Diderot and d'Alembert); *Extrait du Projet de paix perpétuelle de M. l'abbé de Saint-Pierre* (1761); *Du Contrat Social* (1762); *Lettres écrites de la Montagne* (1764); *Considérations sur le gouvernement de Pologne* (published in MS, 1771). Other surviving works, not published in Rousseau's lifetime, include other works on the Abbé de Saint-Pierre (dating from the late 1750s), and the *Projet de Constitution pour la Corse* (dating from 1765).

Among the more important of Rousseau's other writings are the opera *le Devin du Village* (1753); the novel *Julie, ou la Nouvelle Héloïse* (1761); the partly fictional educational treatise *Émile, ou de l'éducation* (1762); and his autobiographical works (all published posthumously), the *Confessions*, *Rousseau juge de Jean-Jacques: Dialogues*, and *Rêveries du Promeneur Solitaire*.

EDITIONS
(N.B. A *Bibliography of the writings of Rousseau to 1800* is in the course of publication by The Voltaire Foundation, Oxford. Volume 2, on *Émile*, by Jo-Ann McEachern, appeared in 1989.)

Complete works

The first reasonably complete edition of Rousseau's works was published by his friends Du Peyrou and Moultou from 1780 to 1789, and there have been many others since. All previous editions have, however, been superseded by what must now be regarded as the standard edition of Rousseau's works, in the Bibliothèque de la Pléiade, published by Gallimard. This edition comprises scholarly introductions and very full notes and is arranged as follows: Vol. I (1959), autobiographical writings; Vol. II (1964), *Nouvelle Héloïse*, theatre, poetry, etc: Vol. III (1964), political writings; Vol. IV (1969), *Émile* and associated works.

Political Works

Writings of Jean-Jacques Rousseau (2 vols., 1915) also contains the French text, but has excellent introductions and notes in English. There are many good editions of the *Social Contract* including those by C. E. Vaughan, *The Political* (1918, with introduction and notes in English), Beaulavon (1922), de Jouvenel (1947) and Grimsley (1972, with introduction and notes in English). There are good separate editions of the *Discours sur les sciences et les arts* by Havens (1946) and of the *Discours sur l'inegalité* by Lecercle (1971) and Starobinski (Folio, 1989). *Economie politique* has been published, along with *Considérations sur le gouvernement de Pologne* and *Projet de Constitution pour la Corse*, in G-F Flammarion (1990).

Correspondence

Rousseau's *Correspondance complète* edited by R. A. Leigh (published initially in Geneva and subsequently in Oxford by The Voltaire Foundation, 1965–89) is a superb critical edition, completely superseding all others.

Translations

There are other good English translations of the *Social Contract* though none include the important second chapter of the Geneva MS (see below, p. 169 ff.). The two *Discourses* have also been translated by R. D. and J. R. Masters (1964), and *A Discourse on Inequality* by Maurice Cranston (1984). The *Project for Corsica* and the *Considerations on the Government of Poland* are included with the *Social Contract* in the translation by F. Watkins (1953). Of Rousseau's other works, *Émile* is available in Everyman's Library, the *Confessions* in Penguin Classics.

Biography and Criticism

Of the very great number of critical studies on Rousseau and his works, the best one in English is Maurice Cranston's excellent biography, as yet unfinished; the first two (of three) volumes are: *Jean-Jacques: the early life and work of J.-J. Rousseau, 1712–1754* (London, 1983), and *The Noble Savage: J.-J. Rousseau 1754–1762* (London, 1991). A similar type of study on Rousseau's life and work, also in English, is L. G. Crocker's *Jean-Jacques Rousseau* (2 vols., New York and London, 1968–73), stimulating and scholarly, if sometimes inclined to be tendentious. To some extent, these two works supersede the still excellent biography by J. Guéhenno, *Jean-Jacques, Histoire d'une Conscience* (Paris, 1948–52) (English translation by J. and D. Weightman, London, 1966). More specifically on Rousseau's works and ideas, there are two particularly good studies in English: J. H. Broome, *Rousseau – a Study of his Thought* (London, 1963), and R. Grimsley, *The Philosophy of Rousseau* (Oxford, 1973), both of them concise, clear and very readable. However, a good introductory book for the English-speaking general reader is John Hope Mason's *The Indispensable Rousseau* (London, 1979), which combines exposition of Rousseau's ideas with plentiful extracts (in English translation), including some from the less well-known works. Among the great number of works in French on Rousseau's thought, the excellent books by P. Burgelin, *La Philosophie de l'existence de Rousseau* (Paris, 1952), and R. Derathé, *Le Rationalisme de Rousseau* (Paris, 1948), are still authoritative. There have been many perceptive psychological studies of Rousseau's personality, and among these two are quite outstanding, J. Starobinski, *La Transparence et l'Obstacle* (Paris, 1958) (available in English translation as *Transparency and Obstruction*, Chicago and London, 1988), and P.-P. Clément, *Jean-Jacques Rousseau, de l'éros coupable à l'éros glorieux* (Neuchâtel, 1976). R. Grimsley has also published an illuminating study of a similar kind, *Jean-Jacques Rousseau, a Study in Self Awareness* (Cardiff, 1969).

There have been a number of very useful works in English devoted principally or entirely to Rousseau's political thought – some of which offer diverse, even conflicting interpretations of it: (in order of date) L. G. Crocker's; *Rousseau's Social Contract: an Interpretive Essay* (1968); R. D. Masters's, *The Political Philosophy of Rousseau* (1968); J. C. Hall's *Rousseau* (1973); D. Cameron's *The Social Thought of Rousseau and Burke* (1973); J. Charvet's *The Social Problem in the Philosophy of Rousseau* (1974); S. Ellenburg's *Rousseau's Political Philosophy* (1976); J. Miller's *Rousseau, Dreamer of Democracy* (1984); R. Wokler's *Social Thought of Rousseau* (1987); M. Viroli's *J.-J. Rousseau and the 'well-ordered society'* (1988). Most of the works on Rousseau's thought mentioned above contain important sections on his political writings, and there is valuable material in Volume III of the Pléiade edition of the complete works, especially the introductions by Starobinski to the *Discours sur l'inégalité* and by Derathé to *Economie politique* and the *Contrat social*, as well as the extensive footnotes. The essential work on the sources of Rousseau's political ideas is Derathé's *Jean-Jacques Rousseau et la science politique de son temps* (1950).

Virtually all works on the history of political thought deal to a greater or lesser extent with Rousseau, and of particular interest are the sharply contrasting views on the meaning and influence of his political thought found in J. L. Talmon's *The Origins of Totalitarian Democracy* (1952) and A. Cobban's *Rousseau and the Modern State* (1964). Important collections of articles are to be found in *Études sur le 'Contrat social' de Jean-Jacques Rousseau. Actes des journées d'étude organisées à Dijon* (1964), *Annales de philosophie politique, 5* (1965), *Rousseau after Two Hundred Years* (ed. R. A. Leigh, 1982), and *Etudes sur les Discours de Rousseau* (ed. Terrasse, 1988). Leigh's posthumous *Unsolved Problems in the Bibliography of J.-J. Rousseau* (1990) demonstrates that the *Contrat social* was far more widely known in 18th Century France than was previously supposed. Finally, a periodical devoted to Rousseau studies in general is the *Annales de la Société Jean-Jacques Rousseau.*

P. D. J.

PUBLISHERS' NOTE

This edition presents a revised version of the previous Everyman edition (by G. D. H. Cole) of the *Social Contract* and *Discourses*, now placed in chronological order. The important second chapter of the Geneva MS of the *Social Contract* has been added in its proper place before the main text, and an appendix has been added containing the other major passages of the MS that were omitted from the final version.

Cole's introduction to the former edition, which is something of a classic in its own right, has been retained unchanged, except for minor corrections. A new introduction, dealing with the development of Rousseau's political writings, has been added. The bibliography has been revised.

A certain number of notes have been added, mainly to explain obscure references. No attempt has been made in these notes to explain Rousseau's terminology, which would require a full-scale philosophical commentary.

A DISCOURSE

WHICH WON THE PRIZE AT THE ACADEMY OF DIJON IN 1750, ON THIS QUESTION PROPOSED BY THE ACADEMY:

HAS THE RESTORATION OF THE ARTS AND SCIENCES HAD A PURIFYING EFFECT UPON MORALS?

Barbarus hic ego sum, qui non intelligor illis. – OVID

[Here I am a barbarian, because men understand me not.]

Preface

The following pages contain a discussion of one of the most sublime and interesting of all moral questions. It is not concerned, however, with those metaphysical subtleties, which of late have found their way into every department of literature, and from which even our academic curricula are not always free. We have now to do with one of those truths on which the happiness of mankind depends.

I foresee that I shall not readily be forgiven for having taken up the position I have adopted. Setting myself up against all that is nowadays most admired, I can expect no less than a universal outcry against me: nor is the approbation of a few sensible men enough to make me count on that of the public. But I have taken my stand, and I shall be at no pains to please either wits or those who follow fashion. There are in all ages men born to be in bondage to the opinions of the society in which they live. There are not a few, who today play the free-thinker and the philosopher, who would, if they had lived in the time of the League, have been no more than fanatics. No author, who has a mind to outlive his own age, should write for such readers.

A word more and I have done. As I did not expect the honour conferred on me, I had, since sending in my Discourse, so altered and enlarged it as almost to make it a new work; but in the circumstances I have felt bound to publish it just as it was when it received the prize. I have only added a few notes, and made two additions which are easily recognizable, of which the Academy possibly might not have approved. The respect, gratitude and even justice I owe to that body seemed to me to demand this acknowledgment.

A Discourse on the Moral Effects of the Arts and Sciences

Decipimur specie recti. – HORACE

The question before me is: 'Whether the Restoration of the arts and sciences has had the effect of purifying or corrupting morals.' Which side am I to take? That, gentlemen, which becomes an honest man, who is sensible of his own ignorance, and thinks himself none the worse for it.

I feel the difficulty of treating this subject fittingly, before the tribunal which is to judge of what I advance. How can I presume to belittle the sciences before one of the most learned assemblies in Europe, to commend ignorance in a famous Academy, and reconcile my contempt for study with the respect due to the truly learned?

I was aware of these inconsistencies, but not discouraged by them. It is not science, I said to myself, that I am attacking; it is virtue that I am defending, and that before virtuous men – and probity is even dearer to men of honour than learning to the learned.

What then have I to fear? The sagacity of the assembly before which I am pleading? That, I acknowledge, is to be feared; but rather on account of faults of construction than of the views I hold. Just sovereigns have never hesitated to decide against themselves in doubtful cases; and indeed the most advantageous situation in which a just claim can be, is that of being laid before a just and enlightened arbitrator, who is judge in his own case.

To this motive, which encouraged me, I may add another which finally decided me. And this is, that as I have upheld the cause of truth to the best of my natural abilities, whatever my apparent success, there is one reward which cannot fail me. That reward I shall find in the bottom of my heart.

3

THE FIRST PART

It is a noble and beautiful spectacle to see man raising himself, so to speak, from nothing by his own exertions; dissipating, by the light of reason, all the thick clouds in which he was by nature enveloped; mounting above himself; soaring in thought even to the celestial regions; like the sun, encompassing with giant strides the vast extent of the universe; and, what is still grander and more wonderful, going back into himself, there to study man and get to know his own nature, his duties and his end. All these miracles we have seen renewed within the last few generations.

Europe had relapsed into the barbarism of the earliest ages; the inhabitants of this part of the world, which is at present so highly enlightened, were living, some centuries ago, in a state still worse than ignorance. A scientific jargon, more despicable than mere ignorance, had usurped the name of knowledge, and opposed an almost invincible obstacle to its restoration.[1]

Things had come to such a pass, that it required a complete revolution to bring men back to common sense. This came at last from the quarter from which it was least to be expected. It was the stupid Mussulman, the eternal scourge of letters, who was the immediate cause of their revival among us. The fall of the throne of Constantine brought to Italy the relics of ancient Greece; and with these precious spoils France in turn was enriched. The sciences soon followed literature, and the art of thinking joined that of writing: an order which may seem strange, but is perhaps only too natural. The world now began to perceive the principal advantage of an intercourse with the Muses, that of rendering mankind more sociable by inspiring them with the desire to please one another with performances worthy of their mutual approbation.

The mind, as well as the body, has its needs: those of the body are the basis of society, those of the mind its ornaments.

So long as government and law provide for the security and well-being of men in their common life, the arts, literature, and the sciences, less despotic though perhaps more powerful, fling garlands of flowers over the chains which weigh them down. They stifle in men's breasts that sense of original liberty, for which they seem to have been born; cause them to love their own slavery, and so make of them what is called a civilized people.

Necessity raised up thrones; the arts and sciences have made them strong. Powers of the earth, cherish all talents and protect those who cultivate them.* Civilized peoples, cultivate such pursuits: to them, happy slaves, you owe that delicacy and exquisiteness of taste, which is so much your boast, that sweetness of disposition and urbanity of manners which make intercourse so easy and agreeable among you – in a word, the appearance of all the virtues, without being in possession of one of them.

It was this sort of refined civilization, all the more attractive for its apparent lack of ostentation, which distinguished Athens and Rome in those most celebrated days of their splendour and magnificence: and it is doubtless in the same respect that our own age and nation will excel all periods and peoples. An air of philosophy without pedantry; an address at once natural and engaging, distant equally from Teutonic rusticity and Italian pantomime; these are the effects of a taste acquired by liberal studies and improved by conversation with the world. What happiness would it be for those who live among us, if our external appearance were always a true mirror of our hearts; if decorum were but virtue; if the maxims we professed were the rules of our conduct; and if real philosophy were inseparable from the title of a philosopher! But

* Sovereigns always see with pleasure a taste for the arts of amusement and superfluity, which do not result in the exportation of bullion, increase among their subjects. They very well know that, besides nourishing that littleness of mind which is proper to slavery, the increase of artificial wants only binds so many more chains upon the people. Alexander, wishing to keep the Ichthyophagi in a state of dependence, compelled them to give up fishing, and subsist on the customary food of all other nations. The American savages, who go naked, and live entirely on the products of the chase, have been always impossible to subdue. What yoke, indeed, can be imposed on men who stand in need of nothing?

so many good qualities too seldom go together; virtue rarely appears in so much pomp and state.

Richness of apparel may proclaim the man of fortune, and elegance the man of taste; but true health and manliness are known by different signs. It is under the homespun of the labourer, and not beneath the gilt and tinsel of the courtier, that we should look for strength and vigour of body.

External ornaments are no less foreign to virtue, which is the strength and activity of the mind. The honest man is an athlete, who loves to wrestle stark naked; he scorns all those vile trappings, which prevent the exertion of his strength, and were, for the most part, invented only to conceal some deformity.

Before art had moulded our behaviour, and taught our passions to speak an artificial language, our morals were rude but natural; and the different ways in which we behaved proclaimed at the first glance the difference of our dispositions. Human nature was not at bottom better then than now; but men found their security in the ease with which they could see through one another, and this advantage, of which we no longer feel the value, prevented their having many vices.

In our day, now that more subtle study and a more refined taste have reduced the art of pleasing to a system, there prevails in modern manners a servile and deceptive conformity; so that one would think every mind had been cast in the same mould. Politeness requires this thing; decorum that; ceremony has its forms, and fashion its laws, and these we must always follow, never the promptings of our own nature.

We no longer dare seem what we really are, but lie under a perpetual restraint; in the meantime the herd of men, which we call society, all act under the same circumstances exactly alike, unless very particular and powerful motives prevent them. Thus we never know with whom we have to deal; and even to know our friends we must wait for some critical and pressing occasion; that is, till it is too late; for it is on those very occasions that such knowledge is of use to us.[1]

What a train of vices must attend this uncertainty! Sincere friendship, real esteem, and perfect confidence are banished from among men. Jealousy, suspicion, fear, coldness, reserve, hate, and fraud lie constantly concealed under that uniform and deceitful veil of politeness; that boasted candour and urbanity, for which we are indebted to the enlightened spirit of this age. We shall no longer take in vain by our oaths the name of our Creator; but we shall insult Him with our blasphemies, and our scrupulous ears will take no offence. We have grown too modest to brag of our own merits; but we do not scruple to decry those of others. We do not grossly outrage even our enemies, but artfully calumniate them. Our hatred of other nations diminishes, but patriotism dies with it. Ignorance is held in contempt; but a dangerous scepticism has succeeded it. Some vices indeed are condemned and others grown dishonourable; but we have still many that are honoured with the names of virtues, and it is become necessary that we should either have, or at least pretend to have them. Let who will extol the moderation of our modern sages, I see nothing in it but a refinement of intemperance as unworthy of my commendation as their deceitful simplicity.*

Such is the purity to which our morals have attained; this is the virtue we have made our own. Let the arts and sciences claim the share they have had in this salutary work. I shall add but one reflection more; suppose an inhabitant of some distant country should endeavour to form an idea of European morals from the state of the sciences, the perfection of the arts, the propriety of our public entertainments, the politeness of our behaviour, the affability of our conversation, our constant professions of benevolence, and from those tumultuous assemblies of people of all ranks, who seem, from morning till night, to have no other care

---

* 'I love,' said Montaigne, 'to converse and hold an argument; but only with very few people, and that for my own gratification. For to do so, by way of affording amusement for the great, or of making a parade of one's talents, is, in my opinion, a trade very ill becoming a man of honour.' It is the trade of all our fashionable wits, save one.[1]

than to oblige one another. Such a stranger, I maintain, would arrive at a totally false view of our morality.

Where there is no effect, it is idle to look for a cause: but here the effect is certain and the depravity actual; our minds have been corrupted in proportion as the arts and sciences have improved. Will it be said, that this is a misfortune peculiar to the present age? No, gentlemen, the evils resulting from our vain curiosity are as old as the world. The daily ebb and flow of the tides are not more regularly influenced by the moon than the morals of a people by the progress of the arts and sciences. As their light has risen above our horizon, virtue has taken flight, and the same phenomenon has been constantly observed in all times and places.

Take Egypt, the first school of mankind, that ancient country, famous for its fertility under a brazen sky; the spot from which Sesostris once set out to conquer the world.[1] Egypt became the mother of philosophy and the fine arts; soon she was conquered by Cambyses, and then successively by the Greeks, the Romans, the Arabs, and finally the Turks.

Take Greece, once peopled by heroes, who twice vanquished Asia, once before Troy and once defending their homeland. Letters, as yet in their infancy, had not corrupted the disposition of its inhabitants; but the progress of the sciences soon produced a dissoluteness of manners, and the imposition of the Macedonian yoke: from which time Greece, always learned, always voluptuous, and always a slave, has experienced amid all its revolutions no more than a change of masters. Not all the eloquence of Demosthenes could breathe life into a body which luxury and the arts had once enervated.

It was not till the days of Ennius and Terence that Rome, founded by a shepherd, and made illustrious by peasants, began to degenerate. But after the appearance of an Ovid, a Catullus, a Martial, and the rest of those numerous obscene authors, whose very names are enough to put modesty to the blush, Rome, once the shrine of virtue, became the theatre of vice, a scorn among the nations, and an object of derision even to barbarians. Thus the capital of the world at length submitted to the yoke of slavery it had imposed on others, and the very day of its fall was the eve of that on which it conferred on one of its citizens the title of Arbiter of Good Taste.[1]

What shall I say of that metropolis of the Eastern Empire, which, by its situation, seemed destined to be the capital of the world; that refuge of the arts and sciences, when they were banished from the rest of Europe, more perhaps by wisdom than barbarism? The most profligate debaucheries, the most abandoned villainies, the most atrocious crimes, plots, murders, and assassinations form the warp and woof of the history of Constantinople. Such is the pure source from which have flowed to us the floods of knowledge on which the present age so prides itself.

But wherefore should we seek, in past ages, for proofs of a truth, of which the present affords us ample evidence? There is in Asia a vast empire, where learning is held in honour, and leads to the highest dignities in the State. If the sciences improved our morals, if they inspired us with courage and taught us to lay down our lives for the good of our country, the Chinese should be wise, free, and invincible. But, if there be no vice they do not practise, no crime with which they are not familiar; if the sagacity of their ministers, the supposed wisdom of their laws, and the multitude of inhabitants who people that vast empire, have alike failed to preserve from them the yoke of the rude and ignorant Tartars, of what use were their men of science and literature? What advantage has that country reaped from the honours bestowed on its learned men? Can it be that of being peopled by a race of scoundrels and slaves?

Contrast with these instances the morals of those few nations which, being preserved from the contagion of useless knowledge, have by their virtues become happy in themselves and afforded an example to the rest of the world. Such were the first inhabitants of Persia, a nation so singular that virtue was taught among them in the same manner as the sciences are with us. They very easily subdued Asia, and possess the exclusive glory of having had the history of their political institutions regarded as a philosophical romance. Such were the Scythians, of whom such wonderful eulogies have come down to us. Such were the Germans, whose simplicity, innocence, and virtue afforded a most delightful contrast to the pen of an historian,[1] weary of describing the baseness and villainies of an enlightened, opulent, and voluptuous nation. Such had been even Rome in the days of its poverty and ignorance. And such has shown itself to be, even in our own times, that rustic nation,[2] whose justly renowned courage not even adversity could conquer, and whose fidelity no example could corrupt.*

It is not through stupidity that the people have preferred other activities to those of the mind. They were not ignorant that in other countries there were men with leisure to spend time disputing about the sovereign good, and about vice and virtue. They knew that these proud reasoners were lavish in their own praises, and stigmatized other nations contemptuously as barbarians. But they noted the morals of these people, and so learnt what to think of their learning.†

Can it be forgotten that, in the very heart of Greece, there arose a city as famous for the happy ignorance of its inhabitants, as for the wisdom of its laws; a republic of demi-gods rather than of men, so greatly superior their virtues seemed to those of mere

---

* I dare not speak of those happy nations, who did not even know the name of many vices, which we find it difficult to suppress; the savages of America, whose simple and natural mode of government Montaigne preferred, without hesitation, not only to the laws of Plato, but to the most perfect visions of government philosophy can ever suggest. He cites many examples, striking for those who are capable of appreciating them. But, what of all that, says he, they can't run to a pair of breeches!

† What are we to think was the real opinion of the Athenians themselves about eloquence, when they were so very careful to banish declamation from that upright tribunal, against whose decision even their gods made no appeal? What did the Romans think of physicians, when they expelled medicine from the republic? And when the relics of humanity left among the Spaniards induced them to forbid their lawyers to set foot in America, what must they have thought of jurisprudence? May it not be said that they thought, by this single expedient, to make reparation for all the outrages they had committed against the unhappy Indians?

humanity? Sparta, eternal proof of the vanity of science, while the vices, under the conduct of the fine arts, were being introduced into Athens, even while its tyrant was carefully collecting together the works of the prince of poets, was driving from her walls artists and the arts, the learned and their learning!

The difference was seen in the outcome. Athens became the seat of politeness and taste, the country of orators and philosophers. The elegance of its buildings equalled that of its language; on every side might be seen marble and canvas, animated by the hands of the most skilful artists. From Athens we derive those astonishing performances, which will serve as models to every corrupt age. The picture of Lacedaemon[1] is not so highly coloured. There, the neighbouring nations used to say, 'men were born virtuous, their native air seeming to inspire them with virtue'. But its inhabitants have left us nothing but the memory of their heroic actions: monuments that should not count for less in our eyes than the most curious relics of Athenian marble.

It is true that, among the Athenians, there were some few wise men who withstood the general torrent, and preserved their integrity even in the company of the muses. But hear the judgment which the principal, and most unhappy of them, passed on the artists and learned men of his day.

'I have considered the poets,' says he, 'and I look upon them as people whose talents impose both on themselves and on others; they give themselves out for wise men, and are taken for such; but in reality they are anything sooner than that.'

'From the poets,' continues Socrates, 'I turned to the artists. Nobody was more ignorant of the arts than myself; nobody was more fully persuaded that the artists were possessed of amazing knowledge. I soon discovered, however, that they were in as bad a way as the poets, and that both had fallen into the same misconception. Because the most skilful of them excel others in their particular jobs, they think themselves wiser than all the rest of mankind. This arrogance spoilt all their skill in my eyes, so that, putting myself in the place of the oracle, and asking myself whether

I would rather be what I am or what they are, know what they know, or know that I know nothing, I very readily answered, for myself and the god, that I had rather remain as I am.

'None of us, neither the sophists, nor the poets, nor the orators, nor the artists, nor I, know what is the nature of the *true*, the *good*, or the *beautiful*. But there is this difference between us; that, though none of these people know anything, they all think they know something; whereas for my part, if I know nothing, I am at least in no doubt of my ignorance. So the superiority of wisdom, imputed to me by the oracle, is reduced merely to my being fully convinced that I am ignorant of what I do not know.'[1]

Thus we find Socrates, the wisest of men in the judgment of the gods, and the most learned of all the Athenians in the opinion of all Greece, speaking in praise of ignorance. Were he alive now, there is little reason to think that our modern scholars and artists would induce him to change his mind. No, gentlemen, that honest man would still persist in despising our vain sciences. He would lend no aid to swell the flood of books that flows from every quarter: he would leave to us, as he did to his disciples, only the example and memory of his virtues; that is the noblest method of instructing mankind.

Socrates had begun at Athens, and the elder Cato proceeded at Rome, to inveigh against those seductive and subtle Greeks, who corrupted the virtue and destroyed the courage of their fellow-citizens: culture, however, prevailed. Rome was filled with philosophers and orators, military discipline was neglected, agriculture was held in contempt, men formed sects, and forgot their country. To the sacred names of liberty, disinterestedness, and obedience to law, succeeded those of Epicurus, Zeno, and Arcesilaus. It was even a saying among their own philosophers that since learned men appeared among them, honest men had been in eclipse. Before that time the Romans were satisfied with the practice of virtue; they were undone when they began to study it.

What would the great soul of Fabricius have felt, if it had been his misfortune to be called back to life, when he saw the pomp and magnificence of that Rome, which his arm had saved from ruin, and his honourable name made more illustrious than all its conquests. 'Ye gods!' he would have said, 'what has become of those thatched roofs and rustic hearths, which were formerly the habitations of temperance and virtue? What fatal splendour has succeeded the ancient Roman simplicity? What is this foreign language, this effeminacy of manners? What is the meaning of these statues, paintings, and buildings? Fools, what have you done? You, the lords of the earth, have made yourselves the slaves of the frivolous nations you have subdued. You are governed by rhetoricians, and it has been only to enrich architects, painters, sculptors, and stage-players that you have watered Greece and Asia with your blood. Even the spoils of Carthage are the prize of a flute-player. Romans! Romans! make haste to demolish those amphitheatres, break to pieces those statues, burn those paintings; drive from among you those slaves who keep you in subjection, and whose fatal arts are corrupting your morals. Let other hands make themselves illustrious by such vain talents; the only talent worthy of Rome is that of conquering the world and making virtue its ruler. When Cyneas took the Roman senate for an assembly of kings, he was not struck by either useless pomp or studied elegance. He heard there none of that futile eloquence, which is now the study and the charm of frivolous orators. What then was the majesty that Cyneas beheld? Fellow-citizens, he saw the noblest sight that ever existed under heaven, a sight which not all your riches or your arts can show; an assembly of two hundred virtuous men, worthy to command in Rome, and to govern the world.'

But let pass the distance of time and place, and let us see what has happened in our own time and country; or rather let us banish odious descriptions that might offend our delicacy, and spare ourselves the pains of repeating the same things under different names. It was not for nothing that I invoked the Manes of Fabricius; for what have I put into his mouth that might not have come with as much propriety from Louis the Twelfth or Henry the Fourth? It is true that in France Socrates would not have drunk the hemlock, but he would have drunk of a potion infinitely more bitter, of insult, mockery, and contempt a hundred times worse than death.

Thus it is that luxury, profligacy, and slavery have been, in all ages, the scourge of the efforts of our pride to emerge from that happy state of ignorance, in which the wisdom of providence had placed us. That thick veil with which it has covered all its operations seems to be a sufficient proof that it never designed us for such fruitless researches. But is there, indeed, one lesson it has taught us, by which we have rightly profited, or which we have neglected with impunity? Let men learn for once that nature would have preserved them from science, as a mother snatches a dangerous weapon from the hands of her child. Let them know that all the secrets she hides are so many evils from which she protects them, and that the very difficulty they find in acquiring knowledge is not the least of her bounty towards them. Men are perverse; but they would have been far worse, if they had had the misfortune to be born learned.

How humiliating are these reflections to humanity, and how mortified by them our pride should be! What! it will be asked, is uprightness the child of ignorance? Is virtue inconsistent with learning? What consequences might not be drawn from such suppositions? But to reconcile these apparent contradictions, we need only examine closely the emptiness and vanity of those pompous titles, which are so liberally bestowed on human knowledge, and which so blind our judgment. Let us consider, therefore, the arts and sciences in themselves. Let us see what must result from their advancement, and let us not hesitate to admit the truth of all those points on which our arguments coincide with the inductions we can make from history.

THE SECOND PART

An ancient tradition passed out of Egypt into Greece, that some god, who was an enemy to the repose of mankind, was the inventor of the sciences.* What must the Egyptians, among whom the sciences first arose, have thought of them? And they beheld, near at hand, the sources from which they sprang. In fact, whether we turn to the annals of the world, or eke out with philosophical investigations the uncertain chronicles of history, we shall not find for human knowledge an origin answering to the idea we are pleased to entertain of it at present. Astronomy was born of superstition, eloquence of ambition, hatred, falsehood, and flattery; geometry of avarice; physics of an idle curiosity; all, even moral philosophy, of human pride. Thus the arts and sciences owe their birth to our vices; we should be less doubtful of their advantages, if they had sprung from our virtues.

Their evil origin is, indeed, but too plainly reproduced in their objects. What would become of the arts, were they not nourished by luxury? If men were not unjust, of what use were jurisprudence? What would become of history, if there were no tyrants, wars, or conspiracies? In a word, who would pass his life in barren speculations, if everybody, attentive only to the obligations of humanity and the necessities of nature, spent his whole life in serving his country, obliging his friends, and relieving the unhappy? Are we then made to live and die on the brink of that well at the bottom of which Truth lies hid? This reflection alone is, in my opinion, enough to discourage at first setting out every man who seriously endeavours to instruct himself by the study of philosophy.

What a variety of dangers surrounds us! What a number of

---

* It is easy to see the allegory in the fable of Prometheus: and it does not appear that the Greeks, who chained him to the Caucasus, had a better opinion of him than the Egyptians had of their god Theutus. The Satyr, says an ancient fable, the first time he saw a fire, was going to kiss and embrace it; but Prometheus cried out to him to forbear, or his beard would rue it. It burns, says he, everything that touches it.

wrong paths present themselves in the investigation of the sciences! Through how many errors, more perilous than truth itself is useful, must we not pass to arrive at it? The disadvantages we lie under are evident; for falsehood is capable of an infinite variety of combinations; but the truth has only one manner of being. Besides, where is the man who sincerely desires to find it? Or even admitting his good will, by what characteristic marks is he sure of knowing it? Amid the infinite diversity of opinions where is the criterion* by which we may certainly judge of it? Again, what is still more difficult, should we even be fortunate enough to discover it, who among us will know how to make right use of it?

If our sciences are futile in the objects they propose, they are even more dangerous in the effects they produce. Being the effect of idleness, they generate idleness in their turn; and an irreparable loss of time is the first prejudice which they must necessarily cause to society. To live without doing some good is a great evil as well in the political as in the moral world; and hence every useless citizen should be regarded as a pernicious person. Tell me then, illustrious philosophers, of whom we learn the ratios in which attraction acts *in vacuo*; and in the revolution of the planets, the relations of spaces traversed in equal times; by whom we are taught what curves have conjugate points, points of inflexion, and cusps; how man sees everything in God; how the soul and body correspond, like two clocks, without actual communication; what planets may be inhabited; and what insects reproduce in an extraordinary manner.[1] Answer me, I say, you from whom we receive all this sublime information, whether we should have been less numerous, worse governed, less formidable, less flourishing, or more perverse, supposing you had taught us none of all these fine things.

---

* The less we know, the more we think we know. The Peripatetics doubted of nothing. Did not Descartes construct the universe with cubes and vortices? And is there in all Europe one single physicist who does not boldly explain the inexplicable mysteries of electricity, which will, perhaps, be for ever the despair of real philosophers?

Reconsider therefore the importance of your productions; and, since the labours of the most enlightened of our learned men and the best of our citizens are of so little utility, tell us what we ought to think of that numerous herd of obscure writers and idle *littérateurs*, who devour without any return the substance of the State.

Idle, do I say? Would God they were![1] Society would be more peaceful, and morals less corrupt. But these vain and futile declaimers go forth on all sides, armed with their fatal paradoxes, to sap the foundations of our faith, and nullify virtue. They smile contemptuously at such old names as patriotism and religion, and consecrate their talents and philosophy to the destruction and defamation of all that men hold sacred. Not that they bear any real hatred to virtue or dogma; they are the enemies of public opinion alone; to bring them to the foot of the altar, it would be enough to banish them to a land of atheists. What extravagancies will not the rage of singularity induce men to commit!

The waste of time is certainly a great evil; but still greater evils attend upon literature and the arts. One is luxury,[2] produced like them by indolence and vanity. Luxury is seldom unattended by the arts and sciences; and they are always attended by luxury. I know that our philosophy, fertile in paradoxes, pretends, in contradiction to the experience of all ages, that luxury contributes to the splendour of States. But, without insisting on the necessity of sumptuary laws, can it be denied that rectitude of morals is essential to the duration of empires, and that luxury is diametrically opposed to such rectitude? Let it be admitted that luxury is a certain indication of wealth; that it even serves, if you will, to increase such wealth; what conclusion is to be drawn from this paradox, so worthy of the times? And what will become of virtue if riches are to be acquired at any cost? The politicians of the ancient world were always talking of morals and virtue; ours speak of nothing but commerce and money.[3] One of them will tell you that in such a country a man is worth just as much as he will sell for at Algiers: another, pursuing the same mode of calculation, finds that in some countries a man is worth nothing, and in others still less than nothing; they value men as they do droves of oxen. According to them, a man is worth no more to the State than the amount he consumes; and thus a Sybarite would be worth at least thirty Lacedaemonians. Let these writers tell me, however, which of the two republics, Sybaris or Sparta, was subdued by a handful of peasants, and which became the terror of Asia.

The monarchy of Cyrus was conquered by thirty thousand men, led by a prince poorer than the meanest of Persian Satraps: in like manner the Scythians, the poorest of all nations, were able to resist the most powerful monarchs of the universe. When two famous republics contended for the empire of the world, the one rich and the other poor, the former was subdued by the latter. The Roman empire in its turn, after having engulfed all the riches of the universe, fell a prey to peoples who knew not even what riches were. The Franks conquered the Gauls, and the Saxons England, without any other treasures than their bravery and their poverty. A band of poor mountaineers, whose whole cupidity was confined to the possession of a few sheep-skins, having first given a check to the arrogance of Austria, went on to crush the opulent and formidable house of Burgundy, which at that time made the potentates of Europe tremble.[1] Finally, all the power and wisdom of the heir of Charles the Fifth, backed by all the treasures of the Indies, broke before a few herring-fishers.[2] Let our politicians condescend to lay aside their calculations for a moment, to reflect on these examples; let them learn for once that money, though it buys everything else, cannot buy morals and citizens. What then is the precise point in dispute about luxury? It is to know which is most advantageous to empires, that their existence should be brilliant and momentary, or virtuous and lasting. I say brilliant, but with what lustre? A taste for ostentation never prevails in the same minds as a taste for honesty. No, it is impossible that understandings, degraded by a multitude of futile cares, should ever rise to what is truly great and noble; even if they had the strength, they would want the courage.

Every artist loves applause. The praise of his contemporaries is the most valuable part of his recompense. What then will he do to obtain it, if he have the misfortune to be born among a people, and at a time, when men of learning, who have become fashionable, have enabled frivolous youth to set the tone; when men have sacrificed their taste to those who tyrannize over their liberty, and when, since one sex dare not approve anything but what is proportionate to the pusillanimity of the other,* the greatest masterpieces of dramatic poetry are condemned, and the noblest of musical productions neglected? This is what he will do. He will lower his genius to the level of the age, and will rather submit to compose mediocre works, that will be admired during his lifetime, than labour at sublime achievements which will not be admired till long after he is dead. Let the famous Voltaire tell us how many fine, powerful, masculine passages he has sacrificed to our false delicacy, and how much that is great and noble, that spirit of gallantry, which delights in what is frivolous and petty, has cost him.[1]

It is thus that the dissolution of morals, the necessary consequence of luxury, brings with it in its turn the corruption of taste. Further, if by chance there be found among men of uncommon ability, an individual with enough strength of mind to refuse to comply with the spirit of the age, and to debase himself by puerile productions, his lot will be hard. He will die in indigence and oblivion. This is not so much a prediction as a fact already confirmed by experience! Yes, Carle Vanloo and Pierre,[2] the time

* I am far from thinking that the ascendancy which women have obtained over men is an evil in itself. It is a present which nature has made them for the good of mankind. If better directed, it might be productive of as much good, as it is now of evil. We are not sufficiently sensible of what advantage it would be to society to give a better education to that half of our species which governs the other. Men will always be what women choose to make them. If you wish then that they should be noble and virtuous, let women be taught what greatness of soul and virtue are. The reflections which this subject arouses, and which Plato formerly made, deserve to be more fully developed by a pen worthy of following so great a master, and defending so great a cause.

is already come when your brushes, destined to increase the majesty of our temples by sublime and holy images, must fall from your hands, or else be prostituted to adorn the panels of a coach with lascivious paintings. And you, inimitable Pigalle, rival of Phidias and Praxiteles, whose chisel the ancients would have employed to carve them gods, whose images almost excuse their idolatry in our eyes; even your hand must condescend to fashion the belly of a porcelain monkey, or else remain idle.

We cannot reflect on the morality of mankind without contemplating with pleasure the picture of the simplicity which prevailed in the earliest times. This image may be justly compared to a beautiful coast, adorned only by the hands of nature; towards which our eyes are constantly turned, and which we see receding with regret. While men were innocent and virtuous and loved to have the gods for witnesses of their actions, they dwelt together in the same huts; but when they became vicious, they grew tired of such inconvenient onlookers, and banished them to magnificent temples. Finally, they expelled their deities even from these, in order to dwell there themselves; or at least the temples of the gods were no longer more magnificent than the palaces of the citizens. This was the height of degeneracy; nor could vice ever be carried to greater lengths than when it was seen, supported, as it were, at the doors of the great, on columns of marble, and graven on Corinthian capitals.

As the conveniences of life increase, as the arts are brought to perfection, and luxury spreads, true courage flags, military virtues disappear; and all this is the effect of the sciences and of those arts which are exercised in the privacy of men's dwellings. When the Goths ravaged Greece, the libraries only escaped the flames owing to an opinion that was set on foot among them, that it was best to leave the enemy with a possession so calculated to divert their attention from military exercises, and keep them engaged in indolent and sedentary occupations.[1]

Charles the Eighth found himself master of Tuscany and the kingdom of Naples, almost without drawing sword; and all his court attributed this unexpected success to the fact that the princes and nobles of Italy applied themselves with greater earnestness to the cultivation of their understandings than to active and martial pursuits. In fact, says the sensible person who records these characteristics, experience plainly tells us, that in military matters and all that resemble them application to the sciences tends rather to make men effeminate and cowardly than resolute and vigorous.

The Romans confessed that military virtue was extinguished among them, in proportion as they became connoisseurs in the arts of the painter, the engraver, and the goldsmith, and began to cultivate the fine arts. Indeed, as if this famous country was to be for ever an example to other nations, the rise of the Medici and the revival of letters has once more destroyed, this time perhaps for ever, the martial reputation which Italy seemed a few centuries ago to have recovered.

The ancient republics of Greece, with that wisdom which was so conspicuous in most of their institutions, forbade their citizens to pursue all those inactive and sedentary occupations, which by enervating and corrupting the body diminish also the vigour of the mind. With what courage, in fact, can it be thought that hunger and thirst, fatigues, dangers, and death, can be faced by men whom the smallest want overwhelms and the slightest difficulty repels? With what resolution can soldiers support the excessive toils of war, when they are entirely unaccustomed to them? With what spirits can they make forced marches under officers who have not even the strength to travel on horseback? It is no answer to cite the reputed valour of all the modern warriors who are so scientifically trained. I hear much of their bravery in a day's battle; but I am told nothing of how they support excessive fatigue, how they stand the severity of the seasons and the inclemency of the weather. A little sunshine or snow, or the want of a few superfluities, is enough to cripple and destroy one of our finest armies in a few days. Intrepid warriors! permit me for once to tell you the truth, which you seldom hear. Of your bravery I am fully satisfied. I have no doubt that you would have triumphed with Hannibal at Cannae, and at Trasimene: that you would have passed the Rubicon with Caesar, and enabled him to enslave his country; but you never would have been able to cross the Alps with the former, or with the latter to subdue your own ancestors, the Gauls.

A war does not always depend on the events of battle: there is in generalship an art superior to that of gaining victories. A man may behave with great intrepidity under fire, and yet be a very bad officer. Even in the common soldier, a little more strength and vigour would perhaps be more useful than so much courage, which after all is no protection from death. And what does it matter to the State whether its troops perish by cold and fever, or by the sword of the enemy?

If the cultivation of the sciences is prejudicial to military qualities, it is still more so to moral qualities. Even from our infancy an absurd system of education serves to adorn our wit and corrupt our judgment.[1] We see, on every side, huge institutions, where our youth are educated at great expense, and instructed in everything but their duty. Your children will be ignorant of their own language, when they can talk others which are not spoken anywhere. They will be able to compose verses which they can hardly understand; and, without being capable of distinguishing truth from error, they will possess the art of making them unrecognizable by specious arguments. But magnanimity, equity, temperance, humanity, and courage will be words of which they know not the meaning. The dear name of country will never strike on their ears; and if they ever hear speak of God,* it will be less to fear than to be frightened of Him. I would as soon, said a wise man,[2] that my pupil had spent his time in the tennis court as in this manner; for there his body at least would have got exercise.

I well know that children ought to be kept employed, and that idleness is for them the danger most to be feared. But what should

---

* *Pensées philosophiques* (Diderot).[3]

they be taught? This is undoubtedly an important question. Let them be taught what they are to practise when they come to be men;* not what they ought to forget.

Our gardens are adorned with statues and our galleries with pictures. What would you imagine these masterpieces of art, thus exhibited to public admiration, represent? The great men who have defended their country, or the still greater men who have enriched it by their virtues? Far from it. They are the images of every perversion of heart and mind, carefully selected from ancient mythology, and presented to the early curiosity of our children, doubtless that they may have before their eyes the

---

* Such was the education of the Spartans according to one of the greatest of their kings. It is well worthy of notice, says Montaigne, that the excellent institutions of Lycurgus, which were in truth miraculously perfect, paid as much attention to the bringing up of youth as if this were their principal object, and yet, at the very seat of the Muses, they make so little mention of learning that it seems as if their generous-spirited youth disdained every other restraint, and required, instead of masters of the sciences, instructors in valour, prudence, and justice alone.

Let us hear next what the same writer says of the ancient Persians. Plato, says he, relates that the heir to the throne was thus brought up. At his birth he was committed, to not the care of women, but to eunuchs in the highest authority and near the person of the king, on account of their virtue. These undertook to render his body beautiful and healthy. At seven years of age they taught him to ride and go hunting. At fourteen he was placed in the hands of four, the wisest, the most just, the most temperate, and the bravest persons in the kingdom. The first instructed him in religion, the second taught him to adhere inviolably to truth, the third to conquer his passions, and the fourth to be afraid of nothing. All, I may add, taught him to be a good man; but not one taught him to be learned.

Astyages, in Xenophon, desires Cyrus to give him an account of his last lesson. It was this, answered Cyrus, one of the big boys of the school having a small coat, gave it to a little boy and took away from him his coat, which was larger. Our master having appointed me arbiter in the dispute, I ordered that matters should stand as they were, as each boy seemed to be better suited than before. The master, however, remonstrated with me, saying that I considered only convenience, whereas justice ought to have been the first concern, and justice teaches that no one should suffer forcible interference with what belongs to him. He added that he was punished for his wrong decision, just as boys are punished in our country schools when they forget the first aorist of τύπτω. My tutor must make me a fine harangue, *in genere demonstrativo*, before he will persuade me that his school is as good as this.

representations of vicious actions, even before they are able to read.

Whence arise all those abuses, unless it be from that fatal inequality introduced among men by the distinction of talents and the cheapening of virtue? This is the most evident effect of all our studies, and the most dangerous of all their consequences. The question is no longer whether a man is honest, but whether he is clever. We do not ask whether a book is useful, but whether it is well written. Rewards are lavished on wit and ingenuity, while virtue is left unhonoured. There are a thousand prizes for fine discourses, and none for good actions. I should be glad, however, to know whether the honour attaching to the best discourse that ever wins the prize in this Academy is comparable with the merit of having founded the prize.

A wise man does not go in chase of fortune; but he is by no means insensible to glory, and when he sees it so ill distributed, his virtue, which might have been animated by a little emulation, and turned to the advantage of society, droops and dies away in obscurity and indigence. Preferring the agreeable arts to the useful ones must, in the long run, inevitably result in this; and this truth has been but too much confirmed since the revival of the arts and sciences. We have physicists, geometricians, chemists, astronomers, poets, musicians, and painters in plenty; but we have no longer a citizen among us; or if there be found a few scattered over our abandoned countryside, they are left to perish there unnoticed and neglected. Such is the condition to which those who give us our daily bread, and our children milk, are reduced, and such are our feelings towards them.

I confess, however, that the evil is not so great as it might have become. The eternal providence, in placing salutary simples beside noxious plants, and making poisonous animals contain their own antidote, has taught the sovereigns of the earth, who are its ministers, to imitate its wisdom. It is by following this example that the truly great monarch,[1] to whose glory every age will add new lustre, drew from the very bosom of the arts and sciences the very fountains of a thousand lapses from rectitude, those famous societies, which, while they are depositaries of the dangerous trust of human knowledge, are yet the sacred guardians of morals, by the attention they pay to their maintenance among themselves in all their purity, and by the demands which they make on every member whom they admit.

These wise institutions, confirmed by his august successor and imitated by all the kings of Europe, will serve at least to restrain men of letters, who, all aspiring to the honour of being admitted into these Academies, will keep watch over themselves, and endeavour to make themselves worthy of such honour by useful performances and irreproachable morals. Those Academies also, which, in proposing prizes for literary merit, make choice of such subjects are calculated to arouse the love of virtue in the hearts of citizens, prove that it prevails in themselves, and must give men the rare and real pleasure of finding learned societies devoting themselves to the enlightenment of mankind, not only by agreeable exercises of the intellect, but also by useful instructions.

An objection which may be made is, in fact, only an additional proof of my argument. So much precaution proves but too evidently the need for it. We never seek remedies for evils that do not exist. Why, indeed, must these bear all the marks of ordinary remedies, on account of their inefficacy? The numerous establishments in favour of the learned are only adapted to make men mistake the objects of the sciences, and turn men's attention to the cultivation of them. One would be inclined to think, from the precautions everywhere taken, that we are overstocked with husbandmen, and are afraid of a shortage of philosophers. I will not venture here to enter into a comparison between agriculture and philosophy, as they would not bear it. I shall only ask: What is philosophy? What is contained in the writings of the most celebrated philosophers? What are the lessons of these friends of wisdom? To hear them, should we not take them for so many mountebanks, exhibiting themselves in public, and crying out, *Here, Here, come to me, I am the only true doctor*? One of them teaches that there is no such thing as matter, but that everything exists only in representation.[1] Another declares that there is no other substance than matter, and no other God than the world itself.[2] A third tells you that there are no such things as virtue and vice, and that moral good and evil are chimeras;[3] while a fourth informs you that men are only beasts of prey, and may conscientiously devour one another. Why, my great philosophers, do you not reserve these wise and profitable lessons for your friends and children? You would soon reap the benefit of them, nor should we be under any apprehension of our own becoming your disciples.

Such are the wonderful men, whom their contemporaries held in the highest esteem during their lives, and to whom immortality has been attributed since their decease. Such are the wise maxims we have received from them, and which are transmitted, from age to age, to our descendants. Paganism, though given over to all the extravagances of human reason, has left nothing to compare with the shameful monuments which have been prepared by the art of printing, during the reign of the gospel. The impious writings of Leucippus and Diagoras perished with their authors. The world, in their days, was ignorant of the art of immortalizing the errors and extravagances of the human mind. But thanks to the art of printing* and the use we make of it, the pernicious reflections of

---

* If we consider the frightful disorders which printing has already caused in Europe, and judge of the future by the progress of its evils from day to day, it is easy to foresee that sovereigns will hereafter take as much pains to banish this dreadful art from their dominions, as they ever took to encourage it. The Sultan Achmet, yielding to the importunities of certain pretenders to taste, consented to have a press erected at Constantinople; but it was hardly set to work before they were obliged to destroy it, and throw the plant into a well.

It is related that the Caliph Omar, being asked what should be done with the library at Alexandria, answered in these words: 'If the books in the library contain anything contrary to the Alcoran, they are evil and ought to be burnt; if they contain only what the Alcoran teaches, they are superfluous.' This reasoning has been cited by our men of letters as the height of absurdity; but if Gregory the Great had been in the place of Omar and the Gospel in the place of the Alcoran, the library would still have been burnt, and it would have been perhaps the finest action of his life.

Hobbes and Spinoza will last for ever. Go, famous writings, of which the ignorance and rusticity of our forefathers would have been incapable. Go to our descendants, along with those still more pernicious works which reek of the corrupted manners of the present age! Let them together convey to posterity a faithful history of the progress and advantages of our arts and sciences. If they are read, they will leave not a doubt about the question we are now discussing, and unless mankind should then be still more foolish than we, they will lift up their hands to Heaven and exclaim in bitterness of heart: 'Almighty God! Thou who holdest in Thy hand the minds of men, deliver us from the fatal arts and sciences of our forefathers; give us back ignorance, innocence, and poverty, which alone can make us happy and are precious in Thy sight.'

But if the progress of the arts and sciences has added nothing to our real happiness; if it has corrupted our morals, and if that corruption has vitiated our taste, what are we to think of the herd of text-book authors, who have removed those impediments which nature purposely laid in the way to the Temple of the Muses, in order to guard its approach and try the powers of those who might be tempted to seek knowledge? What are we to think of those compilers who have indiscreetly broken open the door of the sciences, and introduced into their sanctuary a populace unworthy to approach it, when it was greatly to be wished that all who should be found incapable of making a considerable progress in the career of learning should have been repulsed at the entrance, and thereby cast upon those arts which are useful to society. A man who will be all his life a bad versifier, or a third-rate geometrician, might have made nevertheless an excellent clothier. Those whom nature intended for her disciples have not needed masters. Bacon, Descartes, and Newton, those teachers of mankind, had themselves no teachers. What guide indeed could have taken them so far as their sublime genius directed them? Ordinary masters would only have cramped their intelligence, by confining it within the narrow limits of their own capacity. It was from the obstacles they met with at first that they learned to exert them-selves, and bestirred themselves to traverse the vast field which they covered. If it be proper to allow some men to apply themselves to the study of the arts and sciences, it is only those who feel themselves able to walk alone in their footsteps and to outstrip them. It belongs only to these few to raise monuments to the glory of the human understanding. But if we are desirous that nothing should be above their genius, nothing should be beyond their hopes. This is the only encouragement they require. The soul insensibly adapts itself to the objects on which it is employed, and thus it is that great occasions produce great men. The greatest orator in the world was Consul of Rome,[1] and perhaps the greatest of philosophers Lord Chancellor of England.[2] Can it be conceived that, if the former had only been a professor at some University, and the latter a pensioner of some Academy, their works would not have suffered from their situation? Let not princes disdain to admit into their councils those who are most capable of giving them good advice. Let them renounce the old prejudice, which was invented by the pride of the great, that the art of governing mankind is more difficult than that of instructing them; as if it were easier to induce men to do good voluntarily than to compel them to it by force. Let the learned of the first rank find an honourable refuge in their courts; let them there enjoy the only recompense worthy of them, that of promoting by their influence the happiness of the peoples they have enlightened by their wisdom. It is by this means only that we are likely to see what virtue, science, and authority can do, when animated by the noblest emulation, and working unanimously for the happiness of mankind.

But so long as power alone is on one side, and knowledge and understanding alone on the other, the learned will seldom make great objects their study, princes will still more rarely do great actions, and the peoples will continue to be, as they are, mean, corrupt, and miserable.

As for us, ordinary men, on whom Heaven has not been pleased to bestow such great talents; as we are not destined to reap such glory, let us remain in our obscurity. Let us not covet a reputation we should never attain, and which, in the present state of things, would never make up to us for the trouble it would have cost us, even if we were fully qualified to obtain it. Why should we build our happiness on the opinions of others, when we can find it in our own hearts? Let us leave to others the task of instructing mankind in their duty, and confine ourselves to the discharge of our own. We have no occasion for greater knowledge than this.

Virtue! sublime science of simple minds, are such industry and preparation needed if we are to know you? Are not your principles graven on every heart? Need we do more, to learn your laws, than examine ourselves and listen to the voice of conscience, when the passions are silent?

This is the true philosophy, with which we must learn to be content, without envying the fame of those celebrated men, whose names are immortal in the republic of letters. Let us, instead of envying them, endeavour to make, between them and us, that honourable distinction which was formerly seen to exist between two great peoples, that the one knew how to speak, and the other how to act, aright.

A DISCOURSE

ON A SUBJECT PROPOSED BY THE ACADEMY OF DIJON:

WHAT IS THE ORIGIN OF INEQUALITY AMONG MEN, AND IS IT AUTHORIZED BY NATURAL LAW?[1]

Non in depravatis, sed in his quae bene secundum naturam
se habent considerandum est quid sit naturale.
ARISTOTLE, *Politics*, Bk. i, ch. 2.

[We should consider what is natural not in things which are depraved but in those which are rightly ordered according to nature.]

Most honourable, magnificent and sovereign lords, convinced
that only a virtuous citizen can confer on his country honours
which it can accept, I have been for thirty years past working to
make myself worthy to offer you some public homage; and, this
fortunate opportunity supplementing in some degree the in-
sufficiency of my efforts, I have thought myself entitled to follow
in embracing it the dictates of the zeal which inspires me, rather
than the right which should have been my authorization. Having
had the happiness to be born among you, how could I reflect on
the equality which nature has ordained between men, and the
inequality which they have introduced, without reflecting on the
profound wisdom by which both are in this State happily combined
and made to coincide, in the manner that is most in conformity
with natural law, and most favourable to society, to the maintenance of public order and to the happiness of individuals? In my
researches after the best rules common sense can lay down for the
constitution of a government, I have been so struck at finding
them all in actuality in your own, that even had I not been born
within your walls I should have thought it indispensable for me to
offer this picture of human society to that people, which of all
others seems to be possessed of its greatest advantages, and to
have best guarded against its abuses.

If I had had to make choice of the place of my birth, I should
have preferred a society which had an extent proportionate to the
limits of the human faculties; that is, to the possibility of being
well governed: in which every person being equal to his occupation,
no one should be obliged to commit to others the functions with
which he was entrusted: a State, in which all the individuals being
well known to one another, neither the secret machinations of

vice, nor the modesty of virtue should be able to escape the notice and judgment of the public; and in which the pleasant custom of seeing and knowing one another should <u>make the love of country rather a love of the citizens than of its soil.</u>

I should have wished to be born in a country in which the interest of the Sovereign and that of the people must be single and identical; to the end that all the movements of the machine might tend always to the general happiness. And as this could not be the case, unless the Sovereign and the people were one and the same person, it follows that I should have wished to be born under a democratic government, wisely tempered.

I should have wished to live and die free: that is, so far subject to the laws that neither I, nor anybody else, should be able to cast off their honourable yoke: the easy and salutary yoke which the haughtiest necks bear with the greater docility, as they are made to bear no other.

I should have wished then that no one within the State should be able to say he was above the law; and that no one without should be able to dictate so that the State should be obliged to recognize his authority. For, be the constitution of a government what it may, if there be within its jurisdiction a single man who is not subject to the law, all the rest are necessarily at his discretion. And if there be a national ruler within, and a foreign ruler without, however they may divide their authority, it is impossible that both should be duly obeyed, or that the State should be well governed.

I should not have chosen to live in a republic of recent institution, however excellent its laws; for fear the government, being perhaps otherwise framed than the circumstances of the moment might require, might disagree with the new citizens, or they with it, and the State run the risk of overthrow and destruction almost as soon as it came into being. For it is with liberty as it is with those solid and succulent foods, or with those generous wines which are well adapted to nourish and fortify robust constitutions that are used to them, but ruin and intoxicate weak and delicate constitutions to which they are not suited. Peoples once accustomed to masters are not in a condition to do without them. If they attempt to shake off the yoke they still more estrange themselves from freedom, as, by mistaking for it an unbridled licence to which it is diametrically opposed, they nearly always manage, by their revolutions, to hand themselves over to seducers, who only make their chains heavier than before. The Roman people itself, a model for all free peoples, was wholly incapable of governing itself when it escaped from the oppression of the Tarquins. Debased by slavery, and the ignominious tasks which had been imposed upon it, it was at first no better than a stupid mob, which it was necessary to control and govern with the greatest wisdom; in order that, being accustomed by degrees to breathe the health-giving air of liberty, minds which had been enervated or rather brutalized under tyranny, might gradually acquire that severity of morals and spirit of fortitude which made it at length the people of all most worthy of respect. I should, then, have sought out for my country some peaceful and happy Republic, of an antiquity that lost itself, as it were, in the night of time: which had experienced only such shocks as served to manifest and strengthen the courage and patriotism of its subjects; and whose citizens, long accustomed to a wise independence, were not only free, but worthy to be so.

I should have wished to choose myself a country, diverted, by a fortunate impotence, from the brutal love of conquest, and secured, by a still more fortunate situation, from the fear of becoming itself the conquest of other States: a free city situated between several nations, none of which should have any interest in attacking it, while each had an interest in preventing it from being attacked by the others; in short, a Republic which should have nothing to tempt the ambition of its neighbours, but might reasonably depend on their assistance in case of need. It follows that a republican State so happily situated could have nothing to fear but from itself; and that, if its members trained themselves to the use of arms, it would be rather to keep alive that military ardour and courageous spirit which are so proper among freemen, and tend to keep up their taste for liberty, than from the necessity of providing for their defence.

I should have sought a country, in which the right of legislation was vested in all the citizens; for who can judge better than they of the conditions under which they had best dwell together in the same society? Not that I should have approved of *plebiscita*, like those among the Romans; in which the rulers in the State, and those most interested in its preservation, were excluded from the deliberations on which in many cases its security depended; and in which, by the most absurd inconsistency, the magistrates were deprived of rights which the meanest citizens enjoyed.

On the contrary, I should have desired that, in order to prevent self-interested and ill-conceived projects, and all such dangerous innovations as finally ruined the Athenians, each man should not be at liberty to propose new laws at pleasure; but that this right should belong exclusively to the magistrates; and that even they should use it with so much caution, the people, on its side, be so reserved in giving its consent to such laws, and the promulgation of them be attended with so much solemnity, that before the constitution could be upset by them, there might be time enough for all to be convinced, that it is above all the great antiquity of the laws which makes them sacred and venerable, that men soon learn to despise laws which they see daily altered, and that States, by accustoming themselves to neglect their ancient customs under the pretext of improvement, often introduce greater evils than those they endeavour to remove.

I should have particularly avoided, as necessarily ill-governed, a Republic in which the people, imagining themselves in a position to do without magistrates, or at least to leave them with only a precarious authority, should imprudently have kept for themselves the administration of civil affairs and the execution of their own laws. Such must have been the rude constitution of primitive governments, directly emerging from a state of nature; and this was another of the vices that contributed to the downfall of the Republic of Athens.

But I should have chosen a community in which the individuals, content with sanctioning their laws, and deciding the most important public affairs in general assembly and on the motion of

the rulers, had established honoured tribunals, carefully distinguished the several departments, and elected year by year some of
the most capable and upright of their fellow-citizens to administer
justice and govern the State; a community, in short, in which the
virtue of the magistrates thus bearing witness to the wisdom of the
people, each class reciprocally did the other honour. If in such a
case any fatal misunderstandings arose to disturb the public peace,
even these intervals of blindness and error would bear the marks
of moderation, mutual esteem, and a common respect for the
laws; which are sure signs and pledges of a reconciliation as lasting as sincere. Such are the advantages, most honourable,
magnificent, and sovereign lords, which I should have sought in
the country in which I should have chosen to be born. And if
providence had added to all these a delightful situation, a temperate climate, a fertile soil, and the most beautiful countryside under
Heaven, I should have desired only, to complete my felicity, the
peaceful enjoyment of all these blessings, in the bosom of this
happy country; to live at peace in the sweet society of my fellow-
citizens, and practising towards them, from their own example,
the duties of friendship, humanity, and every other virtue, to leave
behind me the honourable memory of a good man, and an upright
and virtuous patriot.

But if, less fortunate or too late grown wise, I had seen myself
reduced to end an infirm and languishing life in other climates,
vainly regretting that peaceful repose which I had forfeited in the
imprudence of youth, I should at least have entertained the same
feelings in my heart, though denied the opportunity of making use
of them in my native country. Filled with a tender and disinterested
love for my distant fellow-citizens, I should have addressed them
from my heart, much in the following terms.

'My dear fellow-citizens, or rather my brothers, since the ties of
blood, as well as the laws, unite almost all of us, it gives me
pleasure that I cannot think of you, without thinking at the same
time of all the blessings you enjoy, and of which none of you,
perhaps, more deeply feels the value than I who have lost them.

The more I reflect on your civil and political condition, the less can I conceive that the nature of human affairs could admit of a better. In all other governments, when there is a question of ensuring the greatest good of the State, nothing gets beyond projects and ideas, or at best bare possibilities. But as for you, your happiness is complete, and you have nothing to do but enjoy it; you require nothing more to be made perfectly happy than to know how to be satisfied with being so. Your sovereignty, acquired or recovered by the sword, and maintained for two centuries past by your valour and wisdom, is at length fully and universally acknowledged. Your boundaries are fixed, your rights confirmed, and your repose secured by honourable treaties. Your constitution is excellent, being not only dictated by the profoundest wisdom, but guaranteed by great and friendly powers. Your State enjoys perfect tranquillity; you have neither wars nor conquerors to fear; you have no other master than the wise laws you have yourselves made; and these are administered by upright magistrates of your own choosing. You are neither so wealthy as to be enervated by effeminacy, and thence to lose, in the pursuit of frivolous pleasures, the tase for real happiness and solid virtue; nor poor enough to require more assistance from abroad than your own industry is sufficient to procure you. In the meantime the precious privilege of liberty, which in great nations is maintained only by submission to the most exorbitant impositions, costs you hardly anything for its preservation.

May a Republic, so wisely and happily constituted, last for ever, for an example to other nations, and for the felicity of its own citizens! This is the only prayer you have left to make, the only precaution that remains to be taken. It depends, for the future, on yourselves alone (not to make you happy, for your ancestors have saved you that trouble), but to render that happiness lasting, by your wisdom in its enjoyment. It is on your constant union, your obedience to the laws, and your respect for their ministers, that your preservation depends. If there remains among you the smallest trace of bitterness or distrust, hasten to destroy it, as an accursed leaven which sooner or later must bring misfortune and ruin on the State. I conjure you all to look into your hearts, and to hearken to the secret voice of conscience. Is there any among you who can find, throughout the universe, a more upright, more enlightened, and more honourable body than your magistracy? Do not all its members set you an example of moderation, of simplicity of manners, of respect for the laws, and of the most sincere harmony? Place, therefore, without reserve, in such wise superiors, that salutary confidence which reason ever owes to virtue. Consider that they are your own choice, that they justify that choice, and that the honours due to those whom you have dignified are necessarily yours by reflection. Not one of you is so ignorant as not to know that, when the laws lose their force and those who defend them their authority, security and liberty are universally impossible. Why, therefore, should you hesitate to do that cheerfully and with just confidence which you would all along have been bound to do by your true interest, your duty, and reason itself?

Let not a culpable and pernicious indifference to the maintenance of the constitution ever induce you to neglect, in case of need, the prudent advice of the most enlightened and zealous of your fellow-citizens; but let equity, moderation, and firmness of resolution continue to regulate all your proceedings, and to exhibit you to the whole universe as the example of a valiant and modest people, jealous equally of their honour and of their liberty. Beware particularly, as the last piece of advice I shall give you, of sinister constructions and venomous rumours, the secret motives of which are often more dangerous than the actions at which they are levelled. A whole house will be awake and take the first alarm given by a good and trusty watch-dog, who barks only at the approach of thieves; but we hate the importunity of those noisy curs, which are perpetually disturbing the public repose, and whose continual ill-timed warnings prevent our attending to them, when they may perhaps be necessary.

And you, most honourable and magnificent lords, the worthy

and revered magistrates of a free people, permit me to offer you in particular my duty and homage. If there is in the world a station capable of conferring honour on those who fill it, it is undoubtedly that which virtue and talents combine to bestow, that of which you have made yourselves worthy, and to which you have been promoted by your fellow-citizens. Their worth adds a new lustre to your own; while, as you have been chosen, by men capable of governing others, to govern themselves, I cannot but hold you as much superior to all other magistrates, as a free people, and particularly that over which you have the honour to preside, is by its wisdom and its reason superior to the populace of other States.

Be it permitted me to cite an example of which there ought to have existed better records, and one which will be ever near to my heart. I cannot recall to mind, without the sweetest emotions, the memory of that virtuous citizen, to whom I owe my being, and by whom I was often instructed, in my infancy, in the respect which is due to you. I see him still, living by the work of his hands, and feeding his soul on the sublimest truths. I see the works of Tacitus, Plutarch, and Grotius, lying before him in the midst of the tools of his trade. At his side stands his dear son, receiving, alas with too little profit, the tender instructions of the best of fathers. But, if the follies of youth made me for a while forget his wise lessons, I have at length the happiness to be conscious that, whatever propensity one may have to vice, it is not easy for an education, with which love has mingled, to be entirely thrown away.

Such, my most honourable and magnificent lords, are the citizens, and even the common inhabitants of the State which you govern; such are those intelligent and sensible men, of whom, under the name of workmen and the people, it is usual, in other nations, to have a low and false opinion. My father, I own with pleasure, was in no way distinguished among his fellow-citizens. He was only such as they all are; and yet, such as he was, there is no country in which his acquaintance would not have been coveted and cultivated even with advantage by men of the highest character. It would not become me, nor is it, thank Heaven, at all necessary for me to remind you of the regard which such men have a right to expect of their magistrates, to whom they are equal both by education and by the rights of nature and birth, and inferior only, by their own will, by that preference which they owe to your merit, and, for giving you, can claim some sort of acknowledgment on your side. It is with a lively satisfaction I understand that the greatest candour and condescension attend, in all your behaviour towards them, on that gravity which becomes the ministers of the law; and that you so well repay them, by your esteem and attention, the respect and obedience which they owe to you. This conduct is not only just but prudent; as it happily tends to obliterate the memory of many unhappy events which ought to be buried in eternal oblivion. It is also so much the more judicious, as it tends to make this generous and equitable people find a pleasure in their duty; to make them naturally love to do you honour, and to cause those who are the most zealous in the maintenance of their own rights to be at the same time the most disposed to respect yours.

It ought not to be thought surprising that the rulers of a civil society should have the welfare and glory of their communities at heart: but it is uncommonly fortunate for the peace of men, when those persons who look upon themselves as the magistrates, or rather the masters, of a more holy and sublime country, show some love for the earthly country which maintains them. I am happy in having it in my power to make so singular an exception in our favour, and to be able to rank, among its best citizens, those zealous depositaries of the sacred articles of faith established by the laws, those venerable shepherds of souls whose powerful and captivating eloquence is so much the better calculated to bear to men's hearts the maxims of the gospel, as they are themselves the first to put them into practice. All the world knows of the great success with which the art of the pulpit is cultivated at Geneva; but men are so used to hearing divines preach one thing and practise another, that few have a chance of knowing how far the spirit of Christianity, holiness of manners, severity towards themselves, and indulgence towards their neighbours, prevail through-

out the whole body of our ministers. It is, perhaps, given to the
city of Geneva alone to produce the edifying example of so perfect
a union between its clergy and men of letters. It is in great measure
on their wisdom, their known moderation, and their zeal for the
prosperity of the State that I build my hopes of its perpetual
tranquillity. At the same time, I notice, with a pleasure mingled
with surprise and veneration, how much they detest the frightful
maxims of those accursed and barbarous men, of whom history
furnishes us with more than one example; who, in order to
support the pretended rights of God, that is to say their own
interests, have been so much the less sparing of human blood, as
they were more hopeful their own in particular would be always
respected.

I must not forget that precious half of the Republic which
makes the happiness of the other; and whose sweetness and
prudence preserve its tranquillity and virtue. Amiable and virtuous
daughters of Geneva, it will be always the lot of your sex to govern
ours. Happy are we, so long as your chaste influence, solely
exercised within the limits of conjugal union, is exerted only for
the glory of the State and the happiness of the public. It was thus
the female sex commanded at Sparta; and thus you deserve to
command at Geneva. What man can be such a barbarian as to
resist the voice of honour and reason, coming from the lips of an
affectionate wife? Who would not despise the vanities of luxury,
on beholding the simple and modest attire which, from the lustre
it derives from you, seems the most favourable to beauty? It is
your task to perpetuate, by your insinuating influence and your
innocent and amiable rule, a respect for the laws of the State, and
harmony among the citizens. It is yours to reunite divided families
by happy marriages; and, above all things, to correct, by the
persuasive sweetness of your lessons and the modest graces of
your conversation, those extravagances which our young people
pick up in other countries, whence, instead of many useful things
by which they might profit, they bring home hardly anything,
besides a puerile air and a ridiculous manner, acquired among

loose women, but an admiration for I know not what so-called grandeur, and paltry recompenses for being slaves, which can never come near the real greatness of liberty. Continue, therefore, always to be what you are, the chaste guardians of our morals, and the sweet security for our peace, exerting on every occasion the privileges of the heart and of nature, in the interests of duty and virtue.

I flatter myself that I shall never be proved to have been mistaken in building on such a foundation my hopes of the general happiness of the citizens and the glory of the Republic. It must be confessed, however, that with all these advantages, it will not shine with that lustre, by which the eyes of most men are dazzled; a puerile and fatal taste for which is the most mortal enemy of happiness and liberty.

Let our dissolute youth seek elsewhere light pleasures and long repentances. Let our pretenders to taste admire elsewhere the grandeur of palaces, the beauty of equipages, sumptuous furniture, the pomp of public entertainments, and all the refinements of luxury and effeminacy. Geneva boasts nothing but men; such a sight has nevertheless a value of its own, and those who have a taste for it are well worth the admirers of all the rest.

Deign, most honourable, magnificent, and sovereign lords, to receive, and with equal goodness, this respectful testimony of the interest I take in your common prosperity. And, if I have been so unhappy as to be guilty of any indiscreet transport in this glowing effusion of my heart, I beseech you to pardon me, and to attribute it to the tender affection of a true patriot, and to the ardent and legitimate zeal of a man, who can imagine for himself no greater felicity than to see you happy.

Most honourable, magnificent, and sovereign lords, I am, with the most profound respect,

Your most humble and obedient servant and fellow-citizen.

CHAMBÉRY,   J. J. ROUSSEAU'
June 12, 1754

PREFACE

Of all human sciences the most useful and most imperfect appears to me to be that of mankind: and I will venture to say, the single inscription on the Temple of Delphi contained a precept more difficult and more important than is to be found in all the huge volumes that moralists have ever written.[1] I consider the subject of the following discourse as one of the most interesting questions philosophy can propose, and unhappily for us, one of the most thorny that philosophers can have to solve. For how shall we know the source of inequality between men, if we do not begin by knowing mankind? And how shall man hope to see himself as nature made him, across all the changes which the succession of place and time must have produced in his original constitution? How can he distinguish what is fundamental in his nature from the changes and additions which his circumstances and the advances he has made have introduced to modify his primitive condition? Like the statue of Glaucus, which was so disfigured by time, seas, and tempests, that it looked more like a wild beast than a god, the human soul, altered in society by a thousand causes perpetually recurring, by the acquisition of a multitude of truths and errors, by the changes happening to the constitution of the body, and by the continual jarring of the passions, has, so to speak, changed in appearance, so as to be hardly recognizable. Instead of a being, acting constantly from fixed and invariable principles, instead of that celestial and majestic simplicity, impressed on it by its divine Author, we find it only the frightful contrast of passion mistaking itself for reason, and of understanding grown delirious.

It is still more cruel that, as every advance made by the human species removes it still farther from its primitive state, the more discoveries we make, the more we deprive ourselves of the means of making the most important of all. Thus it is, in one sense, by our very study of man, that the knowledge of him is put out of our power.

It is easy to perceive that it is in these successive changes in the constitution of man that we must look for the origin of those differences which now distinguish men, who, it is allowed, are as naturally equal among themselves as were the animals of every kind, before physical causes had introduced those varieties now observable among some of them.

It is, in fact, not to be conceived that these primary changes, however they may have arisen, could have altered, all at once and in the same manner, every individual of the species. It is natural to think that, while the condition of some of them grew better or worse, and they were acquiring various good or bad qualities not inherent in their nature, there were others who continued a longer time in their original condition. Such was doubtless the first source of the inequality of mankind, which it is much easier to point out thus in general terms, than to assign with precision to its actual causes.

Let not my readers therefore imagine that I flatter myself with having seen what it appears to me so difficult to discover. I have here entered upon certain arguments, and risked some conjectures, less in the hope of solving the difficulty, than with a view to throwing some light upon it, and reducing the question to its proper form. Others may easily proceed farther on the same road, and yet no one find it very easy to get to the end. For it is by no means a light undertaking to distinguish properly between what is original and what is artificial in the actual nature of man, or to form a true idea of a state which no longer exists, perhaps never did exist, and probably never will exist; and of which it is, nevertheless, necessary to have true ideas, in order to form a proper judgment of our present state. It requires, indeed, more philosophy than can be imagined to enable any one to determine exactly what precautions he ought to take, in order to make solid observations on this subject; and it appears to me that a good solution of the following problem would be not unworthy of the Aristotles and Plinys of the present age. *What experiments would have to be made, to discover the natural man? And how are those experiments to be made in a state of society?*

So far am I from undertaking to solve this problem, that I think I have sufficiently considered the subject, to venture to declare beforehand that our greatest philosophers would not be too good to direct such experiments, and our most powerful sovereigns to make them. Such a combination we have very little reason to expect, especially attended with the perseverance, or rather succession of intelligence and goodwill necessary on both sides to success.

These investigations, which are so difficult to make, and have been hitherto so little thought of, are, nevertheless, the only means that remain of obviating a multitude of difficulties which deprive us of the knowledge of the real foundations of human society. It is this ignorance of the nature of men which casts so much uncertainty and obscurity on the true definition of natural right: for, the idea of right, says Burlamaqui, and more particularly that of natural right, are ideas manifestly relative to the nature of man.[1] It is then from this very nature itself, he goes on, from the constitution and state of man, that we must deduce the first principles of this science.

We cannot see without surprise and disgust how little agreement there is between the different authors who have treated this great subject. Among the more important writers there are scarcely two of the same mind about it. Not to speak of the ancient philosophers, who seem to have done their best purposely to contradict one another on the most fundamental principles, the Roman jurists subjected man and the other animals indiscriminately to the same natural law, because they considered, under that name, rather the law which nature imposes on herself than that which she prescribes to others; or rather because of the particular acceptation of the term 'law' among those jurists; who seem on this occasion to have understood nothing more by it than the general relations established by nature between all animated beings, for their common preservation. The moderns, understanding by the term 'law' merely a rule prescribed to a moral being, that is to say intelligent, free, and considered in his relations to other beings, consequently confine the jurisdiction of natural law to man, as the only animal endowed with reason. But, defining this law, each after his own fashion, they have established it on such metaphysical principles, that there are very few persons among us capable of comprehending them, much less of discovering them for themselves. So that the definitions of these learned men, all differing in everything else, agree only in this, that it is impossible to comprehend the law of nature, and consequently to obey it, without being a very subtle casuist and a profound metaphysician. All which is as much as to say that mankind must have employed, in the establishment of society, a capacity which is acquired only with great difficulty, and by very few persons, even in a state of society.

Knowing so little of nature, and agreeing so ill about the meaning of the word 'law', it would be difficult for us to fix on a good definition of natural law. Thus all the definitions we meet with in books, setting aside their defect in point of uniformity, have yet another fault, in that they are derived from many kinds of knowledge, which men do not possess naturally, and from advantages of which they can have no idea until they have already departed from that state. Modern writers begin by inquiring what rules it would be expedient for me to agree on for their common interest, and then give the name of natural law to a collection of these rules, without any other proof than the good that would result from their being universally practised. This is undoubtedly a simple way of making definitions, and of explaining the nature of things by almost arbitrary conveniences.

But as long as we are ignorant of the natural man, it is in vain for us to attempt to determine either the law originally prescribed to him, or that which is best adapted to his constitution. All we can know with any certainty respecting this law is that, if it is to be a law, not only the wills of those it obliges must be sensible of their submission to it; but also, to be natural, it must come directly from the voice of nature.

Throwing aside, therefore, all those scientific books, which teach us only to see men such as they have made themselves, and contemplating the first and most simple operations of the human soul, I think I can perceive in it <u>two principles prior to reason, one of them deeply interesting us in our own welfare and preservation, and the other exciting a natural repugnance at seeing any other sensible being, and particularly any of our own species, suffer pain or death.</u> It is from the agreement and combination which the understanding is in a position to establish between these two principles, without its being necessary to introduce that of sociability, that all the rules of natural right appear to me to be derived – rules which our reason is afterwards obliged to establish on other foundations, when by its successive developments it has been led to suppress nature itself.

In proceeding thus, we shall not be obliged to make man a philosopher before he is a man. His duties toward others are not dictated to him only by the later lessons of wisdom; and, so long as he does not resist the internal impulse of compassion, he will never hurt any other man, nor even any sentient being, except on those lawful occasions on which his own preservation is concerned and he is obliged to give himself the preference. By this method also we put an end to the time-honoured disputes concerning the participation of animals in natural law: for it is clear that, being destitute of intelligence and liberty, they cannot recognize that law; as they partake, however, in some measure of our nature, in consequence of the sensibility with which they are endowed, they ought to partake of natural right; so that mankind is subjected to a kind of obligation even toward the brutes. It appears, in fact, that if I am bound to do no injury to my fellow-creatures, this is less because they are rational than because they are sentient beings: and this quality, being common both to men and beasts, ought to entitle the latter at least to the privilege of not being wantonly ill-treated by the former.

The very study of the original man, of his real wants, and the fundamental principles of his duty, is besides the only proper method we can adopt to obviate all the difficulties which the origin of moral inequality presents, on the true foundations of the body politic, on the reciprocal rights of its members, and on many other similar topics equally important and obscure.

If we look at human society with a calm and disinterested eye, it seems, at first, to show us only the violence of the powerful and the oppression of the weak. The mind is shocked at the cruelty of the one, or is induced to lament the blindness of the other; and as nothing is less permanent in life than those external relations, which are more frequently produced by accident than wisdom, and which are called weakness or power, riches or poverty, all human institutions seem at first glance to be founded merely on banks of shifting sand. It is only by taking a closer look, and removing the dust and sand that surround the edifice, that we perceive the immovable basis on which it is raised, and learn to respect its foundations. Now, without a serious study of man, his natural faculties and their successive development, we shall never be able to make these necessary distinctions, or to separate, in the actual constitution of things, that which is the effect of the divine will, from the innovations attempted by human art. The political and moral investigations, therefore, to which the important question before us leads, are in every respect useful; while the hypothetical history of government affords a lesson equally instructive to mankind.

In considering what we should have become, had we been left to ourselves, we should learn to bless Him, whose gracious hand, correcting our institutions, and giving them an immovable basis, has prevented those disorders which would otherwise have arisen from them, and caused our happiness to come from those very sources which seemed likely to involve us in misery.

> *Quem te deus esse*
> *Jussit, et humana quà parte locatus es in re,*
> *Disce.*
>
> PERSIUS, *Satires*, iii. 71.

[Learn what God ordered you to be and your place in the human condition.]

A Dissertation
on the Origin and Foundation of the Inequality of Mankind

It is of man that I have to speak; and the question I am investigating shows me that it is to men that I must address myself: for questions of this sort are not asked by those who are afraid to honour truth. I shall then confidently uphold the cause of humanity before the wise men who invite me to do so, and shall not be dissatisfied if I acquit myself in a manner worthy of my subject and of my judges.

I conceive that there are two kinds of inequality among the human species; one, which I call natural or physical, because it is established by nature, and consists in a difference of age, health, bodily strength, and the qualities of the mind or of the soul: and another, which may be called moral or political inequality, because it depends on a kind of convention, and is established, or at least authorized, by the consent of men. This latter consists of the different privileges which some men enjoy to the prejudice of others; such as that of being more rich, more honoured, more powerful, or even in a position to exact obedience.

It is useless to ask what is the source of natural inequality, because that question is answered by the simple definition of the word. Again, it is still more useless to inquire whether there is any essential connection between the two inequalities; for this would be only asking, in other words, whether those who command are necessarily better than those who obey, and if strength of body or of mind, wisdom, or virtue are always found in particular individuals, in proportion to their power or wealth: a question fit perhaps to be discussed by slaves in the hearing of their masters, but highly unbecoming to reasonable and free men in search of the truth.

The subject of the present discourse, therefore, is more precisely this. To mark, in the progress of things, the moment at which right took the place of violence and nature became subject to law, and to explain by what sequence of miracles the strong came to submit to serve the weak, and the people to purchase imaginary repose at the expense of real felicity.

The philosophers, who have inquired into the foundations of society, have all felt the necessity of going back to a state of nature; but not one of them has got there. Some of them have not hesitated to ascribe to man, in such a state, the idea of just and unjust, without troubling themselves to show that he must be possessed of such an idea, or that it could be of any use to him. Others have spoken of the natural right of every man to keep what belongs to him, without explaining what they meant by 'belongs'. Others again, beginning by giving the strong authority over the weak, proceeded directly to the birth of government, without regard to the time that must have elapsed before the meaning of the words 'authority' and 'government' could have existed among men.[1] Every one of them, in short, constantly dwelling on wants, avidity, oppression, desires, and pride, has transferred to the state of nature ideas which were acquired in society; so that, in speaking of the savage, they described the social man. It has not even entered into the heads of most of our writers to doubt whether the state of nature ever existed; but it is clear from the Holy Scriptures that the first man, having received his understanding and commandments immediately from God, was not himself in such a state; and that, if we give such credit to the writings of Moses as every Christian philosopher ought to give, we must deny that, even before the deluge, men were ever in the pure state of nature; unless, indeed, they fell back into it from some very extraordinary circumstance; a paradox which it would be very embarrassing to defend, and quite impossible to prove.

Let us being then by laying all facts aside,[2] as they do not affect the question. The investigations we may enter into, in treating this subject, must not be considered as historical truths, but only as mere conditional and hypothetical reasonings, rather calculated to explain the nature of things, than to ascertain their actual origin; just like the hypotheses which our physicists daily form respecting the formation of the world. Religion commands us to believe that God Himself having taken men out of a state of nature immediately after the creation, they are unequal only because it is His will they should be so: but it does not forbid us to form conjectures based solely on the nature of man, and the beings around him, concerning what might have become of the human race, if it had been left to itself. This then is the question asked me, and that which I propose to discuss in the following discourse. As my subject interests mankind in general, I shall endeavour to make use of a style adapted to all nations, or rather, forgetting time and place, to attend only to men to whom I am speaking. I shall suppose myself in the Lyceum of Athens, repeating the lessons of my masters, with Plato and Xenocrates for judges, and the whole human race for audience.

O man, of whatever country you are, and whatever your opinions may be, behold your history, such as I have thought to read it, not in books written by your fellow-creatures, who are liars, but in nature, which never lies. All that comes from her will be true; nor will you meet with anything false, unless I have involuntarily put in something of my own. The times of which I am going to speak are very remote: how much are you changed from what you once were! It is, so to speak, the life of your species which I am going to write, after the qualities which you have received, which your education and habits may have depraved, but cannot have entirely destroyed. There is, I feel, an age at which the individual man would wish to stop: you are about to inquire about the age at which you would have liked your whole species to stand still. Discontented with your present state, for reasons which threaten your unfortunate descendants with still greater discontent, you will perhaps wish it were in your power to go back; and this feeling should be a panegyric on your first ancestors, a criticism of your contemporaries, and a terror to the unfortunates who will come after you.

THE FIRST PART

Important as it may be, in order to judge rightly of the natural state of man, to consider him from his origin, and to examine him, as it were, in the embryo of his species, I shall not follow his organization through its successive developments, nor shall I stay to inquire what his animal system must have been at the beginning, in order to become at length what it actually is. I shall not ask whether his long nails were at first, as Aristotle supposes, only crooked talons; whether his whole body, like that of a bear, was not covered with hair; or whether the fact that he walked upon all fours, with his looks directed toward the earth, confined to a horizon of a few paces, did not at once point out the nature and limits of his ideas. On this subject I could form none but vague and almost imaginary conjectures. Comparative anatomy has as yet made too little progress, and the observations of naturalists are too uncertain, to afford an adequate basis for any solid reasoning. So that, without having recourse to the supernatural information given us on this head, or paying any regard to the changes which must have taken place in the internal, as well as the external, conformation of man, as he applied his limbs to new uses, and fed himself on new kinds of food, I shall suppose his conformation to have been at all times what it appears to us at this day; that he always walked on two legs, made use of his hands as we do, directed his looks over all nature, and measured with his eyes the vast expanse of the heavens.

If we strip this being, thus constituted, of all the supernatural gifts he may have received, and all the artificial faculties he can have acquired only by a long process; if we consider him, in a word, just as he must have come from the hands of nature, we behold in him an animal weaker than some, and less agile than others; but, taking him all round, the most advantageously organized of any. I see him satisfying his hunger at the first oak, and slaking his thirst at the first brook: finding his bed at the foot of the tree which afforded him a repast; and, with that, all his wants supplied.

While the earth was left to its naturàl fertility and covered with immense forests, whose trees were never mutilated by the axe, it would present on every side both sustenance and shelter for every species of animal. Men, dispersed up and down among the rest, would observe and imitate their industry, and thus attain even to the instinct of the beasts, with the advantage that, whereas every species of brutes was confined to one particular instinct, man, who perhaps has not any one peculiar to himself, would appropriate them all, and live upon most of those different foods, which other animals shared among themselves; and thus would find his subsistence much more easily than any of the rest.

Accustomed from their infancy to the inclemencies of the weather and the rigour of the seasons, inured to fatigue, and forced, naked and unarmed, to defend themselves and their prey from other ferocious animals, or to escape them by flight, men would acquire a robust and almost unalterable constitution. The children, bringing with them into the world the excellent constitution of their parents, and fortifying it by the very exercises which first produced it, would thus acquire all the vigour of which the human frame is capable. Nature in this case treats them exactly as Sparta treated the children of her citizens: those who come well formed into the world she renders strong and robust, and all the rest she destroys; differing in this respect from our modern communities, in which the State, by making children a burden to their parents, kills them indiscriminately before they are born.

The body of a savage man being the only instrument he understands, he uses it for various purposes, of which ours, for want of practice, are incapable: for our industry deprives us of that force and agility which necessity obliges him to acquire. If he had had an axe, would he have been able with his naked arm to break so large a branch from a tree? If he had had a sling, would he have been able to throw a stone with so great velocity? If he had had a ladder, would he have been so nimble in climbing a tree? If he had had a horse, would he have been himself so swift of foot? Give civilized man time to gather all his machines about him, and he will no doubt easily beat the savage; but if you would see a still

more unequal contest, set them together naked and unarmed, and
you will soon see the advantage of having all our forces constantly
at our disposal, of being always prepared for every event, and of
carrying one's self, as it were, perpetually whole and entire about
one.

Hobbes contends that man is naturally intrepid, and is intent
only upon attacking and fighting. Another illustrious philosopher[1]
holds the opposite, and Cumberland[2] and Pufendorf also affirm
that nothing is more timid and fearful than man in the state of
nature; that he is always in a tremble, and ready to fly at the least
noise or the slightest movement. This may be true of things he
does not know; and I do not doubt his being terrified by every
novelty that presents itself, when he neither knows the physical
good or evil he may expect from it, nor can make a comparison
between his own strength and the dangers he is about to encounter. Such circumstances, however, rarely occur in a state of
nature, in which all things proceed in a uniform manner, and the
face of the earth is not subject to those sudden and continual
changes which arise from the passions and caprices of bodies of
men living together. But savage man, living dispersed among
other animals, and finding himself betimes in a situation to
measure his strength with theirs, soon comes to compare himself
with them; and, perceiving that he surpasses them more in adroitness than they surpass him in strength, learns to be no longer
afraid of them. Set a bear, or a wolf, against a robust, agile, and
resolute savage, as they all are, armed with stones and a good
cudgel, and you will see that the danger will be at least on both
sides, and that, after a few trials of this kind, wild beasts, which
are not fond of attacking each other, will not be at all ready to
attack man, whom they will have found to be as wild and ferocious
as themselves. With regard to such animals as have really more
strength than man has adroitness, he is in the same situation as all
weaker animals, which notwithstanding are still able to subsist;
except indeed that he has the advantage that, being equally swift
of foot, and finding an almost certain place of refuge in every tree,

he is at liberty to take or leave it at every encounter, and thus to fight or fly, as he chooses. Add to this that it does not appear that any animal naturally makes war on man, except in case of self-defence or excessive hunger, or betrays any of those violent antipathies, which seem to indicate that one species is intended by nature for the food of another.

This is doubtless why negroes and savages are so little afraid of the wild beasts they may meet in the woods. The Caribs of Venezuela among others live in this respect in absolute security and without the smallest inconvenience. Though they are almost naked, Francis Corréal[1] tells us, they expose themselves freely in the woods, armed only with bows and arrows; but no one has ever heard of one of them being devoured by wild beasts.

But man has other enemies more formidable, against which he is not provided with such means of defence: these are the natural infirmities of infancy, old age, and illness of every kind, melancholy proofs of our weakness, of which the two first are common to all animals, and the last belongs chiefly to man in a state of society. With regard to infancy, it is observable that the mother, carrying her child always with her, can nurse it with much greater ease than the females of many other animals, which are forced to be perpetually going and coming, with great fatigue, one way to find subsistence, and another to suckle or feed their young. It is true that if the woman happens to perish, the infant is in great danger of perishing with her; but this risk is common to so many other species of animals, whose young take a long time before they are able to provide for themselves. And if our infancy is longer than theirs, our lives are longer in proportion; so that all things are in this respect fairly equal; though there are other rules to be considered regarding the duration of the first period of life, and the number of young, which do not affect the present subject. In old age, when men are less active and perspire little, the need for food diminishes with the ability to provide it. As the savage state also protects them from gout and rheumatism, and old age is, of all ills, that which human aid can least alleviate, they cease to be, without others perceiving that they are no more, and almost without perceiving it themselves.

With respect to sickness, I shall not repeat the vain and false declamations which most healthy people pronounce against medicine; but I shall ask if any solid observations have been made from which it may be justly concluded that, in the countries where the art of medicine is most neglected, the mean duration of man's life is less than in those where it is most cultivated. How indeed can this be the case, if we bring on ourselves more diseases than medicine can furnish remedies? The great inequality in manner of living, the extreme idleness of some, and the excessive labour of others, the easiness of exciting and gratifying our sensual appetites, the too exquisite foods of the wealthy which over-heat and fill them with indigestion, and, on the other hand, the unwholesome food of the poor, often, bad as it is, insufficient for their needs, which induces them, when opportunity offers, to eat voraciously and overcharge their stomachs; all these, together with sitting up late, and excesses of every kind, immoderate transports of every passion, fatigue, mental exhaustion, the innumerable pains and anxieties inseparable from every condition of life, by which the mind of man is incessantly tormented; these are too fatal proofs that the greater part of our ills are of our own making, and that we might have avoided them nearly all by adhering to that simple, uniform, and solitary manner of life which nature prescribed. If she destined man to be healthy, I venture to say that a state of reflection is one contrary to nature and that the man who meditates is a depraved animal. When we think of the good constitution of the savages, at least of those whom we have not ruined with our spirituous liquors, and reflect that they are troubled with hardly any disorders, save wounds and old age, we are tempted to believe that, in following the history of civil society, we shall be telling also that of human sickness. Such, at least, was the opinion of Plato, who inferred from certain remedies prescribed, or approved, by Podalirius and Machaon at the siege of Troy, that several sicknesses which these remedies gave rise to in his time, were not then known to mankind; and Celsus tells us that diet, which is now so necessary, was first invented by Hippocrates.

Being subject therefore to so few causes of sickness, man, in the state of nature, can have no need of remedies, and still less of physicians: nor is the human race in this respect worse off than other animals, and it is easy to learn from hunters whether they meet with many infirm animals in the course of the chase. It is certain they frequently meet with such as carry the marks of having been considerably wounded, with many that have had bones or even limbs broken, yet have been healed without any other surgical assistance than that of time, or any other regimen than that of their ordinary life. At the same time their cures seem not to have been less perfect, for their not having been tortured by incisions, poisoned with drugs, or wasted by fasting. In short, however useful medicine, properly administered, may be among us, it is certain that, if the savage, when he is sick and left to himself, has nothing to hope but from nature, he has, on the other hand, nothing to fear but from his disease; which renders his situation often preferable to our own.

We should beware, therefore, of confounding the savage man with the men we have daily before our eyes. Nature treats all the animals left to her care with a predilection that seems to show how jealous she is of that right. The horse, the cat, the bull, and even the ass are generally of greater stature, and always more robust, and have more vigour, strength, and courage, when they run wild in the forests than when bred in the stall. By becoming domesticated, they lose half these advantages; and it seems as if all our care to feed and treat them well serves only to deprave them. It is thus with man also: as he becomes sociable and a slave, he grows weak, timid, and servile; his effeminate way of life totally enervates his strength and courage. To this it may be added that there is still a greater difference between savage and civilized man than between wild and tame beasts; for men and brutes having been treated alike by nature, the several conveniences in which men indulge themselves still more than they do their beasts, are so many additional causes of their deeper degeneracy.

It is not therefore so great a misfortunate to these primitive men, nor so great an obstacle to their preservation, that they go naked, have no dwellings, and lack all the superfluities which we think so necessary. If their skins are not covered with hair, they have no need of such covering in warm climates; and, in cold countries, they soon learn to appropriate the skins of the beasts they have overcome. If they have but two legs to run with, they have two arms to defend themselves with, and provide for their wants. Their children are slowly and with difficulty taught to walk; but their mothers are able to carry them with ease; an advantage which other animals lack, as the mother, if pursued, is forced either to abandon her young, or to regulate her pace by theirs. Unless, in short, we suppose a singular and fortuitous concurrence of circumstances of which I shall speak later, and which could well never come about, it is plain in every state of the case, that the man who first made himself clothes or a dwelling was furnishing himself with things not at all necessary; for he had till then done without them, and there is no reason why he should not have been able to put up in manhood with the same kind of life as had been his in infancy.

Solitary, indolent, and perpetually accompanied by danger, the savage cannot be fond of sleep; his sleep too must be light, like that of the animals, which think but little and may be said to slumber all the time they do not think. Self-preservation being his chief and almost sole concern, he must exercise most those faculties which are most concerned with attack or defence, either for overcoming his prey, or for preventing him from becoming the prey of other animals. On the other hand, those organs which are perfected only by softness and sensuality will remain in a gross and imperfect state, incompatible with any sort of delicacy; so that, his senses being divided on this head, his touch and taste will be extremely coarse, his sight, hearing, and smell exceedingly fine and subtle. Such in general is the animal condition, and such, according to the narratives of travellers, is that of most savage nations. It is therefore no matter for surprise that the Hottentots of the Cape of Good Hope distinguish ships at sea, with the naked eye, at as great a distance as the Dutch can do with their telescopes; or that the savages of America should trace the Spaniards, by their smell, as well as the best dogs could have done; or that these barbarous peoples feel no pain in going naked, or that they use large quantities of pimento with their food, and drink the strongest European liquors like water.

Hitherto I have considered merely the physical man; let us now take a view of him on his metaphysical and moral side.

I see nothing in any animal but an ingenious machine, to which nature hath given senses to wind itself up, and to guard itself, to a certain degree, against anything that might tend to disorder or destroy it. I perceive exactly the same things in the human machine, with this difference, that in the operations of the brute, nature is the sole agent, whereas man has some share in his own operations, in his character as a free agent. The one chooses and refuses by instinct, the other from an act of free will: hence the brute cannot deviate from the rule prescribed to it, even when it would be advantageous for it to do so; and, on the contrary, man frequently deviates from such rules to his own prejudice. Thus a pigeon would be starved to death by the side of a dish of the choicest meats, and a cat on a heap of fruit or grain; though it is certain that either might find nourishment in the foods which it thus rejects with disdain, did it think of trying them. Hence it is that dissolute men run into excesses which bring on fevers and death; because the mind depraves the senses, and the will continues to speak when nature is silent.

Every animal has ideas, since it has senses; it even combines those ideas in a certain degree; and it is only in degree that man differs, in this respect, from the brute. Some philosophers have even maintained that there is a greater difference between one man and another than between some men and some beasts. It is not, therefore, so much the understanding that constitutes the specific difference between the man and the brute, as the human quality of free agency. Nature lays her commands on every animal, and the brute obeys her voice. Man receives the same impulsion, but at the same time knows himself at liberty to acquiesce or resist: and it is particularly in his consciousness of this liberty that the spirituality of his soul is displayed. For physics may explain, in some measure, the mechanism of the senses and the formation of ideas; but in the power of willing or rather of choosing, and in the feeling of this power, nothing is to be found but acts which are purely spiritual and wholly inexplicable by the laws of mechanism.

Yet, if the difficulties attending all these questions should still leave room for dispute about this difference between men and brutes, there is another very specific quality which distinguishes them, and which will admit of no dispute. This is the faculty of self-improvement, which, by the help of circumstances, gradually develops all the rest of our faculties, and is inherent in the species as in the individual: whereas a brute is, at the end of a few months, all he will ever be during his whole life, and his species, at the end of a thousand years, exactly what it was the first year of that thousand. Why is man alone liable to grow into a dotard? Is it not because he returns, in this, to his primitive state; and that, while the brute, which has acquired nothing and has therefore nothing to lose, still retains the force of instinct, man, who loses, by age or accident, all that his *perfectibility* had enabled him to gain, falls by this means lower than the brutes themselves? It would be melancholy, were we forced to admit that this distinctive and almost unlimited faculty is the source of all human misfortunes; that it is this which, in time, draws man out of his original state, in which he would have spent his days insensibly in peace and innocence; that it is this faculty, which, successively producing in different ages his discoveries and his errors, his vices and his virtues, makes him at length a tyrant both over himself and over nature.* It would be shocking to be obliged to regard as a benefactor the man who first suggested to the Oroonoko Indians the use of the boards

* See Appendix, p. 118.

they apply to the temples of their children, which secure to them some part at least of their imbecility and original happiness.

Savage man, left by nature solely to the direction of instinct, or rather indemnified for what he may lack by faculties capable at first of supplying its place, and afterwards of raising him much above it, must accordingly begin with purely animal functions: thus seeing and feeling must be his first condition, which would be common to him and all other animals. To will, and not to will, to desire and to fear, must be the first, and almost the only operations of his soul, till new circumstances occasion new developments of his faculties.

Whatever moralists may hold,[1] the human understanding is greatly indebted to the passions, which, it is universally allowed, are also much indebted to the understanding. It is by the activity of the passions that our reason is improved; for we desire knowledge only because we wish to enjoy; and it is impossible to conceive any reason why a person who has neither fears nor desires should give himself the trouble of reasoning. The passions, again, originate in our wants, and their progress depends on that of our knowledge; for we cannot desire or fear anything, except from the idea we have of it, or from the simple impulse of nature. Now savage man, being destitute of every species of enlightenment, can have no passions save those of the latter kind: his desires never go beyond his physical wants. The only goods he recognizes in the universe are food, a female, and sleep: the only evils he fears are pain and hunger. I say pain, and not death: for no animal can know what it is to die; the knowledge of death and its terrors being one of the first acquisitions made by man in departing from an animal state.

It would be easy, were it necessary, to support this opinion by facts, and to show that, in all the nations of the world, the progress of the understanding has been exactly proportionate to the wants which the peoples had received from nature, or been subjected to by circumstances, and in consequence to the passions that induced them to provide for those necessities. I might instance the arts, rising up in Egypt and expanding with the inundation of the Nile. I might follow their progress into Greece, where they took root afresh, grew up and towered to the skies, among the rocks and sands of Attica, without being able to germinate on the fertile banks of the Eurotas: I might observe that in general, the people of the North are more industrious than those of the South, because they cannot get on so well without being so: as if nature wanted to equalize matters by giving their understandings the fertility she had refused to their soil.

But who does not see, without recurring to the uncertain testimony of history, that everything seems to remove from savage man both the temptation and the means of changing his condition? His imagination paints no pictures; his heart makes no demands on him. His few wants are so readily supplied, and he is so far from having the knowledge which is needful to make him want more, that he can have neither foresight nor curiosity. The face of nature becomes indifferent to him as it grows familiar. He sees in it always the same order, the same successions: he has not understanding enough to wonder at the greatest miracles; nor is it in his mind that we can expect to find that philosophy man needs, if he is to know how to notice for once what he sees every day. His soul, which nothing disturbs, is wholly wrapped up in the feeling of its present existence, without any idea of the future, however near at hand; while his projects, as limited as his views, hardly extend to the close of day. Such, even at present, is the extent of the native Caribbean's foresight: he will improvidently sell you his cotton-bed in the morning, and come crying in the evening to buy it again, not having foreseen he would want it again the next night.

The more we reflect on this subject, the greater appears the distance between pure sensation and the most simple knowledge: it is impossible indeed to conceive how a man, by his own powers alone, without the aid of communication and the spur of necessity, could have bridged so great a gap. How many ages may have elapsed before mankind were in a position to behold any other fire than that of the heavens! What a multiplicity of chances must

have happened to teach them the commonest uses of that element!
How often must they have let it out before they acquired the art of
reproducing it! and how often may not such a secret have died
with him who had discovered it! What shall we say of agriculture,
an art which requires so much labour and foresight, which is so
dependent on others that it is plain it could only be practised in a
society which had at least begun, and which does not serve so
much to draw the means of subsistence from the earth – for these
it would produce of itself – but to compel it to produce what is
most to our taste? But let us suppose that men had so multiplied
that the natural produce of the earth was no longer sufficient for
their support; a supposition, by the way, which would prove such
a life to be very advantageous for the human race; let us suppose
that, without forges or workshops, the instruments of husbandry
had dropped from the sky into the hands of savages; that they had
overcome their natural aversion to continual labour; that they
had learnt so much foresight for their needs; that they had divined
how to cultivate the earth, to sow grain and plant trees; that they
had discovered the arts of grinding corn, and of setting the grape
to ferment – all being things that must have been taught them by
the gods, since it is not to be conceived how they could discover
them for themselves – yet after all this, what man among them
would be so absurd as to take the trouble of cultivating a field,
which might be stripped of its crop by the first comer, man or
beast, that might take a liking to it; and how should each of them
resolve to pass his life in wearisome labour, when, the more
necessary to him the reward of his labour might be, the surer he
would be of not getting it? In a word, how could such a situation
induce men to cultivate the earth, till it was regularly parcelled out
among them; that is to say, till the state of nature had been
abolished?

Were we to suppose savage man as trained in the art of thinking
as philosophers make him; were we, like them, to suppose him a
very philosopher capable of investigating the sublimest truths,
and of forming, by highly abstract chains of reasoning, maxims of

reason and justice, deduced from the love of order in general, or the known will of his Creator; in a word, were we to suppose him as intelligent and enlightened, as he must have been, and is in fact found to have been, dull and stupid, what advantage would accrue to the species, from all such metaphysics, which could not be communicated by one to another, but must end with him who made them? What progress could be made by mankind, while dispersed in the woods among other animals? and how far could men improve or mutually enlighten one another, when, having no fixed habitation, and no need of one another's assistance, the same persons hardly met twice in their lives, and perhaps then, without knowing one another or speaking together?

Let it be considered how many ideas we owe to the use of speech; how far grammar exercises the understanding and facilitates its operations. Let us reflect on the inconceivable pains and the infinite space of time that the first invention of languages must have cost. To these reflections add what preceded, and then judge how many thousand ages must have elapsed in the successive development in the human mind of those operations of which it is capable.

I shall here take the liberty for a moment, of considering the difficulties of the origin of languages, on which subject I might content myself with a simple repetition of the Abbé Condillac's investigations, as they fully confirm my system, and perhaps even first suggested it.[1] But it is plain, from the manner in which this philosopher solves the difficulties he himself raises, concerning the origin of arbitrary signs, that he assumes what I question, viz. that a kind of society must already have existed among the first inventors of language. While I refer, therefore, to his observations on this head, I think it right to give my own, in order to exhibit the same difficulties in a light adapted to my subject. The first which presents itself is to conceive how language can have become necessary; for as there was no communication among men and no need for any, we can neither conceive the necessity of this invention, nor the possibility of it, if it was not somehow indispensable.

I might affirm, with many others, that languages arose in the domestic intercourse between parents and their children. But this expedient would not obviate the difficulty, and would besides involve the blunder made by those who, in reasoning on the state of nature, always import into it ideas gathered in a state of society. Thus they constantly consider families as living together under one roof, and the individuals of each as observing among themselves a union as intimate and permanent as that which exists among us, where so many common interests unite them: whereas, in this primitive state, men had neither houses, nor huts, nor any kind of property whatever; every one lived where he could, seldom for more than a single night; the sexes united without design, as accident, opportunity, or inclination brought them together, nor had they any great needs of words to communicate their designs to each other; and they parted with the same indifference. The mother gave suck to her children at first for her own sake; and afterwards, when habit had made them dear, for theirs: but as soon as they were strong enough to go in search of their own food, they forsook her of their own accord; and, as they had hardly any other method of not losing one another than that of remaining continually within sight, they soon became quite incapable of recognizing one another when they happened to meet again. It is further to be observed that the child, having all his wants to explain, and of course more to say to his mother than the mother could have to say to him, must have borne the brunt of the task of invention, and the language he used would be of his own device, so that the number of languages would be equal to that of the individuals speaking them, and the variety would be increased by the vagabond and roving life they led, which would not give time for any idiom to become constant. For to say that the mother dictated to her child the words he was to use in asking her for one thing or another, is an explanation of how languages already formed are taught, but by no means explains how languages were originally formed.

We will suppose, however, that this first difficulty is obviated.

Let us for a moment then take ourselves as being on this side of the
vast space which must lie between a pure state of nature and that
in which languages had become necessary, and, admitting their
necessity, let us inquire how they could first be established. Here
we have a new and worse difficulty to grapple with; for if men
need speech to learn to think, they must have stood in much
greater need of the art of thinking, to be able to invent that of
speaking. And though we might conceive how the articulate
sounds of the voice came to be taken as the conventional interpreters of our ideas, it would still remain for us to inquire what
could have been the interpreters of this convention for those ideas,
which, answering to no sensible objects, could not be indicated
either by gesture or voice; so that we can hardly form any tolerable
conjectures about the origin of this art of communicating our
thoughts and establishing a correspondence between minds: an
art so sublime, that far distant as it is from its origin, philosophers
still behold it at such an immeasurable distance from perfection,
that there is none rash enough to affirm it will ever reach it, even
though the revolutions time necessarily produces were suspended
in its favour, though prejudice should be banished from our
academies or condemned to silence, and those learned societies
should devote themselves uninterruptedly for whole ages to this
thorny question.

The first language of mankind, the most universal and vivid, in
a word the only language man needed, before he had occasion to
exert his eloquence to persuade assembled multitudes, was the
simple cry of nature. But as this was excited only by a sort of
instinct on urgent occasions, to implore assistance in case of
danger, or relief in case of suffering, it could be of little use in the
ordinary course of life, in which more moderate feelings prevail.
When the ideas of men began to expand and multiply, and closer
communication took place among them, they strove to invent
more numerous signs and a more copious language. They multiplied the inflexions of the voice, and added gestures, which are in
their own nature more expressive, and depend less for their mean-

ing on a prior determination. Visible and movable objects were therefore expressed by gestures, and audible ones by imitative sounds: but, as hardly anything can be indicated by gestures, except objects actually present or easily described, and visible actions; as they are not universally useful – for darkness or the interposition of a material object destroys their efficacy – and as besides they rather request than secure our attention; men at length bethought themselves of substituting for them the articulate sounds of the voice, which, without bearing the same relation to any particular ideas, are better calculated to express them all, as conventional signs. Such an institution could only be made by common consent, and must have been effected in a manner not very easy for men whose gross organs had not been accustomed to any such exercise. It is also in itself still more difficult to conceive, since such a common agreement must have had motives, and it seems that speech must needs have existed before its use could be established.

It is reasonable to suppose that the first words which men used had for them a much wider meaning than the ones we use in languages which have already developed, and that, ignorant as they were of the division of discourse into its constituent parts, they at first gave every single word the sense of a whole proposition. When they began to distinguish subject and attribute, and noun and verb, which was itself no common effort of genius, substantives were at first only so many proper names; the present infinitive was the only tense of verbs; and the very idea of adjectives must have been developed with great difficulty; for every adjective is an abstract idea, and abstractions are painful and unnatural operations.

Every object at first received a particular name[1] without regard to genus or species, which these primitive originators were not in a position to distinguish; every individual presented itself to their minds in isolation, as they are in the picture of nature. If one oak was called A, another was called B; for the primitive idea of two things is that they are not the same, and it often takes a long time for what they have in common to be seen: so that, the narrower the limits of their knowledge of things, the more copious their dictionary must have been. The difficulty of using such a vocabulary could not be easily removed; for, to arrange beings under common and generic denominations, it became necessary to know their distinguishing properties: the need arose for observation and definition, that is to say, for natural history and metaphysics of a far more developed kind than men can at that time have possessed.

Add to this, that general ideas cannot be introduced into the mind without the assistance of words, nor can the understanding seize them except by means of propositions. This is one of the reasons why animals cannot form such ideas, or ever acquire that capacity for self-improvement which depends on them. When a monkey goes from one nut to another, are we to conceive that he entertains any general idea of that kind of fruit, and compares its archetype with the two individual nuts? Assuredly he does not; but the sight of one of these nuts recalls to his memory the sensations which he received from the other, and his eyes, being modified after a certain manner, give information to the palate of the modification it is about to receive. Every general idea is purely intellectual; if the imagination meddles with it ever so little, the idea immediately becomes particular. If you endeavour to trace in your mind the image of a tree in general, you never attain to your end. In spite of all you can do, you will have to see it as great or little, bare or leafy, light or dark, and were you capable of seeing nothing in it but what is common to all trees, it would no longer be like a tree at all. Purely abstract beings are perceivable in the same manner, or are only conceivable by the help of language. The definition of a triangle alone gives you a true idea of it: the moment you imagine a triangle in your mind, it is some particular triangle and not another, and you cannot avoid giving it sensible lines on a coloured area. We must then make use of propositions and of language in order to form general ideas. For no sooner does the imagination cease to operate than the understanding proceeds only by the help of words. If then the first inventors of speech could give names only to ideas they already had, it follows that the first substantives could be nothing more than proper names.

But when our new grammarians, by means of which I have no conception, began to extend their ideas and generalize their terms, the ignorance of the inventors must have confined this method within very narrow limits; and, as they had at first gone too far in multiplying the names of individuals, from ignorance of their genus and species, they made afterwards too few of these, from not having considered beings in all their specific differences. It would indeed have needed more knowledge and experience than they could have, and more pains and inquiry than they would have bestowed, to carry these distinctions to their proper length. If, even today, we are continually discovering new species, which have hitherto escaped observation, let us reflect how many of them must have escaped men who judged things merely from their first appearance! It is superfluous to add that the primitive classes and the most general notions must necessarily have escaped their notice also. How, for instance, could they have understood or thought of the words matter, spirit, substance, mode, figure, motion, when even our philosophers, who have so long been making use of them, have themselves the greatest difficulty in understanding them; and when, the ideas attached to them being purely metaphysical, there are no models of them to be found in nature?

But I stop at this point, and ask my judges to suspend their reading a while, to consider, after the invention of physical substantives, which is the easiest part of language to invent, that there is still a great way to go, before the thoughts of men will have found perfect expression and constant form, such as would answer the purposes of public speaking, and produce their effect on society. I beg of them to consider how much time must have been spent, and how much knowledge needed, to find out numbers, abstract terms, aorists, and all the tenses of verbs, particles, syntax, the method of connecting propositions, the forms of reasoning, and all the logic of speech. For myself, I am so aghast at the increasing difficulties which present themselves, and so well convinced of the almost demonstrable impossibility that languages should owe their original institution to merely human means, that I leave, to any one who will undertake it, the discussion of the difficult problem: which was the more necessary, the existence of society to the invention of language, or the invention of language to the establishment of society. But be the origins of language and society what they may, it may be at least inferred, from the little care which nature has taken to unite mankind by mutual wants, and to facilitate the use of speech, that she has contributed little to make them sociable, and has put little of her own into all they have done to create such bonds of union. It is in fact impossible to conceive why, in a state of nature, one man should stand more in need of the assistance of another, than a monkey or a wolf of the assistance of another of its kind: or, granting that he did, what motives could induce that other to assist him; or, even then, by what means they could agree about the conditions. I know it is incessantly repeated that man would in such a state have been the most miserable of creatures; and indeed, if it be true, as I think I have proved, that he must have lived many ages, before he could have either desire or an opportunity of emerging from it, this would only be an accusation against nature, and not against the being which she had thus unhappily constituted. But as I understand the word 'miserable', it either has no meaning at all, or else signifies only a painful privation of something, or a state of suffering either in body or soul. I should be glad to have explained to me, what kind of misery a free being, whose heart is at ease and whose body is in health, can possibly suffer. I would like to know which is the more likely to become insupportable to those who take part in it: the life of society or the life of nature. We hardly see anyone around us except people who are complaining of their existence; many even deprive themselves of it if they can and all divine and human laws put together can hardly put a stop to this disorder. I would like to know if anyone has heard of a savage who took it into his head, when he was free, to complain of life and to kill himself. Let us be less arrogant, then, when we judge on which side real misery is found. Nothing, on the other hand, could be more miserable than a savage exposed to the dazzling light of our 'civilization', tormented by our passions and reasoning about a state different from his own. It appears that providence most wisely determined that the faculties, which he potentially possessed, should develop themselves only as occasion offered to exercise them, in order that they might not be superfluous or perplexing to him, by appearing before their time, nor slow and useless when the need for them arose. In instinct alone, he had all he required for living in the state of nature; and with a developed understanding he has only just enough to support life in society.

It appears, at first view, that men in a state of nature, having no moral relations or determinate obligations one with another, could not be either good or bad, virtuous or vicious;[1] unless we take these terms in a physical sense, and call, in an individual, those qualities vices which may be injurious to his preservation, and those virtues which contribute to it; in which case, he would have to be accounted most virtuous, who put least check on the pure impulses of nature. But without deviating from the ordinary sense of the words, it will be proper to suspend the judgment we might be led to form on such a state, and be on our guard against our prejudices, till we have weighed the matter in the scales of impartiality, and seen whether virtues or vices preponderate among civilized men: and whether their virtues do them more good than their vices do harm; till we have discovered whether the progress of the sciences sufficiently indemnifies them for the mischiefs they do one another, in proportion as they are better informed of the good they ought to do; or whether they would not be, on the whole, in a much happier condition if they had nothing to fear or to hope from any one, than as they are, subjected to universal dependence, and obliged to take everything from those who engage to give them nothing in return.

Above all, let us not conclude, with Hobbes, that because man has no idea of goodness, he must be naturally wicked; that he is

vicious because he does not know virtue; that he always refuses to
do his fellow-creatures services which he does not think they have
a right to demand; or that by virtue of the right he justly claims to
all he needs, he foolishly imagines himself the sole proprietor of
the whole universe. Hobbes had seen clearly the defects of all the
modern definitions of natural right: but the consequences which
he deduces from his own show that he understands it in an equally
false sense. In reasoning on the principles he lays down, he ought
to have said that the state of nature, being that in which the care
for our own preservation is the least prejudicial to that of others,
was consequently the best calculated to promote peace, and the
most suitable for mankind. He does say the exact opposite, in
consequence of having improperly admitted, as a part of savage
man's care for self-preservation, the gratification of a multitude of
passions which are the work of society, and have made laws
necessary. A bad man, he says, is a robust child. But it remains to
be proved whether man in a state of nature is this robust child:
and, should we grant that he is, what would he infer? Why truly,
that if this man, when robust and strong, were dependent on
others as he is when feeble, there is no extravagance he would not
be guilty of; that he would beat his mother when she was too slow
in giving him her breast; that he would strangle one of his younger
brothers, if he should be troublesome to him, or bite the leg of
another, if he put him to any inconvenience. But that man in the
state of nature is both strong and dependent involves two contrary
suppositions. Man is weak when he is dependent, and is his own
master before he comes to be strong. Hobbes did not reflect that
the same cause, which prevents a savage from making use of his
reason, as our jurists hold, prevents him also from abusing his
faculties, as Hobbes himself allows: so that it may be justly said
that savages are not bad merely because they do not know what it
is to be good: for it is neither the development of the understanding nor the restraint of law that hinders them from doing ill; but
the peacefulness of their passions, and their ignorance of vice:
tanto plus in illis proficit vitiorum ignoratio, quam in his cognitio

virtutis. * There is another principle which has escaped Hobbes; which, having been bestowed on mankind, to moderate, on certain occasions, the impetuosity of *amour-propre*,[1] or, before its birth, the desire of self-preservation, tempers the ardour with which he pursues his own welfare, by an innate repugnance at seeing a fellow-creature suffer.† I think I need not fear contradiction in holding man to be possessed of the only natural virtue, which could not be denied him by the most violent detractor of human virtue. I am speaking of compassion, which is a disposition suitable to creatures so weak and subject to so many evils as we certainly are: by so much the more universal and useful to mankind, as it comes before any kind of reflection; and at the same time so natural, that the very brutes themselves sometimes give evident proofs of it. Not to mention the tenderness of mothers for their offspring and the perils they encounter to save them from danger, it is well known that horses show a reluctance to trample on living

* [Justin, *Hist.* ii, 2. So much more does the ignorance of vice profit the one sort than the knowledge of virtue the other.]

† *Amour-propre* must not be confused with love of self: for they differ both in themselves and in their effects. Love of self is a natural feeling which leads every animal to look to its own preservation, and which, guided in man by reason and modified by compassion, creates humanity and virtue. *Amour-propre* is a purely relative and factitious feeling, which arises in the state of society, leads each individual to make more of himself than of any other, causes all the mutual damage men inflict one on another, and is the real source of the 'sense of honour'. This being understood, I maintain that, in our primitive condition, in the true state of nature, *amour-propre* did not exist; for as each man regarded himself as the only observer of his actions, the only being in the universe who took any interest in him, and the sole judge of his deserts, no feeling arising from comparisons he could not be led to make could take root in his soul; and for the same reason, he could know neither hatred nor the desire for revenge, since these passions can spring only from a sense of injury: and as it is the contempt or the intention to hurt, and not the harm done, which constitutes the injury, men who neither valued nor compared themselves could do one another much violence, when it suited them, without feeling any sense of injury. In a word, each man, regarding his fellows almost as he regarded animals of different species, might seize the prey of a weaker or yield up his own to a stronger, and yet consider these acts of violence as mere natural occurrences, without the slightest emotion of insolence or despite, or any other feeling than the joy or grief of success or failure.

bodies. One animal never passes by the dead body of another of its species without disquiet: some even give their fellows a sort of burial; while the mournful lowings of the cattle when they enter the slaughter-house show the impressions made on them by the horrible spectacle which meets them. We find, with pleasure, the author of *The Fable of the Bees*[1] obliged to own that man is a compassionate and sensible being, and laying aside his cold subtlety of style, in the example he gives, to present us with the pathetic description of a man who, from a place of confinement, is compelled to behold a wild beast tear a child from the arms of its mother, grinding its tender limbs with its murderous teeth, and tearing its palpitating entrails with its claws. What horrid agitation must not the eye-witness of such a scene experience, although he would not be personally concerned! What anguish would he not suffer at not being able to give any assistance to the fainting mother and the dying infant!

Such is the pure emotion of nature, prior to all kinds of reflection! Such is the force of natural compassion, which the greatest depravity of morals has as yet hardly been able to destroy! for we daily find at our theatres men affected, nay, shedding tears at the sufferings of a wretch who, were he in the tyrant's place, would probably even add to the torments of his enemies; like the blood-thirsty Sulla, who was so sensitive to ills he had not caused, or that Alexander of Pheros who did not dare to go and see any tragedy acted, for fear of being seen weeping with Andromache and Priam, though he could listen without emotion to the cries of all the citizens who were daily strangled at his command.

> *Mollissima corda*
> *Humano generi dare se natura fatetur*
> *Quae lacrimas dedit.*
>
> JUVENAL, *Satires*, XV.131*

Mandeville well knew that, in spite of all their morality, men

---

* [Nature avows she gave the human race the softest hearts, who gave them tears.]

would have never been better than monsters, had not nature bestowed on them a sense of compassion, to aid their reason: but he did not see that from this quality alone flow all those social virtues, of which he denied man the possession. But what is generosity, clemency, or humanity but compassion applied to the weak, to the guilty, or to mankind in general? Even benevolence and friendship are, if we judge rightly, only the effects of compassion, constantly set upon a particular object: for how is it different to wish that another person may not suffer pain and uneasiness and to wish him happy? Were it even true that pity is no more than a feeling, which puts us in the place of the sufferer, a feeling obscure yet lively in a savage, developed yet feeble in civilized man; this truth would have no other consequence than to confirm my argument. Compassion must, in fact, be the stronger, the more the animal beholding any kind of distress identifies himself with the animal that suffers. Now, it is plain that such identification must have been much more perfect in a state of nature than it is in a state of reason. It is reason that engenders *amour-propre*, and reflection that confirms it: it is reason which turns man's mind back upon itself, and divides him from everything that could disturb or afflict him. It is philosophy that isolates him, and bids him say, at sight of the misfortunes of others: 'Perish if you will, I am secure.' Nothing but such general evils as threaten the whole community can disturb the tranquil sleep of the philosopher, or tear him from his bed. A murder may with impunity be committed under his window; he has only to put his hands to his ears and argue a little with himself, to prevent nature, which is shocked within him, from identifying itself with the unfortunate sufferer. Uncivilized man has not this admirable talent; and for want of reason and wisdom, is always foolishly ready to obey the first promptings of humanity. It is the populace that flocks together at riots and street brawls, while the wise man prudently makes off. It is the mob and the market-women, who part the combatants, and stop decent people from cutting one another's throats.

It is then certain that compassion is a natural feeling, which, by moderating the activity of love of self in each individual, contributes to the preservation of the whole species. It is this compassion that hurries us without reflection to the relief of those who are in distress: it is this which in a state of nature supplies the place of laws, morals, and virtues, with the advantage that none are tempted to disobey its gentle voice: it is this which will always prevent a sturdy savage from robbing a weak child or a feeble old man of the sustenance they may have with pain and difficulty acquired, if he sees a possibility of providing for himself by other means: it is this which, instead of inculcating that sublime maxim of rational justice, *Do to others as you would have them do unto you*, inspires all men with that other maxim of natural goodness, much less perfect indeed, but perhaps more useful; *Do good to yourself with as little evil as possible to others*. In a word, it is rather in this natural feeling than in any subtle arguments that we must look for the cause of that repugnance, which every man would experience in doing evil, even independently of the maxims of education. Although it might belong to Socrates and other minds of the like craft to acquire virtue by reason, the human race would long since have ceased to be, had its preservation depended only on the reasonings of the individuals composing it.

With passions so little active, and so good a curb, men, being rather wild than wicked, and more intent to guard themselves against the mischief that might be done them, than to do mischief to others, were by no means subject to very perilous dissensions. They maintained no kind of intercourse with one another, and were consequently strangers to vanity, deference, esteem, and contempt; they had not the least idea of 'mine' and 'thine', and no true conception of justice; they looked upon every violence to which they were subjected, rather as an injury that might easily be repaired than as a crime that ought to be punished; and they never thought of taking revenge, unless perhaps mechanically and on the spot, as a dog will sometimes bite the stone which is thrown at him. Their quarrels therefore would seldom have very bloody consequences; for the subject of them would be merely the question of subsistence. But I am aware of one greater danger, which remains to be noticed.

Of the passions that stir the heart of man, there is one which makes the sexes necessary to each other, and is extremely ardent and impetuous; a terrible passion that braves danger, surmounts all obstacles, and in its transports seems calculated to bring destruction on the human race which it is really destined to preserve. What must become of men who are left to this brutal and boundless rage, without modesty, without shame, and daily upholding their amours at the price of their blood?

It must, in the first place, be allowed that, the more violent the passions are, the more are laws necessary to keep them under restraint. But, setting aside the inadequacy of laws to effect this purpose, which is evident from the crimes and disorders to which these passions daily give rise among us, we should do well to inquire if these evils did not spring up with the laws themselves; for in this case, even if the laws were capable of repressing such evils, it is the least that could be expected from them, that they should check a mischief which would not have arisen without them.

Let us begin by distinguishing between the physical and moral ingredients in the feeling of love. The physical part of love is that general desire which urges the sexes to union with each other. The moral part is that which determines and fixes this desire exclusively upon one particular object; or at least gives it a greater degree of energy toward the object thus preferred. It is easy to see that the moral part of love is a factitious feeling, born of social usage, and enhanced by the women with much care and cleverness, to establish their empire, and put in power the sex which ought to obey. This feeling, being founded on certain ideas of beauty and merit which a savage is not in a position to acquire, and on comparisons which he is incapable of making, must be for him almost non-existent; for, as his mind cannot form abstract ideas of proportion and regularity, so his heart is not susceptible of the feelings of love and admiration, which are even insensibly produced by the application of these ideas. He follows solely the character nature has implanted in him, and not tastes which he could never have acquired; so that every woman equally answers his purpose.

Men in a state of nature being confined merely to what is physical in love, and fortunate enough to be ignorant of those excellences, which whet the appetite while they increase the difficulty of gratifying it, must be subject to fewer and less violent fits of passion, and consequently fall into fewer and less violent disputes. The imagination, which causes such ravages among us, never speaks to the heart of savages, who quietly await the impulses of nature, yield to them involuntarily, with more pleasure than ardour, and, their wants once satisfied, lose the desire. It is therefore incontestable that love, as well as all other passions, must have acquired in society that glowing impetuosity, which makes it so often fatal to mankind. And it is the more absurd to represent savages as continually cutting one another's throats to indulge their brutality, because this opinion is directly contrary to experience; the Caribbeans, who have as yet least of all deviated from the state of nature, being in fact the most peaceable of people in their amours, and the least subject to jealousy, though they live in a hot climate which seems always to inflame the passions.

With regard to the inferences that might be drawn, in the case of several species of animals, the males of which fill our poultry-yards with blood and slaughter, or in spring make the forests resound with their quarrels over their females; we must begin by excluding all those species, in which nature has plainly established, in the comparative power of the sexes, relations different from those which exist among us: thus we can base no conclusion about men on the habits of fighting cocks. In those species where the proportion is better observed, these battles must be entirely due to the scarcity of females in comparison with males; or, what amounts to the same thing, to the intervals during which the female constantly refuses the advances of the male: for if each female admits the male but during two months in the year, it is the same as if the number of females were five-sixths less. Now, neither of these two cases is applicable to the human species, in which the number of females usually exceeds that of males, and among whom it has never been observed, even among savages, that the females have, like those of other animals, their stated times of passion and indifference. Moreover, in several of these species, the individuals all take fire at once, and there comes a fearful moment of universal passion, tumult, and disorder among them; a scene which is never beheld in the human species, whose love is not thus seasonal. We must not then conclude from the combats of such animals for the enjoyment of the females, that the case would be the same with mankind in a state of nature: and, even if we drew such a conclusion, we see that such contests do not exterminate other kinds of animals, and we have no reason to think they would be more fatal to ours. It is indeed clear that they would do still less mischief than is the case in a state of society; especially in those countries in which, morals being still held in some repute, the jealousy of lovers and the vengeance of husbands are the daily cause of duels, murders, and even worse crimes; where the obligation of eternal fidelity only occasions adultery, and the very laws of honour and continence necessarily increase debauchery and lead to the multiplication of abortions.

Let us conclude then that man in a state of nature, wandering up and down the forests, without industry, without speech, and without home, an equal stranger to war and to all ties, neither standing in need of his fellow-creatures nor having any desire to hurt them, and perhaps even not distinguishing them one from another; let us conclude that, being self-sufficient and subject to so few passions, he could have no feelings or knowledge but such as befitted his situation; that he felt only his actual necessities, and disregarded everything he did not think himself immediately concerned to notice, and that his understanding made no greater progress than his vanity. If by accident he made any discovery, he was the less able to communicate it to others, as he did not know even his own children. Every art would necessarily perish with its inventor, where there was no kind of education among men, and generations succeeded generations without the least advance; when, all setting out from the same point, centuries must have elapsed in the barbarism of the first ages; when the race was already old, and man remained a child.

If I have expatiated at such length on this supposed primitive state, it is because I had so many ancient errors and inveterate prejudices to eradicate, and therefore thought it incumbent on me to dig down to their very root, and show, by means of a true picture of the state of nature, how far even the natural inequalities of mankind are from having that reality and influence which modern writers suppose.

It is in fact easy to see that many of the differences between men which are ascribed to nature stem rather from habit and the diverse modes of life of men in society. Thus a robust or delicate constitution, and the strength or weakness attaching to it, are more frequently the effects of a hardy or effeminate method of education than of the original endowment of the body. It is the same with the powers of the mind; for education not only makes a difference between such as are cultured and such as are not, but even increases the differences which exist among the former, in proportion to their respective degrees of culture: as the distance between a giant and a dwarf on the same road increases with every step they take. If we compare the prodigious diversity, which obtains in the education and manner of life of the various orders of men in the state of society, with the uniformity and simplicity of animal and savage life, in which every one lives on the same kind of food and in exactly the same manner, and does exactly the same things, it is easy to conceive how much less the difference between man and man must be in a state of nature than in a state of society, and how greatly the natural inequality of mankind must be increased by the inequalities of social institutions.

But even if nature really affected, in the distribution of her gifts, that partiality which is imputed to her, what advantage would the greatest of her favourites derive from it, to the detriment of others, in a state that admits of hardly any kind of relation between them? Where there is no love, of what advantage is beauty? Of what use is wit to those who do not converse, or cunning to those who have no business with others? I hear it constantly repeated that, in such a state, the strong would oppress the weak; but what is here meant by oppression? Some, it is said, would violently domineer over others, who would groan under a servile submission to their caprices. This indeed is exactly what I observe to be the case among us; but I do not see how it can be inferred of men in a state of nature, who could not easily be brought to conceive what we mean by dominion and servitude. One man, it is true, might seize the fruits which another had gathered, the game he had killed, or the cave he had chosen for shelter; but how would he ever be able to exact obedience, and what ties of dependence could there be among men without possessions? If, for instance, I am driven from one tree, I can go to the next; if I am disturbed in one place, what hinders me from going to another? Again, should I happen to meet with a man so much stronger than myself, and at the same time so depraved, so indolent, and so barbarous, as to compel me to provide for his sustenance while he himself remains idle; he must take care not to have his eyes off me for a single moment; he must bind me fast before he goes to sleep, or I shall certainly either knock him on the head or make my escape. That is to say, he must in such a case voluntarily expose himself to much greater trouble than he seeks to avoid, or can give me. After all this, let him be off his guard ever so little; let him but turn his head aside at any sudden noise, and I shall be instantly twenty paces off, lost in the forest, and, my fetters burst asunder, he would never see me again.

Without my expatiating thus uselessly on these details, every one must see that as the bonds of servitude are formed merely by the mutual dependence of men on one another and the reciprocal needs that unite them, it is impossible to make any man a slave, unless he be first reduced to a situation in which he cannot do without the help of others: and, since such a situation does not exist in a state of nature, every one is there his own master, and the law of the strongest is of no effect.

Having proved that the inequality of mankind is hardly felt, and that its influence is next to nothing in a state of nature, I must next show its origin and trace its progress in the successive developments of the human mind. Having shown that human *perfectibility*, the social virtues, and the other faculties which natural man potentially possessed, could never develop of themselves, but must require the fortuitous concurrence of many foreign causes that might never arise, and without which he would have remained for ever in his primitive conditions, I must now collect and consider the different accidents which may have improved the human understanding while depraving the species, and made man wicked while making him sociable; so as to bring him and the world from that distant period to the point at which we now behold them.

I confess that, as the events I am going to describe might have happened in various ways, I have nothing to determine my choice but conjectures: but such conjectures become reasons when they are the most probable that can be drawn from the nature of things, and the only means of discovering the truth. The consequences, however, which I mean to deduce will not be barely conjectural; as, on the principles just laid down, it would be impossible to form any other theory that would not furnish the same results, and from which I could not draw the same conclusions.

This will be a sufficient apology for my not dwelling on the manner in which the lapse of time compensates for the little probability in the events; on the surprising power of trivial causes, when their action is constant; on the impossibility, on the one hand, of destroying certain hypotheses, though on the other we cannot give them the certainty of known matters of fact; on its being within the province of history, when two facts are given as real, and have to be connected by a series of intermediate facts, which are unknown or supposed to be so, to supply such facts as may connect them; and on its being in the province of philosophy when history is silent, to determine similar facts to serve the same end; and lastly, on the influence of similarity, which, in the case of events, reduces the facts to a much smaller number of different classes than is commonly imagined. It is enough for me to offer these hints to the consideration of my judges, and to have so arranged that the general reader has no need to consider them at all.

THE SECOND PART

The first man who, having enclosed a piece of ground, bethought himself of saying 'This is mine', and found people simple enough to believe him, was the real founder of civil society. From how many crimes, wars, and murders, from how many horrors and misfortunes might not any one have saved mankind, by pulling up the stakes, or filling up the ditch, and crying to his fellows: 'Beware of listening to this impostor; you are undone if you once forget that the fruits of the earth belong to us all, and the earth itself to nobody.' But there is great probability that things had then already come to such a pitch, that they could no longer continue as they were; for the idea of property depends on many prior ideas, which could only be acquired successively, and cannot have been formed all at once in the human mind. Mankind must have made very considerable progress, and acquired considerable knowledge and industry which they must also have transmitted and increased from age to age, before they arrived at this last point of the state of nature. Let us then go farther back, and endeavour to unify under a single point of view that slow succession of events and discoveries in the most natural order.

Man's first feeling was that of his own existence, and his first care that of self-preservation. The produce of the earth furnished him with all he needed, and instinct told him how to use it. Hunger and other appetites made him at various times experience various modes of existence; and among these was one which urged him to propagate his species – a blind propensity that, having nothing to do with the heart, produced a merely animal act. The want once gratified, the two sexes knew each other no more; and even the offspring was nothing to its mother, as soon as it could do without her.

Such was the condition of infant man; the life of an animal limited at first to mere sensations, and hardly profiting by the gifts nature bestowed on him, much less capable of entertaining a thought of forcing anything from her. But difficulties soon presented themselves, and it became necessary to learn how to surmount them: the height of the trees, which prevented him from gathering their fruits, the competition of other animals desirous of the same fruits, and the ferocity of those who sought to deprive man himself of life, all obliged him to apply himself to bodily exercises. He had to be active, swift of foot, and vigorous in fight. Natural weapons, stones, and sticks, were easily found: he learnt to surmount the obstacles of nature, to contend in case of necessity with other animals, and to dispute for the means of subsistence even with other men, or to indemnify himself for what he was forced to give up to a stronger.

In proportion as the human race grew more numerous, men's cares increased. The difference of soils, climates, and seasons, must have introduced some differences into their manner of living. Barren years, long and sharp winters, scorching summers which parched the fruits of the earth, must have demanded a new industry. On the seashore and the banks of rivers, they invented the hook and line, and became fishermen and eaters of fish. In the forests they made bows and arrows, and became huntsmen and warriors. In cold countries they clothed themselves with the skins of the beasts they had slain. The lightning, a volcano, or some lucky chance acquainted them with fire, a new resource against the rigours of winter: they next learned how to preserve this element, then how to reproduce it, and finally how to prepare with it the flesh of animals which before they had eaten raw.

The way these different beings and phenomena impinged on him and on each other must naturally have engendered in man's mind the awareness of certain relationships. Thus the relationships which we denote by the terms great, small, strong, weak, swift, slow, fearful, bold, and the like, almost insensibly compared at need, must have at length produced in him a kind of reflection, or rather a mechanical prudence, which would indicate to him the precautions most necessary to his security.

The new intelligence which resulted from this development increased his superiority over other animals, by making him sensible of it. He would now endeavour, therefore, to ensnare them, would play them a thousand tricks, and though many of them might surpass him in swiftness or in strength, would in time become the master of some and the scourge of others. Thus, the first time he looked into himself, he felt the first emotion of pride; and, at a time when he scarce knew how to distinguish the different orders of beings, by looking upon his species as of the highest order, he prepared the way for assuming pre-eminence as an individual.

Other men, it is true, were not then to him what they now are to us, and he had no greater intercourse with them than with other animals; yet they were not neglected in his observations. The conformities, which he would in time discover between them, and between himself and his female, led him to judge of others which were not then perceptible; and finding that they all behaved as he himself would have done in like circumstances, he naturally inferred that their manner of thinking and acting was altogether in conformity with his own. This important truth, once deeply impressed on his mind, must have induced him, from an intuitive feeling more certain and much more rapid than any kind of reasoning, to pursue the rules of conduct, which he had best observe towards them, for his own security and advantage.

Taught by experience that the love of well-being is the sole motive of human actions, he found himself in a position to distinguish the few cases, in which mutual interest might justify him in relying upon the assistance of his fellows; and also the still fewer cases in which a conflict of interests might give cause to suspect them. In the former case, he joined in the same herd with them, or at most in some kind of loose association, that laid no restraint on its members, and lasted no longer than the transitory occasion that formed it. In the latter case, every one sought his own private advantage, either by open force, if he thought himself strong enough, or by address and cunning, if he felt himself the weaker.

In this manner, men may have insensibly acquired some gross ideas of mutual undertakings, and of the advantages of fulfilling them: that is, just so far as their present and apparent interest was concerned: for they were perfect strangers to foresight, and were so far from troubling themselves about the distant future, that they hardly thought of the morrow. If a deer was to be taken, every one saw that, in order to succeed, he must abide faithfully by his post: but if a hare happened to come within the reach of any one of them, it is not to be doubted that he pursued it without scruple, and, having seized his prey, cared very little, if by so doing he caused his companions to miss theirs.

It is easy to understand that such intercourse would not require a language much more refined than that of rooks or monkeys, who associate together for much the same purpose. Inarticulate cries, plenty of gestures, and some imitative sounds, must have been for a long time the universal language; and by the addition, in every country, of some conventional articulate sounds (of which, as I have already intimated, the first institution is not too easy to explain) particular languages were produced; but these were rude and imperfect, and nearly such as are now to be found among some savage nations.

Hurried on by the rapidity of time, by the abundance of things I have to say, and by the almost insensible progress of things in their beginnings, I pass over in an instant a multitude of ages; for the slower the events were in their succession, the more rapidly may they be described.

These first advances enabled men to make others with greater rapidity. In proportion as they grew enlightened, they grew industrious. They ceased to fall asleep under the first tree, or in the first cave that afforded them shelter; they invented several kinds of implements of hard and sharp stones, which they used to dig up the earth, and to cut wood; then they made huts out of branches, and afterwards learnt to plaster them over with mud and clay. This was the epoch of a first revolution, which established and distinguished families, and introduced a kind of property, in itself the source of a thousand quarrels and conflicts. As, however, the strongest were probably the first to build themselves huts which they felt themselves able to defend, it may be concluded that the weak found it much easier and safer to imitate, than to attempt to dislodge them: and of those who were once provided with huts, none could have any inducement to appropriate that of his neighbour; not indeed so much because it did not belong to him, as because it could be of no use, and he could not make himself master of it without exposing himself to a desperate battle with the family which occupied it.

The first expansions of the human heart were the effects of a novel situation, which united husbands and wives, fathers and children, under one roof. The habit of living together soon gave rise to the finest feelings known to humanity, conjugal love and paternal affection. Every family became a little society, the more united because liberty and reciprocal attachment were the only bonds of its union. The sexes, whose manner of life had been hitherto the same, began now to adopt different ways of living. The women became more sedentary, and accustomed themselves to mind the hut and their children, while the men went abroad in search of their common subsistence. From living a softer life, both sexes also began to lose something of their strength and ferocity: but, if individuals became to some extent less able to encounter wild beasts separately, they found it, on the other hand, easier to assemble and resist in common.

The simplicity and solitude of man's life in this new condition, the paucity of his wants, and the implements he had invented to satisfy them, left him a great deal of leisure, which he employed to furnish himself with many conveniences unknown to his fathers: and this was the first yoke he inadvertently imposed on himself, and the first source of the evils he prepared for his descendants. For, besides continuing thus to enervate both body and mind, these conveniences lost with use almost all their power to please, and even degenerated into real needs, till the want of them became far more disagreeable than the possession of them had been pleasant. Men would have been unhappy at the loss of them, though the possession did not make them happy.

We can here see a little better how the use of speech became established, and insensibly improved in each family, and we may form a conjecture also concerning the manner in which various causes may have extended and accelerated the progress of language, by making it more and more necessary. Floods or earthquakes surrounded inhabited districts with precipices or waters: revolutions of the globe tore off portions from the continent, and made them islands. It is readily seen that among men thus collected and compelled to live together, a common idiom must have arisen much more easily than among those who still wandered through the forests of the continent. Thus it is very possible that after their first essays in navigation the islanders brought over the use of speech to the continent: and it is at least very probable that communities and languages were first established in islands, and even came to perfection there before they were known on the mainland.

Everything now begins to change its aspect. Men, who have up to now been roving in the woods, by taking to a more settled manner of life, come gradually together, form separate bodies, and at length in every country arises a distinct nation, united in character and manners, not by regulations or laws, but by uniformity of life and food, and the common influence of climate. Permanent neighbourhood could not fail to produce, in time, some connection between different families. Young people of opposite sexes lived in neighbouring huts and the casual unions between them which resulted from the call of nature soon led, as they came to know each other better, to another kind which was no less pleasant and more permanent. They became accustomed to looking more closely at the different objects of their desires and to making comparisons; imperceptibly they acquired ideas of beauty and merit which led to feelings of preference. In consequence of seeing each other often, they could not do without seeing each other constantly. A tender and pleasant feeling insinuated itself into their souls, and the least opposition turned it into an impetuous fury: with love arose jealousy; discord triumphed, and human blood was sacrificed to the gentlest of all passions.

As ideas and feelings succeeded one another, and heart and head were brought into play, men continued to lay aside their original wildness; their private connections became every day more intimate as their limits extended. They accustomed themselves to assemble before their huts round a large tree; singing and dancing, the true offspring of love and leisure, became the amusement, or rather the occupation, of men and women thus assembled together with nothing else to do. Each one began to consider the rest, and to wish to be considered in turn; and thus a value came to be attached to public esteem. Whoever sang or danced best, whoever was the handsomest, the strongest, the most dexterous, or the most eloquent, came to be of most consideration; and this was the first step towards inequality, and at the same time towards vice. From these first distinctions arose on the one side vanity and contempt and on the other shame and envy: and the fermentation caused by these new leavens ended by producing combinations fatal to innocence and happiness.

As soon as men began to value one another, and the idea of consideration had got a footing in the mind, every one put in his claim to it, and it became impossible to refuse it to any with impunity. Hence arose the first obligations of civility even among savages; and every intended injury became an affront; because, besides the hurt which might result from it, the party injured was certain to find in it a contempt for his person, which was often more insupportable than the hurt itself.

Thus, as every man punished the contempt shown him by others, in proportion to his opinion of himself, revenge became terrible, and men bloody and cruel. This is precisely the state reached by most of the savage nations known to us: and it is for want of having made a proper distinction in our ideas, and seen how very far they already are from the state of nature, that so many writers have hastily concluded that man is naturally cruel, and requires civil institutions to make him more mild;[1] whereas nothing is more gentle than man in his primitive state, as he is placed by nature at an equal distance from the stupidity of brutes, and the fatal ingenuity of civilized man. Equally confined by instinct and reason to the sole care of guarding himself against the mischiefs which threaten him, he is restrained by natural compassion from doing any injury to others, and is not led to do such a thing even in return for injuries received. For, according to the axiom of the wise Locke, 'There can be no injury, where there is no property.'

But it must be remarked that the society thus formed, and the relations thus established among men, required of them qualities different from those which they possessed from their primitive constitution. Morality began to appear in human actions, and every one, before the institution of law, was the only judge and avenger of the injuries done him, so that the goodness which was suitable in the pure state of nature was no longer proper in the new-born state of society. Punishments had to be made more severe, as opportunities of offending became more frequent, and the dread of vengeance had to take the place of the rigour of the law. Thus, though men had become less patient, and their natural compassion had already suffered some diminution, this period of expansion of the human faculties, keeping a just mean between the indolence of the primitive state and the petulant activity of our *amour-propre*, must have been the happiest and most stable of epochs. The more we reflect on it, the more we shall find that this state was the least subject to revolutions, and altogether the very best man could experience; so that he can have departed from it only through some fatal accident, which, for the public good, should never have happened. The example of savages, most of whom have been found in this state, seems to prove that men were meant to remain in it, that it is the real youth of the world, and that all subsequent advances have been apparently so many steps towards the perfection of the individual, but in reality towards the decrepitude of the species.

So long as men remained content with their rustic huts, so long as they were satisfied with clothes made of the skins of animals and sewn together with thorns and fish-bones, adorned themselves only with feathers and shells, and continued to paint their bodies different colours, to improve and beautify their bows and arrows, and to make with sharp-edged stones fishing boats or clumsy musical instruments; in a word, so long as they undertook only what a single person could accomplish, and confined themselves to such arts as did not require the joint labour of several hands, they lived free, healthy, honest, and happy lives, in so far as their nature allowed, and they continued to enjoy the pleasures of mutual and independent intercourse. But from the moment one man began to stand in need of the help of another; from the moment it appeared advantageous to any one man to have enough provisions for two, equality disappeared, property was introduced, work became indispensable, and vast forests became smiling fields, which man had to water with the sweat of his brow, and where slavery and misery were soon seen to germinate and grow up with the crops.

Metallurgy and agriculture were the two arts which produced this great revolution. The poets tell us it was gold and silver, but, for the philosophers, it was iron and corn, which first civilized men, and ruined humanity. Thus both were unknown to the savages of America, who for that reason are still savage: the other nations also seem to have continued in a state of barbarism while they practised only one of these arts. One of the best reasons, perhaps, why Europe has been, if not longer, at least more constantly and highly civilized than the rest of the world, is that it is at once the most abundant in iron and the most fertile in corn.

It is difficult to conjecture how men first came to know and use iron; for it is impossible to suppose they would of themselves think of digging the ore out of the mine, and preparing it for smelting, before they knew what would be the result. On the other hand, we have the less reason to suppose this discovery the effect of any accidental fire, as mines are only formed in barren places, bare of trees and plants; so that it looks as if nature had taken pains to keep the fatal secret from us. There remains, therefore, only the extraordinary accident of some volcano which, by ejecting metallic substances already in fusion, suggested to the spectators the idea of imitating the natural operation. And we must further conceive them as possessed of uncommon courage and foresight, to undertake so laborious a work, with so distant a prospect of drawing advantage from it; yet these qualities are united only in minds more advanced than we can suppose those of these first discoverers to have been.

With regard to agriculture, the principles of it were known long before they were put in practice; and it is indeed hardly possible that men, constantly employed in drawing their subsistence from plants and trees, should not readily acquire a knowledge of the means made use of by nature for the propagation of plant life. It was in all probability very long, however, before their industry took that turn, either because trees, which together with hunting and fishing afforded them food, did not require their attention; or because they were ignorant of the use of corn, or without instruments to cultivate it; or because they lacked foresight to future needs; or lastly, because they were without means of preventing others from robbing them of the fruit of their labour.

When they grew more industrious, it is natural to believe that they began, with the help of sharp stones and pointed sticks, to cultivate a few vegetables or roots around their huts; though it was long before they knew how to prepare corn, or were provided with the implements necessary for raising it in any large quantity; not to mention how essential it is, for husbandry, to consent to immediate loss, in order to reap a future gain – a precaution very foreign to the turn of a savage's mind; for, as I have said, he hardly foresees in the morning what he will need at night.

The invention of the other arts must therefore have been necessary to compel mankind to apply themselves to agriculture. No sooner were artificers wanted to smelt and forge iron, than others were required to maintain them; the more hands that were employed in manufactures, the fewer were left to provide for the common subsistence, though the number of mouths to be furnished with food remained the same: and as some required commodities in exchange for their iron, the rest at length discovered the method of making iron serve for the multiplication of commodities. By this means the arts of husbandry and agriculture were established on the one hand, and the art of working metals and multiplying their uses on the other.

The cultivation of the earth necessarily brought about its distribution; and property, once recognized, gave rise to the first rules of justice; for, to secure each man his own, it had to be possible for each to have something. Besides, as men began to look forward to the future, and all had something to lose, every one had reason to apprehend that reprisals would follow any injury he might do to another. This origin is so much the more natural, as it is impossible to conceive how property can come from anything but manual labour: for what else can a man add to things which he does not originally create, so as to make them his own property? It is the husbandman's labour alone that, giving him a title to the produce of the ground he has tilled, gives him a claim also to the land itself, at least till harvest; and so, from year to year, a constant possession which is easily transformed into property. When the ancients, says Grotius, gave to Ceres the title of Legislatrix, and to a festival celebrated in her honour the name of Thesmophoria, they meant by that that the distribution of lands had produced a new kind of right: that is to say, the right of property, which is different from the right deducible from the law of nature.

In this state of affairs, equality might have been sustained, had the talents of individuals been equal, and had, for example, the use of iron and the consumption of commodities always exactly balanced each other; but, as there was nothing to preserve this balance, it was soon distributed; the strongest did most work; the most skilful turned his labour to best account; the most ingenious devised methods of diminishing his labour: the husbandman wanted more iron, or the smith more corn, and, while both laboured equally, the one gained a great deal by his work, while the other could hardly support himself. Thus natural inequality unfolds itself insensibly with that of combination, and the difference between men, developed by their different circumstances, becomes more sensible and permanent in its effects, and begins to have an influence, in the same proportion, over the lot of individuals.

Matters once at this pitch, it is easy to imagine the rest. I shall not detain the reader with a description of the successive invention of other arts, the development of language, the trial and utilization of talents, the inequality of fortunes, the use and abuse of riches, and all the details connected with them which the reader can easily supply for himself. I shall confine myself to a glance at mankind in this new situation.

Behold then all human faculties developed, memory and imagination in full play, *amour-propre* interested, reason active, and the mind almost at the highest point of its perfection. Behold all the natural qualities in action, the rank and condition of every man assigned him; not merely his share of property and his power to serve or injure others, but also his wit, beauty, strength or skill, merit or talents: and these being the only qualities capable of commanding respect, it soon became necessary to possess or to affect them.

It now became the interest of men to appear what they really were not. To be and to seem became two totally different things; and from this distinction sprang insolent pomp and cheating trickery, with all the numerous vices that go in their train. On the other hand, free and independent as men were before, they were now, in consequence of a multiplicity of new wants, brought into subjection, as it were, to all nature, and particularly to one another; and each became in some degree a slave even in becoming the master of other men: if rich, they stood in need of the services of others; if poor, of their assistance; and even a middle condition did not enable them to do without one another. Man must now, therefore, have been perpetually employed in getting others to interest themselves in his lot, and in making them, apparently at least, if not really, find their advantage in promoting his own. Thus he must have been sly and artful in his behaviour to some, and imperious and cruel to others; being under a kind of necessity to ill-use all the persons of whom he stood in need, when he could not frighten them into compliance, and did not judge it his interest to be useful to them. Insatiable ambition, the thirst of raising their respective fortunes, not so much from real want as from the desire to surpass others, inspired all men with a vile propensity to injure one another, and with a secret jealousy, which is the more dangerous, as it puts on the mask of benevolence, to carry its point with greater security. In a word, there arose rivalry and competition on the one hand, and conflicting interests on the other, together with a secret desire on both of profiting at the expense of others. All these evils were the first effects of property, and the inseparable attendants of growing inequality.

Before the invention of signs to represent riches, wealth could hardly consist in anything but lands and cattle, the only real possessions men can have. But, when inheritances so increased in number and extent as to occupy the whole of the land, and to border on one another, one man could aggrandize himself only at the expense of another; at the same time the supernumeraries, who had been too weak or too indolent to make such acquisitions, and had grown poor without sustaining any loss, because, while they saw everything change around them, they remained still the same, were obliged to receive their subsistence, or steal it, from the rich; and this soon bred, according to their different characters, dominion and slavery, or violence and rapine. The wealthy, on their part, had no sooner begun to taste the pleasure of command, than they disdained all others, and, using their old slaves to acquire new, thought of nothing but subduing and enslaving their neighbours; like ravenous wolves, which, having once tasted human flesh, despise every other food and thenceforth seek only men to devour.

Thus, as the most powerful or the most miserable considered their might or misery as a kind of right to the possessions of others, equivalent, in their opinion, to that of property, the destruction of equality was attended by the most terrible disorders. Usurpations by the rich, robbery by the poor, and the unbridled passions of both, suppressed the cries of natural compassion and the still feeble voice of justice, and filled men with avarice, ambition, and vice. Between the title of the strongest and that of the first occupier, there arose perpetual conflicts, which never ended but in battles and bloodshed. The new-born state of society thus gave rise to a horrible state of war; men thus harassed and depraved were no longer capable of retracing their steps or renouncing the fatal acquisitions they had made, but, labouring by the abuse of the faculties which do them honour, merely to their own confusion, brought themselves to the brink of ruin.

> *Attonitus novitate mali, divesque miserque,*
> *Effugere optat opes; et quae modo voverat odit.* *

It is impossible that men should not at length have reflected on so wretched a situation, and on the calamities that overwhelmed them. The rich, in particular, must have felt how much they suffered by a constant state of war, of which they bore all the expense; and in which, though all risked their lives, they alone risked their property. Besides, however speciously they might disguise their usurpations, they knew that they were founded on precarious and false titles; so that, if others took from them by force what they themselves had gained by force, they would have no reason to complain. Even those who had been enriched by their own industry, could hardly base their proprietorship on better claims. It was in vain to repeat: 'I built this well; I gained this spot by my industry.' Who gave you your standing, it might be answered, and what right have you to demand payment of us for doing what we never asked you to do? Do you not know that

---

* [Ovid, *Metamorphoses*, xi. 127.

   Both rich and poor, shocked at their new-found ills,
   Would fly from wealth, and lose what they had sought.]

numbers of your fellow-creatures are starving, for want of what you have too much of? You ought to have had the express and universal consent of mankind, before appropriating more of the common subsistence than you needed for your own maintenance. Destitute of valid reasons to justify and sufficient strength to defend himself, able to crush individuals with ease, but easily crushed himself by a troop of bandits, one against all, and incapable, on account of mutual jealousy, of joining with his equals against numerous enemies united by the common hope of plunder, the rich man, thus urged by necessity, conceived at length the profoundest plan that ever entered the mind of man: this was to employ in his favour the forces of those who attacked him, to make allies of his adversaries, to inspire them with different maxims, and to give them other institutions as favourable to himself as the law of nature was unfavourable.

With this view, after having represented to his neighbours the horror of a situation which armed every man against the rest, and made their possessions as burdensome to them as their wants, and in which no safety could be expected either in riches or in poverty, he readily devised plausible arguments to make them close with his design. 'Let us join,' said he, 'to guard the weak from oppression, to restrain the ambitious, and secure to every man the possession of what belongs to him: let us institute rules of justice and peace, to which all without exception may be obliged to conform; rules that may in some measure make amends for the caprices of fortune, by subjecting equally the powerful and the weak to the observance of reciprocal obligations. Let us, in a word, instead of turning our forces against ourselves, collect them in a supreme power which may govern us by wise laws, protect and defend all the members of the association, repulse their common enemies, and maintain eternal harmony among us.'

Far fewer words to this purpose would have been enough to impose on men so barbarous and easily seduced; especially as they had too many disputes among themselves to do without arbitrators, and too much ambition and avarice to go long without masters. All ran headlong to their chains, in hopes of securing their liberty; for they had just wit enough to perceive the advantages of political institutions, without experience enough to enable them to foresee the dangers. The most capable of foreseeing the dangers were the very persons who expected to benefit by them; and even the most prudent judged it not inexpedient to sacrifice one part of their freedom to ensure the rest; as a wounded man has his arm cut off to save the rest of his body.

Such was, or may well have been, the origin of society and law, which bound new fetters on the poor, and gave new powers to the rich; which irretrievably destroyed natural liberty, eternally fixed the law of property and inequality, converted clever usurpation into unalterable right, and, for the advantage of a few ambitious individuals, subjected all mankind to perpetual labour, slavery, and wretchedness. It is easy to see how the establishment of one community made that of all the rest necessary, and how, in order to make head against united forces, the rest of mankind had to unite in turn. Societies soon multiplied and spread over the face of the earth, till hardly a corner of the world was left in which a man could escape the yoke, and withdraw his head from beneath the sword which he saw perpetually hanging over him by a thread. Civil right having thus become the common rule among the members of each community, the law of nature maintained its place only between different communities, where, under the name of the right of nations, it was qualified by certain tacit conventions, in order to make commerce practicable, and serve as a substitute for natural compassion, which lost, when applied to societies, almost all the influence it had over individuals, and survived no longer except in some great cosmopolitan spirits, who, breaking down the imaginary barriers that separate different peoples, follow the example of our Sovereign Creator, and include the whole human race in their benevolence.

But bodies politic, remaining thus in a state of nature among themselves, presently experienced the inconveniences which had obliged individuals to forsake it; for this state became still more fatal to these great bodies than it had been to the individuals of whom they were composed. Hence arose national wars, battles, murders, and reprisals, which shock nature and outrage reason; together with all those horrible prejudices which class among the virtues the honour of shedding human blood.[1] The most distinguished men hence learned to consider cutting each other's throats a duty; at length men massacred their fellow-creatures by thousands without so much as knowing why, and committed more murders in a single day's fighting, and more violent outrages in the sack of a single town, than were committed in the state of nature during whole ages over the whole earth. Such were the first effects which we can see to have followed the division of mankind into different communities. But let us return to their institution.

I know that some writers have given other explanations of the origin of political societies, such as the conquest of the powerful, or the association of the weak.[2] It is, indeed, indifferent to my argument which of these causes we choose. That which I have just laid down, however, appears to me the most natural for the following reasons. First: because, in the first case, the right of conquest, being no right in itself, could not serve as a foundation on which to build any other; the victor and the vanquished people still remained with respect to each other in the state of war, unless the vanquished, restored to the full possession of their liberty, voluntarily made choice of the victor for their chief. For till then, whatever capitulation may have been made being founded on violence, and therefore *ipso facto* void, there could not have been on this hypothesis either a real society or body politic, or any law other than that of the strongest. Secondly: because the words 'strong' and 'weak' are, in the second case, ambiguous; for during the interval between the establishment of a right of property, or prior occupancy, and that of political government, the meaning of these words is better expressed by the terms 'rich' and 'poor'; because, in fact, before the institution of laws, men had no other way of reducing their equals to submission, than by attacking their goods, or making some of their own over to them. Thirdly:

because, as the poor had nothing but their freedom to lose, it would have been in the highest degree absurd for them to resign voluntarily the only good they still enjoyed, without getting anything in exchange: whereas the rich having feelings, if I may so express myself, in every part of their possessions, it was much easier to harm them, and therefore more necessary for them to take precautions against it; and, in short, because it is more reasonable to suppose a thing to have been invented by those to whom it would be of service, than by those whom it must have harmed.

Government had, in its infancy, no regular and constant form. The want of experience and philosophy prevented men from seeing any but present inconveniences, and they thought of providing against others only as they presented themselves. In spite of the endeavours of the wisest legislators, the political state remained imperfect, because it was little more than the work of chance; and, as it had begun ill, though time revealed its defects and suggested remedies, the original faults were never repaired. It was continually being patched up, when the first task should have been to get the site cleared and all the old materials removed, as was done by Lycurgus at Sparta, if a stable and lasting edifice was to be erected. Society consisted at first merely of a few general conventions, which every member bound himself to observe; and for the performance of covenants the whole body went security to each individual. Experience only could show the weakness of such a constitution, and how easily it might be infringed with impunity, from the difficulty of convicting men of faults, where the public alone was to be witness and judge: the laws could not but be eluded in many ways; disorders and inconveniences could not but multiply continually, till it became necessary to commit the dangerous trust of public authority to private persons, and the care of enforcing obedience to the deliberations of the people to the magistrate. For to say that chiefs were chosen before the confederacy was formed, and that the administrators of the laws were there before the laws themselves, is too absurd a supposition to consider seriously.

It would be as unreasonable to suppose that men at first threw themselves irretrievably and unconditionally into the arms of an absolute master, and that the first expedient which proud and unsubdued men hit upon for their common security was to run headlong into slavery. For what reason, in fact, did they take to themselves superiors, if it was not in order that they might be defended from oppression, and have protection for their lives, liberties, and properties, which are, so to speak, the constituent elements of their being? Now, in the relations between man and man, the worst that can happen is for one to find himself at the mercy of another, and it would have been inconsistent with common sense to begin by bestowing on a chief the only things they wanted his help to preserve. What equivalent could he offer them for so great a right? And if he had presumed to exact it under pretext of defending them, would he not have received the answer recorded in the fable: 'What more can the enemy do to us?' It is therefore beyond dispute, and indeed the fundamental maxim of all political right, that people have set up chiefs to protect their liberty, and not to enslave them. 'If we have a prince,' said Pliny to Trajan, 'it is to save ourselves from having a master.'

Politicians indulge in the same sophistry about the love of liberty as philosophers about the state of nature. They judge, by what they see, of very different things, which they have not seen; they attribute to man a natural propensity to servitude, because the slaves within their observation are seen to bear the yoke with patience; they fail to reflect that it is with liberty as with innocence and virtue; the value is known only to those who possess them, and the taste for them is forfeited when they are forfeited themselves. 'I know the charms of your country,' said Brasidas to a Satrap, who was comparing the life at Sparta with that at Persepolis, 'but you cannot know the pleasures of mine.'

An unbroken horse erects his mane, paws the ground and starts back impetuously at the sight of the bridle; while one which is properly trained suffers patiently even whip and spur: so savage man will not bend his neck to the yoke to which civilized man submits without a murmur, but prefers the most turbulent state of liberty to the most peaceful slavery. We cannot therefore, from the servility of nations already enslaved, judge of the natural disposition of mankind for or against slavery; we should go by the prodigious efforts of every free people to save itself from oppression. I know that the former are for ever holding forth in praise of the tranquillity they enjoy in their chains, and that they call a state of wretched servitude a state of peace: *miserrimam servitutem pacem appellant.** But when I observe the latter sacrificing pleasure, peace, wealth, power, and life itself to the preservation of that one treasure, which is so disdained by those who have lost it; when I see free-born animals dash their brains out against the bars of their cage, from an innate impatience of captivity; when I behold numbers of naked savages, that despise European pleasures, braving hunger, fire, the sword, and death, to preserve nothing but their independence, I feel that it is not for slaves to argue about liberty.

With regard to paternal authority, from which some writers have derived absolute government and all society,¹ it is enough, without going back to the contrary arguments of Locke and Sidney, to remark that nothing on earth can be farther from the ferocious spirit of despotism than the mildness of that authority which looks more to the advantage of him who obeys than to that of him who commands; that, by the law of nature, the father is the child's master no longer than his help is necessary; that from that time they are both equal, the son being perfectly independent of the father, and owing him only respect, and not obedience. For gratitude is a duty which ought to be paid, but not a right to be exacted: instead of saying that civil society is derived from paternal authority, we ought to say rather that the latter derives its principal force from the former. No individual was ever acknowledged as the father of many, till his sons and daughters remained settled around him. The goods of the father, of which he is really the master, are the ties which keep his children in depen-

---

* [Tacitus, *Hist.* iv. 17. The most wretched slavery they call peace.]

dence, and he may bestow on them, if he pleases, no share of his property, unless they merit it by constant deference to his will. But the subjects of an arbitrary despot are so far from having the like favour to expect from their chief, that they themselves and everything they possess are his property, or at least are considered by him as such; so that they are forced to receive, as a favour, the little of their own he is pleased to leave them. When he despoils them, he does but justice, and mercy in that he permits them to live.

By proceeding thus to test fact by right, we should discover as little reason as truth in the voluntary establishment of tyranny. It would also be no easy matter to prove the validity of a contract binding on only one of the parties, where all the risk is on one side, and none on the other; so that no one could suffer but he who bound himself. This hateful system is indeed, even in modern times, very far from being that of wise and good monarchs, and especially of the kings of France; as may be seen from several passages in their edicts; particularly from the following passage in a celebrated edict published in 1667 in the name and by order of Louis XIV.

'Let it not, therefore, be said that the Sovereign is not subject to the laws of his State; since the contrary is a true proposition of the right of nations, which flattery has sometimes attacked but good princes have always defended as the tutelary divinity of their dominions. How much more legitimate is it to say with the wise Plato, that the perfect felicity of a kingdom consists in the obedience of subjects to their prince, and of the prince to the laws, and in the laws being just and constantly directed to the public good!'*

I shall not stay here to inquire whether, as liberty is the noblest faculty of man, it is not degrading our very nature, reducing ourselves to the level of the brutes, which are mere slaves of instinct, and even an affront to the Author of our being, to

---

* *Of the Rights of the Most Christian Queen over various States of the Monarchy of Spain, 1667.*

renounce without reserve the most precious of all His gifts, and to bow to the necessity of committing all the crimes He has forbidden, merely to gratify a mad or a cruel master; or if this sublime craftsman ought not to be less angered at seeing His workmanship entirely destroyed than thus dishonoured. I will waive (if my opponents please) the authority of Barbeyrac,[1] who, following Locke, roundly declares that no man can so far sell his liberty as to submit to an arbitrary power which may use him as it likes. *For, he adds, this would be to sell his own life, of which he is not master.* I shall ask only what right those who were not afraid thus to debase themselves could have to subject their posterity to the same ignominy, and to renounce for them those blessings which they do not owe to the liberality of their progenitors, and without which life itself must be a burden to all who are worthy of it.

Pufendorf says that we may divest ourselves of our liberty in favour of other men, just as we transfer our property from one to another by contracts and agreements. But this seems a very weak argument. For in the first place, the property I alienate becomes quite foreign to me, nor can I suffer from the abuse of it; but it very nearly concerns me that my liberty should not be abused, and I cannot without incurring the guilt of the crimes I may be compelled to commit, expose myself to become an instrument of crime. Besides, the right of property being only a convention of human institution, men may dispose of what they possess as they please: but this is not the case with the essential gifts of nature, such as life and liberty, which every man is permitted to enjoy, and of which it is at least doubtful whether any have a right to divest themselves. By giving up the one, we degrade our being; by giving up the other, we do our best to annul it; and, as no temporal good can indemnify us for the loss of either, it would be an offence against both reason and nature to renounce them at any price whatsoever. But, even if we could transfer our liberty, as we do our property, there would be a great difference with regard to the children, who enjoy the father's substance only by the transmission of his right; whereas, liberty being a gift which they hold from nature as being men, their parents have no right whatever to deprive them of it. As then, to establish slavery, it was necessary to do violence to nature, so, in order to perpetuate such a right, nature would have to be changed. Jurists who have gravely determined that the child of a slave comes into the world a slave, have decided, in other words, that a man shall come into the world not a man.

I regard it then as certain, that government did not begin with arbitrary power, but that this is the depravation, the extreme term, of government, and brings it back, finally, to just the law of the strongest, which it was originally designed to remedy. Supposing, however, it had begun in this manner, such power, being in itself illegitimate, could not have served as a basis for the laws of society, nor, consequently, for the inequality they instituted.

Without entering at present upon the investigations which still remain to be made into the nature of the fundamental compact underlying all government, I content myself with adopting the common opinion concerning it, and regard the establishment of the political body as a real contract between the people and the chiefs chosen by them: a contract by which both parties bind themselves to observe the laws therein expressed, which form the ties of their union. The people having in respect of their social relations concentrated all their wills in one, the several articles, concerning which this will is explained, become so many fundamental laws, obligatory on all the members of the State without exception, and one of these articles regulates the choice and power of the magistrates appointed to watch over the execution of the rest. This power extends to everything which may maintain the constitution, without going so far as to alter it. It is accompanied by honours, in order to bring the laws and their administrators into respect. The ministers are also distinguished by personal prerogatives, in order to recompense them for the cares and labour which good administration involves. The magistrate, on his side, binds himself to use the power he is entrusted with only in conformity with the intention of his constituents, to maintain them all in the peaceable possession of what belongs to them, and to prefer on every occasion the public interest to his own.

Before experience had shown, or knowledge of the human heart enabled men to foresee, the unavoidable abuses of such a constitution, it must have appeared so much the more excellent, as those who were charged with the care of its preservation had themselves most interest in it; for magistracy and the rights attaching to it being based solely on the fundamental laws, the magistrates would cease to be legitimate as soon as these ceased to exist; the people would no longer owe them obedience; and as not the magistrates, but the laws, are essential to the being of a State, the members of it would regain the right to their natural liberty.

If we reflect with ever so little attention on this subject, we shall find new arguments to confirm this truth, and be convinced from the very nature of the contract that it cannot be irrevocable; for, if there were no superior power capable of ensuring the fidelity of the contracting parties, or compelling them to perform their reciprocal engagements, the parties would be sole judges in their own cause, and each would always have a right to renounce the contract, as soon as he found that the other had violated its terms, or that they no longer suited his convenience. It is upon this principle that the right of abdication may possibly be founded. Now, if, as here, we consider only what is human in this institution, it is certain that, if the magistrate, who has all the power in his own hands, and appropriates to himself all the advantages of the contract, has none the less a right to renounce his authority, the people, who suffer for all the faults of their chief, must have a much better right to renounce their dependence. But the terrible and innumerable quarrels and disorders that would necessarily arise from so dangerous a privilege, show, more than anything else, how much human governments stood in need of a more solid basis than mere reason, and how expedient it was for the public tranquillity that the divine will should interpose to invest the sovereign authority with a sacred and inviolable character, which might deprive subjects of the fatal right of disposing of it. If the world had received no other advantages from religion, this would be enough to impose on men the duty of adopting and cultivating it, abuses and all, since it has been the means of saving more blood than fanaticism has ever spilt. But let us follow the thread of our hypothesis.

The different forms of government owe their origin to the differing degrees of inequality which existed between individuals at the time of their institution. If there happened to be any one man among them pre-eminent in power, virtue, riches, or personal influence, he became sole magistrate, and the State assumed the form of monarchy. If several, nearly equal in point of eminence, stood above the rest, they were elected jointly, and formed an aristocracy. Again, among a people who had deviated less from a state of nature, and between whose fortune or talents there was less disproportion, the supreme administration was retained in common, and a democracy was formed. It was discovered in process of time which of these forms suited men the best. Some peoples continued to be ruled solely by their laws; others soon came to obey masters. Citizens wished to preserve their liberty; subjects, however, irritated at seeing others enjoying a blessing they had lost, thought only of making slaves of their neighbours. In a word, on the one side arose riches and conquests, and on the other happiness and virtue.

In these different governments, all the offices were at first elective; and when the influence of wealth did not carry the day, the preference was given to merit, which gives a natural ascendancy, and to age, which is experienced in business and deliberate in council. The Elders of the Hebrews, the Gerontes at Sparta, the Senate at Rome, and the very etymology of our word Seigneur, show how old age was once held in veneration. But the more often the choice fell upon old men, the more often elections had to be repeated, and the more they became a nuisance; intrigues set in, factions were formed, party feeling grew bitter, civil wars broke out; the lives of individuals were sacrificed to the pretended happiness of the State; and at length men were on the point of relapsing into their primitive anarchy. Ambitious chiefs profited by these circumstances to perpetuate their offices in their own families: at the same time the people, already used to dependence, ease, and the conveniences of life, and already incapable of breaking its fetters, agreed to an increase of its slavery, in order to secure its tranquillity. Thus magistrates, having become hereditary, contracted the habit of considering their offices as a family estate, and themselves as proprietors of the communities of which they were at first only the officers, of regarding their fellow-citizens as their slaves, and numbering them, like cattle, among their belongings, and of calling themselves the equals of the gods and kings of kings.

If we follow the progress of inequality in these various revolutions, we shall find that the establishment of laws and of the right of property was its first term, the institution of magistracy the second, and the conversion of legitimate into arbitrary power the third and last; so that the condition of rich and poor was authorized by the first period; that of powerful and weak by the second; and only by the third that of master and slave, which is the last degree of inequality, and the term at which all the rest remain, when they have got so far, till the government is either entirely dissolved by new revolutions, or brought back again to legitimacy.

To understand this progress as necessary we must consider not so much the motives for the establishment of the body politic, as the forms it assumes in actuality, and the faults that necessarily attend it: for the flaws which make social institutions necessary are the same as make the abuse of them unavoidable. If we except Sparta, where the laws were mainly concerned with the education of children, and where Lycurgus established such morality as practically made laws needless – for laws as a rule, being weaker than the passions, restrain men without altering them – it would not be difficult to prove that every government, which scrupulously complied with the ends for which it was instituted, and guarded carefully against change and corruption, was set up unnecessarily. For a country in which no one evaded the laws and no one made a bad use of the powers of a magistrate would require neither laws nor magistrates.

Political distinctions necessarily produce civil distinctions. The growing inequality between the people and its leaders is soon felt by individuals and among them it takes a thousand different forms according to their passions, their talents and their circumstances. The magistrate could not usurp illegitimate power without the help of creatures to whom he is forced to give a share of that power. Besides, individuals only allow themselves to be oppressed so far as they are hurried on by blind ambition, and, looking rather below than above them, come to love authority more than independence, and submit to slavery, that they may in turn enslave others. It is no easy matter to reduce to obedience a man who has no ambition to command; nor would the most adroit politician find it possible to enslave a people whose only desire was to be independent. But inequality easily makes its way among cowardly and ambitious minds, which are ever ready to run the risks of fortune, and almost indifferent whether they command or obey, as it is favourable or adverse. Thus, there must have been a time, when the eyes of the people were so fascinated, that their rulers had only to say to the least of men, 'Be great, you and all your posterity,' to make him immediately appear great in the eyes of every one as well as in his own. His descendants took still more upon them, in proportion to their distance from him; the more obscure and uncertain the cause, the greater the effect: the greater the number of idlers one could count in a family, the more illustrious it was held to be.

If this were the place to go into details, I could readily explain how, even without the intervention of government, inequality of credit and authority became unavoidable among private persons, as soon as their union in a single society made them compare themselves one with another, and take into account the differences which they found out from the continual intercourse every man had to have with his neighbours.* These differences are of several kinds; but riches, nobility or rank, power and personal merit being the principal distinctions by which men form an estimate of each other in society, I could prove that the harmony or conflict of these different forces is the surest indication of the good or bad constitution of a State. I could show that among these four kinds of inequality, personal qualities being the origin of all the others, wealth is the one to which they are all reduced in the end; for, as riches tend most immediately to the prosperity of individuals, and are easiest to communicate, they are used to purchase every other distinction. By this observation we are enabled to judge pretty exactly how far a people has departed from its primitive constitution, and of its progress towards the extreme term of corruption.

* Distributive justice would oppose this rigorous equality of the state of nature, even were it practicable in civil society; as all the members of the State owe it their services in proportion to their talents and abilities, they ought, on their side, to be distinguished and favoured in proportion to the services they have actually rendered. It is in this sense we must understand that passage of Isocrates, in which he extols the primitive Athenians, for having determined which of the two kinds of equality was the most useful, viz. that which consists in dividing the same advantages indiscriminately among all the citizens, or that which consists in distributing them to each according to his deserts. These able politicians, adds the orator, banishing that unjust inequality which makes no distinction between good and bad men, adhered inviolably to that which rewards and punishes every man according to his deserts.

But in the first place, there never existed a society, however corrupt some may have become, where no difference was made between the good and the bad; and with regard to morality, where no measures can be prescribed by law exact enough to serve as a practical rule for a magistrate, it is with great prudence that, in order not to leave the fortune or quality of the citizens to his discretion, it prohibits him from passing judgment on persons and confines his judgment to actions. Only morals such as those of the ancient Romans can bear censors, and such a tribunal among us would throw everything into confusion. The difference between good and bad men is determined by public esteem; the magistrate being strictly a judge of right alone; whereas the public is the truest judge of morals, and is of such integrity and penetration on this head, that although it may be sometimes deceived, it can never be corrupted. The rank of citizens ought, therefore, to be regulated, not according to their personal merit – for this would put it in the power of the magistrate to apply the law almost arbitrarily – but according to the actual services done to the State, which are capable of being more exactly estimated.

I could explain how much this universal desire for reputation, honours, and advancement, which inflames us all, exercises and holds up to comparison our faculties and powers; how it excites and multiplies our passions, and, by creating universal competition and rivalry, or rather enmity, among men, occasions numberless failures, successes, and disturbances of all kinds by making so many aspirants run the same course. I could show that it is to this desire of being talked about, and this unremitting rage of distinguishing ourselves, that we owe the best and the worst things we possess, both our virtues and our vices, our science and our errors, our conquerors and our philosophers; that is to say, a great many bad things, and a very few good ones. In a word, I could prove that, if we have a few rich and powerful men on the pinnacle of fortune and grandeur, while the crowd grovels in want and obscurity, it is because the former prize what they enjoy only in so far as others are destitute of it; and because, without changing their condition, they would cease to be happy the moment the people ceased to be wretched.

These details alone, however, would furnish matter for a considerable work, in which the advantages and disadvantages of every kind of government might be weighed, as they are related to man in the state of nature, and at the same time all the different aspects, under which inequality has up to the present appeared, or may appear in ages yet to come, according to the nature of the several governments, and the alterations which time must unavoidably occasion in them, might be demonstrated. We should then see the multitude oppressed from within, in consequence of the very precautions it had taken to guard against foreign tyranny. We should see oppression continually gain ground without its being possible for the oppressed to know where it would stop, or what legitimate means was left them of checking its progress. We should see the rights of citizens and the freedom of nations slowly extinguished, and the complaints, protests, and appeals of the weak treated as seditious murmurings. We should see the honour of defending the common cause confined by statecraft to a mercenary part of the people. We should see taxes made necessary by such means, and the disheartened husbandman deserting his fields even in the midst of peace, and leaving the plough to gird on the sword. We should see fatal and capricious codes of honour established; and the champions of their country sooner or later becoming its enemies, and for ever holding their daggers to the breasts of their fellow-citizens. The time would come when they would be heard saying to the oppressor of their country:

> *Pectore si fratris gladium juguloque parentis*
> *Condere me jubeas, gravidaeque in viscera partu*
> *Conjugis, invita peragam tamen omnia dextra.*
>   LUCAN, i. 376.*

From great inequality of fortunes and conditions, from the vast variety of passions and of talents, of useless and pernicious arts, of vain sciences, would arise a multitude of prejudices equally contrary to reason, happiness, and virtue. We should see the magistrates fomenting everything that might weaken men united in society, by promoting dissension among them; everything that might sow in it the seeds of actual division, while it gave society the air of harmony; everything that might inspire the different ranks of people with mutual hatred and distrust, by setting the rights and interests of one against those of another, and so strengthen the power which comprehended them all.

It is from the midst of this disorder and these revolutions, that despotism, gradually raising up its hideous head and devouring everything that remained sound and untainted in any part of the State, would at length trample on both the laws and the people, and establish itself on the ruins of the republic. The times which immediately preceded this last change would be times of trouble and calamity; but at length the monster would swallow up every-

---

* [If you order me to thrust my sword into my brother's breast or my father's throat or the bowels of my pregnant wife, I will do all this though with an unwilling right arm.]

thing, and the people would no longer have either chiefs or laws, but only tyrants. From this moment there would be no question of virtue or morality; for despotism (*cui ex honesto nulla est spes*), wherever it prevails, admits no other master; it no sooner speaks than probity and duty lose their weight and blind obedience is the only virtue which slaves can still practise.

This is the last term of inequality, the extreme point that closes the circle, and meets that from which we set out. Here all private persons return to their first equality, because they are nothing; and, subjects having no law but the will of their master, and their master no restraint but his passions, all notions of good and all principles of equity again vanish. There is here a complete return to the law of the strongest, and so to a new state of nature, differing from that we set out from; for the one was a state of nature in its first purity, while this is the consequence of excessive corruption. There is so little difference between the two states in other respects, and the contract of government is so completely dissolved by despotism, that the despot is master only so long as he remains the strongest; as soon as he can be expelled, he has no right to complain of violence. The popular insurrection that ends in the death or deposition of a Sultan is as lawful an act as those by which he disposed, the day before, of the lives and fortunes of his subjects. As he was maintained by force alone, it is force alone that overthrows him. Thus everything takes place according to the natural order; and, whatever may be the result of such frequent and precipitate revolutions, no one man has reason to complain of the injustice of another, but only of his own ill-fortune or indiscretion.

If the reader thus discovers and retraces the lost and forgotten road, by which man must have passed from the state of nature to the state of society; if he carefully restores, along with the intermediate situations which I have just described, those which want of time has compelled me to suppress, or my imagination has failed to suggest, he cannot fail to be struck by the vast distance which separates the two states. It is in tracing this slow succession that he will find the solution of a number of problems of politics and morals, which philosophers cannot settle. He will feel that, men being different in different ages, the reason why Diogenes could not find a man was that he sought among his contemporaries a man of an earlier period. He will see that Cato died with Rome and liberty, because he did not fit the age in which he lived; the greatest of men served only to astonish a world which he would certainly have ruled, had he lived five hundred years sooner. In a word, he will explain how the soul and the passions of men insensibly change their very nature; why our wants and pleasures in the end seek new objects; and why, the original man having vanished by degrees, society offers to us only an assembly of artificial men and factitious passions, which are the work of all these new relations, and without any real foundation in nature. We are taught nothing on this subject, by reflection, that is not entirely confirmed by observation. The savage and the civilized man differ so much in the bottom of their hearts and in their inclinations, that what constitutes the supreme happiness of one would reduce the other to despair. The former breathes only peace and liberty; he desires only to live and be free from labour; even the *ataraxia* of the Stoic falls far short of his profound indifference to every other object. Civilized man, on the other hand, is always moving, sweating, toiling, and racking his brains to find still more laborious occupations: he goes on in drudgery to his last moment, and even seeks death to put himself in a position to live, or renounces life to acquire immortality. He pays his court to men in power, whom he hates, and to the wealthy, whom he despises; he stops at nothing to have the honour of serving them; he is not ashamed to value himself on his own meanness and their protection; and, proud of his slavery, he speaks with disdain of those, who have not the honour of sharing it. What a sight would the perplexing and envied labours of a European minister of State present to the eyes of a Caribbean! How many cruel deaths would not this indolent savage prefer to the horrors of such a life, which is seldom even sweetened by the pleasure of doing good! But, for him to see into the motives of all this solicitude the words 'power' and 'reputation' would have to bear some meaning in his mind; he would have to know that there are men who set a value on the opinion of the rest of the world; who can be made happy and satisfied with themselves rather on the testimony of other people than on their own. In reality, the source of all these differences is, that the savage lives within himself, while social man lives constantly outside himself, and only knows how to live in the opinion of others, so that he seems to receive the consciousness of his own existence merely from the judgment of others concerning him. It is not to my present purpose to insist on the indifference to good and evil which arises from this disposition, in spite of our many fine works on morality, or to show how, everything being reduced to appearances, there is but art and mummery in even honour, friendship, virtue, and often vice itself, of which we at length learn the secret of boasting; to show, in short, how, always asking others what we are, and never daring to ask ourselves, in the midst of so much philosophy, humanity, and civilization, and of such sublime codes of morality, we have nothing to show for ourselves but a frivolous and deceitful appearance, honour without virtue, reason without wisdom, and pleasure without happiness. It is sufficient that I have proved that this is not by any means the original state of man, but that it is merely the spirit of society, and the inequality which society produces, that thus transform and alter all our natural inclinations.

I have endeavoured to trace the origin and progress of inequality, and the institution and abuse of political societies, as far as these are capable of being deduced from the nature of man merely by the light of reason, and independently of those sacred dogmas which give the sanction of divine right to sovereign authority. It follows from this survey that, as there is hardly any inequality in the state of nature, all the inequality which now prevails owes its strength and growth to the development of our faculties and the advance of the human mind, and becomes at last permanent and legitimate by the establishment of property and laws. Secondly, it follows that moral inequality, authorized by positive right alone, clashes with natural right, whenever it is not proportionate to physical inequality – a distinction which sufficiently determines what we ought to think of that species of inequality which prevails in all civilized countries; since it is plainly contrary to the law of nature, however defined, that children should command old men, fools wise men, and that the privileged few should gorge themselves with superfluities, while the starving multitude are in want of the bare necessities of life.

APPENDIX[1]

A famous author,[2] reckoning up the good and evil of human life, and comparing the aggregates, finds that our pains greatly exceed our pleasures: so that, all things considered, human life is not at all a valuable gift. This conclusion does not surprise me; for the writer drew all his arguments from man in civilization. Had he gone back to the state of nature, his inquiries would clearly have had a different result, and man would have been seen to be subject to very few evils not of his own creation. It has indeed cost us not a little trouble to make ourselves as wretched as we are. When we consider, on the one hand, the immense labours of mankind, the many sciences brought to perfection, the arts invented, the powers employed, the deeps filled up, the mountains levelled, the rocks shattered, the rivers made navigable, the tracts of land cleared, the lakes emptied, the marshes drained, the enormous structures erected on land, and the teeming vessels that cover the sea; and, on the other hand, estimate with ever so little thought, the real advantages that have accrued from all these works to mankind, we cannot help being amazed at the vast disproportion there is between these things, and deploring the infatuation of man, which, to gratify his silly pride and vain self-admiration, induces him eagerly to pursue all the miseries he is capable of feeling, though beneficent nature had kindly placed them out of his way.

That men are actually wicked, a sad and continual experience of them proves beyond doubt: but, all the same I think I have shown that man is naturally good.[3] What then can have depraved him to such an extent, except the changes that have happened in his constitution, the advances he has made, and the knowledge he has acquired? We may admire human society as much as we please; it will be none the less true that it necessarily leads men to hate each other in proportion as their interests clash, and to do one another apparent services, while they are really doing every imaginable mischief. What can be thought of a relation, in which the interest of every individual dictates rules directly opposite to those the public reason dictates to the community in general – in which every man finds his profit in the misfortunes of his neighbour? There is not perhaps any man in a comfortable position who has not greedy heirs, and perhaps even children, secretly wishing for his death; not a ship at sea, of which the loss would not be good news to some merchant or other; not a house, which some debtor of bad faith would not be glad to see reduced to ashes with all the papers it contains; not a nation which does not rejoice at the disasters that befall its neighbours. Thus it is that we find our advantage in the misfortunes of our fellow-creatures, and that the loss of one man almost always constitutes the prosperity of another. But it is still more pernicious that public calamities are the objects of the hopes and expectations of innumerable individuals. Some desire sickness, some mortality, some war, and some famine. I have seen men wicked enough to weep for sorrow at the prospect of a plentiful season; and the great and fatal fire of London, which cost so many unhappy persons their lives or their fortunes, made the fortunes of perhaps ten thousand others. I know that Montaigne censures Demades the Athenian for having caused to be punished a workman who, by selling his coffins very dear, was a great gainer by the deaths of his fellow-citizens; but, the reason alleged by Montaigne being that everybody ought to be punished, my point is clearly confirmed by it. Let us penetrate, therefore, the superficial appearances of benevolence, and survey what passes in the inmost recesses of the heart. Let us reflect what must be the state of things, when men are forced to caress and destroy one another at the same time; when they are born enemies by duty, and knaves by interest. It will perhaps be said that society is so formed that every man gains by serving the rest. That would be all very well, if he did not gain still more by injuring them. There is no legitimate profit so great, that it cannot be greatly exceeded by what may be made illegitimately; we always gain more by hurting our neighbours than by doing them good. Nothing is required but to know how to act with impunity; and to this end the powerful employ all their strength, and the weak all their cunning.

Savage man, when he has dined, is at peace with all nature, and the friend of all his fellow-creatures. If a dispute arises about a meal, he rarely comes to blows, without having first compared the difficulty of conquering his antagonist with the trouble of finding subsistence elsewhere: and, as pride does not come in, it all ends in a few blows; the victor eats, and the vanquished seeks provision somewhere else, and all is at peace. The case is quite different with man in the state of society, for whom first necessaries have to be provided, and then superfluities; delicacies follow next, then immense wealth, then subjects, and then slaves. He enjoys not a moment's relaxation; and what is yet stranger, the less natural and pressing his wants, the more headstrong are his passions, and, still worse, the more he has it in his power to gratify them; so that after a long course of prosperity, after having swallowed up treasures and ruined multitudes, the hero ends up by cutting every throat till he finds himself, at last, sole master of the world. Such is in miniature the moral picture, if not of human life, at least of the secret pretensions of the heart of civilized man.

Compare without partiality the state of the citizen with that of the savage, and trace out, if you can, how many inlets the former has opened to pain and death, besides those of his vices, his wants, and his misfortunes. If you reflect on the mental afflictions that prey on us, the violent passions that waste and exhaust us, the excessive labour with which the poor are burdened, the still more dangerous indolence to which the wealthy give themselves up, so that the poor perish of want, and the rich of surfeit; if you reflect but a moment on the heterogeneous mixtures and pernicious seasonings of foods; the corrupt state in which they are frequently eaten; on the adulteration of medicines, the wiles of those who sell them, the mistakes of those who administer them, and the poisonous vessels in which they are prepared; on the epidemics bred by foul air in consequence of great numbers of men being crowded together, or those which are caused by our delicate way of living, by our passing from our houses into the open air and back again, by the putting on or throwing off our clothes with too little care, and by all the precautions which sensuality has converted into necessary habits, and the neglect of which sometimes costs us our life or health; if you take into account the conflagrations and earthquakes, which, devouring or overwhelming whole cities, destroy the inhabitants by thousands; in a word, if you add together all the dangers with which these causes are always threatening us, you will see how dearly nature makes us pay for the contempt with which we have treated her lessons.

I shall not here repeat, what I have elsewhere said of the calamities of war; but wish that those, who have sufficient knowledge, were willing or bold enough to make public the details of the villainies committed in armies by the contractors for commissariat and hospitals: we should see plainly that their monstrous frauds, already none too well concealed, which cripple the finest armies in less than no time, occasion greater destruction among the soldiers than the swords of the enemy.

The number of people who perish annually at sea, by famine, the scurvy, pirates, fire, and shipwrecks, affords matter for another shocking calculation. We must also place to the credit of the establishment of property, and consequently to the institution of society, assassinations, poisonings, highway robberies, and even the punishments inflicted on the wretches guilty of these crimes; which, though expedient to prevent greater evils, yet by making the murder of one man cost the lives of two or more, double the loss to the human race.

What shameful methods are sometimes practised to prevent the birth of men, and cheat nature; either by brutal and depraved appetites which insult her most beautiful work – appetites unknown to savages or mere animals, which can spring only from the corrupt imagination of mankind in civilized countries; or by secret abortions, the fitting effects of debauchery and vitiated notions of honour; or by the exposure or murder of multitudes of infants, who fall victims to the poverty of their parents, or the cruel shame of their mothers; or, finally, by the mutilation of unhappy wretches, part of whose life, with their hope of posterity, is given up to vain singing, or, still worse, the brutal jealousy of other men: a mutilation which, in the last case, becomes a double outrage against nature from the treatment of those who suffer it, and from the use to which they are destined. But is it not a thousand times more common and more dangerous for paternal rights openly to offend against humanity? How many talents have not been thrown away, and inclinations forced, by the unwise constraint of fathers? How many men, who would have distinguished themselves in a fitting estate, have died dishonoured and wretched in another for which they had no taste! How many happy, but unequal, marriages have been broken or disturbed, and how many chaste wives have been dishonoured, by an order of things continually in contradiction with that of nature! How many good and virtuous husbands and wives are reciprocally punished for having been ill-assorted! How many young and unhappy victims of their parents' avarice plunge into vice, or pass their melancholy days in tears, groaning in the indissoluble bonds which their hearts repudiate and gold alone has formed! Fortunate sometimes are those whose courage and virtue remove them from life before inhuman violence makes them spend it in crime or in despair. Forgive me, fathers and mothers, who are ever to be pitied: I regret having to increase your pain; I only hope it may serve as an eternal and terrible example to anyone who dares, in the very name of nature, to violate the most sacred of natural rights.

If I have spoken only of those ill-starred unions which are the result of our system, is it to be thought that those over which love and sympathy preside are free from disadvantages? What if I should undertake to show humanity attacked in its very source, and even in the most sacred of all ties, in which fortune is consulted before nature, and, the disorders of society confounding all virtue and vice, continence becomes a criminal precaution, and a refusal to give life to a fellow-creature, an act of humanity? But, without drawing aside the veil which hides all these horrors, let us content ourselves with pointing out the evil which others will have to remedy.

To all this add the multiplicity of unhealthy trades, which shorten men's lives or destroy their bodies, such as working in the mines, and the preparing of metals and minerals, particularly lead, copper, mercury, cobalt, and arsenic: add those other dangerous trades which are daily fatal to many tilers, carpenters, masons, and miners; put all these together and we can see, in the establishment and perfection of societies, the reasons for that diminution of our species, which has been noticed by many philosophers.

Luxury, which cannot be avoided among men greedy for their own comfort and for the respect of others, soon completes the evil which society had begun and, under the pretence of giving bread to the poor whom it should never have made such, impoverishes all the rest, and sooner or later depopulates the State. Luxury is a remedy much worse than the disease it sets up to cure; or rather it is in itself the greatest of all evils, for every State, great or small: for, in order to maintain all the servants and vagabonds it creates, it brings oppression and ruin on the citizen and the labourer; it is like those scorching winds, which, covering the trees and plants with devouring insects, deprive useful animals of their subsistence and spread famine and death wherever they blow.

From society and the luxury to which it gives birth arise the liberal and mechanical arts, commerce, letters, and all those superfluities which make industry flourish, and enrich and ruin nations. The reason for such destruction is plain. It is easy to see, from the very nature of agriculture, that it must be the least lucrative of all the arts; for, its produce being the most universally necessary, the price must be proportionate to the abilities of the very poorest of mankind.

From the same principle may be deduced this rule, that the arts in general are more lucrative in proportion as they are less useful; and that, in the end, the most useful becomes the most neglected. From this we may learn what to think of the real advantages of industry and the actual effects of its progress.

Such are the sensible causes of all the miseries, into which opulence at length plunges the most celebrated nations. In proportion as arts and industry flourish, the despised husbandman, burdened with the taxes necessary for the support of luxury, and condemned to pass his days between labour and hunger, forsakes his native field, to seek in towns the bread he ought to carry thither. The more our capital cities strike the vulgar eye with admiration, the greater reason is there to lament the sight of the abandoned countryside, the large tracts of land that lie uncultivated, the roads crowded with unfortunate citizens turned beggars or highwaymen, and doomed to end their wretched lives either on a dunghill or on the gallows. Thus the State grows rich on the one hand, and feeble and depopulated on the other; the mightiest monarchies, after having taken immense pains to enrich and depopulate themselves, fall at last a prey to some poor nation, which has yielded to the fatal temptation of invading them, and then, growing opulent and weak in its turn, is itself invaded and ruined by some other.

Would someone be so kind as to explain to us what produced the hordes of barbarians who overran Europe, Asia and Africa for so many centuries? Was their prodigious increase due to their industry and arts, to the wisdom of their laws, or to the excellence of their political system? Let the learned tell us why, instead of multiplying to such a degree, these fierce and brutal men, without sense or science, without education, without restraint, did not destroy each other hourly in quarrelling over the productions of their fields and woods. Let them tell us how these wretches could have the presumption to oppose such clever people as we were, so well trained in military discipline, and possessed of such excellent laws and institutions: and why, since society has been brought to perfection in northern countries, and so much pains taken to instruct their inhabitants in their social duties and in the art of living happily and peaceably together, we see them no longer produce such numberless hosts as they used once to send forth to be the plague and terror of other nations. I fear someone may at last answer me by saying, that all these fine things, arts, sciences, and laws, were wisely invented by men, as a salutary plague, to prevent the too great multiplication of mankind, lest the world, which was given us for a habitation, should in time be too small for its inhabitants.

What, then, is to be done? Must we destroy society, abolish *mine* and *yours* and go back to living in the forests with the bears? This is the sort of conclusion my adversaries would come to and I would sooner forestall it than leave to them the shame of drawing it. O you, who have never heard the voice of heaven, who think man destined only to live this little life and die in peace; you, who can resign in the midst of populous cities your fatal acquisitions, your restless spirits, your corrupt hearts and endless desires; resume, since it depends entirely on yourselves, your ancient and primitive innocence: retire to the woods, there to lose the sight and remembrance of the crimes of your contemporaries; and be not apprehensive of degrading your species, by renouncing its advances in order to renounce its vices. As for men like me, whose passions have destroyed their original simplicity, who can no longer subsist on plants or acorns, or live without laws and magistrates; those who were honoured in their first father with supernatural instructions; those who discover, in the design of giving human actions at the start a morality which they must otherwise have been so long in acquiring, the reason for a precept in itself indifferent and inexplicable on every other system; those, in short, who are persuaded that the Divine Being has called all mankind to be partakers in the happiness and perfection of celestial intelligences, all these will endeavour to merit the eternal prize they are to expect from the practice of those virtues, which they make themselves follow in learning to know them. They will respect the sacred bonds of their respective communities; they will love their fellow-citizens, and serve them with all their might: they will scrupulously obey the laws, and all those who make or administer them; they will particularly honour those wise and good princes, who find means of preventing, curing, or even palliating all these evils and abuses, by which we are constantly threatened; they will animate the zeal of their deserving rulers, by showing them, without flattery or fear, the importance of their office and the severity of their duty. But they will not therefore have less contempt for a constitution that cannot support itself without the aid of so many splendid characters, much oftener wished for than found; and from which, notwithstanding all their pains and solicitude, there always arise more real calamities than even apparent advantages.

A DISCOURSE ON
POLITICAL ECONOMY

A Discourse on
Political Economy

The word Economy, or Oeconomy, is derived from οἰκός, a house, and νόμος, law, and meant originally only the wise and legitimate government of the house for the common good of the whole family. The meaning of the term was then extended to the government of that great family, the State. To distinguish these two senses of the word, the latter is called *general* or *political* economy, and the former domestic or particular economy. The first only is discussed in the present discourse.

Even if there were as close an analogy as many authors maintain between the State and the family, it would not follow that the rules of conduct proper for one of these societies would be also proper for the other. They differ too much in extent to be regulated in the same manner; and there will always be a great difference between domestic government, in which a father can see everything for himself, and civil government, where the chief sees hardly anything save through the eyes of others. To put both on an equality in this respect, the talents, strength, and all the faculties of the father would have to increase in proportion to the size of his family, and the soul of a powerful monarch would have to be, to that of an ordinary man, as the extent of his empire is to that of a private person's estate.

But how could the government of the State be like that of the family, when the basis on which they rest is so different? The father being physically stronger than his children, his paternal authority, as long as they need his protection, may be reasonably said to be established by nature. But in the great family, all the members of which are naturally equal, the political authority, being purely arbitrary as far as its institution is concerned, can be founded only on conventions, and the Magistrate can have no authority over the rest, except by virtue of the laws. The duties of a father are dictated to him by natural feelings, and in a manner that seldom allows him to neglect them. For rulers there is no such principle, and they are really obliged to the people only by what they themselves have promised to do, and the people have therefore a right to require of them. Another more important difference is that since the children have nothing but what they receive from their father, it is plain that all the rights of property belong to him or emanate from him; but quite the opposite is the case in the great family, where the general administration is established only to secure individual property, which is antecedent to it. The principal object of the work of the whole house is to preserve and increase the patrimony of the father, in order that he may be able some day to distribute it among his children without impoverishing them; whereas the wealth of the exchequer is only a means, often ill understood, of keeping the individuals in peace and plenty. In a word, the little family is destined to be extinguished, and to resolve itself some day into several families of a similar nature; but the great family, being constituted to endure for ever in the same condition, need not, like the small one, increase for the purpose of multiplying, but need only maintain itself; and it can easily be proved that any increase does it more harm than good.

In the family, it is clear, for several reasons which lie in its very nature, that the father ought to command. In the first place, the authority ought not to be equally divided between father and mother; the government must be single, and in every division of opinion there must be one preponderant voice to decide. Secondly, however lightly we may regard the disadvantages peculiar to women, yet, as they necessarily occasion intervals of inaction, this is a sufficient reason for excluding them from this supreme authority: for when the balance is perfectly even, a straw is enough to turn the scale. Besides, the husband ought to be able to superintend his wife's conduct, because it is of importance for him to be assured that the children, whom he is obliged to acknowledge and maintain, belong to no one but himself. Thirdly, children should be obedient to their father, at first of necessity, and afterwards from gratitude: after having had their wants satisfied by him during one half of their lives, they ought to consecrate the other half to providing for his. Fourthly, servants owe him their services in exchange for the provision he makes for them, though they may break off the bargain as soon as it ceases to suit them. I say nothing here of slavery, because it is contrary to nature, and cannot be authorized by any right or law.

There is nothing of all this in political society, in which the chief is so far from having any natural interest in the happiness of the individuals, that it is not uncommon for him to seek his own in their misery. If the magistracy is hereditary, a community of men is often governed by a child. If it be elective, innumerable inconveniences arise from such election; while in both cases all the advantages of paternity are lost. If you have but a single ruler, you lie at the discretion of a master who has no reason to love you: and if you have several, you must bear at once their tyranny and their divisions. In a word, abuses are inevitable and their consequences fatal in every society where the public interest and the laws have no natural force, and are perpetually attacked by personal interest and the passions of the ruler and the members.

Although the functions of the father of a family and those of the chief magistrate ought to make for the same object, they must do so in such different ways, and their duty and rights are so essentially distinct, that we cannot confound them without forming very false ideas about the fundamental laws of society, and falling into errors which are fatal to mankind. In fact, if the voice of nature is the best counsellor to which a father can listen in the discharge of his duty, for the Magistrate it is a false guide, which continually prevents him from performing his, and leads sooner or later to the ruin of himself and of the State, if he is not restrained by the most sublime virtue. The only precaution necessary for the father of a family is to guard himself against depravity, and prevent his natural inclinations from being corrupted; whereas it is these themselves which corrupt the Magistrate. In order to act aright, the first has only to consult his heart; the other becomes a traitor the moment he listens to his. Even his own reason should be suspect to him, nor should he follow any rule other than the public reason, which is the law. Thus nature has made a multitude of good fathers of families; but it is doubtful whether, from the very beginning of the world, human wisdom has made ten men capable of governing their peers.

From all that has just been said, it follows that *public* economy, which is my subject, has been rightly distinguished from *private* economy, and that, the State having nothing in common with the family except the obligations which their heads lie under of making both of them happy, the same rules of conduct cannot apply to both. I have considered these few lines enough to overthrow the detestable system which Sir Robert Filmer has endeavoured to establish in his *Patriarcha*; a work to which two celebrated writers have done too much honour in writing books to refute it.[1] Moreover, this error is of very long standing; for Aristotle himself thought proper to combat it with arguments which may be found in the first book of his *Politics*.

I must here ask my readers to distinguish also between *public economy*, which is my subject and which I call *government*, and the supreme authority, which I call *Sovereignty*;[2] a distinction which consists in the fact that the latter has the right of legislation, and in certain cases binds the body of the nation itself, while the former has only the right of execution, and is binding only on individuals.

I shall take the liberty of making use of a very common, and in some respects inaccurate, comparison, which will serve to illustrate my meaning.

The body politic, taken individually, may be considered as an organized, living body, resembling that of man. The sovereign power represents the head; the laws and customs are the brain, the source of the nerves and seat of the understanding, will, and senses, of which the Judges and Magistrates are the organs: commerce, industry and agriculture are the mouth and stomach which prepare the common subsistence; the public income is the blood, which a prudent *economy*, in performing the functions of the heart, causes to distribute through the whole body nutriment and life: the citizens are the body and the members, which make the machine live, move, and work; and no part of this machine can be damaged without the painful impression being at once conveyed to the brain, if the animal is in a state of health.

The life of both bodies is the self common to the whole, the reciprocal sensibility and internal correspondence of all the parts. Where this communication ceases, where the formal unity disappears, and the contiguous parts belong to one another only by juxtaposition, the man is dead, or the State is dissolved.

The body politic, therefore, is also a corporate being possessed of a will; and this general will, which tends always to the preservation and welfare of the whole and of every part, and is the source of the laws, constitutes for all the members of the State, in their relations to one another and to it, the rule of what is just or unjust: a truth which shows, by the way, how idly some writers have treated as theft the subtlety prescribed to children at Sparta for obtaining their frugal repasts, as if everything ordained by the law were not lawful.[1]

It is important to observe that this rule of justice, though certain with regard to all citizens, may be defective with regard to foreigners. The reason is clear. The will of the State, though general in relation to its own members, is no longer so in relation to other States and their members, but becomes, for them, a particular and individual will, which has its rule of justice in the law of nature. This, however, enters equally into the principle here laid down; for in such a case, the great city of the world becomes the body politic, whose general will is always the law of nature, and of which the different States and peoples are individual members. From these distinctions, applied to each political society and its members, are derived the most certain and universal rules, by which we can judge whether a government is good or bad, and in general of the morality of all human actions.

Every political society is composed of other smaller societies of different kinds, each of which has its interests and its rules of conduct: but those societies which everybody perceives, because they have an external and authorized form, are not the only ones that actually exist in the State: all individuals who are united by a common interest compose as many others, either transitory or permanent, whose influence is none the less real because it is less apparent, and the proper observation of whose various relations is the true knowledge of public morals and manners. The influence of all these tacit or formal associations causes, by the influence of their will, as many different modifications of the public will. The will of these particular societies has always two relations; for the members of the association, it is a general will; for the great society, it is a particular will; and it is often right with regard to the first object, and wrong as to the second. An individual may be a devout priest, a brave soldier, or a zealous senator, and yet a bad citizen. A particular resolution may be advantageous to the smaller community, but pernicious to the greater. It is true that, particular societies always being subordinate to those that contain them, the latter should be obeyed rather than the former; the duty of a citizen takes precedence of that of a senator, and a man's duty of that of a citizen: but unhappily personal interest is always found in inverse ratio to duty, and increases in proportion as association grows narrower, and the engagement less sacred; which irrefragably proves that the most general will is always the most just also, and that the voice of the people is in fact the voice of God.

It does not follow that the public decisions are always equitable; they may possibly, for reasons which I have given, not be so when they have to do with foreigners. Thus it is not impossible that a Republic, though in itself well governed, should enter upon an unjust war. Not is it less possible for the Council of a Democracy to pass unjust decrees, and condemn the innocent; but this never happens unless the people is seduced by private interests, which the credit or eloquence of some clever persons substitutes for those of the State: in which case the general will

will be one thing, and the result of the public deliberation another. This is not contradicted by the case of the Athenian Democracy; for Athens was in fact not a Democracy, but a very tyrannical Aristocracy, governed by philosophers and orators. Carefully determine what happens in every public deliberation, and it will be seen that the general will is always for the common good; but very often there is a secret division, a tacit confederacy, which, for particular ends, causes the natural disposition of the assembly to be set at naught. In such a case the body of society is really divided into other bodies, the members of which acquire a general will, which is good and just with respect to these new bodies, but unjust and bad with regard to the whole, from which each is thus dismembered.

We see then how easy it is, by the help of these principles, to explain those apparent contradictions, which are noticed in the conduct of many persons who are scrupulously honest in some respects, and cheats and scoundrels in others, who trample under foot the most sacred duties, and yet are faithful to the death to engagements that are often illegitimate. Thus the most depraved of men always pay some sort of homage to public faith; and even robbers, who are the enemies of virtue in the great society, pay some respect to the shadow of it in their secret caves.[1]

In establishing the general will as the first principle of public *economy*, and the fundamental rule of government, I have not thought it necessary to inquire seriously whether the Magistrates belong to the people, or the people to the Magistrates; or whether in public affairs the good of the State should be taken into account, or only that of its rulers. That question indeed has long been decided one way in theory, and another in practice; and in general it would be ridiculous to expect that those who are in fact masters will prefer any other interest to their own. It would not be improper, therefore, further to distinguish public economy as popular or tyrannical. The former is that of every State, in which there reigns between the people and the rulers unity of interest and will: the latter will necessarily exist wherever the government and the people have different interests, and, consequently, opposing wills. The rules of the latter are written at length in the archives of history, and in the satires of Machiavelli.[1] The rules of the former are found only in the writings of those philosophers who venture to proclaim the rights of humanity.

I. The first and most important rule of legitimate or popular government, that is to say, of government whose object is the good of the people, is therefore, as I have observed, to follow in everything the general will. But to follow this will it is necessary to know it, and above all to distinguish it from the particular will, beginning with one's self: this distinction is always very difficult to make, and only the most sublime virtue can afford sufficient illumination for it. As, in order to will, it is necessary to be free, a difficulty no less great than the former arises – that of preserving at once the public liberty and the authority of government. Look into the motives which have induced men, once united by their common needs in a general society, to unite themselves still more intimately by means of civil societies: you will find no other motive than that of assuring the property, life, and liberty of each member by the protection of all. But can men be forced to defend the liberty of any one among them, without trespassing on that of others? And how can they provide for the public needs, without alienating the individual property of those who are forced to contribute to them? With whatever sophistry all this may be covered over, it is certain that if any constraint can be laid on my will, I am no longer free, and that I am no longer master of my own property, if any one else can lay a hand on it. This difficulty, which would have seemed insurmountable, has been removed, like the first, by the most sublime of all human institutions, or rather by a divine inspiration, which teaches mankind to imitate here below the unchangeable decrees of the Deity. By what inconceivable art has a means been found of making men free by making them subject; of using in the service of the State the properties, the persons, and even the lives of all its members, without constraining and without consulting them; of confining their will by their own admission; of overcoming their refusal by that consent, and forcing them to punish themselves, when they act against their own will? How can it be that all should obey, yet nobody take upon him to command, and that all should serve, and yet have no masters, but be the more free, as, in apparent subjection, each loses no part of his liberty but what might be hurtful to that of another? These wonders are the work of law. It is to law alone that men owe justice and liberty. It is this salutary organ of the will of all which establishes, in civil right, the natural equality between men. It is this celestial voice which dictates to each citizen the precepts of public reason, and teaches him to act according to the rules of his own judgment, and not to behave inconsistently with himself. It is with this voice alone that political rulers should speak when they command; for no sooner does one man, setting aside the law, claim to subject another to his private will, than he departs from the state of civil society, and confronts him face to face in the pure state of nature, in which obedience is prescribed solely by necessity.

The most pressing interest of the ruler, and even his most indispensable duty, therefore, is to watch over the observation of the laws of which he is the minister, and on which his whole authority is founded. At the same time, if he exacts the observance of them from others, he is the more strongly bound to observe them himself, since he enjoys all their favour. For his example is of such force, that even if the people were willing to permit him to release himself from the yoke of the law, he ought to be cautious in availing himself of so dangerous a prerogative, which others might soon claim to usurp in their turn, and often use to his prejudice. At bottom, as all social engagements are mutual in nature, it is impossible for any one to set himself above the law, without renouncing its advantages; for nobody is bound by any obligation to one who claims that he is under no obligations to others. For this reason no exemption from the law will ever be granted, on any ground whatsoever, in a well-regulated government. Those citizens who have deserved well of their country ought to be rewarded with honours, but never with privileges: for the Republic is at the eve of its fall, when any one can think it fine not to obey the laws. If the nobility or the soldiery should ever adopt such a maxim, all would be lost beyond redemption.

The power of the laws depends still more on their own wisdom than on the severity of their administrators, and the public will derives its greatest weight from the reason which has dictated it. Hence Plato looked upon it as a very necessary precaution to place at the head of all edicts a preamble, setting forth their justice and utility. In fact, the first of all laws is to respect the laws: the severity of penalties is only a vain resource, invented by little minds in order to substitute terror for that respect which they have no means of obtaining. It has constantly been observed that in those countries where legal punishments are most severe, they are also most frequent; so that the cruelty of such punishments is a proof only of the multitude of criminals, and, punishing everything with equal severity, induces those who are guilty to commit crimes, in order to escape being punished for their faults.

But though the government be not master of the law, it is much to be its guarantor, and to possess a thousand means of inspiring the love of it. In this alone the talent of reigning consists. With force in one's hands, there is no art required to make the whole world tremble, nor indeed much to gain men's hearts; for experience has long since taught the people to give its rulers great credit for all the evil they abstain from doing it, and to adore them if they do not absolutely hate it. A fool, if he be obeyed, may punish crimes as well as another: but the true statesman is he who knows how to prevent them: it is over the wills, even more than the actions, of his subjects that his honourable rule is extended. If he could secure that every one should act aright, he would no longer have anything to do; and the masterpiece of his labours would be to be able to remain unemployed. It is certain, at least, that the greatest talent a ruler can possess is to disguise his power, in order to render it less odious, and to conduct the State so peaceably as to make it seem to have no need of conductors.

I conclude, therefore, that, as the first duty of the Legislator is to make the laws conformable to the general will, the first rule of public economy is that the administration of justice should be conformable to the laws. It will even be enough to prevent the State from being ill governed, that the Legislator shall have provided, as he should, for every need of place, climate, soil, custom, neighbourhood, and all the rest of the relations peculiar to the people he had to institute. Not but what there still remains an infinity of details of administration and economy, which are left to the wisdom of the government: but there are two infallible rules for its good conduct on these occasions; one is, that the spirit of the law ought to decide in every particular case that could not be foreseen; the other is that the general will, the source and supplement of all laws, should be consulted wherever they fail. But how, I shall be asked, can the general will be known in cases in which it has not expressed itself? Must the whole nation be assembled together at every unforeseen event? Certainly not. It ought the less to be assembled, because it is by no means certain that its decision would be the expression of the general will; besides, the method would be impracticable in a great people, and is hardly ever necessary where the government is well-intentioned: for the rulers well know that the general will is always on the side which is most favourable to the public interest, that is to say, most equitable; so that it is needful only to act justly, to be certain of following the general will. When this is flouted too openly, it makes itself felt, in spite of the formidable restraint of the public authority. I shall cite the nearest possible examples that may be followed in such cases.

In China, it is the constant maxim of the Prince to decide against his officers, in every dispute that arises between them and the people. If bread be too dear in any province, the intendant of that province is thrown into prison. If there be an insurrection in another, the governor is dismissed, and every mandarin answers with his head for all the mischief that happens in his department. Not that these affairs do not subsequently undergo a regular examination; but long experience has caused the judgment to be thus anticipated. There is seldom any injustice to be repaired; in the meantime, the Emperor, being satisfied that public outcry does not arise without cause, always discovers, through the seditious clamours which he punishes, just grievances to redress.

It is a great thing to preserve the rule of peace and order through all parts of the Republic; it is a great thing that the State should be tranquil, and the law respected: but if nothing more is done, there will be in all this more appearance than reality; for that government which confines itself to mere obedience will find difficulty in getting itself obeyed. If it is good to know how to deal with men as they are, it is much better to make them what there is need that they should be. The most absolute authority is that which penetrates into a man's inmost being, and concerns itself no less with his will than with his actions. It is certain that all peoples become in the long run what the government makes them: warriors, citizens, men, when it so pleases; or merely populace and rabble, when it chooses to make them so. Hence every prince who despises his subjects, dishonours himself, in confessing that he does not know how to make them worthy of respect. Make men, therefore, if you would command men: if you would have them obedient to the laws, make them love the laws, and then they will need only to know what is their duty to do it. This was the great art of ancient governments, in those distant times when philosophers gave laws to men, and made use of their authority only to render them wise and happy. Thence arose the numerous sumptuary laws, the many regulations of morals, and all the public rules of conduct which were admitted or rejected with the greatest care. Even tyrants did not forget this important part of administration, but took as great pains to corrupt the morals of their slaves, as Magistrates took to correct those of their fellow-citizens. But our modern governments, which imagine they have done everything when they have raised money, conceive that it is unnecessary and even impossible to go a step farther.

II. The second essential rule of public economy is no less

important than the first. If you would have the general will accomplished, bring all the particular wills into conformity with it; in other words, as virtue is nothing more than this conformity of the particular wills with the general will, establish the reign of virtue.

If our politicians were less blinded by their ambition, they would see how impossible it is for any establishment whatever to act in the spirit of its institution, unless it is guided in accordance with the law of duty; they would feel that the greatest support of public authority lies in the hearts of the citizens, and that nothing can take the place of morality in the maintenance of government. It is not only upright men who know how to administer the laws; but at bottom only good men know how to obey them. The man who once gets the better of remorse, will not shrink before punishments which are less severe, and less lasting, and from which there is at least the hope of escaping: whatever precautions are taken, those who only require impunity in order to do wrong will not fail to find means of eluding the law, and avoiding its penalties. In this case, as all particular interests unite against the general interest, which is no longer that of any individual, public vices have a greater effect in enervating the laws than the laws in the repression of such vices: so that the corruption of the people and of their rulers will at length extend to the government, however wise it may be. The worst of all abuses is to pay an apparent obedience to the laws, only in order actually to break them with security. For in this case the best laws soon become the most pernicious; and it would be a hundred times better that they should not exist. In such a situation, it is vain to add edicts to edicts and regulations to regulations. Everything serves only to introduce new abuses, without correcting the old. The more laws are multiplied, the more they are despised, and all the new officials appointed to supervise them are only so many more people to break them, and either to share the plunder with their predecessors, or to plunder apart on their own. The reward of virtue soon becomes that of robbery; the vilest of men rise to the greatest credit; the greater they are the more despicable they become; their infamy appears even in their dignities, and their very honours dishonour them. If they buy the influence of the leaders or the protection of women, it is only that they may sell justice, duty, and the State in their turn: in the meantime, the people, feeling that its vices are not the first cause of its misfortunes, murmurs and complains that all its misfortunes come solely from those whom it pays to protect it from such things.

It is under these circumstances that the voice of duty no longer speaks in men's hearts, and their rulers are obliged to substitute the cry of terror, or the lure of an apparent interest, of which they subsequently trick their creatures. In this situation they are compelled to have recourse to all the petty and despicable shifts which they call *rules of State* and *mysteries of the Cabinet*. All the vigour that is left in the government is used by its members in ruining and supplanting one another, while the public business is neglected, or is transacted only as personal interest requires and directs. In short, the whole art of those great politicians lies in so mesmerizing those they stand in need of, that each may think he is labouring for his own interest in working for theirs: I say *theirs* on the false supposition that it is the real interest of rulers to annihilate a people in order to make it subject, and to ruin their own property in order to secure their possession of it.

But when the citizens love their duty, and the guardians of the public authority sincerely apply themselves to the fostering of that love by their own example and assiduity, every difficulty vanishes; and government becomes so easy that it needs none of that art of darkness, whose blackness is its only mystery. Those enterprising spirits, so dangerous and so much admired, all those great ministers, whose glory is inseparable from the miseries of the people, are no longer regretted: public morality supplies what is wanting in the genius of the rulers; and the more virtue reigns, the less need there is for talent. Even ambition is better served by duty than by usurpation: when the people is convinced that its rulers are labouring only for its happiness, its deference saves them the trouble of labouring to strengthen their power: and history shows us, in a thousand cases, that the authority of one who is beloved over those whom he loves is a hundred times more absolute than all the tyranny of usurpers. This does not mean that the government ought to be afraid to make use of its power, but that it ought to make use of it only in a lawful manner. We find in history a thousand examples of pusillanimous or ambitious rulers, who were ruined by their slackness or their pride; not one who suffered for having been strictly just. But we ought not to confound negligence with moderation, or clemency with weakness. To be just, it is necessary to be severe; to permit vice, when one has the right and the power to suppress it, is to be oneself vicious.

It is not enough to say to the citizens, *be good*; they must be taught to be so; and even example, which is in this respect the first lesson, is not the sole means to be employed; patriotism is the most efficacious: for, as I have said already, every man is virtuous when his particular will is in all things conformable to the general will, and we voluntarily will what is willed by those whom we love. It appears that the feeling of humanity evaporates and grows feeble in embracing all mankind, and that we cannot be affected by the calamities of Tartary or Japan, in the same manner as we are by those of European nations. It is necessary in some degree to confine and limit our interest and compassion in order to make it active. Now, as this sentiment can be useful only to those with whom we have to live, it is proper that our humanity should confine itself to our fellow-citizens, and should receive a new force because we are in the habit of seeing them, and by reason of the common interest which unites them. It is certain that the greatest miracles of virtue have been produced by patriotism: this fine and lively feeling, which gives to the force of self-love all the beauty of virtue, lends it an energy which, without disfiguring it, makes it the most heroic of all passions. This it is that produces so many immortal actions, the glory of which dazzles our feeble eyes; and so many great men, whose old-world virtues pass for fables now that patriotism is made mock of. This is not surprising; the transports of susceptible hearts appear altogether fanciful to any one who has never felt them; and the love of one's country, which is a hundred times more lively and delightful than the love of a mistress, cannot be conceived except by experiencing it. But it is easy to perceive in every heart that is warmed by it, in all the actions it inspires, a glowing and sublime ardour which does not attend the purest virtue, when separated from it. Contrast Socrates even with Cato; the one was the greater philosopher, the other more of the citizen. Athens was already ruined in the time of Socrates, and he had no other country than the world at large. Cato had the cause of his country always at heart; he lived for it alone, and could not bear to outlive it. The virtue of Socrates was that of the wisest of men; but, compared with Caesar and Pompey, Cato seems a god among mortals. Socrates instructed a few individuals, opposed the Sophists, and died for truth: but Cato defended his country, its liberty, and its laws, against the conquerors of the world, and at length departed from the earth, when he had no longer a country to serve. A worthy pupil of Socrates would be the most virtuous of his contemporaries; but a worthy follower of Cato would be one of the greatest. The virtue of the former would be his happiness; the latter would seek his happiness in that of all. We should be taught by the one, and led by the other; and this alone is enough to determine which to prefer: for no people has ever been made into a nation of philosophers, but it is not impossible to make a people happy.

Do we wish men to be virtuous? Then let us begin by making them love their country: but how can they love it, if their country be nothing more to them than to strangers, and afford them nothing but what it can refuse nobody? It would be still worse, if they did not enjoy even the privilege of social security, and if their lives, liberties, and property lay at the mercy of persons in power, without their being permitted, or its being possible for them, to make an appeal to the laws. For in that case, being subjected to the duties of the state of civil society, without enjoying even the common privileges of the state of nature, and without being able to use their strength in their own defence, they would be in the worst condition in which freemen could possibly find themselves, and the word 'country' would mean for them something merely odious and ridiculous. It must not be imagined that a man can break or lose an arm, without the pain being conveyed to his head: nor it is any more credible that the general will should consent that any one member of the State, whoever he might be, should wound or destroy another, than it is that the fingers of a man in his senses should wilfully scratch his eyes out. The security of individuals is so intimately connected with the public confederation that, apart from the regard that must be paid to human weakness, that convention would in point of right be dissolved, if in the State a single citizen who might have been relieved were allowed to perish, or if one were wrongfully confined in prison, or if in one case an obviously unjust sentence were given. For the fundamental conventions being broken, it is impossible to conceive of any right or interest that could retain the people in the social union; unless they were restrained by force, which alone causes the dissolution of the state of civil society.

In fact, does not the undertaking entered into by the whole body of the nation bind it to provide for the security of the least of its members with as much care as for that of all the rest? Is the welfare of a single citizen any less the common cause than that of the whole State? It may be said that it is good that one should perish for all. I am ready to admire such a saying when it comes from the lips of a virtuous and worthy patriot voluntarily and dutifully sacrificing himself for the good of his country: but if we are to understand by it, that it is lawful for the government to sacrifice an innocent man for the good of the multitude, I look upon it as one of the most execrable rules tyranny ever invented, the greatest falsehood that can be advanced, the most dangerous admission that can be made, and a direct contradiction of the fundamental laws of society. So little is it the case that any one person ought to perish for all, that all have pledged their lives and properties for the defence of each, in order that the weakness of individuals may always be protected by the strength of the public, and each member by the whole State. Suppose we take from the whole people one individual after another, and then press the advocates of this rule to explain more exactly what they mean by the *body of the State*, and we shall see that it will at length be reduced to a small number of persons, who are not the people, but the officers of the people, and who, having bound themselves by personal oath to perish for the welfare of the people, would thence infer that the people is to perish for their own.

Need we look for examples of the protection which the State owes to its members, and the respect it owes to their persons? It is only among the most illustrious and courageous nations that they are to be found; it is only among free peoples that the dignity of man is realized. It is well known into what perplexity the whole republic of Sparta was thrown, when the question of punishing a guilty citizen arose.

In Macedon, the life of a man was a matter of such importance, that Alexander the Great, at the height of his glory, would not have dared to put a Macedonian criminal to death in cold blood, till the accused had appeared to make his defence before his fellow-citizens, and had been condemned by them. But the Romans distinguished themselves above all other peoples by the regard which their government paid to the individual, and by its scrupulous attention to the preservation of the inviolable rights of all the members of the State. Nothing was so sacred among them as the life of a citizen; and no less than an assembly of the whole people was needed to condemn one. Not even the senate, nor the consuls, in all their majesty, possessed the right; but the crime and punishment of a citizen were regarded as a public calamity among the most powerful people in the world. So hard indeed did it seem to shed blood for any crime whatsoever, that by the Lex Porcia, the penalty of death was commuted into that of banishment for all those who were willing to survive the loss of so great a country. Everything both at Rome, and in the Roman armies, breathed that love of fellow-citizens one for another, and that respect for the Roman name, which raised the courage and inspired the virtue of every one who had the honour to bear it. The cap of a citizen delivered from slavery, the civic crown of him who had saved the life of another, were looked upon with the greatest pleasure amid the pomp of their triumphs; and it is remarkable that among the crowns which were bestowed in honour of splendid actions in war, the civic crown and that of the triumphant general alone were of laurel, all the others being merely of gold. It was thus that Rome was virtuous and became the mistress of the world. Ambitious rulers! A herdsman governs his dogs and cattle, and yet is only the meanest of mankind. If it be a fine thing to command, it is when those who obey us are capable of doing us honour. Show respect, therefore, to your fellow-citizens, and you will render yourselves worthy of respect; show respect to liberty, and your power will increase daily. Never exceed your rights, and they will soon become unlimited.

Let our country then show itself the common mother of her citizens; let the advantages they enjoy in their country endear it to them; let the government leave them enough share in the public administration to make them feel that they are at home; and let the laws be in their eyes only the guarantees of the common liberty. These rights, great as they are, belong to all men: but without seeming to attack them directly, the ill-will of rulers may in fact easily reduce their effect to nothing. The law, which they thus abuse, serves the powerful at once as a weapon of offence, and as a shield against the weak; and the pretext of the public good is always the most dangerous scourge of the people. What is most necessary, and perhaps most difficult, in government, is rigid integrity in doing strict justice to all, and above all in protecting the poor against the tyranny of the rich. The greatest evil has already come about, when there are poor men to be defended, and rich men to be restrained. It is on the middle classes alone that the whole force of the law is exerted; they are equally powerless against the treasures of the rich and the penury of the poor. The first mocks them, the second escapes them. The one breaks the meshes, the other passes through them.

It is therefore one of the most important functions of government to prevent extreme inequality of fortunes; not by taking away wealth from its possessors, but by depriving all men of means to accumulate it; not by building hospitals for the poor, but by securing the citizens from becoming poor. The unequal distribution of inhabitants over the territory, when men are crowded together in one place, while other places are depopulated; the encouragement of the arts that minister to luxury and of purely superfluous arts at the expense of useful and laborious crafts; the sacrifice of agriculture to commerce; the necessitation of the tax-farmer by the maladministration of the funds of the State; and in short, venality pushed to such an extreme that even public esteem is reckoned at a cash value, and virtue rated at a market price: these are the most obvious causes of opulence and of poverty, of public interest, of mutual hatred among citizens, of indifference to the common cause, of the corruption of the people, and of the weakening of all the springs of government. Such are the evils, which are with difficulty cured when they make themselves felt, but which a wise administration ought to prevent, if it is to maintain, along with good morals, respect for the laws, patriotism, and the influence of the general will.

But all these precautions will be inadequate, unless rulers go still more to the root of the matter. I conclude this part of public economy where I ought to have begun it. There can be no patriotism without liberty, no liberty without virtue, no virtue without citizens; create citizens, and you have everything you need; without them, you will have nothing but debased slaves, from the rulers of the State downwards. To form citizens is not the work of a day; and in order to have men it is necessary to educate them when they are children. It will be said, perhaps, that whoever has men to govern, ought not to seek, beyond their nature, a perfection of which they are incapable; that he ought not to desire to destroy their passions; and that the execution of such an attempt is no more desirable than it is possible. I will agree, further, that a man without passions would certainly be a bad citizen; but it must be agreed also that, if men are not taught not to love some things, it is impossible to teach them to love one object more than another – to prefer that which is truly beautiful to that which is deformed. If, for example, they were early accustomed to regard their individuality only in its relation to the body of the State, and to be aware, so to speak, of their own existence merely as a part of that of the State, they might at length come to identify themselves in some degree with this greater whole, to feel themselves members of their country, and to love it with that exquisite feeling which no isolated person has save for himself; to lift up their spirits perpetually to this great object, and thus to transform into a sublime virtue that dangerous disposition which gives rise to all our vices. Not only does philosophy demonstrate the possibility of taking steps in these new directions; history furnishes us with a thousand striking examples. If they are so rare among us moderns, it is because nobody troubles himself whether citizens exist or not, and still less does anybody think of attending to the matter soon enough to make them. It is too late to change our natural inclinations, when they have taken their course, and egoism is confirmed by habit: and it is too late to lead us out of ourselves when once the human ego, concentrated in our hearts, has acquired that contemptible activity which absorbs all virtue and constitutes the life and being of little minds. How can patriotism germinate in the midst of so many other passions which smother it? And what can remain, for fellow-citizens, of a heart already divided between avarice, a mistress, and vanity?

From the first moment of life, men ought to begin learning to deserve to live; and, as at the instant of birth we partake of the rights of citizenship, that instant ought to be the beginning of the exercise of our duty. If there are laws for the age of maturity, there ought to be laws for infancy, teaching obedience to others: and as the reason of each man is not left to be the sole arbiter of his duties, government ought the less indiscriminately to abandon to the intelligence and prejudices of fathers the education of their children, as that education is of still greater importance to the

State than to the fathers: for, according to the course of nature, the death of the father often deprives him of the final fruits of education; but his country sooner or later perceives its effects. Families dissolve, but the State remains.

Should the public authority, by taking the place of the father, and charging itself with that important function, acquire his rights by discharging his duties, he would have the less cause to complain, as he would only be changing his title, and would have in common, under the name of *citizen*, the same authority over his children, as he was exercising separately under the name of *father*, and would not be less obeyed when speaking in the name of the law, than when he spoke in that of nature. Public education, therefore, under regulations prescribed by the government, and under magistrates established by the Sovereign, is one of the fundamental rules of popular or legitimate government. If children are brought up in common in the bosom of equality; if they are imbued with the laws of the State and the precepts of the general will; if they are taught to respect these above all things; if they are surrounded by examples and objects which constantly remind them of the tender mother who nourishes them, of the love she bears them, of the inestimable benefits they receive from her, and of the return they owe her, we cannot doubt that they will learn to cherish one another mutually as brothers, to will nothing contrary to the will of society, to substitute the actions of men and citizens for the futile and vain babbling of sophists, and to become in time defenders and fathers of the country of which they will have been so long the children.

I shall say nothing of the Magistrates destined to preside over such an education, which is certainly the most important business of the State. It is easy to see that if such marks of public confidence were conferred on slight grounds, if this sublime function were not, for those who have worthily discharged all other offices, the reward of labour, the pleasant and honourable repose of old age, and the crown of all honours, the whole enterprise would be useless and the education void of success. For wherever the lesson is not supported by authority, and the precept by example, all instruction is fruitless; and virtue itself loses its credit in the mouth of one who does not practise it. But let illustrious warriors, bent under the weight of their laurels, preach courage: let upright Magistrates, grown white in the purple and on the bench teach justice. Such teachers as these would thus get themselves virtuous successors, and transmit from age to age, to generations to come, the experience and talents of rulers, the courage and virtue of citizens, and common emulation in all to live and die for their country.

I know of but three peoples which once practised public education, the Cretans, the Lacedaemonians, and the ancient Persians: among all these it was attended with the greatest success, and indeed it did wonders among the two last. Since the world has been divided into nations too great to admit of being well governed, this method has been no longer practicable, and the reader will readily perceive other reasons why such a thing has never been attempted by any modern people. It is very remarkable that the Romans were able to dispense with it; but Rome was for five hundred years one continued miracle which the world cannot hope to see again. The virtue of the Romans, engendered by their horror of tyranny and the crimes of tyrants, and by an innate patriotism, made all their houses so many schools of citizenship; while the unlimited power of fathers over their children made the individual authority so rigid that the father was more feared than the Magistrate, and was in his family tribunal both censor of morals and avenger of the laws.[1]

Thus a careful and well-intentioned government, vigilant incessantly to maintain or restore patriotism and morality among the people, provides beforehand against the evils which sooner or later result from the indifference of the citizens to the fate of the Republic, keeping within narrow bounds that personal interest which so isolates the individual that the State is enfeebled by his power, and has nothing to hope from his goodwill. Wherever men love their country, respect the laws, and live simply, little remains to be done in order to make them happy; and in public administration, where chance has less influence than in the lot of individuals, wisdom is so nearly allied to happiness, that the two objects are confounded.

III. It is not enough to have citizens and to protect them, it is also necessary to consider their subsistence. Provision for the public wants is an obvious inference from the general will, and the third essential duty of government. This duty is not, we should feel, to fill the granaries of individuals and thereby to grant them a dispensation from labour, but to keep plenty so within their reach that labour is always necessary and never useless for its acquisition. It extends also to everything regarding the management of the exchequer, and the expenses of public administration. Having thus treated of general economy with reference to the government of persons, we must now consider it with reference to the administration of property.

This part presents no fewer difficulties to solve, and contradictions to remove, than the preceding. It is certain that the right of property is the most sacred of all the rights of citizenship, and even more important in some respects than liberty itself; either because it more nearly affects the preservation of life, or because, property being more easily usurped and more difficult to defend than life, the law ought to pay a greater attention to what is most easily taken away; or finally, because property is the true foundation of civil society, and the real guarantee of the undertakings of citizens: for if property were not answerable for personal actions, nothing would be easier than to evade duties and laugh at the laws. On the other hand, it is no less certain that the maintenance of the State and the government involves costs and outgoings; and as every one who agrees to the end must acquiesce in the means, it follows that the members of a society ought to contribute from their property to its support. Besides, it is difficult to secure the property of individuals on one side, without attacking it on another; and it is impossible that all the regulations which govern the order of succession, will, contracts, etc., should not lay individuals under some constraint as to the disposition of their goods, and should not consequently restrict the right of property.

But besides what I have said above of the agreement between the authority of law and the liberty of the citizen, there remains to be made, with respect to the disposition of goods, an important observation which removes many difficulties. As Pufendorf has shown, the right of property, by its very nature, does not extend beyond the life of the proprietor, and the moment a man is dead his goods cease to belong to him. Thus, to prescribe the conditions according to which he can dispose of them, is in reality less to alter his right as it appears, than to extend it in fact.

In general, although the institution of the laws which regulate the power of individuals in the disposition of their own goods belongs only to the Sovereign, the spirit of these laws, which the government ought to follow in their application, is that, from father to son, and from relation to relation, the goods of a family should go as little out of it and be as little alienated as possible. There is a sensible reason for this in favour of children, to whom the right of property would be quite useless, if the father left them nothing, and who besides, having often contributed by their labour to the acquisition of their father's wealth, are in their own right associates with him in his right of property. But another reason, more distant, though not less important, is that nothing is more fatal to morality and to the Republic than the continual shifting of rank and fortune among the citizens: such changes are both the proof and the source of a thousand disorders, and overturn and confound everything; for those who were brought up to one thing find themselves destined for another; and neither those who rise nor those who fall are able to assume the rules of conduct, or to possess themselves of the qualifications requisite for their new condition, still less to discharge the duties it entails. I proceed to the object of public finance.

If the people governed itself and there were no intermediary between the administration of the State and the citizens, they would have no more to do than to assess themselves occasionally, in proportion to the public needs and the abilities of individuals: and as they would all keep in sight the recovery and employment of such assessments, no fraud or abuse could slip into the management of them; the State would never be involved in debt, or the people overburdened with taxes; or at least the knowledge of how the money would be used would be a consolation for the severity of the tax. But things cannot be carried on in this manner: on the contrary, however small any State may be, civil societies are always too populous to be under the immediate government of all their members. It is necessary that the public money should go through the hands of the rulers, all of whom have, besides the interests of the State, their own individual interests, which are not the last to be listened to. The people, on its side, perceiving rather the cupidity and ridiculous expenditure of its rulers than the public needs, murmurs at seeing itself stripped of necessaries to furnish others with superfluities; and when once these complaints have reached a certain degree of bitterness, the most upright administration will find it impossible to restore confidence. In such a case, voluntary contributions bring in nothing, and forced contributions are illegitimate. This cruel alternative of letting the State perish, or of violating the sacred right of property, which is its support, constitutes the great difficulty of just and prudent economy.

The first step which the founder of a republic ought to take after the establishment of laws, is to settle a sufficient fund for the maintenance of the Magistrates and other officials, and for other public expenses. This fund, if it consist of money, is called *aerarium* or *fisc*, and *public demesne* if it consist of lands. This, for obvious reasons, is much to be preferred. Whoever has reflected on this matter must be of the opinion of Bodin, who looks upon the public demesne as the most reputable and certain means of providing for the needs of the State. It is noteworthy also that Romulus, in his division of lands, made it his first care to set apart a third for the use of the State. I confess it is not impossible for the produce of the demesne, if it be badly managed, to be reduced to nothing; but it is not of the essence of public demesnes to be badly administered.

Before any use is made of this fund, it should be assigned or accepted by an assembly of the people, or of the estates of the country, which should determine its future use. After this solemnity, which makes such funds inalienable, their very nature is, in a manner, changed, and the revenues become so sacred, that it is not only the most infamous theft, but actual treason, to misapply them or pervert them from the purpose for which they were destined. It reflects great dishonour on Rome that the integrity of Cato the censor was something so very remarkable, and that an Emperor, on rewarding the talents of a singer with a few crowns, thought it necessary to observe that the money came from his own private purse, and not from that of the State. But if we find few Galbas, where are we to look for a Cato? For when vice is no longer dishonourable, what chiefs will be so scrupulous as to abstain from touching the public revenues that are left to their discretion, and even not in time to impose on themselves, by pretending to confound their own expensive and scandalous dissipations with the glory of the State, and the means of extending their own authority with the means of augmenting its power? It is particularly in this delicate part of the administration that virtue is the only effective instrument, and that the integrity of the Magistrate is the only real check upon his avarice. Books and auditing of accounts, instead of exposing frauds, only conceal them; for prudence is never so ready to conceive new precautions as knavery is to elude them. Never mind, then, about account books and papers; place the management of finance in honest hands: that is the only way to get it faithfully conducted.

When public funds are once established, the rulers of the State become of right the administrators of them: for this administration constitutes a part of government which is always essential, though not always equally so. Its influence increases in proportion as that of other resources is diminished; and it may justly be said that a government has reached the last stage of corruption, when it has ceased to have sinews other than money. Now as every government constantly tends to become lax, this is enough to show why no State can subsist unless its revenues constantly increase.

The first sense of the necessity of this increase is also the first sign of the internal disorder of the State; and the prudent administrator, in his endeavours to find means to provide for the present necessity, will neglect nothing to find out the distant cause of the new need; just as a mariner, when he finds the water gaining on his vessel, does not neglect, while he is working the pumps, to discover and stop the leak.

From this rule is deduced the most important rule in the administration of finance, which is, to take more pains to guard against needs than to increase revenues. For, whatever diligence be employed, the relief which only comes after, and more slowly than, the evil, always leaves some injury behind. While a remedy is being found for one evil, another is beginning to make itself felt, and even the remedies themselves produce new difficulties: so that at length the nation is involved in debt and the people oppressed, while the government loses its influence and can do very little with a great deal of money. I imagine it was owing to the recognition of this rule that such wonders were done by ancient governments, which did more with their parsimony than ours do with all their treasures; and perhaps from this comes the common use of the word 'economy', which means rather the prudent management of what one has than ways of getting what one has not.

But apart from the public demesne, which is of service to the State in proportion to the uprightness of those who govern, any one sufficiently acquainted with the whole force of the general administration, especially when it confines itself to legitimate methods, would be astonished at the resources the rulers can make use of for safeguarding all public needs, without trespassing on the goods of individuals. As they are masters of the whole commerce of the State, nothing is easier for them than to direct it into such channels as to provide for every need, without appearing to interfere. The distribution of provisions, money, and merchandise in just proportions, according to times and places, is the true secret of finance and the source of wealth, provided those who administer it have foresight enough to suffer a present apparent loss, in order really to obtain immense profits in the future. When we see a government paying bounties, instead of receiving duties, on the exportation of corn in time of plenty, and on its importation in time of scarcity, we must have such facts before our eyes if we are to be persuaded of their reality. We should hold such facts to be idle tales, if they had happened in ancient times. Let us suppose that, in order to prevent a scarcity in bad years, a proposal were made to establish public granaries; would not the maintenance of so useful an institution serve in most countries as an excuse for new taxes? At Geneva, such granaries, established and kept up by a prudent administration, are a public resource in bad years, and the principal revenue of the State at all times. *Alit et ditat* is the inscription which stands, rightly and properly, on the front of the building. To set forth in this place the economic system of a good government, I have often turned my eyes to that of this Republic, rejoicing to find in my own country an example of that wisdom and happiness which I should be glad to see prevail in every other.

If we ask how the needs of a State grow, we shall find they generally arise, like the wants of individuals, less from any real necessity than from the increase of useless desires, and that expenses are often augmented only to give a pretext for raising receipts: so that the State would sometimes gain by not being rich, and apparent wealth is in reality more burdensome than poverty itself would be. Rulers may indeed hope to keep the peoples in stricter dependence, by thus giving them with one hand what they take from with the other; and this was in fact the policy of Joseph towards the Egyptians; but this political sophistry is the more fatal to the State, as the money never returns into the hands it went out of. Such principles only enrich the idle at the expense of the industrious.

A desire for conquest is one of the most evident and dangerous causes of this increase. This desire, occasioned often by a different species of ambition from that which it seems to proclaim, is not always what it appears to be, and has not so much, for its real motive, the apparent desire to aggrandize the Nation as a secret desire to increase the authority of the rulers at home, by increasing the number of troops, and by the diversion which the objects of war occasion in the minds of the citizens.

It is at least certain, that no peoples are so oppressed and wretched as conquering nations, and that their successes only increase their misery. Did not history inform us of the fact, reason would suffice to tell us that, the greater a State grows, the heavier and more burdensome in proportion its expenses become: for every province has to furnish its share to the general expense of government, and besides has to be at the expense of its own administration, which is as great as if it were really independent. Add to this that great fortunes are always acquired in one place and spent in another. Production therefore soon ceases to balance consumption, and a whole country is impoverished merely to enrich a single town.

Another source of the increase of public wants, which depends on the foregoing, is this. There may come a time when the citizens, no longer looking upon themselves as interested in the common cause, will cease to be the defenders of the country, and the Magistrates will prefer the command of mercenaries to that of freemen; if for no other reason than that, when the time comes, they may use them to reduce freemen to submission. Such was the state of Rome towards the end of the Republic and under the Emperors: for all the victories of the early Romans, like those of Alexander, had been won by brave citizens, who were ready, at need, to give their blood in the service of their country, but would never sell it. Only at the siege of Veii did the practice of paying the Roman infantry begin. Marius, in the Jugurthine war, dishonoured the legions by introducing freedmen, vagabonds, and other mercenaries. Tyrants, the enemies of the very people it was their duty to make happy, maintained regular troops, apparently to withstand the foreigner, but really to enslave their countrymen. To form such troops, it was necessary to take men from the land; the lack of their labour then diminished the amount of provisions, and their maintenance introduced those taxes which increased prices. The first disorder gave rise to murmurs among the people; in order to suppress them, the number of troops had to be increased, and consequently the misery of the people also got worse; and the growing despair led to still further increases in the cause in order to guard against its effects. On the other hand, the mercenaries, whose merit we may judge of by the price at which they sold themselves, proud of their own meanness, and despising the laws that protected them, as well as their fellows whose bread they ate, imagined themselves more honoured in being Caesar's satellites than in being defenders of Rome. As they were given over to blind obedience, their swords were always at the throats of their fellow-citizens, and they were prepared for general butchery at the first sign. It would not be difficult to show that this was one of the principal causes of the ruin of the Roman Empire.

The invention of artillery and fortifications has forced the princes of Europe, in modern times, to return to the use of regular troops, in order to garrison their towns; but, however lawful their motives, it is to be feared the effect may be no less fatal. It will be no less necessary than formerly to depopulate the country to form armies and garrisons; it will be no less necessary to oppress the peoples; in a word, these dangerous establishments have increased of late years with such rapidity in this part of the world, that they evidently threaten to depopulate Europe, and sooner or later to ruin its inhabitants.

Be this as it may, it ought to be seen that such institutions necessarily subvert the true economic system, which draws the principal revenue of the State from the public demesne, and leave only the troublesome resource of subsidies and imposts; with which it remains to deal.

It should be remembered that the foundation of the social

compact is property; and its first condition, that every one should be maintained in the peaceful possession of what belongs to him. It is true that, by the same treaty, every one binds himself, at least tacitly, to be assessed toward the public wants: but as this undertaking cannot prejudice the fundamental law, and presupposes that the need is clearly recognized by all who contribute to it, it is plain that such assessment, in order to be lawful, must be voluntary; it must depend, not indeed on particular will, as if it were necessary to have the consent of each individual, and that he should give no more than just what he pleased, but on a general will, decided by vote of a majority, and on the basis of a proportional rating which leaves nothing arbitrary in the imposition of the tax.

That taxes cannot be legitimately established except by the consent of the people or its representatives, is a truth generally admitted by all philosophers and jurists of any repute on questions of public right, not even excepting Bodin. If any of them have laid down rules which seem to contradict this, their particular motives for doing so may easily be seen; and they introduce so many conditions and restrictions that the argument comes at bottom to the same thing: for whether the people has it in its power to refuse, or the Sovereign ought not to exact, is a matter of indifference with regard to right; and if the point in question concerns only power, it is useless to inquire whether it is legitimate or not. Contributions levied on the people are two kinds; real, levied on commodities, and personal, paid by the head. Both are called taxes or subsidies: when the people fixes the sum to be paid, it is called subsidy; but when it grants the product of an imposition, it is called a tax. We are told in *The Spirit of the Laws* that a capitation tax is most suited to slavery, and a real tax most in accordance with liberty. This would be incontestable, if the circumstances of every person were equal; for otherwise nothing can be more disproportionate than such a tax; and it is in the observations of exact proportions that the spirit of liberty consists. But if a tax by heads were exactly proportioned to the circumstances of individuals, as what is called the capitation tax in France might be, it would be the most equitable and consequently the most proper for freemen.

These proportions appear at first very easy to note, because, being relative to each man's position in the world, their incidence is always public: but proper regard is seldom paid to all the elements that should enter into such a calculation, even apart from deception arising from avarice, fraud, and self-interest. In the first place, we have to consider the relation of quantities, according to which, *ceteris paribus*, the person who has ten times the property of another man ought to pay ten times as much to the State. Secondly, the relation of the use made, that is to say, the distinction between necessaries and superfluities. He who possesses only the common necessaries of life should pay nothing at all, while the tax on him who is in possession of superfluities may justly be extended to everything he has over and above necessaries. To this he will possibly object that, when his rank is taken into account, what may be superfluous to a man of inferior station is necessary for him. But this is false: for a grandee has two legs just like a cowherd, and, like him again, but one belly. Besides, these pretended necessaries are really so little necessary to his rank, that if he should renounce them on any worthy occasion, he would only be the more honoured. The populace would be ready to adore a minister who went to council on foot, because he had sold off his carriages to supply a pressing need of the State. Lastly, to no man does the law prescribe magnificence; and propriety is no argument against right.

A third relation, which is never taken into account, though it ought to be the chief consideration, is the advantage that every person derives from the social confederacy; for this provides a powerful protection for the immense possessions of the rich, and hardly leaves the poor man in quiet possession of the cottage he builds with his own hands. Are not all the advantages of society for the rich and powerful? Are not all lucrative posts in their hands? Are not all privileges and exemptions reserved for them alone? Is not the public authority always on their side? If a man of eminence robs his creditors, or is guilty of other knaveries, is he not always assured of impunity? Are not the assaults, acts of violence, assassinations, and even murders committed by the great, matters that are hushed up in a few months, and of which nothing more is thought? But if a great man himself is robbed or insulted, the whole police force is immediately in motion, and woe even to innocent persons who chance to be suspected. If he has to pass through any dangerous road, the country is up in arms to escort him. If the axle-tree of his chaise breaks, everybody flies to his assistance. If there is a noise at his door, he speaks but a word, and all is silent. If he is incommoded by the crowd, he waves his hand and every one makes way. If his coach is met on the road by a wagon, his servants are ready to beat the driver's brains out, and fifty honest pedestrians going quietly about their business had better be crushed to death than an idle jackanapes be delayed in his coach. Yet all this respect costs him not a farthing: it is the rich man's right, and not what he buys with his wealth. How different is the case of the poor man! the more humanity owes him, the more society denies him. Every door is shut against him, even whem he has a right to its being opened: and if ever he obtains justice, it is with much greater difficulty than others obtain favours. If the militia is to be raised or the highway to be mended, he is always given the preference; he always bears the burden which his richer neighbour has influence enough to get exempted from. On the least accident that happens to him, everybody avoids him: if his cart be overturned in the road, so far is he from receiving any assistance, that he is lucky if he does not get horse-whipped by the impudent lackeys of some young duke: in a word, all gratuitous assistance is denied to the poor when they need it, just because they cannot pay for it. I look upon any poor man as totally undone, if he has the misfortune to have an honest heart, a fine daughter, and a powerful neighbour.

Another no less important fact is that the losses of the poor are much harder to repair than those of the rich, and that the difficulty of acquisition is always greater in proportion as there is more need for it. 'Nothing comes out of nothing,' is as true of life as in physics: money is the seed of money, and the first guinea is sometimes more difficult to acquire than the second million. Add to this that what the poor pay is lost to them for ever, and remains in, or returns to, the hands of the rich: and as, to those who share in the government or to their dependants, the whole produce of the taxes must sooner or later pass, although they pay their share, these persons have always a sensible interest in increasing them.

The terms of the social compact between these two estates of men may be summed up in a few words: 'You have need of me, because I am rich and you are poor. We will therefore come to an agreement. I will permit you to have the honour of serving me, on condition that you bestow on me the little you have left, in return for the pains I shall take to command you.'

Putting all these considerations carefully together, we shall find that, in order to levy taxes in a truly equitable and proportionate manner, the imposition ought not to be in simple ratio to the property of the contributors, but in compound ratio to the difference of their conditions and the superfluity of their possessions. This very important and difficult operation is daily made by numbers of honest clerks, who know their arithmetic; but a Plato or a Montesquieu would not venture to undertake it without the greatest diffidence, or without praying to Heaven for understanding and integrity.

Another disadvantage of personal taxes is that they may be too much felt or raised with too great severity. This, however, does not prevent them from being frequently evaded; for it is much easier for persons to escape a tax than for their possessions.

Of all impositions, that on land, or real taxation, has always been regarded as most advantageous in countries where more attention is paid to what the tax will produce, and to the certainty of recovering the product, than to securing the least discomfort for the people. It has been even maintained that it is necessary to burden the peasant in order to rouse him from indolence, and that he would never work if he had no taxes to pay. But in all countries experience confutes this ridiculous notion. In England and Holland the farmer pays very little, and in China nothing: yet these are the countries in which the land is best cultivated. On the other hand, in those countries where the husbandman is taxed in proportion to the produce of his lands, he leaves them uncultivated, or reaps just as much from them as suffices for bare subsistence. For to him who loses the fruit of his labour, it is some gain to do nothing. To lay a tax on industry is a very singular expedient for banishing idleness.

Taxes on land or corn, especially when they are excessive, lead to two results so fatal in their effect that they cannot but depopulate and ruin, in the long run, all countries in which they are established.

The first of these arises from the defective circulation of specie; for industry and commerce draw all the money from the country into the capitals: and as the tax destroys the proportion there might otherwise be between the needs of the husbandman and the price of his corn, money is always leaving and never returning. Thus the richer the city the poorer the country. The product of the taxes passes from the hands of the prince or his financial officers into those of artists and traders; and the husbandman, who receives only the smallest part of it, is at length exhausted by paying always the same, and receiving constantly less. How could a human body subsist if it had veins and no arteries, or if its arteries conveyed the blood only within four inches of the heart? Chardin tells us that in Persia the royal dues on commodities are paid in kind: this custom, which, Herodotus informs us, prevailed long ago in the same country down to the time of Darius, might prevent the evil of which I have been speaking. But unless intendants, directors, commissioners, and warehousemen in Persia are a different kind of people from what they are elsewhere, I can hardly believe that the smallest part of this produce ever reaches the king, or that the corn is not spoilt in every granary, and the greater part of the warehouses not consumed by fire.

The second evil effect arises from an apparent advantage, which aggravates the evil before it can be perceived. That is that corn is a commodity whose price is not enhanced by taxes in the country producing it, and which, in spite of its absolute necessity, may be diminished in quantity without the price being increased. Hence, many people die of hunger, although corn remains cheap, and the husbandman bears the whole charge of a tax, for which he cannot indemnify himself by the price of his corn. It must be observed that we ought not to reason about a land-tax in the same manner as about duties laid on various kinds of merchandise; for the effect of such duties is to raise the price, and they are paid by the buyers rather than the sellers. For these duties, however heavy, are still voluntary, and are paid by the merchant only in proportion to the quantity he buys; and as he buys only in proportion to his sale, he himself gives the law its particular application; but the farmer who is obliged to pay his rent at stated times, whether he sells or not, cannot wait till he can get his own price for his commodity: even if he is not forced to sell for mere subsistence, he must sell to pay the taxes; so that it is frequently the heaviness of the tax that keeps the price of corn low.

It is further to be noticed that the resources of commerce and industry are so far from rendering the tax more supportable through abundance of money, that they only render it more burdensome. I shall not insist on what is very evident; i.e. that, although a greater or less quantity of money in a State may give it the greater or less credit in the eye of the foreigner, it makes not the least difference to the real fortune of the citizens, and does not make their condition any more or less comfortable. But I must make these two important remarks: First, unless a State possesses superfluous commodities, and abundance of money results from foreign trade, only trading cities are sensible of the abundance; while the peasant only becomes relatively poorer. Secondly, as the price of everything is enhanced by the increase of money, taxes also must be proportionately increased; so that the farmer will find himself still more burdened without having more resources.

It ought to be observed that the tax on land is a real duty on the produce. It is universally agreed, however, that nothing is so dangerous as a tax on corn paid by the purchaser: but how comes it we do not see that it is a hundred times worse when the duty is paid by the cultivator himself? Is not this an attack on the substance of the State at its very source? Is it not the directest possible method of depopulating a country, and therefore in the end ruining it? For the worst kind of scarcity a nation can suffer from is lack of inhabitants.

Only the real statesman can rise, in imposing taxes, above the mere financial object: he alone can transform heavy burdens into useful regulations, and make the people even doubtful whether such establishments were not calculated rather for the good of the nation in general, than merely for the raising of money.

Duties on the importation of foreign commodities, of which the natives are fond, without the country standing in need of them; on the exportation of those of the growth of the country which are not too plentiful, and which foreigners cannot do without; on the productions of frivolous and all too lucrative arts; on the importation of all pure luxuries; and in general on all objects of luxury; will answer the two-fold end in view. It is by such taxes, indeed, by which the poor are eased, and the burdens thrown on the rich, that it is possible to prevent the continual increase of inequality of fortune; the subjection of such a multitude of artisans and useless servants to the rich, the multiplication of idle persons in our cities, and the depopulation of the countryside.

It is important that the value of any commodity and the duties laid on it should be so proportioned that the avarice of individuals may not be too strongly tempted to fraud by the greatness of the possible profit. To make smuggling difficult, those commodities should be singled out which are hardest to conceal. All duties should be rather paid by the consumer of the commodity taxed than by him who sells it; as the quantity of duty he would be obliged to pay would lay him open to greater temptations, and afford him more opportunities for fraud.

This is the constant custom in China, a country where the taxes are greater and yet better paid than in any other part of the world. The merchant himself there pays no duty; the buyer alone, without murmuring or sedition, meets the whole charge; for as the necessaries of life, such as rice and corn, are absolutely exempt from taxation, the common people is not oppressed, and the duty falls only on those who are well-to-do. Precautions against smuggling ought not to be dictated so much by the fear of its occurring, as by the attention which the government should pay to securing individuals from being seduced by illegitimate profits, which first make them bad citizens, and afterwards soon turn them into dishonest men.

Heavy taxes should be laid on servants in livery, on equipages, rich furniture, fine clothes, on spacious courts and gardens, on public entertainments of all kinds, on useless professions, such as dancers, singers, players, and in a word, on all that multiplicity of objects of luxury, amusement, and idleness, which strike the eyes of all, and can the less be hidden, as their whole purpose is to be seen, without which they would be useless. We need be under no apprehension of the produce of these taxes being arbitrary, because they are laid on things not absolutely necessary. They must know but little of mankind who imagine that, after they have been once seduced by luxury, they can ever renounce it: they would a hundred times sooner renounce common necessaries, and had much rather die of hunger than of shame. The increase in their expense is only an additional reason for supporting them, when the vanity of appearing wealthy reaps its profit from the price of the thing and the charge of the tax. As long as there are rich people in the world, they will be desirous of distinguishing themselves from the poor, nor can the State devise a revenue less burdensome or more certain than what arises from this distinction.

For the same reason, industry would have nothing to suffer from an economic system which increased the revenue, encouraged agriculture by relieving the husbandman, and insensibly tended to bring all fortunes nearer to that middle condition which constitutes the genuine strength of the State. These taxes might, I admit, bring certain fashionable articles of dress and amusement to an untimely end; but it would be only to substitute others, by which the artificer would gain, and the exchequer suffer no loss. In a word, suppose the spirit of government was constantly to tax only the superfluities of the rich, one of two things must happen: either the rich would convert their superfluous expenses into useful ones, which would redound to the profit of the State, and thus the imposition of taxes would have the effect of the best sumptuary laws, the expenses of the State would necessarily diminish with those of individuals, and the treasury would not receive so much less as it would gain by having less to pay; or, if the rich did not become less extravagant, the exchequer would have such resources in the product of taxes on their expenditure as would provide for the needs of the State. In the first case the treasury would be the richer by what it would save, from having the less to do with its money; and in the second, it would be enriched by the useless expenses of individuals.

We may add to all this a very important distinction in matters of political right, to which governments, constantly tenacious of doing everything for themselves, ought to pay great attention. It has been observed that personal taxes and duties on the necessaries of life, as they directly trespass on the right of property, and consequently on the true foundation of political society, are always liable to have dangerous results, if they are not established with the express consent of the people or its representatives. It is not the same with articles the use of which we can deny ourselves; for as the individual is under no absolute necessity to pay, his contribution may count as voluntary. The particular consent of each contributor then takes the place of the general consent of the whole people: for why should a people oppose the imposition of a tax which falls only on those who desire to pay it? It appears to me certain that everything, which is not prescribed by law, or contrary to morality, and yet may be prohibited by the government, may also be permitted on payment of a certain duty. Thus, for example, if the government may prohibit the use of coaches, it may certainly impose a tax on them; and this is a prudent and useful method of censuring their use without absolutely forbidding it. In this case, the tax may be regarded as a sort of fine, the product of which compensates for the abuse it punishes.

It may perhaps be objected that those, whom Bodin calls *impostors*, i.e. those who impose or contrive the taxes, being in the class of the rich, will be far from sparing themselves to relieve the poor. But this is quite beside the point. If, in every nation, those to whom the Sovereign commits the government of the people, were, from their position, its enemies, it would not be worth while to inquire what they ought to do to make the people happy.

The General Society of the Human Race

(This Chapter, the second in the original draft of the *Social Contract* (the 'Geneva manuscript'), was omitted from the final published version. The passages contained in square brackets have been crossed out in the manuscript.)

Let us begin by inquiring whence the need for political institutions arises.

Man's strength is so strictly proportionate to his natural needs and to his primitive state that when this state changes, or these needs increase, be it ever so slightly, the help of his fellow-men becomes necessary to him. When, finally, his desires encompass the whole of nature, the co-operation of the whole human race is hardly sufficient to satisfy them. Thus the same causes which make us wicked also make us slaves; we are simultaneously subjected and depraved. The sense of our weakness stems less from our nature than from our cupidity. Our needs bring us together at the same time as our passions divide us, and the more we become enemies of our fellow-men, the less we can do without them. Such are the first bonds of general society; such are the foundations of that universal benevolence which seems to be stifled in our hearts just when our minds recognize the need for it, and whose fruits everyone wants to gather without having to cultivate it. For the fact that men are identical by nature is of no importance here; it can lead them to quarrel just as much as to unite, and fosters competition and jealousy as often as it does good understanding and agreement.

From this new order of things there arises a multitude of relationships without measure, without rule, and without consistency. Men are continually deforming and changing them, and for every one who tries to fix them there are a hundred working to destroy them. And as the relative existence of a man in the state of nature depends on a thousand other relationships which are continually changing, he can never be sure he is going to stay the same for two moments of his life. Peace and happiness are only momentary flashes for him; nothing is permanent but the wretchedness that results from all these vicissitudes. Even if his feelings and his ideas could rise as far as the love of order and the sublime notions of virtue, he could never make any sure application of his principles; the state of things would not allow him to discern good or evil, the honest man or the wicked.

So general society of the sort to which our mutual needs can give rise does not offer any effective assistance to man when he has entered this state of wretchedness; or rather it only gives new strength to the man who already has too much, whilst the weak man, lost, stifled, crushed in the multitude, finds no haven of refuge and no support in his weakness, and finally perishes as the victim of this deceitful union which he expected would bring him happiness.

[When men first join together on a voluntary basis, they do so for motives which bear no relation to the essential function of such a union. Far from proposing as their aim a common happiness of which each could have his share, they create a situation in which one's good fortune is another's misfortune. Once we are convinced of this, and once we recognize that, far from aiming at the general good, men only come together because they are moving away from it, then we shall come to feel that, even if such a state could exist, it would only be a source of crimes and misfortunes for men, since each would only see his own interest, follow his own inclinations, and listen to the voice of his own passions.]

So the sweet voice of Nature is no longer an infallible guide for us, nor is the independence we have received from her a desirable state. Peace and innocence escaped us for ever, even before we tasted their delights. Beyond the range of thought and feeling of the brutish men of the earliest times, and no longer within the grasp of the 'enlightened' men of later periods, the happy life of the Golden Age could never really have existed for the human race. When men could have enjoyed it they were unaware of it; and when they could have understood it they had already lost it.[1]

There is yet another point: if this perfect independence and this liberty without rules had remained united with primitive innocence, it would still have had an essential vice harmful to the development of our most excellent faculties: It would have lacked that link between the parts which constitutes them into a whole. The earth would have been covered with men between whom there would have been almost no communication; we should have made contact with one another at some points without becoming united at any; each one of us would have remained isolated among the others, each one of us would have thought only of himself; our understanding would have been unable to develop; we should have lived without feeling anything, and we should have died without having lived; all our happiness would have consisted in not being conscious of our wretchedness; there would have been neither kindness in our hearts nor morality in our actions and we should never have enjoyed that most delicious sentiment of the soul which is the love of virtue.

[It is certain that the words 'human race' bring to mind a purely collective idea which does not imply any real union among the individuals which constitute it. To this let us add the following supposition: let us think of the human race as a corporate[2] person having, together with a feeling of common existence which gives it individuality and makes it a unity, a universal motive force which makes each part act for a general end relative to the whole. Let us assume that this common feeling is that of humanity and the natural law is the active principle of the whole machine. Then let us observe what results from the constitution of man in his relations with his fellows. Entirely contrary to what we have supposed we shall find that the progress of society stifles humanity in men's hearts by arousing personal interest, and that the notions of natural law, which it would be more appropriate to call the law of reason, only begin to develop when the earlier development of the passions is making all its precepts powerless. From this it is apparent that this so-called social treaty, dictated by nature, is a pure fantasy, since its conditions are always unknown or impracticable and men must either be unaware of them or infringe them.

If the general society existed elsewhere than in the systems of philosophers, it would, as I have said, be a corporate[1] being with its own qualities distinct from those of the particular beings who constitute it, in the same sort of way as chemical compounds have properties which they do not obtain from any of the elements which constitute them. There would be a universal language which nature would teach to all men and which would be the first instrument of their mutual communication. There would be a sort of common sensorium which would ensure the correspondence of all the parts. Public good or evil would not be merely the sum of individual goods and evils, as in a simple aggregation, but it would reside in the liaison which unites them; it would be greater than this sum; and public felicity, far from being established on the happiness of individuals, would itself be the source of that happiness.]

It is false to assert that, in the state of independence, reason leads us to contribute to the common good through a consideration of our own interests. Far from being allied, private interest and the common good are mutually exclusive in the natural order of things. Social laws are a yoke which every one is very willing to impose on others, but which he does not want to bear himself. '*I sense that I am bringing terror and strife into the midst of the human race*,' says the independent man whom the wise man wishes to stifle; '*but either I must be unhappy, or I must make others unhappy, and no one is more dear to me than myself.*[2] It is useless,' he might add, 'for me to try to reconcile my interest with that of others; everything you tell me about the advantages of the social law would be excellent if, whilst I was scrupulously observing it towards others, I could be sure that they would all observe it towards me. But what assurance can you give me on this? Could I find myself in any worse situation than that of being exposed to all the harm which stronger men might wish to do to me without daring to get my own back on weaker ones? Either you must give me guarantees against any unjust undertaking, or you must not expect me to abstain from similar actions in my turn. It is no good your telling me that by renouncing the duties which natural law imposes on me I at the same time deprive myself of its rights, and that my violent actions will authorize all those which anyone may wish to commit against me. I accept this state of affairs all the more willingly because I cannot see how my moderation could offer me any guarantee. It will be up to me, moreover, to get the strong on my side by sharing with them the spoils of the weak. That way, I shall be both better off and safer than if I followed the paths of justice.' The proof that enlightened and independent man would have reasoned in this way is that this is precisely how any sovereign society reasons when it is accountable for its conduct to no one but itself.

How can one reply convincingly to such arguments without bringing in religion to aid morality and making the will of God intervene directly to bind men together in society? But the sublime notions of the God of wise men, the laws of kindness and brotherhood which He imposes on us, the social virtues of pure minds, which are the only form of worship He wishes from us, all these will never be understood by the multitude. The multitude will always be given Gods as stupid as itself and will make slight material sacrifices to them and then honour them by giving itself over to a thousand horrible and destructive passions. The whole world would be swimming in blood and the human race would soon perish, if philosophy and the laws did not restrain the furies of fanaticism and if the voice of men was not stronger than that of the Gods.

Indeed, if the concepts of the Supreme Being and of natural law were innate in every heart, it was very superfluous to take the trouble to teach them both directly. To do so was to inform us of what we already knew, and the way in which this was undertaken would have been more appropriate if the aim had been to make us forget them. If they were not innate, then all those to whom God has not given them are dispensed from knowing them. The moment particular instructions were required for this purpose, each people had its own, together with proofs that they were the only good ones. This resulted in bloodshed and murder far more often than in concord and peace.

So let us leave on one side the sacred precepts of the different religions, the abuse of which causes as many crimes as their use can spare us from. Let us leave to the philosopher the examination of a question which the theologian has never treated except to the prejudice of the human race.

But the philosopher will refer me back *to the human race* itself, which *alone has the right to decide, for its only passion is for the* greatest possible *well-being of all men.* He will tell me that *it is to the general will that the individual must address himself to know how far he must be a man, a citizen, a subject, a father and a child, and when it is fitting for him to live and when to die.*[1] 'I admit that I can clearly see there the rule that I must consult,' our independent man will say, 'but I still do not see the reason why I should be subject to this rule. It is not a question of teaching me what justice is; it is a question of showing me what interest I have in being just.' No one, indeed, will disagree with the view *that the general will is, in each individual, a pure act of the understanding which reasons, when the passions are silent, about what a man can ask of his fellows and what his fellows have the right to ask of him.* But where is the man who can thus separate himself from himself? If self-preservation is the first precept of nature, can he be forced to consider, in this way, the human race in general and to impose on himself duties whose relation with his own individual constitution he cannot see? Do not the objections mentioned above continue to exist? Do we not still need to show how this personal interest demands that he submit himself to the general will?

Moreover, as the ability thus to generalize his ideas is one of the most difficult and one of the last to be acquired achievements of the human understanding, it is questionable whether the ordinary man will ever be in a state to derive the rules of his conduct from this sort of reasoning. Would it not often happen, if the general will had to be consulted about a particular action, that a well-intentioned man would make a mistake, either in the rule or in its application, and would follow his own inclinations whilst thinking he was obeying the law? What will he do to save himself from such errors? Will he listen to his inner voice? But it is said that this voice is only formed by the habit of judging and feeling in the bosom of society and according to the laws; it cannot, then, serve to establish them. It would moreover be necessary for his heart to be exempt from those passions which speak louder than conscience, drown its timid voice, and make some philosophers assert that this voice does not exist. Should he consult *the principles of written law, the social actions of* all *peoples, the tacit conventions of the* very *enemies of the human race?*[1] He would still always come up against the first difficulty for it is only from the social order established among us that we derive our ideas of the order we imagine. We conceive of general society on the model of our particular societies; the establishment of little republics makes us dream of the great one, and we really only begin to be men after having first been citizens. From this we can see what we should think of those so-called cosmopolitans who, justifying their love of their country through their love of the human race, boast of loving the whole world so as to have the right to love no one at all.

What reasoning proves to us in this respect is amply confirmed by the facts. One does not have to go very far back into remote antiquity to see clearly that sound ideas of natural law and the common brotherhood of all men arrived fairly late on the scene and made such slow progress in the world that only with Christianity have they become sufficiently generalized. Even in the laws of Justinian one still finds the violent actions of former times authorized in many ways, not only against declared enemies, but against all those who were not subject to the Empire;

the humanity of the Romans thus extended no further than their dominion.

It was indeed long believed, as Grotius points out, that it was permitted to rob, pillage and ill-treat foreigners, especially barbarians, even to the point of enslaving them. That is why it was possible, without giving offence, to ask strangers if they were brigands or pirates; for such occupations, far from being shameful, then passed for honourable. The first heroes, like Hercules and Theseus, who made war on brigands, were still quite capable of acting as brigands themselves; the Greeks often called 'treaties of peace' those which were made between peoples which had never been at war. The words 'foreigners' and 'enemies' were for a long time synonymous among a number of ancient peoples, even among the Latins. 'Hostis enim,' says Cicero, 'apud majores nostros dicebatur, quem nunc peregrinum dicimus.'* Hobbes's error, then, is not that of having established that a state of war existed between men who were independent and had become sociable; where he went wrong was in supposing that this state was natural to the human race, and in considering it the cause of vices of which it is really the effect.

Yet although there is no natural and general society among men, although they become unhappy and wicked in becoming sociable, although the laws of justice and equality mean nothing to those who live at one and the same time in the liberty of the state of nature and subject to the needs of the social state, yet we should not think that there is neither virtue nor happiness for us and that heaven has abandoned us without remedy to depravity. We should rather try to extract from the evil itself the remedy which can cure it. If possible, we must make up for the lack of any general association by creating new associations. Let our violent interlocutor himself be the judge of our success. Let us show him that the art of living together can, as it develops, repair the evils which, in its initial stages, it caused to human nature; let us show

* The man we would now call a stranger was, in former times, usually referred to as an enemy.

him all the wretchedness of the state which he believed a happy one, and all the falsity of the reasoning which he believed sound. Let him see, in a better constitution of things, the reward of good actions, the punishment of bad ones, and the felicitous accord of justice and happiness. Let us enlighten his reason with new knowledge, let us warm his heart with new feelings; let him learn to multiply his being and his felicity by sharing them with his fellows. If my zeal does not blind me in this enterprise, I do not doubt that if he has a strong soul and an upright mind, this enemy of the human race will finally abjure his hatred together with his errors; reason, which led him astray, will bring him back to humanity; he will learn to prefer to his apparent interest his interest properly understood; he will become good, virtuous and compassionate. In short, this man who wanted to be a fierce brigand will become the most firm support of a well-ordered society.

THE SOCIAL CONTRACT

OR

PRINCIPLES OF POLITICAL

RIGHT

Foederis aequas
Dicamus leges.
Vergil, *Aeneid* xi.

[Let us establish just laws for our contract.]

FOREWORD

This little treatise is part of a longer work, which I began years ago without realizing my limitations, and long since abandoned. Of the various fragments that might have been extracted from what I wrote, this is the most considerable, and, I think, the least unworthy of being offered to the public. The rest no longer exists.[1]

Book I

I mean to inquire if, in the civil order, there can be any sure and legitimate rule of administration, men being taken as they are and laws as they might be. In this inquiry I shall endeavour always to unite what right sanctions with what is prescribed by interest, in order that justice and utility may in no case be divided.

I enter upon my task without proving the importance of the subject. I shall be asked if I am a prince or a legislator, to write on politics. I answer that I am neither, and that is why I do so. If I were a prince or a legislator, I should not waste time in saying what wants doing; I should do it, or hold my peace.

As I was born a citizen of a free State, and a member of the Sovereign,[1] I feel that, however feeble the influence my voice can have on public affairs, the right of voting on them makes it my duty to study them: and I am happy, when I reflect upon governments, to find my inquiries always furnish me with new reasons for loving that of my own country.

Chapter 1
Subject of the First Book

Man is born free;[2] and everywhere he is in chains. One thinks himself the master of others, and still remains a greater slave than they. How did this change come about? I do not know. What can make it legitimate? That question I think I can answer.

If I took into account only force, and the effects derived from it, I should say: 'As long as a people is compelled to obey, and obeys, it does well; as soon as it can shake off the yoke, and shakes it off, it does still better; for, regaining its liberty by the same right as took it away, either it is justified in resuming it, or there was no justification for those who took it away.' But the social order is a sacred right which is the basis of all other rights. Nevertheless, this right does not come from nature, and must therefore be founded on conventions. Before coming to that, I have to prove what I have just asserted.

CHAPTER 2

The First Societies

The most ancient of all societies, and the only one that is natural, is the family: and even so the children remain attached to the father only so long as they need him for their preservation. As soon as this need ceases, the natural bond is dissolved. The children, released from the obedience they owed to the father, and the father, released from the care he owed his children, return equally to independence. If they remain united, they continue so no longer naturally, but voluntarily; and the family itself is then maintained only by convention.

This common liberty results from the nature of man. His first law is to provide for his own preservation, his first cares are those which he owes to himself; and, as soon as he reaches years of discretion, he is the sole judge of the proper means of preserving himself, and consequently becomes his own master.

The family then may be called the first model of political societies: the ruler corresponds to the father, and the people to the children; and all, being born free and equal, alienate their liberty only for their own advantage. The whole difference is that, in the family, the love of the father for his children repays him for the care he takes of them, while, in the State, the pleasure of commanding takes the place of the love which the chief cannot have for the peoples under him.

Grotius denies that all human power is established in favour of the governed, and quotes slavery as an example. His usual method of reasoning is constantly to establish right by fact.* It would be possible to employ a more logical method, but none could be more favourable to tyrants.

It is then, according to Grotius, doubtful whether the human race belongs to a hundred men, or that hundred men to the human race: and, throughout his book, he seems to incline to the former alternative, which is also the view of Hobbes.[1] On this showing, the human species is divided into so many herds of cattle, each with its ruler, who keeps guard over them for the purpose of devouring them.

As a shepherd is of a nature superior to that of his flock, the shepherds of men, i.e. their rulers, are of a nature superior to that of the peoples under them. Thus, Philo tells us, the Emperor Caligula reasoned, concluding equally well either that kings were gods, or that men were beasts.

The reasoning of Caligula agrees with that of Hobbes and Grotius. Aristotle, before any of them, had said that men are by no means equal naturally, but that some are born for slavery, and others for dominion.

Aristotle was right; but he took the effect for the cause. Nothing can be more certain than that every man born in slavery is born for slavery. Slaves lose everything in their chains, even the desire of escaping from them: they love their servitude, as the comrades of Ulysses loved their brutish conditions.† If then there are slaves by nature, it is because there have been slaves against nature. Force made the first slaves, and their cowardice perpetuated the condition.

I have said nothing of King Adam,[2] or Emperor Noah, father of the three great monarchs who shared out the universe, like the children of Saturn, whom some scholars have recognized in them.

---

* 'Learned inquiries into public right are often only the history of past abuses; and troubling to study them too deeply is a profitless infatuation' (*Essay on the Interests of France in Relation to its Neighbours*, by the Marquis d'Argenson). This is exactly what Grotius has done.

† See a short treatise of Plutarch's entitled 'That Animals Reason'.

I trust to getting due thanks for my moderation; for, being a direct descendant of one of these princes, perhaps of the eldest branch, how do I know that a verification of titles might not leave me the legitimate king of the human race? In any case, there can be no doubt that Adam was sovereign of the world, as Robinson Crusoe was of his island, as long as he was its only inhabitant; and this empire had the advantage that the monarch, safe on his throne, had no rebellions, wars, or conspirators to fear.

CHAPTER 3

The Right of the Strongest

The strongest is never strong enough to be always the master, unless he transforms strength into right, and obedience into duty. Hence the right of the strongest, which, though to all seeming meant ironically, is really laid down as a fundamental principle. But are we never to have an explanation of this phrase? Force is a physical power, and I fail to see what moral effect it can have. To yield to force is an act of necessity, not of will — at the most, an act of prudence. In what sense can it be a duty?

Suppose for a moment that this so-called 'right' exists. I maintain that the sole result is a mass of inexplicable nonsense. For, if force creates right, the effect changes with the cause: every force that is greater than the first succeeds to its right. As soon as it is possible to disobey with impunity, disobedience is legitimate; and, the strongest being always in the right, the only thing that matters is to act so as to become the strongest. But what kind of right is that which perishes when force fails? If we must obey perforce, there is no need to obey because we ought; and if we are not forced to obey, we are under no obligation to do so. Clearly, the word 'right' adds nothing to force: in this connection, it means absolutely nothing.

Obey the powers that be. If this means yield to force, it is a good precept, but superfluous: I can answer for its never being violated. All power comes from God, I admit; but so does all sickness: does that mean that we are forbidden to call in the doctor? A brigand surprises me at the edge of a wood: must I not merely surrender my purse on compulsion; but, even if I could withhold it, am I in conscience bound to give it up? For certainly the pistol he holds is also a power.

Let us then admit that force does not create right, and that we are obliged to obey only legitimate powers. In that case, my original question recurs.

CHAPTER 4

Slavery

Since no man has a natural authority over his fellow, and force creates no right, we must conclude that conventions form the basis of all legitimate authority among men.

If an individual, says Grotius, can alienate his liberty and make himself the slave of a master, why could not a whole people do the same and make itself subject to a king? There are in this passage plenty of ambiguous words which would need explaining; but let us confine ourselves to the word *alienate*. To alienate is to give or to sell. Now, a man who becomes the slave of another does not give himself; he sells himself, at the least for his subsistence: but for what does a people sell itself? A king is so far from furnishing his subjects with their subsistence that he gets his own only from them; and, as Rabelais says, kings do not live on nothing. Do subjects then give their persons on condition that the king takes their goods also? I fail to see what they have left to preserve.

It will be said that the despot assures his subjects civil

tranquillity. Granted; but what do they gain, if the wars his ambition brings down upon them, his insatiable avidity, and the vexatious conduct of his ministers press harder on them than their own dissensions would have done? What do they gain, if the very tranquillity they enjoy is one of their miseries? Tranquillity is found also in dungeons; but is that enough to make them desirable places to live in? The Greeks imprisoned in the cave of the Cyclops lived there very tranquilly, while they were awaiting their turn to be devoured.

To say that a man gives himself freely, is to say what is absurd and inconceivable; such an act is null and illegitimate, from the mere fact that he who does it is out of his mind. To say the same of a whole people is to suppose a people of madmen; and madness creates no right.

Even if each man could alienate himself, he could not alienate his children: they are born men and free; their liberty belongs to them, and no one but they has the right to dispose of it. Before they come to years of discretion, the father can, in their name, lay down conditions for their preservation and well-being, but he cannot give them irrevocably and without conditions: such a gift is contrary to the ends of nature, and exceeds the rights of paternity. It would therefore be necessary, in order to legitimize an arbitrary government, that in every generation the people should be in a position to accept or reject it; but, were this so, the government would be no longer arbitrary.

To renounce liberty is to renounce being a man, to surrender the rights of humanity and even its duties. For him who renounces everything no indemnity is possible. Such a renunciation is incompatible with man's nature; to remove all liberty from his will is to remove all morality from his acts. Finally, it is an empty and contradictory convention that sets up, on the one side, absolute authority, and, on the other, unlimited obedience. It is not clear that we can be under no obligation to a person from whom we have the right to exact everything? Does not this condition alone, in the absence of equivalence or exchange, in itself involve the nullity of the act? For what right can my slave have against me, when all that he has belongs to me, and, his right being mine, this right of mine against myself is a phrase devoid of meaning?

Grotius and the rest find in war another origin for the so-called right of slavery. The victor having, as they hold, the right of killing the vanquished, the latter can buy back his life at the price of his liberty; and this convention is the more legitimate because it is to the advantage of both parties.

But it is clear that this supposed right to kill the conquered is by no means deducible from the state of war. Men, from the mere fact that, while they are living in their primitive independence, they have no mutual relations stable enough to constitute either the state of peace or the state of war, cannot be naturally enemies. War is constituted by a relation between things, and not between persons; and, as the state of war cannot arise out of simple personal relations, but only out of real relations, private war, or war of man with man, can exist neither in the state of nature, where there is no constant property, nor in the social state, where everything is under the authority of the laws.

Individual combats, duels, and encounters, are acts which cannot constitute a state; while the private wars, authorized by the Establishments of Louis IX, King of France, and suspended by the Peace of God, are abuses of feudalism, in itself an absurd system if ever there was one, and contrary to the principles of natural right and to all good polity.

War then is a relation, not between man and man, but between State and State, and individuals are enemies only accidentally, not as men, nor even as citizens,* but as soldiers; not as members of

---

* The Romans, who understood and respected the right of war more than any other nation on earth, carried their scruples on this head so far that a citizen was not allowed to serve as a volunteer without engaging himself expressly against the enemy, and against such and such an enemy by name. A legion in which the younger Cato was seeing his first service under Popilius having been reconstructed, the elder Cato wrote to Popilius that, if he wished his son to continue serving under him, he must administer to him a new military oath, because, the first having been annulled, he was no longer able to bear arms against the enemy. The same Cato

their country, but as its defenders. Finally, each State can have for enemies only other States, and not men; for between things disparate in nature there can be no real relation.

Furthermore, this principle is in conformity with the established rules of all times and the constant practice of all civilized peoples. Declarations of war are intimations less to powers than to their subjects. The foreigner, whether king, individual, or people, who robs, kills, or detains the subjects, without declaring war on the prince, is not an enemy, but a brigand. Even in real war, a just prince, while laying hands, in the enemy's country, on all that belongs to the public, respects the lives and goods of individuals: he respects rights on which his own are founded. The object of the war being the destruction of the hostile State, the other side has a right to kill its defenders, while they are bearing arms; but as soon as they lay them down and surrender, they cease to be enemies or instruments of the enemy, and become once more merely men, whose life no one has any right to take. Sometimes it is possible to kill the State without killing a single one of its members; and war gives no right which is not necessary to the gaining of its object. These principles are not those of Grotius: they are not based on the authority of poets, but derived from the nature of reality and based on reason.

The right of conquest has no foundation other than the right of the strongest. If war does not give the conqueror the right to massacre the conquered peoples, the right to enslave them cannot be based upon a right which does not exist. No one has a right to kill an enemy except when he cannot make him a slave, and the right to enslave him cannot therefore be derived from the right to kill him. It is accordingly an unfair exchange to make him buy at the price of his liberty his life, over which the victor holds no right.

---

wrote to his son telling him to take great care not to go into battle before taking this new oath. I know that the siege of Clusium and other isolated events can be quoted against me; but I am citing laws and customs. The Romans are the people that least often transgressed its laws; and no other people has had such good ones. [Added in the edition of 1782 from Rousseau's MS notes.]

Is it not clear that there is a vicious circle in founding the right of life and death on the right of slavery, and the right of slavery on the right of life and death?

Even if we assume this terrible right to kill everybody, I maintain that a slave made in war, or a conquered people, is under no obligation to a master, except to obey him as far as he is compelled to do so. By taking an equivalent for his life, the victor has not done him a favour; instead of killing him without profit, he has killed him usefully. So far then is he from acquiring over him any authority in addition to that of force, that the state of war continues to subsist between them: their mutual relation is the effect of it, and the usage of the right of war does not imply a treaty of peace. A convention has indeed been made; but this convention, so far from destroying the state of war, presupposes its continuance.

So, from whatever aspect we regard the question, the right of slavery is null and void, not only as being illegitimate, but also because it is absurd and meaningless. The words *slave* and *right* contradict each other, and are mutually exclusive. It will always be equally foolish for a man to say to a man or to a people: 'I make with you a convention wholly at your expense and wholly to my advantage; I shall keep it as long as I like, and you will keep it as long as I like.'

CHAPTER 5

That We Must Always Go back to a First Convention

Even if I granted all that I have been refuting, the friends of despotism would be no better off. There will always be a great difference between subduing a multitude and ruling a society. Even if scattered individuals were successively enslaved by one man, however numerous they might be, I still see no more than a master and his slaves, and certainly not a people and its ruler; I see what may be termed an aggregation, but not an association; there is as yet neither public good nor body politic. The man in question, even if he has enslaved half the world, is still only an individual; his interest, apart from that of others, is still a purely private interest. If this same man comes to die, his empire, after him, remains scattered and without unity, as an oak falls and dissolves into a heap of ashes when the fire has consumed it.

A people, says Grotius, can give itself to a king. Then, according to Grotius, a people is a people before it gives itself. The gift is itself a civil act, and implies public deliberation. It would be better, before examining the act by which a people chooses a king, to examine that by which it has become a people; for this act, being necessarily prior to the other, is the true foundation of society.

Indeed, if there were no prior convention, where, unless the election were unanimous, would be the obligation on the minority to submit to the choice of the majority? How have a hundred men who wish for a master the right to vote on behalf of ten who do not? The law of majority voting is itself something established by convention, and presupposes unanimity, on one occasion at least.

CHAPTER 6

The Social Compact

I suppose men to have reached the point at which the obstacles in the way of their preservation in the state of nature show their power of resistance to be greater than the resources at the disposal of each individual for his maintenance in that state. That primitive condition can then subsist no longer; and the human race would perish unless it changed its manner of existence.

But, as men cannot engender new forces, but only unite and direct existing ones, they have no other means of preserving themselves than the formation, by aggregation, of a sum of forces great enough to overcome the resistance. These they have to bring into play by means of a single motive power, and cause to act in concert.

This sum of forces can arise only where several persons come together: but, as the force and liberty of each man are the chief instruments of his self-preservation, how can he pledge them without harming his own interests, and neglecting the care he owes to himself? This difficulty, in its bearing on my present subject, may be stated in the following terms:

'The problem is to find a form of association which will defend and protect with the whole common force the person and goods of each associate, and in which each, while uniting himself with all, may still obey himself alone, and remain as free as before.' This is the fundamental problem of which the social contract provides the solution.

The clauses of this contract are so determined by the nature of the act that the slightest modification would make them vain and ineffective; so that, although they have perhaps never been formally set forth, they are everywhere the same and everywhere tacitly admitted and recognized, until, on the violation of the social compact, each regains his original rights and resumes his natural liberty, while losing the conventional liberty in favour of which he renounced it.

These clauses, properly understood, may be reduced to one – the total alienation of each associate, together with all his rights, to the whole community; for, in the first place, as each gives himself absolutely, the conditions are the same for all; and, this being so, no one has any interest in making them burdensome to others.

Moreover, the alienation being without reserve, the union is as perfect as it can be, and no associate has anything more to demand: for, if the individuals retained certain rights, as there would be no common superior to decide between them and the public, each, being on one point his own judge, would ask to be so on all; the state of nature would thus continue, and the association would necessarily become inoperative or tyrannical.

Finally, each man, in giving himself to all, gives himself to nobody; and as there is no associate over which he does not acquire the same right as he yields others over himself, he gains an equivalent for everything he loses, and an increase of force for the preservation of what he has.

If then we discard from the social compact what is not of its essence, we shall find that it reduces itself to the following terms:

'*Each of us puts his person and all his power in common under the supreme direction of the general will, and, in our corporate capacity, we receive each member as an indivisible part of the whole.*'

At once, in place of the individual personality of each contracting party, this act of association creates a corporate[1] and collective body, composed of as many members as the assembly contains voters, and receiving from this act its unity, its common identity, its life, and its will. This public person, so formed by the union of all other persons, formerly took the name of *city*,* and now takes that of *Republic* or *body politic*; it is called by its

---

* The real meaning of this word has been almost wholly lost in modern times; most people mistake a town for a city, and a townsman for a citizen. They do not know that houses make a town, but citizens a city. The same mistake long ago cost the Carthaginians dear. I have never read of the title of citizens being given to the subjects of any prince, not even the ancient Macedonians or the English of today, though they are nearer liberty than any one else. The French alone everywhere familiarly adopt the name of citizens, because, as can be seen from their dictionaries, they have no idea of its meaning; otherwise they would be guilty of usurping it, of the crime of *lèse-majesté*; among them, the name expresses a virtue, and not a right. When Bodin spoke of our citizens and townsmen, he fell into a bad blunder in taking the one class for the other. M. d'Alembert has avoided the error, and, in his article on Geneva, has clearly distinguished the four orders of men (or even five, counting mere foreigners) who dwell in our town, of which two only compose the Republic. No other French writer, to my knowledge, has understood the real meaning of the word citizen.

members *State* when passive, *Sovereign* when active, and *Power* when compared with others like itself. Those who associated in it take collectively the name of *people*, and severally are called *citizens*, as sharing in the sovereign authority, and *subjects*, as being under the laws of the State. But these terms are often confused and taken one for another: it is enough to know how to distinguish them when they are being used with precision.

CHAPTER 7

The Sovereign

This formula shows us that the act of association comprises a mutual undertaking between the public and the individuals, and that each individual, in making a contract, as we may say, with himself, is bound in a double relation; as a member of the Sovereign he is bound to the individuals, and as a member of the State to the Sovereign. But the maxim of civil right, that no one is bound by undertakings made to himself, does not apply in this case; for there is a great difference between incurring an obligation to yourself and incurring one to a whole of which you form a part.

Attention must further be called to the fact that public deliberation, while competent to bind all the subjects to the Sovereign, because of the two different capacities in which each of them may be regarded, cannot, for the opposite reason, bind the Sovereign to itself; and that it is consequently against the nature of the body politic for the Sovereign to impose on itself a law which it cannot infringe. Being able to regard itself in only one capacity, it is in the position of an individual who makes a contract with himself; and this makes it clear that there neither is nor can be any kind of fundamental law binding on the body of the people – not even the social contract itself. This does not mean that the body politic cannot enter into undertakings with others, provided the contract is not infringed by them; for in relation to the foreigner, it becomes a simple being, an individual.

But the body politic or the Sovereign, drawing its being wholly from the sanctity of the contract, can never bind itself, even to an outsider, to do anything derogatory to the original act, for instance, to alienate any part of itself, or to submit to another Sovereign. Violation of the act by which it exists would be self-annihilation; and that which is itself nothing can create nothing.

As soon as this multitude is so united in one body, it is impossible to offend against one of the members without attacking the body, and still more to offend against the body without the members resenting it. Duty and interest therefore equally oblige the two contracting parties to give each other help; and the same men should seek to combine, in their double capacity, all the advantages dependent upon that capacity.

Again, the Sovereign, being formed wholly of the individuals who compose it, neither has nor can have any interest contrary to theirs; and consequently the sovereign power need give no guarantee to its subjects, because it is impossible for the body to wish to hurt all its members. We shall also see later on that it cannot hurt any in particular. The Sovereign, merely by virtue of what it is, is always what it should be.

This, however, is not the case with the relation of the subjects to the Sovereign, which, despite the common interest, would have no security that they would fulfil their undertakings, unless it found means to assure itself of their fidelity.

In fact, each individual, as a man, may have a particular will contrary or dissimilar to the general will which he has as a citizen. His particular interest may speak to him quite differently from the common interest: his absolute and naturally independent existence may make him look upon what he owes to the common cause as a gratuitous contribution, the loss of which will do less harm to others than the payment of it is burdensome to himself; and, regarding the corporate[1] person which constitutes the State as a *persona ficta*, because not a man, he may wish to enjoy the rights of citizenship without being ready to fulfil the duties of a subject. The continuance of such an injustice could not but prove the undoing of the body politic.

In order then that the social compact may not be an empty formula, it tacitly includes the undertaking, which alone can give force to the rest, that whoever refuses to obey the general will shall be compelled to do so by the whole body. This means nothing less than that he will be forced to be free; for this is the condition which, by giving each citizen to his country, secures him against all personal dependence. In this lies the key to the working of the political machine; this alone legitimizes civil undertakings, which, without it, would be absurd, tyrannical and liable to the most frightful abuses.

CHAPTER 8

The Civil State

The passage from the state of nature to the civil state produces a very remarkable change in man, by substituting justice for instinct in his conduct, and giving his actions the morality they had formerly lacked. Then only, when the voice of duty takes the place of physical impulses and right of appetite, does man, who so far had considered only himself, find that he is forced to act on different principles, and to consult his reason before listening to his inclinations. Although, in this state, he deprives himself of some advantages which he got from nature, he gains in return others so great, his faculties are so stimulated and developed, his ideas so extended, his feelings so ennobled, and his whole soul so uplifted, that, did not the abuses of this new condition often degrade him below that which he left, he would be bound to bless continually the happy moment which took him from it for ever, and, instead of a stupid and unimaginative animal, made him an intelligent being and a man.

Let us draw up the whole account in terms easily commensurable. What man loses by the social contract is his natural liberty and an unlimited right to everything he tries to get and succeeds in getting; what he gains is civil liberty and the proprietorship of all he possesses. If we are to avoid mistake in weighing one against the other, we must clearly distinguish natural liberty, which is bounded only by the strength of the individual, from civil liberty, which is limited by the general will; and possession, which is merely the effect of force or the right of the first occupier, from property, which can be founded only on a positive title.

We might, over and above all this, add, to what man acquires in the civil state, moral liberty, which alone makes him truly master of himself; for the mere impulse of appetite is slavery, while obedience to a law which we prescribe to ourselves is liberty. But I have already said too much on this head, and the philosophical meaning of the word liberty is not what concerns us here.

CHAPTER 9

Real Property

Each member of the community gives himself to it, at the moment of its foundation, just as he is, with all the resources at his command, including the goods he possesses. This act does not make possession, in changing hands, change its nature, and become property in the hands of the Sovereign; but, as the forces of the city are incomparably greater than those of an individual, public possession is also, in fact, stronger and more irrevocable, without being any more legitimate, at any rate from the point of view of foreigners. For the State, in relation to its members, is master of all their goods by the social contract, which, within the State, is the basis of all rights; but, in relation to other powers, it is so only by the right of the first occupier, which it holds from its members.

The right of the first occupier, though more real than the right of the strongest, becomes a real right only when the right of property has already been established. Every man has naturally a right to everything he needs; but the positive act which makes him proprietor of one thing excludes him from everything else. Having his share, he ought to keep to it, and can have no further right against the community. This is why the right of the first occupier, which in the state of nature is so weak, claims the respect of every man in civil society. In this right we are respecting not so much what belongs to another as what does not belong to ourselves.

In general, to establish the right of the first occupier over a plot of ground, the following conditions are necessary: first, the land must not yet be inhabited; secondly, a man must occupy only the amount he needs for his subsistence; and, in the third place, possession must be taken, not by an empty ceremony, but by labour and cultivation, the only sign of proprietorship that should be respected by others, in default of a legal title.

In granting the right of first occupancy to necessity and labour, are we not really stretching it as far as it can go? Is it possible to leave such a right unlimited? Is it to be enough to set foot on a plot of common ground, in order to be able to call yourself at once the master of it? Is it to be enough that a man has the strength to expel others for a moment, in order to establish his right to prevent them from ever returning? How can a man or a people seize an immense territory and keep it from the rest of the world except by a punishable usurpation, since all others are being robbed, by such an act, of the place of habitation and the means of subsistence which nature gave them in common? When Nuñez Balbao, standing on the seashore, took possession of the South Seas and the whole of South America in the name of the crown of Castille, was that enough to dispossess all their actual inhabitants, and to shut out from them all the princes of the world? If this was the case, it was quite unnecessary to multiply these ceremonies, and all the King of Spain had to do was, from his apartment, to take possession all at once of the whole universe, allowing himself subsequently to exclude from his empire what had formerly been possessed by other princes.

We can imagine how the lands of individuals, where they were contiguous and came to be united, became the public territory, and how the right of Sovereignty, extending from the subjects over the lands they held, became at once real and personal. The possessors were thus made more dependent, and the forces at their command used to guarantee their fidelity. The advantage of this does not seem to have been felt by ancient monarchs, who called themselves King of the Persians, Scythians, or Macedonians, and seemed to regard themselves more as rulers of men than as masters of a country. Those of the present day more cleverly call themselves Kings of France, Spain, England, etc.: thus holding the land, they are quite confident of holding the inhabitants.

The peculiar fact about this alienation is that, in taking over the goods of individuals, the community so far from despoiling them, only assures them legitimate possession, and changes usurpation into a true right and enjoyment into proprietorship. Thus the possessors, being regarded as depositaries of public property, and having their rights respected by all the members of the State and maintained against foreign aggression by all its forces, have, by a cession which benefits both the public and still more themselves, acquired, so to speak, all that they gave up. This paradox may easily be explained by the distinction between the rights which the Sovereign and the proprietor have over the same estate, as we shall see later on.

It may also happen that men begin to unite one with another before they possess anything, and that, subsequently occupying a tract of country which is enough for all, they enjoy it in common, or share it out among themselves, either equally or according to a scale fixed by the Sovereign. However the acquisition be made, the right which each individual has to his own estate is always subordinate to the right which the community has over all: without this, there would be neither stability in the social tie, nor real force in the exercise of Sovereignty.

I shall end this chapter and this book by remarking on a fact on which the whole social system should rest: i.e. that, instead of destroying natural equality, the fundamental compact substitutes, for such physical inequality as nature may have set up between men, an equality that is moral and legitimate, and that men, who may be unequal in strength or intelligence, become every one equal by convention and legal right.*

---

* Under bad governments, this equality is only apparent and illusory; it serves only to keep the pauper in his poverty and the rich man in the position he has usurped. In fact, laws are always of use to those who possess and harmful to those who have nothing: from which it follows that the social state is advantageous to men only when all have something and none too much.

Book II

Chapter 1

That Sovereignty Is Inalienable

The first and most important deduction from the principles we have so far laid down is that the general will alone can direct the State according to the object for which it was instituted, i.e. the common good: for if the clashing of particular interests made the establishment of societies necessary, the agreement of these very interests made it possible. The common element in these different interests is what forms the social tie; and, were there no point of agreement between them all, no society could exist. It is solely on the basis of this common interest that every society should be governed.

I hold then that Sovereignty, being nothing less than the exercise of the general will, can never be alienated, and that the Sovereign, who is no less than a collective being, cannot be represented except by himself: the power indeed may be transmitted, but not the will.

In reality, if it is not impossible for a particular will to agree on some point with the general will, it is at least impossible for the agreement to be lasting and constant; for the particular will tends, by its very nature, to partiality, while the general will tends to equality. It is even more impossible to have any guarantee of this agreement; for even if it should always exist, it would be the effect not of art, but of chance. The Sovereign may indeed say: 'I now will actually what this man wills, or at least what he says he wills'; but it cannot say: 'What he wills tomorrow, I too shall will' because it is absurd for the will to bind itself for the future, nor is it incumbent on any will to consent to anything that is not for the good of the being who wills. If then the people promises simply to obey, by that very act it dissolves itself and loses what makes it a people; the moment a master exists, there is no longer a Sovereign, and from that moment the body politic has ceased to exist.

This does not mean that the commands of the rulers cannot pass for general wills, so long as the Sovereign, being free to oppose them, offers no opposition. In such a case, universal silence is taken to imply the consent of the people. This will be explained later on.

CHAPTER 2

That Sovereignty Is Indivisible

Sovereignty, for the same reason as makes it inalienable, is indivisible; for will either is, or is not, general;* it is the will either of the body of the people, or only of a part of it. In the first case, the will, when declared, is an act of Sovereignty and constitutes law: in the second, it is merely a particular will, or act of magistracy – at the most a decree.

But our political theorists,[1] unable to divide Sovereignty in its principle, divide it according to its object; into force and will; into legislative power and executive power; into rights of taxation, justice, and war; into internal administration and power of foreign treaty. Sometimes they confuse all these sections, and sometimes they distinguish them; they turn the Sovereign into a fantastic being composed of several connected pieces; it is as if they were making man of several bodies, one with eyes, one with arms, another with feet, and each with nothing besides. We were told that the jugglers of Japan dismember a child before the eyes of the spectators; then they throw all the members into the air one after another, and the child falls down alive and whole. The conjuring tricks of our political theorists are very like that; they first dismember the body politic by an illusion worthy of a fair, and then join it together again we know not how.

* To be general, a will need not always be unanimous; but every vote must be counted: any formal exclusion is a breach of generality.

This error is due to a lack of exact notions concerning the Sovereign authority, and to taking for parts of it what are only emanations from it. Thus, for example, the acts of declaring war and making peace have been regarded as acts of Sovereignty; but this is not the case, as these acts do not constitute law, but merely the application of a law, a particular act which decides how the law applies, as we shall see clearly when the idea attached to the word 'law' has been defined.

If we examined the other divisions in the same manner, we should find that, whenever Sovereignty seems to be divided, there is an illusion: the rights which are taken as being part of Sovereignty are really all subordinate, and always imply supreme wills of which they only sanction the execution.

It would be impossible to estimate the obscurity this lack of exactness has thrown over the decisions of writers who have dealt with political right, when they have used the principles laid down by them to pass judgment on the respective rights of kings and peoples. Every one can see, in Chapters III and IV of the first book of Grotius, how the learned man and his translator, Barbeyrac, entangle and tie themselves up in their own sophistries, for fear of saying too little or too much of what they think, and so offending the interests they have to conciliate. Grotius, a refugee in France, ill content with his own country, and desirous of paying his court to Louis XIII, to whom his book is dedicated, spares no pains to rob the peoples of all their rights and invest kings with them by every conceivable artifice. This would also have been much to the taste of Barbeyrac, who dedicated his translation to George I of England. But unfortunately the expulsion of James II, which he called his 'abdication', compelled him to use all reserve, to shuffle and to tergiversate, in order to avoid making William out a usurper. If these two writers had adopted the true principles, all difficulties would have been removed, and they would have been always consistent; but it would have been a sad truth for them to tell, and would have paid court for them to no one save the people. Moreover, truth is no road to fortune, and the people dispenses neither ambassadorships, nor professorships, nor pensions.

CHAPTER 3

Whether the General Will Is Fallible

It follows from what has gone before that the general will is always upright and always tends to the public advantage; but it does not follow that the deliberations of the people always have the same rectitude. Our will is always for our own good, but we do not always see what that is; the people is never corrupted, but it is often deceived, and on such occasions only does it seem to will what is bad.

There is often a great deal of difference between the will of all and the general will; the latter considers only the common interest, while the former takes private interest into account, and is no more than a sum of particular wills: but take away from these same wills the pluses and minuses that cancel one another,* and the general will remains as the sum of the differences.

If, when the people, being furnished with adequate information, held its deliberations, the citizens had no communication one with another, the grand total of the small differences would always give the general will, and the decision would always be good. But when intrigues arise, and partial associations are formed at the expense of the great association, the will of each of these associations becomes general in relation to its members, while it remains particular in relation to the State: it may then be said that there are no longer as many votes as there are men, but only as many as there are associations. The differences become less numerous and give a less general result. Lastly, when one of these associations is so great as to prevail over all the rest, the result is no longer a sum of small differences, but a single

---

* 'Every interest,' says the Marquis d'Argenson, 'has different principles. The agreement of two particular interests is formed by opposition to a third.' He might have added that the agreement of all interests is formed by opposition to that of each. If there were no different interests, the common interest would be barely felt, as it would encounter no obstacle; all would go on of its own accord, and politics would cease to be an art.

difference; in this case there is no longer a general will, and the opinion which prevails is purely particular.

It is therefore essential, if the general will is to be able to make itself known, that there should be no partial society in the state and that each citizen should express only his own opinion:* which was indeed the sublime and unique system established by the Great Lycurgus. But if there are partial societies, it is best to have as many as possible and to prevent them from being unequal, as was done by Solon, Numa, and Servius.[1] These precautions are the only ones that can guarantee that the general will shall be always enlightened, and that the people shall in no way deceive itself.

CHAPTER 4

The Limits of the Sovereign Power

If the State is a corporate body whose life is in the union of its members, and if the most important of its cares is the care for its own preservation, it must have a universal and compelling force, in order to move and dispose each part as may be most advantageous to the whole. As nature gives each man absolute power over all his members, the social compact gives the body politic absolute power over all its members also; and it is this power which, under the direction of the general will, bears, as I have said, the name of Sovereignty.

---

* 'In fact,' says Machiavelli, 'there are some divisions that are harmful to a Republic and some that are advantageous. Those which stir up sections and followers[2] are harmful; those attended by neither are advantageous. Since, then, the founder of a Republic cannot help enmities arising, he ought at least to prevent them from growing into sections' (*History of Florence*, Book VII). [Rousseau quotes the Italian.]

But, besides the public person, we have to consider the private persons composing it, whose life and liberty are naturally independent of it. We are bound then to distinguish clearly between the respective rights of the citizens and the Sovereign,* and between the duties the former have to fulfil as subjects, and the natural rights they should enjoy as men.

Each man alienates, I admit, by the social compact, only such part of his powers, goods, and liberty as it is important for the community to control; but it must also be granted that the Sovereign is sole judge of what is important.

Every service a citizen can render the State he ought to render as soon as the Sovereign demands it; but the Sovereign, for its part, cannot impose upon its subjects any fetters that are useless to the community, nor can it even wish to do so; for no more by the law of reason than by the law of nature can anything occur without a cause.

The undertakings which bind us to the social body are obligatory only because they are mutual; and their nature is such that in fulfilling them we cannot work for others without working for ourselves. Why is it that the general will is always upright, and that all continually will the happiness of each one, unless it is because there is not a man who does not think of 'each' as meaning him, and consider himself in voting for all? This proves that equality of rights and the idea of justice which such equality creates originate in the preference each man gives to himself, and accordingly in the very nature of man. It proves that the general will, to be really such, must be general in its object as well as its essence; that it must both come from all and apply to all; and that it loses its natural rectitude when it is directed to some particular and determinate object, because in such a case we are judging of something foreign to us, and have no true principle of equity to guide us.

* Attentive readers, do not, I pray, be in a hurry to charge me with contradicting myself. The terminology made it unavoidable, considering the poverty of the language; but wait and see.

Indeed, as soon as a question of particular fact or right arises on a point not previously regulated by a general convention, the matter becomes contentious. It is a case in which the individuals concerned are one party, and the public the other, but in which I can see neither the law that ought to be followed nor the judge who ought to give the decision. In such a case, it would be absurd to propose to refer the question to an express decision of the general will, which can be only the conclusion reached by one of the parties and in consequence will be, for the other party, merely an external and particular will, inclined on this occasion to injustice and subject to error. Thus, just as a particular will cannot stand for the general will, the general will, in turn, changes its nature, when its object is particular, and, as general, cannot pronounce on a man or a fact. When, for instance, the people of Athens nominated or displaced its rulers, decreed honours to one, and imposed penalties on another, and, by a multitude of particular decrees, exercised all the functions of government indiscriminately, it had in such cases no longer a general will in the strict sense; it was acting no longer as Sovereign, but as magistrate. This will seem contrary to current views; but I must be given time to expound my own.

It should be seen from the foregoing that what makes the will general is less the number of voters than the common interest uniting them; for, under this system, each necessarily submits to the conditions he imposes on others: and this admirable agreement between interest and justice gives to the common deliberations an equitable character which at once vanishes when any particular question is discussed, in the absence of a common interest to unite and identify the ruling of the judge with that of the party.

From whatever side we approach our principle, we reach the same conclusion, that the social compact sets up among the citizens an equality of such a kind, that they all bind themselves to observe the same conditions and should therefore all enjoy the same rights. Thus, from the very nature of the compact, every act of Sovereignty, i.e. every authentic act of the general will, binds or favours all the citizens equally; so that the Sovereign recognizes only the body of the nation, and draws no distinctions between those of whom it is made up. What, then, strictly speaking, is an act of Sovereignty? It is not a convention between a superior and an inferior, but a convention between the body and each of its members. It is legitimate, because based on the social contract, and equitable, because common to all; useful, because it can have no other object than the general good, and stable, because guaranteed by the public force and the supreme power. So long as the subjects have to submit only to conventions of this sort, they obey no one but their own will; and to ask how far the respective rights of the Sovereign and the citizens extend, is to ask up to what point the latter can enter into undertakings with themselves, each with all, and all with each.

We can see from this that the sovereign power, absolute, sacred, and inviolable as it is, does not and cannot exceed the limits of general conventions, and that every man may dispose at will of such goods and liberty as these conventions leave him; so that the Sovereign never has a right to lay more charges on one subject than on another, because, in that case, the question becomes particular, and ceases to be within its competency.

When these distinctions have once been admitted, it is seen to be so untrue that there is, in the social contract, any real renunciation on the part of the individuals, that the position in which they find themselves as a result of the contract is really preferable to that in which they were before. Instead of a renunciation, they have made an advantageous exchange: instead of an uncertain and precarious way of living they have got one that is better and more secure; instead of natural independence they have got liberty, instead of the power to harm others security for themselves, and instead of their strength, which others might overcome, a right which social union makes invincible. Their very life, which they have devoted to the State, is by it constantly protected; and when they risk it in the State's defence, what more are they doing than giving back what they have received from it? What are they doing that they would not do more often and with greater danger in the state of nature, in which they would inevitably have to fight battles at the peril of their lives in defence of that which is the means of their preservation? All have indeed to fight when their country needs them; but then no one has ever to fight for himself. Do we not gain something by running, on behalf of what gives us our security, only some of the risks we should have to run for ourselves, as soon as we lost it?

CHAPTER 5

The Right of Life and Death

The question is often asked how individuals, having no right to dispose of their own lives, can transfer to the Sovereign a right which they do not possess. The difficulty of answering this question seems to me to lie in its being wrongly stated. Every man has a right to risk his own life in order to preserve it. Has it ever been said that a man who throws himself out of the window to escape from a fire is guilty of suicide? Has such a crime ever been laid to the charge of him who perishes in a storm because, when he went on board, he knew of the danger?

The social treaty has for its end the preservation of the contracting parties. He who wills the end wills the means also, and the means must involve some risks, and even some losses. He who wishes to preserve his life at others' expense should also, when it is necessary, be ready to give it up for their sake. Furthermore, the citizen is no longer the judge of the dangers to which the law desires him to expose himself; and when the prince says to him: 'It is expedient for the State that you should die,' he ought to die, because it is only on that condition that he has been living in security up to the present, and because his life is no longer a mere bounty of nature, but a gift made conditionally by the State.

The death-penalty inflicted upon criminals may be looked on in much the same light: it is in order that we may not fall victims to an assassin that we consent to die if we ourselves turn assassins. In this treaty, so far from disposing of our own lives, we think only of securing them, and it is not to be assumed that any of the parties then expects to get hanged.

Again, every malefactor, by attacking social rights, becomes on forfeit a rebel and a traitor to his country; by violating its laws he ceases to be a member of it; he even makes war upon it. In such a case the preservation of the State is inconsistent with his own, and one or the other must perish; in putting the guilty to death, we slay not so much the citizen as an enemy. The trial and the judgment are the proofs that he has broken the social treaty, and is in consequence no longer a member of the State. Since, then, he has recognized himself to be such by living there, he must be removed by exile as a violator of the compact, or by death as a public enemy; for such an enemy is not a moral person, but merely a man; and in such a case the right of war is to kill the vanquished.

But, it will be said, the condemnation of a criminal is a particular act. I admit it: but such condemnation is not a function of the Sovereign; it is a right the Sovereign can confer without being able itself to exert it. All my ideas are consistent, but I cannot expound them all at once.

We may add that frequent punishments are always a sign of weakness or remission on the part of the government. There is not a single ill-doer who could not be turned to some good. The State has no right to put to death, even for the sake of making an example, any one whom it can leave alive without danger.

The right of pardoning or exempting the guilty from a penalty imposed by the law and pronounced by the judge belongs only to the authority which is superior to both judge and law, i.e. the Sovereign; even in its right in this matter is far from clear, and the cases for exercising it are extremely rare. In a well-governed State, there are few punishments, not because there are many pardons, but because criminals are rare; it is when a State is in decay that the multitude of crimes is a guarantee of impunity. Under the Roman Republic, neither the senate nor the consuls ever attempted to pardon; even the people never did so, though it sometimes revoked its own decision. Frequent pardons mean that crime will soon need them no longer, and no one can help seeing whither that leads. But I feel my heart protesting and restraining my pen; let us leave these questions to the just man who has never offended, and has never himself stood in need of pardon.

CHAPTER 6
Law

By the social compact we have given the body politic existence and life; we have now by legislation to give it movement and will. For the original act by which the body is formed and united still in no respect determines what it ought to do for its preservation.

What is well and in conformity with order is so by the nature of things and independently of human conventions. All justice comes from God, who is its sole source; but if we knew how to receive so high an inspiration, we should need neither government nor laws. Doubtless, there is a universal justice emanating from reason alone; but this justice, to be admitted among us, must be mutual. Humanly speaking, in default of natural sanctions, the laws of justice are ineffective among men: they merely make for the good of the wicked and the undoing of the just, when the just man observes them towards everybody and nobody observes them towards him. Conventions and laws are therefore needed to join rights to duties and refer justice to its object. In the state of nature, where everything is common, I owe nothing to him whom I have promised nothing; I recognize as belonging to others only what is of no use to me. In the state of society all rights are fixed by law, and the case becomes different.

But what, after all, is a law? As long as we remain satisfied with attaching purely metaphysical ideas to the word, we shall go on arguing without arriving at an understanding; and when we have defined a law of nature, we shall be no nearer the definition of a law of the State.

I have already said that there can be no general will directed to a particular object. Such an object must be either within or outside the State. If outside, a will which is alien to it cannot be, in relation to it, general; if within, it is part of the State, and in that case there arises a relation between whole and part which makes them two separate beings, of which the part is one, and the whole minus the part the other. But the whole minus a part cannot be the whole; and while this relation persists, there can be no whole, but only two unequal parts; and it follows that the will of one is no longer in any respect general in relation to the other.

But when the whole people decrees for the whole people, it is considering only itself; and if a relation is then formed, it is between two aspects of the entire object, without there being any division of the whole. In that case the matter about which the decree is made is, like the decreeing will, general. This act is what I call a law.

When I say that the object of laws is always general, I mean that law considers subjects *en masse* and actions in the abstract, and never a particular person or action. Thus the law may indeed decree that there shall be privileges, but cannot confer them on anybody by name. It may set up several classes of citizens, and even lay down the qualifications for membership of these classes, but it cannot nominate such and such persons as belonging to them; it may establish a monarchical government and hereditary succession, but it cannot choose a king, or nominate a royal family. In a word, no function which has a particular object belongs to the legislative power.

On this view, we at once see that it can no longer be asked

whose business it is to make laws, since they are acts of the general will; nor whether the prince is above the law, since he is a member of the State; nor whether the law can be unjust, since no one is unjust to himself; nor how we can be both free and subject to the laws, since they are but registers of our wills.

We see further that, as the law unites universality of will with universality of object, what a man, whoever he be, commands of his own motion cannot be a law; and even what the Sovereign commands with regard to a particular matter is no nearer being a law, but is a decree, an act, not of sovereignty, but of magistracy.

I therefore give the name 'Republic' to every State that is governed by laws, no matter what the form of its administration may be: for only in such a case does the public interest govern, and the *res publica* rank as a *reality*. Every legitimate government is republican;* what government is I will explain later on.

Laws are, properly speaking, only the conditions of civil association. The people, being subject to the laws, ought to be their author: the conditions of the society ought to be regulated solely by those who come together to form it. But how are they to regulate them? Is it to be by common agreement, by a sudden inspiration? Has the body politic an organ to declare its will? Who can give it the foresight to formulate and announce its acts in advance? Or how is it to announce them in the hour of need? How can a blind multitude, which often does not know what it wills, because it rarely knows what is good for it, carry out for itself so great and difficult an enterprise as a system of legislation? Of itself the people wills always the good, but of itself it by no means always sees it. The general will is always upright, but the judgment which guides it is not always enlightened. It must be got to see objects as they are, and sometimes as they ought to appear to

---

* I understand by this word, not merely an aristocracy or a democracy, but generally any government directed by the general will, which is the law. To be legitimate, the government must be, not one with the Sovereign, but its minister. In such a case even a monarchy is a Republic. This will be made clearer in the following book [added in edition of 1782 from Rousseau's MS notes].

it; it must be shown the good road it is in search of, secured from the seductive influences of individual wills, taught to see the relationship of times and spaces, and made to weigh the attractions of present and sensible advantages against the danger of distant and hidden evils. The individuals see the good they reject; the public wills the good it does not see. All stand equally in need of guidance. The former must be compelled to bring their wills into conformity with their reason; the latter must be taught to know what it wills. If that is done, public enlightenment leads to the union of understanding and will in the social body: the parts are made to work exactly together, and the whole is raised to its highest power. This makes a legislator necessary.

CHAPTER 7

The Legislator

In order to discover the rules of society best suited to nations, a superior intelligence beholding all the passions of men without experiencing any of them would be needed. This intelligence would have to be wholly unrelated to our nature, while knowing it through and through; its happiness would have to be independent of us, and yet ready to occupy itself with ours; and lastly, it would have, in the march of time, to look forward to a distant glory, and, working in one century, to be able to enjoy in the next.* It would take gods to give men laws.

What Caligula argued from the facts, Plato, in the dialogue called the *Politicus*, argued in defining the civil or kingly man, on

---

* A people becomes famous only when its legislation begins to decline. We do not know for how many centuries the system of Lycurgus made the Spartans happy before the rest of Greece took any notice of it.

the basis of right. But if great princes are rare, how much more so are great legislators! The former have only to follow the pattern which the latter have to lay down. The legislator is the engineer who invents the machine, the prince merely the mechanic who sets it up and makes it go. 'At the birth of societies,' says Montesquieu, 'the rulers of Republics establish institutions, and afterwards the institutions mould the rulers.'

He who dares to undertake the making of a people's institutions ought to feel himself capable, so to speak, of changing human nature, of transforming each individual, who is by himself a complete and solitary whole, into part of a greater whole from which he in a manner receives his life and being; of altering man's constitution for the purpose of strengthening it; and of substituting a partial and moral existence for the physical and independent existence nature has conferred on us all. He must, in a word, take away from man his own resources and give him instead new ones alien to him, and incapable of being made use of without the help of other men. The more completely these natural resources are annihilated, the greater and the more lasting are those which he acquires, and the more stable and perfect the new institutions; so that if each citizen is nothing and can do nothing without the rest, and the resources acquired by the whole are equal or superior to the aggregate of the resources of all the individuals, it may be said that legislation is at the highest possible point of perfection.

The legislator occupies in every respect an extraordinary position in the State. If he should do so by reason of his genius, he does so no less by reason of his office, which is neither magistracy, nor Sovereignty. This office, which sets up the Republic, nowhere enters into its constitution; it is an individual and superior function, which has nothing in common with human empire; for if he who holds command over men ought not to have command over the laws, he who has command over the laws ought not any more to have it over men; or else his laws would be the ministers of his passions and would often merely serve to perpetuate his injustices: his private aims would inevitably mar the sanctity of his work.

When Lycurgus gave laws to his country, he began by resigning the throne. It was the custom of most Greek towns to entrust the establishment of their laws to foreigners. The Republics of modern Italy in many cases followed this example; Geneva did the same and profited by it.* Rome, when it was most prosperous, suffered a revival of all the crimes of tyranny, and was brought to the verge of destruction, because it put the legislative authority and the sovereign power into the same hands.[1]

Nevertheless, the decemvirs themselves never claimed the right to pass any law merely on their own authority. 'Nothing we propose to you,' they said to the people, 'can pass into law without your consent. Romans, be yourselves the authors of the laws which are to make you happy.'

He, therefore, who draws up the laws has, or should have, no right of legislation, and the people cannot, even if it wishes, deprive itself of this incommunicable right, because, according to the fundamental compact, only the general will can bind the individuals, and there can be no assurance that a particular will is in conformity with the general will, until it has been put to the free vote of the people. This I have said already; but it is worth while to repeat it.

Thus in the task of legislation we find together two things which appear to be incompatible: an enterprise too difficult for human powers, and, for its execution, an authority that is no authority.

There is a further difficulty that deserves attention. Wise men, if they try to speak their language to the common herd instead of its own, cannot possibly make themselves understood. There are a thousand kinds of ideas which it is impossible to translate into popular language. Conceptions that are too general and objects

---

* Those who know Calvin only as a theologian much underestimate the extent of his genius. The codification of our wise edicts, in which he played a large part, does him no less honour than his *Institute*. Whatever revolution time may bring in our religion, so long as the spirit of patriotism and liberty still lives among us, the memory of this great man will be for ever blessed.

that are too remote are equally out of its range: each individual, having no taste for any other plan of government than that which suits his particular interest, finds it difficult to realize the advantages he might hope to draw from the continual privations good laws impose. For a young people to be able to relish sound principles of political theory and follow the fundamental rules of statecraft, the effect would have to become the cause; the social spirit, which should be created by these institutions, would have to preside over their very foundation; and men would have to be before law what they should become by means of law. The legislator therefore, being unable to appeal to either force or reason, must have recourse to an authority of a different order, capable of constraining without violence and persuading without convincing.

This is what has, in all ages, compelled the fathers of nations to have recourse to divine intervention and credit the gods with their own wisdom, in order that the peoples, submitting to the laws of the State as to those of nature, and recognizing the same power in the formation of the city as in that of man, might obey freely, and bear with docility the yoke of the public happiness.

This sublime reason, far above the range of the common herd, is that whose decisions the legislator puts into the mouth of the immortals, in order to constrain by divine authority those whom human prudence could not move.* But it is not anybody who can make the gods speak, or get himself believed when he proclaims himself their interpreter. The great soul of the legislator is the only miracle that can prove his mission. Any man may grave tablets of stone, or buy an oracle, or feign secret intercourse with some divinity, or train a bird to whisper in his ear, or find other vulgar

---

* 'In truth,' says Machiavelli, 'there has never been, in any country, an extraordinary legislator who has not had recourse to God; for otherwise his laws would not have been accepted: there are, in fact, many useful truths of which a wise man may have knowledge without their having in themselves such clear reasons for their being so as to be able to convince others' (*Discourses on Livy*, Bk v, ch. xi). [Rousseau quotes the Italian.]

ways of imposing on the people. He whose knowledge goes no further may perhaps gather round him a band of fools; but he will never found an empire, and his extravagances will quickly perish with him. Idle tricks form a passing tie; only wisdom can make it lasting. The Judaic law, which still subsists, and that of the child of Ishmael,[1] which, for ten centuries, has ruled half the world, still proclaim the great men who laid them down; and, while the pride of philosophy or the blind spirit of faction sees in them no more than lucky impostures, the true political theorist admires, in the institutions they set up, the great and powerful genius which presides over things made to endure.

We should not, with Warburton,[2] conclude from this that politics and religion have among us a common object, but that, in the first periods of nations, the one is used as an instrument for the other.

CHAPTER 8

The People

As, before putting up a large building, the architect surveys and sounds the site to see if it will bear the weight, the wise legislator does not begin by laying down laws good in themselves, but by investigating the fitness of the people, for which they are destined, to receive them. Plato refused to legislate for the Arcadians and the Cyrenaeans,[3] because he knew that both peoples were rich and could not put up with equality; and good laws and bad men were found together in Crete,[4] because Minos had inflicted discipline on a people already burdened with vice.

A thousand nations have achieved earthly greatness, that could never have endured good laws; even such as could have endured them could have done so only for a very brief period of their long history. Most peoples, like most men, are docile only in youth; as they grow old they become incorrigible. When once customs have become established and prejudices inveterate, it is dangerous and useless to attempt their reformation; the people, like the foolish and cowardly patients who rave at sight of the doctor, can no longer bear that any one should lay hands on its faults to remedy them.

There are indeed times in the history of States when, just as some kinds of illness turn men's heads and make them forget the past, periods of violence and revolutions do to peoples what these crises do to individuals: horror of the past takes the place of forgetfulness, and the State, set on fire by civil wars, is born again, so to speak, from its ashes, and takes on anew, fresh from the jaws of death, the vigour of youth. Such were Sparta at the time of Lycurgus, Rome after the Tarquins, and, in modern times, Holland and Switzerland after the expulsion of the tyrants.

But such events are rare; they are exceptions, the cause of which is always to be found in the particular constitution of the State concerned. They cannot even happen twice to the same people, for it can make itself free as long as it remains barbarous, but not when the civic impulse has lost its vigour. Then disturbances may destroy it, but revolutions cannot mend it: it needs a master, and not a liberator. Free peoples, be mindful of this maxim: 'Liberty may be gained, but can never be recovered.'

Youth is not infancy. There is for nations, as for men, a period of youth, or, shall we say, maturity, before which they should not be made subject to laws; but the maturity of a people is not always easily recognizable, and, if it is anticipated, the work is spoilt. One people is amenable to discipline from the beginning; another, not after ten centuries. Russia will never be really civilized, because it was civilized too soon. Peter had a genius for imitation; but he lacked true genius, which is creative and makes all from nothing. He did some good things, but most of what he did was out of place. He saw that his people was barbarous, but did not see that it was not ripe for civilization: he wanted to civilize it when it needed only hardening. His first wish was to make Germans or Englishmen, when he ought to have been making Russians; and he prevented his subjects from ever becoming what they might have been by persuading them that they were what they are not. In this fashion too a French teacher turns out his pupil to be an infant prodigy, and for the rest of his life to be nothing whatsoever. The empire of Russia will aspire to conquer Europe, and will itself be conquered. The Tartars, its subjects or neighbours, will become its masters and ours, by a revolution which I regard as inevitable. Indeed, all the kings of Europe are working in concert to hasten its coming.

CHAPTER 9
The People (continued)

As nature has set bounds to the stature of a well-made man, and, outside those limits, makes nothing but giants or dwarfs, similarly, for the constitution of a State to be it its best, it is possible to fix limits that will make it neither too large for good government, nor too small for self-maintenance. In every body politic there is a maximum strength which it cannot exceed and which it only loses by increasing in size. Every extension of the social tie means its relaxation; and, generally speaking, a small State is stronger in proportion than a great one.

A thousand arguments could be advanced in favour of this principle. First, long distances make administration more difficult, just as a weight becomes heavier at the end of a longer lever. Administration therefore becomes more and more burdensome as its stages are multiplied; for, in the first place, each city has its own, which is paid for by the people: each district its own, still paid for by the people: then comes each province, and then the great governments, satrapies, and viceroyalties, always costing more the higher you go, and always at the expense of the unfortunate people. Last of all comes the supreme administration, which eclipses all the rest. All these overcharges are a continual drain upon the subjects; so far from being better governed by all these different orders, they are worse governed than if there were only a single authority over them. In the meantime, there scarce remain resources enough to meet emergencies; and, when recourse must be had to these, the State is always on the eve of destruction.

This is not all; not only has the government less vigour and promptitude for securing the observance of the laws, preventing nuisances, correcting abuses, and guarding against seditious undertakings begun in distant places; the people has less affection for its rulers, whom it never sees, for its country, which, to its eyes, seems like the world, and for its fellow citizens, most of whom are unknown to it. The same laws cannot suit so many diverse provinces with different customs, situated in the most various climates, and incapable of enduring a uniform government. Different laws lead only to trouble and confusion among peoples which, living under the same rulers and in constant communication one with another, intermingle and intermarry, and, coming under the sway of new customs, never know if they can call their very patrimony their own. Talent is buried, virtue unknown, and vice unpunished, among such a multitude of men who do not know one another, gathered together in one place at the seat of the central administration. The leaders, overwhelmed with business, see nothing for themselves; the State is governed by clerks. Finally, the measures which have to be taken to maintain the general authority, which all these distant officials wish to escape or to impose upon, absorb all the energy of the public, so that there is none left for the happiness of the people. There is hardly enough to defend it when need arises, and thus a body which is too big for its constitution gives way and falls crushed under its own weight.

Again, the State must assure itself a safe foundation, if it is to have stability, and to be able to resist the shocks it cannot help experiencing, as well as the efforts it will be forced to make for its maintenance; for all peoples have a kind of centrifugal force that makes them continually act one against another, and tend to aggrandize themselves at their neighbours' expense, like the vortices of Descartes. Thus the weak run the risk of being soon swallowed up; and it is almost impossible for any one to preserve itself except by putting itself in a state of equilibrium with all, so that the pressure is on all sides practically equal.

It may therefore be seen that there are reasons for expansion and reasons for contraction; and it is no small part of the statesman's skill to hit between them the mean that is most favourable to the preservation of the State. It may be said that the reason for expansion, being merely external, and relative, ought to be subordinate to the reasons for contraction, which are internal and absolute. A strong and healthy constitution is the first thing to look for; and it is better to count on the vigour which comes of good government than on the resources a great territory furnishes.

It may be added that there have been known States so constituted that the necessity of making conquests entered into their very constitution, and that, in order to maintain themselves, they were forced to expand ceaselessly. It may be that they congratulated themselves greatly on this fortunate necessity, which none the less indicated to them, along with the limits of their greatness, the inevitable moment of their fall.

CHAPTER 10

The People (continued)

A body politic may be measured in two ways – either by the extent of its territory, or by the number of its people; and there is, between these two measurements, a right relation which makes the State really great. The men make the State, and the territory sustains the men; the right relation therefore is that the land should suffice for the maintenance of the inhabitants, and that there should be as many inhabitants as the land can maintain. In this proportion lies the maximum strength of a given number of people; for, if there is too much land, it is troublesome to guard and inadequately cultivated, produces more than is needed, and soon gives rise to wars of defence; if there is not enough, the State depends on its neighbours for what it needs over and above, and this soon gives rise to wars of offence. Every people, to which its situation gives no choice save that between commerce and war, is weak in itself: it depends on its neighbours, and on circumstances; its existence can never be more than short and uncertain. It either conquers others, and changes its situation, or it is conquered and becomes nothing. Only insignificance or greatness can keep it free.

No fixed relation can be stated between the extent of territory and the population that are adequate one to the other, both because of the differences in the quality of land, in its fertility, in the nature of its products, and in the influence of climate, and because of the different tempers of those who inhabit it; for some in a fertile country consume little, and others on an ungrateful soil much. The greater or less fecundity of women, the conditions that are more or less favourable in each country to the growth of population, and the influence the legislator can hope to exercise by his institutions, must also be taken into account The legislator therefore should not go by what he sees, but by what he foresees; he should stop not so much at the state in which he actually finds the population, as at that to which it ought naturally to attain. Lastly, there are countless cases in which the particular local circumstances demand or allow the acquisition of a greater territory than seems necessary. Thus, men will spread out in a mountainous country, where the natural products, i.e. woods and pastures, need less labour, where we know from experience that women are more fertile than in the plains, and where a great expanse of slope affords only a small level tract that can be counted on for vegetation. On the other hand, men can live close together on the coast, even in lands or rocks and nearly barren sands, because there fishing makes up to a great extent for the lack of land produce, because the inhabitants have to congregate together more in order to repel pirates, and further because it is easier to unburden the country of its superfluous inhabitants by means of colonies.

To these conditions of law-giving must be added one other which, though it cannot take the place of the rest, renders them all useless when it is absent. This is the enjoyment of peace and plenty; for the moment at which a State sets its house in order is, like the moment when a battalion is forming up, that when its body is least capable of offering resistance and easiest to destroy. A better resistance could be made at a time of absolute disorganization than at a moment of fermentation, when each is occupied with his own position and not with the danger. If war, famine, or sedition arises at this time of crisis, the State will inevitably be overthrown.

Not that many governments have not been set up during such storms; but in such cases these governments are themselves the State's destroyers. Usurpers always bring about or select troublous times to get passed, under cover of the public terror, destructive laws, which the people would never adopt in cold blood. The moment chosen is one of the surest means of distinguishing the work of the legislator from that of the tyrant.

What people, then, is a fit subject for legislation? One which, already bound by some unity of origin, interest, or convention, has never yet felt the real yoke of law; one that has neither customs nor superstitions deeply ingrained, one which stands in no fear of being overwhelmed by sudden invasion; one which, without entering into its neighbours' quarrels, can resist each of them single-handed, or get the help of one to repel another; one in which every member may be known by every other, and there is no need to lay on any man burdens too heavy for a man to bear; one which can do without other peoples, and without which all others can do;* one which is neither rich nor poor, but self-sufficient; and, lastly, one which unites the consistency of an ancient people with the docility of a new one. Legislation is made difficult less by what it is necessary to build up than by what has to be destroyed; and what makes success so rare is the impossibility of finding natural simplicity together with social requirements. All these conditions are indeed rarely found united, and therefore few States have good constitutions.

There is still in Europe one country capable of being given laws – Corsica.[1] The valour and persistency with which that brave people has regained and defended its liberty well deserve that some wise man should teach it how to preserve what it has won. I have a feeling that some day that little island will astonish Europe.

---

* If there were two neighbouring peoples, one of which could not do without the other, it would be very hard on the former, and very dangerous for the latter. Every wise nation, in such a case, would make haste to free the other from dependence. The Republic of Thlascala, enclosed by the Mexican Empire, preferred doing without salt to buying from the Mexicans, or even getting it from them as a gift. The Thlascalans were wise enough to see the snare hidden under such liberality. They kept their freedom, and that little State, shut up in that great Empire, was finally the instrument of its ruin.

CHAPTER 11

The Various Systems of Legislation

If we ask in what precisely consists the greatest good of all, which should be the end of every system of legislation, we shall find it reduce itself to two main objects, liberty and equality — liberty, because all particular dependence means so much force taken from the body of the State, and equality, because liberty cannot exist without it.

I have already defined civil liberty; by equality, we should understand, not that the degrees of power and riches are to be absolutely identical for everybody; but that power shall never be great enough for violence, and shall always be exercised by virtue of rank and law; and that, in respect of riches, no citizen shall ever be wealthy enough to buy another, and none poor enough to be forced to sell himself;* which implies, on the part of the great, moderation in goods and position, and, on the side of the common sort, moderation in avarice and covetousness.

Such equality, we are told, is an unpractical ideal that cannot actually exist. But if its abuse is inevitable, does it follow that we should not at least make regulations concerning it? It is precisely because the force of circumstances tends continually to destroy equality that the force of legislation should always tend to its maintenance.

But these general objects of every good legislative system need modifying in every country in accordance with the local situation and the temper of the inhabitants; and these circumstances should determine, in each case, the particular system of institutions

* If the object is to give the State consistency, bring the two extremes as near to each other as possible; allow neither rich men nor beggars. These two estates, which are naturally inseparable, are equally fatal to the common good; from the one come the friends of tyranny, and from the other tyrants. It is always between them that public liberty is put up to auction; the one buys, and the other sells.

which is best, not perhaps in itself, but for the State for which it is destined. If, for instance, the soil is barren and unproductive, or the land too crowded for its inhabitants, the people should turn to industry and the crafts, and exchange what they produce for the commodities they lack. If, on the other hand, a people dwells in rich plains and fertile slopes, or, in a good land, lacks inhabitants, it should give all its attention to agriculture, which causes men to multiply, and should drive out the crafts, which would only result in depopulation, by grouping in a few localities the few inhabitants there are.* If a nation dwells on an extensive and convenient coast-line, let it cover the sea with ships and foster commerce and navigation. It will have a life that will be short and glorious. If, on its coasts, the sea washes nothing but almost inaccessible rocks, let it remain barbarous and ichthyophagous: it will have a quieter, perhaps a better, and certainly a happier life. In a word, besides the principles that are common to all, every nation has in itself something that gives them a particular application, and makes its legislation peculiarly its own. Thus, among the Jews long ago and more recently among the Arabs, the chief object was religion, among the Athenians letters, at Carthage and Tyre commerce, at Rhodes shipping, at Sparta war, at Rome virtue. The author of *The Spirit of the Laws*[1] has shown with many examples by what art the legislator directs the constitution towards each of these objects.

What makes the constitution of a State really solid and lasting is the due observance of what is proper, so that the natural relations are always in agreement with the laws on every point, and law only serves, so to speak, to assure, accompany and rectify them. But if the legislator mistakes his object and adopts a principle other than circumstances naturally direct; if his principle makes for servitude, while they make for liberty, or if it makes for riches,

---

* 'Any branch of foreign commerce,' says M. d'Argenson, 'creates on the whole only apparent advantage for the kingdom in general; it may enrich some individuals, or even some towns; but the nation as a whole gains nothing by it, and the people is no better off.'

while they make for populousness, or if it makes for peace, while they make for conquest – the laws will insensibly lose their influence, the constitution will alter, and the State will have no rest from trouble till it is either destroyed or changed, and nature has resumed her invincible sway.

CHAPTER 12
The Division of the Laws

If the whole is to be set in order, and the commonwealth put into the best possible shape, there are various relations to be considered. First, there is the action of the complete body upon itself, the relation of the whole to the whole, of the Sovereign to the State; and this relation, as we shall see, is made up of the relations of the intermediate terms.

The laws which regulate this relation bear the name of political laws, and are also called fundamental laws, not without reason if they are wise. For, if there is, in each State, only one good system, the people that is in possession of it should hold fast to this; but if the established order is bad, why should laws that prevent men from being good be regarded as fundamental? Besides, in any case, a people is always in a position to change its laws, however good; for, if it choose to do itself harm, who can have a right to stop it?

The second relation is that of the members one to another, or to the body as a whole; and this relation should be in the first respect as unimportant, and in the second as important, as possible. Each citizen would then be perfectly independent of all the rest, and at the same time very dependent on the city; which is brought about always by the same means, as the strength of the State can alone secure the liberty of its members. From this second relation arise civil laws.

We may consider also a third kind of relation between the individual and the law, a relation of disobedience to its penalty. This gives rise to the setting up of criminal laws, which, at bottom, are less a particular class of law than the sanction behind all the rest.

Along with these three kinds of law goes a fourth, most important of all, which is graven not on tablets of marble or brass, but on the hearts of the citizens. This forms the real constitution of the State, takes on every day new powers, when other laws decay or die out, restores them or takes their place, keeps a people in the ways in which it was meant to go, and insensibly replaces authority by the force of habit. I am speaking of morality, of custom, above all of public opinion; a power unknown to political thinkers, on which none the less success in everything else depends. With this the great legislator concerns himself in secret, though he seems to confine himself to particular regulations; for these are only the arc of the arch, while manners and morals, slower to arise, form in the end its immovable keystone.

Among the different classes of laws, the political, which determine the form of the government, are alone relevant to my subject.

Book III

Before speaking of the different forms of government, let us try to fix the exact sense of the word, which has not yet been very clearly explained.

Chapter 1

Government in General

I warn the reader that this chapter requires careful reading, and that I am unable to make myself clear to those who refuse to be attentive.

Every free action is produced by the concurrence of two causes; one moral, i.e. the will which determines the act; the other physical, i.e. the power which executes it. When I walk towards an object, it is necessary first that I should will to go there, and, in the second place, that my feet should carry me. If a paralytic wills to run and an active man wills not to, they will both stay where they are. The body politic has the same motive powers; here too force and will are distinguished, will under the name of *legislative power* and force under that of *executive power*. Without their concurrence, nothing is, or should be, done.

We have seen that the legislative power belongs to the people, and can belong to it alone. It may, on the other hand, readily be seen, from the principles laid down above, that the executive power cannot belong to the generality as legislature or Sovereign, because it consists wholly of particular acts which fall outside the competency of the law, and consequently of the Sovereign, whose acts must always be laws.

The public force therefore needs an agent of its own to bind it together and set it to work under the direction of the general will, to serve as a means of communication between the State and the Sovereign, and to do for the collective person more or less what the union of soul and body does for man. Here we have what is, in the State, the basis of government, often wrongly confused with the Sovereign, whose minister it is.

What then is government? An intermediate body set up between the subjects and the Sovereign, to secure their mutual correspondence, charged with the execution of the laws and the maintenance of liberty, both civil and political.

The members of this body are called magistrates or *kings*, that is to say *governors*, and the whole body bears the name *prince*.* Thus those who hold that the act, by which a people puts itself under a prince, is not a contract, are certainly right. It is simply and solely a commission, an employment, in which the rulers, mere officials of the Sovereign, exercise in their own name the power of which it makes them depositaries. This power it can limit, modify, or recover at pleasure; for the alienation of such a right is incompatible with the nature of the social body, and contrary to the aim of the association.

I call then *government*, or supreme administration, the legitimate exercise of the executive power, and *prince* or *magistrate* the man or the body entrusted with that administration.

In government reside the intermediate forces whose relations make up that of the whole to the whole, or of the Sovereign to the State. This last relation may be represented as that between the extreme terms of a continuous proportion, which has government as its mean proportional.[1] The government gets from the Sovereign the orders it gives the people, and, for the State to be properly balanced, there must, when everything is reckoned in, be equality between the product or power of the government taken in itself, and the product or power of the citizens, who are on the one hand sovereign and on the other subject.

* Thus at Venice the College, even in the absence of the Doge, is called 'Most Serene Prince'.

Furthermore, none of these three terms can be altered without the equality being instantly destroyed. If the Sovereign desires to govern, or the magistrate to give laws, or if the subjects refuse to obey, disorder takes the place of regularity, force and will no longer act together, and the State is dissolved and falls into despotism or anarchy. Lastly, as there is only one mean proportional between each relation, there is also only one good government possible for a State. But, as countless events may change the relations of a people, not only may different governments be good for different peoples, but also for the same people at different times.

In attempting to give some idea of the various relations that may hold between these two extreme terms, I shall take as an example the number of a people, which is the most easily expressible.

Suppose the State is composed of ten thousand citizens. The Sovereign can only be considered collectively and as a body; but each member, as being a subject, is regarded as an individual: thus the Sovereign is to the subject as ten thousand to one, i.e. each member of the State has as his share only a ten-thousandth part of the sovereign authority, although he is wholly under its control. If the people numbers a hundred thousand, the condition of the subject undergoes no change, and each equally is under the whole authority of the laws, while his vote, being reduced to one hundred-thousandth part, has ten times less influence in drawing them up. The subject therefore remaining always a unit, the relation between him and the Sovereign increases with the number of the citizens. From this it follows that, the larger the State, the less the liberty.

When I say the relation increases, I mean that it grows more unequal. Thus the greater it is in the geometrical sense, the less relation there is in the ordinary sense of the word. In the former sense, the relation, considered according to quantity, is expressed by the quotient; in the latter, considered according to identity, it is reckoned by similarity.

Now, the less relation the particular wills have to the general will, that is, morals and manners to laws, the more should the repressive force be increased. The government, then, to be good, should be proportionately stronger as the people is more numerous.

On the other hand, as the growth of the State gives the depositaries of the public authority more temptations and chances of abusing their power, the greater the force with which the government ought to be endowed for keeping the people in hand, the greater too should be the force at the disposal of the Sovereign for keeping the government in hand. I am speaking, not of absolute force, but of the relative force of the different parts of the State.

It follows from this double relation that the continuous proportion between the Sovereign, the prince, and the people, is by no means an arbitrary idea, but a necessary consequence of the nature of the body politic. It follows further that, one of the extreme terms, viz. the people, as subject, being fixed and represented by unity, whenever the duplicate ratio increases or diminishes, the simple ratio does the same, and is changed accordingly. From this we see that there is not a single unique and absolute form of government, but as many governments differing in nature as there are States differing in size.

If, ridiculing this system, any one were to say that, in order to find the mean proportional and give form to the body of the government, it is only necessary, according to me, to find the square root of the number of people, I should answer that I am here taking this number only as an instance; that the relations of which I am speaking are not measured by the number of men alone, but generally by the amount of action, which is a combination of a multitude of causes; and that, further, if, to save words, I borrow for a moment the terms of geometry, I am none the less well aware that moral quantities do not allow of geometrical accuracy.

The government is on a small scale what the body politic which includes it is on a great one. It is a corporate body endowed with certain faculties, active like the Sovereign and passive like the State, and capable of being resolved into other similar relations. This accordingly gives rise to a new proportion, within which there is yet another, according to the arrangement of the magistracies, till an indivisible middle term is reached, i.e. a single ruler or supreme magistrate, who may be represented, in the midst of this progression, as the unity between the fractional and the ordinal series.

Without encumbering ourselves with this multiplication of terms, let us rest content with regarding government as a new body within the State, distinct from the people and the Sovereign, and intermediate between them.

There is between these two bodies this essential difference, that the State exists by itself, and the government only through the Sovereign. Thus the dominant will of the prince is, or should be, nothing but the general will or the law; his force is only the public force concentrated in his hands, and, as soon as he tries to base any absolute and independent act on his own authority, the tie that binds the whole together begins to be loosened. If finally the prince should come to have a particular will more active than the will of the Sovereign, and should employ the public force in his hands in obedience to this particular will, there would be, so to speak, two Sovereigns, one rightful and the other actual, the social union would evaporate instantly, and the body politic would be dissolved.

However, in order that the government may have a true existence and a real life distinguishing it from the body of the State, and in order that all its members may be able to act in concert and fulfil the end for which it was set up, it must have a particular personality, a sensibility common to its members, and a force and will of its own making for its preservation. This particular existence implies assemblies, councils, power of deliberation and decision, rights, titles, and privileges belonging exclusively to the prince and making the office of magistrate more honourable in proportion as it is more troublesome. The difficulties lie in the manner of so ordering this subordinate whole within the whole, that it in no way alters the general constitution by affirmation of its own, and always distinguishes the particular force it possesses, which is destined to aid in its preservation, from the public force, which is destined to the preservation of the State; and, in a word, is always ready to sacrifice the government to the people, and never to sacrifice the people to the government.

Furthermore, although the artificial body of the government is the work of another artificial body, and has, we may say, only a borrowed and subordinate life, this does not prevent it from being able to act with more or less vigour or promptitude, or from being, so to speak, in more or less robust health. Finally, without departing directly from the end for which it was instituted, it may deviate more or less from it, according to the manner of its constitution.

From all these differences arise the various relations which the government ought to bear to the body of the State, according to the accidental and particular relations by which the State itself is modified, for often the government that is best in itself will become the most pernicious, if the relations in which it stands have altered according to the defects of the body politic to which it belongs.

CHAPTER 2

The Constituent Principle in the Various Forms of Government

To set forth the general cause of the above differences, we must here distinguish between the prince and the Government, as we did before between the State and the Sovereign.

The body of the magistrates may be composed of a greater or a less number of members. We said that the relation of the Sovereign to the subjects was greater in proportion as the people was more numerous, and, by a clear analogy, we may say the same of the relation of the government to the magistrates.

But the total force of the government, being always that of the State, is invariable; so that, the more of this force it expends on its own members, the less it has left to employ on the whole people.

The more numerous the magistrates, therefore, the weaker the government. This principle being fundamental, we must do our best to make it clear.

In the person of the magistrate we can distinguish three essentially different wills: first, the private will of the individual, tending only to his personal advantage; secondly, the common will of the magistrates, which is relative solely to the advantage of the prince, and may be called corporate will, being general in relation to the government, and particular in relation to the State, of which the government forms part; and, in the third place, the will of the people or the sovereign will, which is general both in relation to the State regarded as the whole, and to the government regarded as a part of the whole.

In a perfect act of legislation, the individual or particular will should be at zero; the corporate will belonging to the government should occupy a very subordinate position; and, consequently, the general or sovereign will should always predominate and should be the sole guide of all the rest.

According to the natural order, on the other hand, these different wills become more active in proportion as they are concentrated. Thus, the general will is always the weakest, the corporate will second, and the individual will strongest of all: so that, in the government, each member is first of all himself, then a magistrate, and then a citizen – in an order exactly the reverse of what the social system requires.

This granted, if the whole government is in the hands of one man, the particular and the corporate will are wholly united, and consequently the latter is at its highest possible degree of intensity.

But, as the use to which the force is put depends on the degree reached by the will, and as the absolute force of the government is invariable, it follows that the most active government is that of one man.

Suppose, on the other hand, we unite the government with the legislative authority, and make the Sovereign prince also, and all the citizens so many magistrates: then the corporate will, being confounded with the general will, can possess no greater activity than that will, and must leave the particular will as strong as it can possibly be. Thus, the government, having always the same absolute force, will be at the lowest point of its relative force or activity.

These relations are incontestable, and there are other considerations which still further confirm them. We can see, for instance, that each magistrate is more active in the body to which he belongs than each citizen in that to which he belongs, and that consequently the particular will has much more influence on the acts of government than on those of the Sovereign; for each magistrate is almost always charged with some governmental function, while each citizen, taken singly, exercises no function of Sovereignty. Furthermore, the bigger the State grows, the more its real force increases, though not in direct proportion to its growth; but, the State remaining the same, the number of magistrates may increase to any extent, without the government gaining any greater real force; for its force is that of the State, the dimension of which remains equal. Thus the relative force or activity of the government decreases, while its absolute or real force cannot increase.

Moreover, it is a certainty that promptitude in execution diminishes as more people are put in charge of it: where prudence is made too much of, not enough is made of fortune; opportunity is let slip, and deliberation results in the loss of its object.

I have just proved that the government grows remiss in proportion as the number of the magistrates increases; and I previously proved that, the more numerous the people, the greater should be the repressive force. From this it follows that the relation of the magistrates to the government should vary inversely to the relation of the subjects to the Sovereign; that is to say, the larger the State, the more should the government be tightened, so that the number of the rulers diminish in proportion to the increase of that of the people.

It should be added that I am here speaking of the relative strength of the government, and not of its rectitude: for, on the other hand, the more numerous the magistracy, the nearer the corporate will comes to the general will; while, under a single magistrate, the corporate will is, as I said, merely a particular will. Thus, what may be gained on one side is lost on the other, and the art of the legislator is to know how to fix the point at which the force and the will of the government, which are always in inverse proportion, meet in the relation that is most to the advantage of the State.

CHAPTER 3

The Division of Governments

We saw in the last chapter what causes the various kinds or forms of government to be distinguished according to the number of the members composing them: it remains in this to discover how the division is made.

In the first place, the Sovereign may commit the charge of the government to the whole people or to the majority of the people, so that more citizens are magistrates than are mere private individuals. This form of government is called *democracy*.

Or it may restrict the government to a small number, so that there are more private citizens than magistrates; and this is named *aristocracy*.

Lastly, it may concentrate the whole government in the hands of a single magistrate from whom all others hold their power. This third form is the most usual, and is called *monarchy*, or royal government.

It should be remarked that all these forms, or at least the first two, admit of degree, and even of very wide differences; for democracy may include the whole people, or may be restricted to half. Aristocracy, in its turn, may be restricted indefinitely from half the people down to the smallest possible number. Even royalty is susceptible of a measure of distribution. Sparta always had two kings, as its constitution provided; and the Roman Empire saw as many as eight emperors at once, without its being possible to say that the Empire was split up. Thus there is a point at which each form of government passes into the next, and it becomes clear that, under three comprehensive denominations, government is really susceptible of as many diverse forms as the State has citizens.

Nor is this all: for, as the government may also, in certain aspects, be subdivided into other parts, one administered in one fashion and one in another, the combination of the three forms may result in a multitude of mixed forms, each of which admits of multiplication by all the simple forms.

There has been at all times much dispute concerning the best form of government, without consideration of the fact that each is in some cases the best, and in others the worst.

If, in the different States, the number of supreme magistrates should be in inverse ratio to the number of citizens, it follows that, generally, democratic government suits small States, aristocratic government those of middle size, and monarchy great ones. This rule is immediately deducible from the principle laid down. But it is impossible to count the innumerable circumstances which may furnish exceptions.

CHAPTER 4

Democracy

He who makes the law knows better than any one else how it should be executed and interpreted. It seems then impossible to have a better constitution than that in which the executive and legislative powers are united; but this very fact renders the government in certain respects inadequate, because things which should be distinguished are confounded, and the prince and the Sovereign, being the same person, form, so to speak, no more than a government without government.

It is not good for him who makes the laws to execute them, or for the body of the people to turn its attention away from a general standpoint and devote it to particular objects. Nothing is more dangerous than the influence of private interests in public affairs, and the abuse of the laws by the government is a less evil than the corruption of the legislator, which is the inevitable sequel to private points of view. In such a case, the State being altered in substance, all reformation becomes impossible. A people that would never misuse governmental powers would never misuse independence; a people that would always govern well would not need to be governed.

If we take the term in the strict sense, there never has been a real democracy, and there never will be. It is against the natural order for the many to govern and the few to be governed. It is unimaginable that the people should remain continually assembled to devote their time to public affairs, and it is clear that they cannot set up commissions for that purpose without the form of administration being changed.

In fact, I can confidently lay down as a principle that, when the functions of government are shared by several tribunals, the less numerous sooner or later acquire the greatest authority, if only because they are in a position to expedite affairs, and power thus naturally comes into their hands.

Besides, how many conditions that are difficult to unite does such a government presuppose! First, a very small State, where the people can readily be got together and where each citizen can with ease know all the rest; secondly, great simplicity of manners, to prevent business from multiplying and raising thorny problems; next, a large measure of equality in rank and fortune, without which equality of rights and authority cannot long subsist; lastly, little or no luxury — for luxury either comes of riches or makes them necessary; it corrupts at once rich and poor, the rich by possession and the poor by covetousness; it sells the country to softness and vanity, and takes away from the State all its citizens, to make them slaves one to another, and one and all to public opinion.

This is why a famous writer[1] has made virtue the fundamental principle of Republics; for all these conditions could not exist without virtue. But, for want of the necessary distinctions, that great thinker was often inexact, and sometimes obscure, and did not see that, the sovereign authority being everywhere the same, the same principle should be found in every well-constituted State, in a greater or less degree, it is true, according to the form of the government.

It may be added that there is no government so subject to civil wars and intestine agitations as democratic or popular government, because there is none which has so strong and continual a tendency to change to another form, or which demands more vigilance and courage for its maintenance as it is. Under such a constitution above all, the citizen should arm himself with strength and constancy, and say, every day of his life, what a virtuous Count Palatine* said in the Diet of Poland: 'Malo periculosam libertatem quam quietum servitium.'

Were there a people of gods, their government would be democratic. So perfect a government is not for men.

---

* The Palatine of Posen, father of the King of Poland, Duke of Lorraine. [I prefer liberty with danger to peace with slavery.]

CHAPTER 5
Aristocracy

We have here two quite distinct corporate bodies, the government and the Sovereign, and in consequence two general wills, one general in relation to all the citizens, the other only for the members of the administration. Thus, although the government may regulate its internal policy as it pleases, it can never speak to the people save in the name of the Sovereign, that is, of the people itself, a fact which must not be forgotten.

The first societies governed themselves aristocratically. The heads of families took counsel together on public affairs. The young bowed without question to the authority of experience. Hence such names as *priests, elders, senate,* and *gerontes.* The savages of North America govern themselves in this way even now, and their government is admirable.

But, in proportion as artificial inequality produced by institutions became predominant over natural inequality, riches or power* were put before age, and aristocracy became elective. Finally, the transmission of the father's power along with his goods to his children, by creating patrician families, made government hereditary, and there came to be senators of twenty.

There are then three sorts of aristocracy – natural, elective, and hereditary. The first is only for simple peoples; the third is the worst of all governments; the second is the best, and is aristocracy properly so called.

Besides the advantage that lies in the distinction between the two powers, it presents that of its members being chosen; for, in popular government, all the citizens are born magistrates; but here magistracy is confined to a few, who become such only by

---

* It is clear that the word *optimates* meant, among the ancients, not the best, but the most powerful.

election.* By this means uprightness, understanding, experience, and all other claims to pre-eminence and public esteem become so many further guarantees of wise government.

Moreover, assemblies are more easily held, affairs better discussed and carried out with more order and diligence, and the credit of the State is better sustained abroad by venerable senators than by a multitude that is unknown or despised.

In a word, it is the best and most natural arrangement that the wisest should govern the many, when it is assured that they will govern for its profit, and not for their own. There is no need to multiply instruments, or get twenty thousand men to do what a hundred picked men can do even better. But it must not be forgotten that corporate interest here begins to direct the public power less under the regulation of the general will, and that a further inevitable propensity takes away from the laws part of the executive power.

If we are to speak of what is individually desirable, neither should the State be so small, nor a people so simple and upright, that the execution of the laws follows immediately from the public will, as it does in a good democracy. Nor should the nation be so great that the rulers have to scatter in order to govern it and are able to play the Sovereign each in his own department, and, beginning by making themselves independent, end by becoming masters.

But if aristocracy does not demand all the virtues needed by popular government, it demands others which are peculiar to itself; for instance, moderation on the side of the rich and contentment on that of the poor; for it seems that thorough-going equality would be out of place, as it was not found even at Sparta.

---

* It is of great importance that the form of the election of magistrates should be regulated by law; for if it is left at the discretion of the prince, it is impossible to avoid falling into hereditary aristocracy, as the Republics of Venice and Berne actually did. The first of these has therefore long been a State dissolved; the second, however, is maintained by the extreme wisdom of the senate, and forms an honourable and highly dangerous exception.

Furthermore, if this form of government carries with it a certain inequality of fortune, this is justifiable in order that as a rule the administration of public affairs may be entrusted to those who are most able to give them their whole time, but not, as Aristotle maintains, in order that the rich may always be put first. On the contrary, it is of importance that an opposite choice should occasionally teach the people that the deserts of men offer claims to pre-eminence more important than those of riches.

CHAPTER 6

Monarchy

So far, we have considered the prince as a collective, corporate body, unified by the force of the laws, and the depositary in the State of the executive power. We have now to consider this power when it is gathered together into the hands of a natural person, a real man, who alone has the right to dispose of it in accordance with the laws. Such a person is called a monarch or king.

In contrast with other forms of administration, in which a collective being stands for an individual, in this form an individual stands for a collective being; so that the moral unity that constitutes the prince is at the same time a physical unity, and all the qualities, which in the other case are only with difficulty brought together by the law, are found naturally united.

Thus the will of the people, the will of the prince, the public force of the State, and the particular force of the government, all answer to a single motive power; all the springs of the machine are in the same hands, the whole moves towards the same end; there are no conflicting movements to cancel one another, and no kind of constitution can be imagined in which a less amount of effort produces a more considerable amount of action. Archimedes, seated quietly on the bank and easily drawing a great vessel afloat, stands to my mind for a skilful monarch, governing vast states from his study, and moving everything while he seems himself unmoved.

But if no government is more vigorous than this, there is also none in which the particular will holds more sway and rules the rest more easily. Everything moves towards the same end indeed, but this end is by no means that of the public happiness; the very strength of the administration is constantly prejudicial to the State.

Kings desire to be absolute, and men are always crying out to them from afar that the best means of being so is to get themselves loved by their people. This precept is all very well, and even in some respects very true. Unfortunately, it will always be derided at court. The power which comes of a people's love is no doubt the greatest; but it is precarious and conditional, and princes will never rest content with it. The best kings desire to be in a position to be wicked, if they please, without forfeiting their mastery: political sermonizers may tell them to their hearts' content that, the people's strength being their own, their first interest is that the people should be prosperous, numerous, and formidable; they are well aware that this is untrue. Their first personal interest is that the people should be weak, wretched, and unable to resist them. I admit that, provided the subjects remained always in submission, the prince's interest would indeed be that it should be powerful, in order that its power, being his own, might make him formidable to his neighbours; but, this interest being merely secondary and subordinate, and strength being incompatible with submission, princes naturally give the preference always to the principle that is more to their immediate advantage. This is what Samuel put strongly before the Hebrews, and what Machiavelli has clearly shown. He professed to teach kings; but it was the people he really taught. His *Prince* is the book of Republicans.*

---

* Machiavelli was a proper man and a good citizen; but, being attached to the

We found, on general grounds, that monarchy is suitable only for great States, and this is confirmed when we examine it in itself. The more numerous the public administration, the smaller becomes the relation between the prince and the subjects, and the nearer it comes to equality, so that in democracy the ratio is unity, or absolute equality. Again, as the government is restricted in numbers the ratio increases and reaches its maximum when the government is in the hands of a single person. There is then too great a distance between prince and people, and the State lacks a bond of union. To form such a bond, there must be intermediate orders, and princes, personages, and nobility to compose them. But no such things suit a small State, to which all class differences mean ruin.

If, however, it is hard for a great State to be well governed, it is much harder for it to be so by a single man; and every one knows what happens when kings substitute others for themselves.

An essential and inevitable defect, which will always rank monarchical below republican government, is that in a republic the public voice hardly ever raises to the highest positions men who are not enlightened and capable, and such as to fill them with honour; while in monarchies those who rise to the top are most often merely petty blunderers, petty swindlers, and petty intriguers, whose petty talents cause them to get into the highest positions at court, but, as soon as they have got there, serve only to make their ineptitude clear to the public. The people is far less often mistaken in its choice than the prince; and a man of real worth among the king's ministers is almost as rare as a fool at the

court of the Medici, he could not help veiling his love of liberty in the midst of his country's oppression. The choice of his detestable hero, Caesar Borgia, clearly enough shows his hidden aim: and the contradiction between the teaching of the *Prince* and that of the *Discourses on Livy* and the *History of Florence* shows that this profound political thinker has so far been studied only by superficial or corrupt readers. The court of Rome sternly prohibited his book. I can well believe it; for it is that court it most clearly portrays. [Added in the edition of 1782 from Rousseau's MS notes.]

head of a republican government. Thus, when, by some fortunate chance, one of these born governors takes the helm of State in some monarchy that has been nearly overwhelmed by swarms of bumbling administrators, there is nothing but amazement at the resources he discovers, and his coming marks an era in his country's history.

For a monarchical State to have a chance of being well governed, its population and extent must be proportionate to the abilities of its governor. It is easier to conquer than to rule. With a long enough lever, the world could be moved with a single finger; to sustain it needs the shoulders of Hercules. However small a State may be, the prince is hardly ever big enough for it. When, on the other hand, it happens that the State is too small for its ruler, in these rare cases too it is ill governed, because the ruler, constantly pursuing his great designs, forgets the interests of the people, and makes it no less wretched by misusing the talents he has, than a ruler of less capacity would make it for want of those he had not. A kingdom should, so to speak, expand or contract with each reign, according to the prince's capabilities; but, the abilities of a senate being more constant in quantity, the State can then have permanent frontiers without the administration suffering.

The disadvantage that is most felt in monarchical government is the want of the continuous succession which, in both the other forms, provides an unbroken bond of union. When one king dies, another is needed; elections leave dangerous intervals and are full of storms; and unless the citizens are disinterested and upright to a degree which very seldom goes with this kind of government, intrigue and corruption abound. He to whom the State has sold itself can hardly help selling it in his turn and repaying himself, at the expense of the weak, the money the powerful have wrung from him. Under such an administration, venality sooner or later spreads through every part, and peace so enjoyed under a king is worse than the disorders of an interregnum.

What has been done to prevent these evils? Crowns have been made hereditary in certain families, and an order of succession has been set up, to prevent disputes from arising on the death of kings. That is to say, the disadvantages of regency have been put in place of those of election, apparent tranquillity has been preferred to wise administration, and men have chosen rather to risk having children, monstrosities, or imbeciles as rulers than to have disputes over the choice of good kings. It has not been taken into account that, in so exposing ourselves to the risks this possibility entails, we are setting almost all the chances against us. There was sound sense in what the younger Dionysius said to his father, who reproached him for doing some shameful deed by asking: 'Did I set you the example?' 'No,' answered his son, 'but your father was not king.'

Everything conspires to take away from a man who is set in authority over others the sense of justice and reason. Much trouble, we are told, is taken to teach young princes the art of reigning; but their education seems to do them no good. It would be better to begin by teaching them the art of obeying. The greatest kings whose praises history tells were not brought up to reign: reigning is a science we are never so far from possessing as when we have learnt too much of it, and one we acquire better by obeying than by commanding. 'Nam utilissimus idem ac brevissimus bonarum malarumque rerum delectus cogitare quid aut nolueris sub alio principe, aut volueris.'*

One result of this lack of coherence is the inconstancy of royal government, which, regulated now on one scheme and now on another, according to the character of the reigning prince or those who reign for him, cannot for long have a fixed object or a consistent policy – and this variability, not found in the other forms of government, where the prince is always the same, causes the State to be always shifting from principle to principle and from project to project. Thus we may say that generally, if a court

---

* Tacitus, *Histories*, i. 16. 'For the best, and also the shortest way of finding out what is good and what is bad is to consider what you would have wished to happen or not to happen, had another than you been Emperor.'

is more subtle in intrigue, there is more wisdom in a senate, and Republics advance towards their ends by more consistent and better considered policies; while every revolution in a royal ministry creates a revolution in the State; for the principle common to all ministers and nearly all kings is to do in every respect the reverse of what was done by their predecessors.

This incoherence further clears up a sophism that is very familiar to royalist political writers; not only is civil government likened to domestic government, and the prince to the father of a family – this error has already been refuted – but the prince is also freely credited with all the virtues he ought to possess, and is supposed to be always what he should be. This supposition once made, royal government is clearly preferable to all others, because it is incontestably the strongest, and, to be the best also, wants only a corporate will more in conformity with the general will.

But if, according to Plato,* the 'king by nature' is such a rarity, how often will nature and fortune conspire to give him a crown? And, if royal education necessarily corrupts those who receive it, what is to be hoped from a series of men brought up to reign? It is, then, wanton self-deception to confuse royal government with government by a good king. To see such government as it is in itself, we must consider it as it is under princes who are incompetent or wicked: for either they will come to the throne wicked or incompetent, or the throne will make them so.

These difficultes have not escaped our writers, who, all the same, are not troubled by them. The remedy, they say, is to obey without a murmur: God sends bad kings in His wrath, and they must be borne as the scourges of Heaven. Such talk is doubtless edifying; but it would be more in place in a pulpit than in a political book. What are we to think of a doctor who promises miracles, and whose whole art is to exhort the sufferer to patience? We know for ourselves that we must put up with a bad

---

* In the *Politicus*.

government when it is there; the question is how to find a good one.

CHAPTER 7

Mixed Governments

Strictly speaking, there is no such thing as a simple government. An isolated ruler must have subordinate magistrates; a popular government must have a head. There is therefore, in the distribution of the executive power, always a gradation from the greater to the lesser number, with the difference that sometimes the greater number is dependent on the smaller, and sometimes the smaller on the greater.

Sometimes the distribution is equal, when either the constituent parts are in mutual dependence, as in the government of England, or the authority of each section is independent, but imperfect, as in Poland. This last form is bad; for it secures no unity in the government, and the State is left without a bond of union.

Is a simple or a mixed government the better? Political writers are always debating the question, which must be answered as we have already answered a question about all forms of government.

Simple government is better in itself, just because it is simple. But when the executive power is not sufficiently dependent upon the legislative power, i.e. when the prince is more closely related to the Sovereign than the people to the prince, this lack of proportion must be cured by the division of the government; for all the parts have then no less authority over the subjects, while their division makes them all together less strong against the Sovereign.

The same disadvantage is also prevented by the appointment of intermediate magistrates, who leave the government entire, and have the effect only of balancing the two powers and maintaining their respective rights. Government is then not mixed, but moderated.

The opposite disadvantages may be similarly cured, and when the government is too lax, tribunals may be set up to concentrate it. This is done in all democracies. In the first case, the government is divided to make it weak; in the second, to make it strong: for the maxima of both strength and weakness are found in simple governments, while the mixed forms result in a mean strength.

Chapter 8
That All Forms of Government Do Not Suit All Countries

Liberty, not being a fruit of all climates, is not within the reach of all peoples. The more this principle, laid down by Montesquieu, is considered, the more its truth is felt; the more it is combated, the more chance is given to confirm it by new proofs.

In all the governments that there are, the public person consumes without producing. Whence then does it get what it consumes? From the labour of its members. The necessities of the public are supplied out of the superfluities of individuals. It follows that the civil State can subsist only so long as men's labour brings them a return greater than their needs.

The amount of this excess is not the same in all countries. In some it is considerable, in others middling, in yet others nil, in some even negative. The relation of product to subsistence depends on the fertility of the climate, on the sort of labour the land demands, on the nature of its products, on the strength of its inhabitants, on the greater or less consumption they find necessary, and on several further considerations of which the whole relation is made up.

On the other side, all governments are not of the same nature: some are less voracious than others, and the differences between them are based on this second principle, that the further from their source the public contributions are removed, the more burdensome they become. The charge should be measured not by the amount of the impositions, but by the path they have to travel in order to get back to those from whom they came. When the circulation is prompt and well established, it does not matter whether much or little is paid; the people is always rich and, financially speaking, all is well. On the contrary, however little the people gives, if that little does not return to it, it is soon exhausted by giving continually: the State is then never rich, and the people is always a people of beggars.

It follows that, the more the distance between people and government increases, the more burdensome tribute becomes: thus, in a democracy, the people bears the least charge; in an aristocracy, a greater charge; and, in monarchy, the weight becomes heaviest. Monarchy therefore suits only wealthy nations; aristocracy, States of middling size and wealth; and democracy, States that are small and poor.

In fact, the more we reflect, the more we find the difference between free and monarchical States to be this: in the former, everything is used for the public advantage; in the latter, the public forces and those of individuals are affected by each other, and either increases as the other grows weak; finally, instead of governing subjects to make them happy, despotism makes them wretched in order to govern them.

We find then, in every climate, natural causes according to which the form of government which it requires can be assigned, and we can even say what sort of inhabitants it should have.

Unfriendly and barren lands, where the product does not repay the labour, should remain desert and uncultivated, or peopled only by savages; lands where men's labour brings in no more than the exact minimum necessary to subsistence should be inhabited by barbarous peoples: in such places all polity is impossible.

Lands where the surplus of product over labour is only middling are suitable for free peoples; those in which the soil is abundant and fertile and gives a great product for a little labour call for monarchical government, in order that the surplus of superfluities among the subjects may be consumed by the luxury of the prince: for it is better for this excess to be absorbed by the government than dissipated among the individuals. I am aware that there are exceptions; but these exceptions themselves confirm the rule, in that sooner or later they produce revolutions which restore things to the natural order.

General laws should always be distinguished from individual causes that may modify their effects. If all the South were covered with Republics and all the North with despotic States, it would be none the less true that, in point of climate, despotism is suitable to hot countries, barbarism to cold countries, and good polity to temperate regions. I see also that, the principle being granted, there may be disputes on its application; it may be said that there are cold countries that are very fertile, and tropical countries that are very unproductive. But this difficulty exists only for those who do not consider the question in all its aspects. We must, as I have already said, take labour, strength, consumption, etc., into account.

Take two tracts of equal extent, one of which brings in five and the other ten. If the inhabitants of the first consume four and those of the second nine, the surplus of the first product will be a fifth and that of the second a tenth. The ratio of these two surpluses will then be inverse to that of the products, and the tract which produces only five will give a surplus double that of the tract which produces ten.

But there is no question of a double product, and I think no one would put the fertility of cold countries, as a general rule, on an equality with that of hot ones. Let us, however, suppose this equality to exist: let us, if you will, regard England as on the same level as Sicily, and Poland as Egypt — further south, we shall have Africa and the Indies; further north, nothing at all. To get this equality of product, what a difference there must be in tillage: in Sicily, there is only need to scratch the ground; in England, how men must toil! But, where more hands are needed to get the same product, the superfluity must necessarily be less.

Consider, besides, that the same number of men consume much less in hot countries. The climate requires sobriety for the sake of health; and Europeans who try to live there as they would at home all perish of dysentery and indigestion. 'We are,' says Chardin, 'carnivorous animals, wolves, in comparison with the Asiatics. Some attribute the sobriety of the Persians to the fact that their country is less cultivated; but it is my belief that their country abounds less in commodities because the inhabitants need less. If their frugality,' he goes on, 'were the effect of the nakedness of the land, only the poor would eat little; but everybody does so. Again, less or more would be eaten in various provinces, according to the land's fertility; but the same sobriety is found throughout the kingdom. They are very proud of their manner of life, saying that you have only to look at their hue to recognize how far it excels that of the Christians. In fact, the Persians are of an even hue; their skins are fair, fine and smooth; while the hue of their subjects, the Armenians, who live after the European fashion, is rough and blotchy, and their bodies are gross and unwieldy.'

The nearer you get to the equator, the less people live on. Meat they hardly touch; rice, maize, couscous, millet and cassava are their ordinary food. There are in the Indies millions of men whose subsistence does not cost a halfpenny a day. Even in Europe we find considerable differences of appetite between Northern and Southern peoples. A Spaniard will live for a week on a German's dinner. In the countries in which men are more voracious, luxury therefore turns in the direction of consumption. In England, luxury appears in a well-filled table; in Italy, you feast on sugar and flowers.

Luxury in clothes shows similar differences. In climates in which the changes of season are prompt and violent, men have better and simpler clothes; where they clothe themselves only for adornment, what is striking is more thought of than what is useful; clothes themselves are then a luxury. At Naples, you may see daily walking in the Pausilippeum men in gold-embroidered upper garments and nothing else. It is the same with buildings; magnificence is the sole consideration where there is nothing to fear from the air. In Paris and London, you desire to be lodged warmly and comfortably; in Madrid, you have superb salons, but not a window that closes, and you go to bed in a mere hole.

In hot countries foods are much more substantial and succulent; and the third difference cannot but have an influence on the second. Why are so many vegetables eaten in Italy? Because there they are good, nutritious, and excellent in taste. In France, where they are nourished only on water, they are far from nutritious and are thought nothing of at table. They take up all the same no less ground, and cost at least as much pains to cultivate. It is a proved fact that the wheat of Barbary, in other respects inferior to that of France, yields much more flour, and that the wheat of France in turn yields more than that of northern countries; from which it may be inferred that a like gradation in the same direction, from equator to pole, is found generally. But is it not an obvious disadvantage for an equal product to contain less nourishment?

To all these points may be added another, which at once depends on and strengthens them. Hot countries need inhabitants less than cold countries, and can support more of them. There is thus a double surplus, which is all to the advantage of despotism. The greater the territory occupied by a fixed number of inhabitants, the more difficult revolt becomes, because rapid or secret concerted action is impossible, and the government can easily unmask projects and cut communications; but the more a numerous people is gathered together, the less can the government usurp the Sovereign's place: the people's leaders can deliberate as safely in their houses as the prince in council, and the crowd gather as rapidly in the squares as the prince's troops in their quarters. The advantage of tyrannical government therefore lies in acting at great distances. With the help of the rallying-points it establishes, its strength, like that of the lever,* grows with distance. The strength of the people, on the other hand, acts only when concentrated: when spread abroad, it evaporates and is lost, like powder scattered on the ground, which catches fire only grain by grain. The least populous countries are thus the fittest for tyranny: fierce animals reign only in deserts.

CHAPTER 9

The Signs of a Good Government

The question 'What absolutely is the best government?' is unanswerable as well as indeterminate; or rather, there are as many good answers as there are possible combinations in the absolute and relative situations of all nations.

But if it is asked by what sign we may know that a given people is well or ill governed, that is another matter, and the question, being one of fact, admits of an answer.

It is not, however, answered, because every one wants to answer it in his own way. Subjects extol public tranquillity, citizens individual liberty; the one class prefers security of possessions, the other that of person; the one regards as the best government that which is most severe, the other maintains that the mildest is the best; the one wants crimes punished, the other wants them prevented; the one wants the State to be feared by its neighbours, the

* This does not contradict what I said before (Bk. II, ch. 9) about the disadvantages of great States; for we were then dealing with the authority of the government over the members, while here we are dealing with its force against the subjects. Its scattered members serve it as rallying-points for action against the people at a distance, but it has no rallying-point for direct action on to members themselves. Thus the length of the lever is its weakness in the one case, and its strength in the other.

other prefers that it should be ignored; the one is content if money circulates, the other demands that the people shall have bread. Even if an agreement were come to on these and similar points, should we have got any further? As moral qualities do not admit of exact measurement, agreement about the sign does not mean agreement about the valuation.

For my part, I am continually astonished that a sign so simple is not recognized, or that men are of so bad faith as not to admit it. What is the end of political association? The preservation and prosperity of its members. And what is the surest sign of their preservation and prosperity? Their numbers and population. Seek then nowhere else this sign that is in dispute. The rest being equal, the government under which, without external aids, without naturalization or colonies, the citizens increase and multiply most is beyond question the best. The government under which a people wanes and diminishes is the worst. Calculators, it is left for you to count, to measure, to compare.*

---

* On the same principle it should be judged what centuries deserve the preference for human prosperity. Those in which letters and arts have flourished have been too much admired, because the hidden object of their culture has not been fathomed, and their fatal effects not taken into account. 'Idque apud imperitos humanitas vocabatur, cum pars servitutis esset.' ['Fools called "humanity" what was a part of slavery,' Tacitus, *Agricola*, 31.] Shall we never see in the maxims books lay down the vulgar interest that makes their writers speak? No, whatever they may say, when, despite its renown, a country is depopulated, it is not true that all is well, and it is not enough that a poet should have an income of 100,000 francs to make his age the best of all. Less attention should be paid to the apparent repose and tranquillity of the rulers than to the well-being of their nations as wholes, and above all of the most numerous States. A hail-storm lays several cantons waste, but it rarely makes a famine. Outbreaks and civil wars give rulers rude shocks, but they are not the real ills of peoples, who may even get a respite, while there is a dispute as to who shall tyrannize over them. Their true prosperity and calamities come from their permanent condition: it is when the whole remains crushed beneath the yoke, that decay sets in, and that the rulers destroy them at will, and 'ubi solitudinem faciunt, pacem appellant'. [Where they create solitude, they call it peace,' Tacitus, *Agricola*, 31.] When the bickering of the great disturbed the kingdom of France, and the Coadjutor of Paris[1] took a dagger in his pocket to the Parliament, these things did not prevent the people of France from prospering and

CHAPTER 10

The Abuse of Government and Its Tendency to Degenerate

As the particular will acts constantly in opposition to the general will, the government continually exerts itself against the Sovereignty. The greater this exertion becomes, the more the constitution changes; and, as there is in this case no other corporate will to create an equilibrium by resisting the will of the prince, sooner or later the prince must inevitably suppress the Sovereign and break the social treaty. This is the unavoidable and inherent defect which, from the very birth of the body politic, tends ceaselessly to destroy it, as age and death end by destroying the human body.

There are two general courses by which government degenerates: i.e. when it undergoes contraction, or when the State is dissolved.

Government undergoes contraction when it passes from the many to the few, that is, from democracy to aristocracy, and from aristocracy to royalty. To do so is its natural propensity.* If it

multiplying in dignity, ease, and freedom. Long ago Greece flourished in the midst of the most savage wars; blood ran in torrents, and yet the whole country was covered with inhabitants. It appeared, says Machiavelli, that in the midst of murder, proscription, and civil war, our republic only throve: the virtue, morality, and independence of the citizens did more to strengthen it than all their dissensions had done to enfeeble it. A little disturbance gives the soul elasticity; what makes the race truly prosperous is not so much peace as liberty.

* The slow formation and the progress of the Republic of Venice in its lagoons are a notable instance of this sequence; and it is most astonishing that, after more than twelve hundred years' existence, the Venetians seem to be still at the second stage, which they reached with the *Serrar di Consiglio* in 1198.[1] As for the ancient Dukes who are brought up against them, it is proved, whatever the *Squittinio della libertà veneta*[2] may say of them, that they were in no sense Sovereigns.

A case certain to be cited against my view is that of the Roman Republic, which, it will be said, followed exactly the opposite course, and passed from monarchy to aristocracy and from aristocracy to democracy. I by no means take this view of it.

(continued)

took the backward course from the few to the many, it could be said that it was relaxed; but this inverse sequence is impossible.

Indeed, governments never change their form except when their energy is exhausted and leaves them too weak to keep what they have. If a government at once extended its sphere and relaxed its stringency, its force would become absolutely nil, and it would persist still less. It is therefore necessary to wind up the spring and tighten the hold as it gives way: or else the State it sustains will come to grief.

The dissolution of the State may come about in either of two ways.

First, when the prince ceases to administer the State in accordance with the laws, and usurps the Sovereign power. A remarkable change then occurs: not the government, but the State,

---

What Romulus first set up was a mixed government, which soon deteriorated into despotism. From special causes, the State died an untimely death, as newborn children sometimes perish without reaching manhood. The expulsion of the Tarquins was the real period of the birth of the Republic. But at first it took on no constant form, because, by not abolishing the patriciate, it left half its work undone. For, by this means, hereditary aristocracy, the worst of all legitimate forms of administration, remained in conflict with democracy, and the form of the government, as Machiavelli has proved, was only fixed on the establishment of the tribunate: only then was there a true government and a veritable democracy. In fact, the people was then not only Sovereign, but also magistrate and judge: the senate was only a subordinate tribunal, to temper and concentrate the government, and the consuls themselves, though they were patricians, first magistrates, and absolute generals in war, were in Rome itself no more than presidents of the people.

From that point, the government followed its natural tendency, and inclined strongly to aristocracy. The patriciate, we may say, abolished itself, and the aristocracy was found no longer in the body of patricians as at Venice and Genoa, but in the body of the senate, which was composed of patricians and plebeians, and even in the body of tribunes when they began to usurp an active function: for names do not affect facts, and, when the people has rulers who govern for it, whatever name they bear, the government is an aristocracy.

The abuse of aristocracy led to the civil wars and the triumvirate. Sulla, Julius Caesar, and Augustus became in fact real monarchs; and finally, under the despotism of Tiberius, the State was dissolved. Roman history then confirms, instead of invalidating, the principle I have laid down.

undergoes contraction; I mean that the great State is dissolved, and another is formed within it, composed solely of the members of the government, which becomes for the rest of the people merely master and tyrant. So that the moment the government usurps the Sovereignty, the social compact is broken, and all private citizens recover by right their natural liberty, and are forced, but not bound, to obey.

The same thing happens when the members of the government severally usurp the power they should exercise only as a body; this is as great an infraction of the laws, and results in even greater disorders. There are then, so to speak, as many princes as there are magistrates, and the State, no less divided than the government, either perishes or changes its form.

When the State is dissolved, the abuse of government, whatever it is, bears the common name of *anarchy*. To distinguish, democracy degenerates into *ochlocracy*, and aristocracy into *oligarchy*; and I would add that royalty degenerates into *tyranny*; but this last word is ambiguous and needs explanation.

In vulgar usage, a tyrant is a king who governs violently and without regard for justice and law. In the exact sense, a tyrant is an individual who arrogates to himself the royal authority without having a right to it. This is how the Greeks understood the word 'tyrant': they applied it indifferently to good and bad princes whose authority was not legitimate.* *Tyrant* and *usurper* are thus perfectly synonymous terms.

In order that I may give different things different names, I call him who usurps the royal authority a *tyrant*, and him who usurps

---

* 'Omnes enim et habentur et dicuntur tyranni, qui potestate utuntur perpetua in ea civitate quae libertate usa est' (Cornelius Nepos, *Life of Miltiades*). ['For all those are called and considered tyrants, who hold perpetual power in a State that has known liberty.'] It is true that Aristotle (*Nicomachean Ethics*, Bk., viii, ch. x) distinguishes the tyrant from the king by the fact that the former governs in his own interest, and the latter only for the good of his subjects; but not only did all Greek authors in general use the word 'tyrant' in a different sense, as appears most clearly in Xenophon's *Hiero*, but also it would follow from Aristotle's distinction that, from the very beginning of the world, there has not yet been a single king.

the sovereign power a *despot*. The tyrant is he who thrusts himself in contrary to the laws to govern in accordance with the laws; the despot is he who sets himself above the laws themselves. Thus the tyrant cannot be a despot, but the despot is always a tyrant.

CHAPTER 11

The Death of the Body Politic

Such is the natural and inevitable tendency of the best constituted governments. If Sparta and Rome perished, what State can hope to endure for ever? If we would set up a long-lived form of government, let us not even dream of making it eternal. If we are to succeed, we must not attempt the impossible, or flatter ourselves that we are endowing the work of man with a stability of which human conditions do not permit.

The body politic, as well as the human body, begins to die as soon as it is born, and carries in itself the causes of its destruction. But both may have a constitution that is more or less robust and suited to preserve them a longer or a shorter time. The constitution of man is the work of nature; that of the State the work of art. It is not in men's power to prolong their own lives; but it is for them to prolong as much as possible the life of the State, by giving it the best possible constitution. The best constituted State will have an end; but it will end later than any other, unless some unforeseen accident brings about its untimely destruction.

The life-principle of the body politic lies in the sovereign authority. The legislative power is the heart of the State; the executive power is its brain, which causes the movement of all the parts. The brain may become paralysed and the individual still live. A man may remain an imbecile and live; but as soon as the heart ceases to perform its functions, the animal is dead.

The State subsists by means not of the laws, but of the legislative power. Yesterday's law is not binding today; but silence is taken for tacit consent, and the Sovereign is held to confirm incessantly the laws it does not abrogate as it might. All that it has once declared itself to will it wills always, unless it revokes its declaration.

Why then is so much respect paid to old laws? For this very reason. We must believe that nothing but the excellence of old acts of will can have preserved them so long: if the Sovereign had not recognized them as throughout salutary, it would have revoked them a thousand times. This is why, so far from growing weak, the laws continually gain new strength in any well constituted State; the precedent of antiquity makes them daily more venerable: while wherever the laws grow weak as they become old, this proves that there is no longer a legislative power, and that the State is dead.

CHAPTER 12

How the Sovereign Authority Maintains Itself

The Sovereign, having no force other than the legislative power, acts only by means of the laws; and the laws being solely the authentic acts of the general will, the Sovereign cannot act save when the people is assembled. The people in assembly, I shall be told, is a mere chimera. It is so today, but two thousand years ago it was not so. Has man's nature changed?

The bounds of possibility, in moral matters, are less narrow than we imagine: it is our weaknesses, our vices, and our prejudices that confine them. Base souls have no belief in great men; vile slaves smile in mockery at the name of liberty.

Let us judge of what can be done by what has been done. I shall say nothing of the Republics of ancient Greece; but the Roman Republic was, to my mind, a great State, and the town of Rome a great town. The last census showed that there were in Rome four hundred thousand citizens capable of bearing arms, and the last computation of the population of the Empire showed over four million citizens, excluding subjects, foreigners, women, children, and slaves.

What difficulties might not be supposed to stand in the way of the frequent assemblage of the vast population of this capital and its neighbourhood. Yet few weeks passed without the Roman people being in assembly, and even being so several times. It exercised not only the rights of Sovereignty, but also a part of those of government. It dealt with certain matters, and judged certain cases, and this whole people was found in the public meeting-place hardly less often as magistrates than as citizens.

If we went back to the earliest history of nations, we should find that most ancient governments, even those of monarchical form, such as the Macedonian and the Frankish, had similar councils. In any case, the one incontestable fact I have given is an answer to all difficulties; it is good logic to reason from the actual to the possible.

CHAPTER 13
The Same (continued)

It is not enough for the assembled people to have once fixed the constitution of the State by giving its sanction to a body of law; it is not enough for it to have set up a perpetual government, or provided once for all for the election of magistrates. Besides the extraordinary assemblies unforeseen circumstances may demand, there must be fixed periodical assemblies which cannot be abrogated or prorogued, so that on the proper day the people is legitimately called together by law, without need of any formal summoning.

But, apart from these assemblies authorized by their date alone, every assembly of the people not summoned by the magistrates appointed for that purpose, and in accordance with the prescribed forms, should be regarded as unlawful, and all its acts as null and void, because the command to assemble should itself proceed from the law.

The greater or less frequency with which lawful assemblies should occur depends on so many considerations that no exact rules about them can be given. It can only be said generally that the stronger the government the more often should the Sovereign show itself.

This, I shall be told, may do for a single town; but what is to be done when the State includes several? Is the sovereign authority to be divided? Or is it to be concentrated in a single town to which all the rest are made subject?

Neither the one nor the other, I reply. First, the sovereign authority is one and simple, and cannot be divided without being destroyed. In the second place, one town cannot, any more than one nation, legitimately be made subject to another, because the essence of the body politic lies in the reconciliation of obedience and liberty, and the words subject and Sovereign are identical correlatives the ideas of which meets in the single word 'citizen'.

I answer further that the union of several towns in a single city is always bad, and that, if we wish to make such a union, we should not expect to avoid its natural disadvantages. It is useless to bring up abuses that belong to great States against one who desires to see only small ones; but how can small States be given the strength to resist great ones? In the same way as formerly the Greek towns resisted the Great King, and more recently Holland and Switzerland have resisted the House of Austria.

Nevertheless, if the State cannot be reduced to the right limits, there remains still one resource; this is, to allow no capital, to make the seat of government move from town to town, and to assemble by turn in each the Provincial Estates of the country.

People the territory evenly, extend everywhere the same rights, bear to every place in it abundance and life: by these means will the State become at once as strong and as well governed as possible. Remember that the walls of towns are built of the ruins of the houses of the countryside. For every palace I see raised in the capital, my mind's eye sees a whole country made desolate.

CHAPTER 14

The Same (continued)

The moment the people is legitimately assembled as a sovereign body, the jurisdiction of the government wholly lapses, the executive power is suspended, and the person of the meanest citizen is as sacred and inviolable as that of the first magistrate; for in the presence of the person represented, representatives no longer exist. Most of the tumults that arose in the comitia at Rome were due to ignorance or neglect of this rule. The consuls were in them merely the presidents of the people; the tribunes were mere speakers;* the senate was nothing at all.

These intervals of suspension, during which the prince recognizes or ought to recognize an actual superior, have always been viewed by him with alarm; and these assemblies of the people, which are the aegis of the body politic and the curb on the government, have at all times been the horror of rulers: who therefore never spare pains, objections, difficulties, and promises,

---

* In nearly the same sense as this word has in the English Parliament. The similarity of these functions would have brought the consuls and the tribunes into conflict, even had all jurisdiction been suspended.

to stop the citizens from having them. When the citizens are greedy, cowardly, and pusillanimous, and love ease more than liberty, they do not long hold out against the redoubled efforts of the government; and thus, as the resisting force incessantly grows, the sovereign authority ends by disappearing, and most cities fall and perish before their time.

But between the sovereign authority and arbitrary government there sometimes intervenes a mean power of which something must be said.

CHAPTER 15

Deputies or Representatives

As soon as public service ceases to be the chief business of the citizens, and they would rather serve with their money than with their persons, the State is not far from its fall. When it is necessary to march out to war, they pay troops and stay at home: when it is necessary to meet in council, they name deputies and stay at home. By reason of idleness and money, they end by having soldiers to enslave their country and representatives to sell it.

It is through the hustle of commerce and the arts, through the greedy self-interest of profit, and through softness and love of amenities that personal services are replaced by money payments. Men surrender a part of their profits in order to have time to increase them at leisure. Make gifts of money, and you will not be long without chains. The word 'finance' is a slavish word, unknown in the city-state. In a country that is truly free, the citizens do everything with their own arms and nothing by means of money; so far from paying to be exempted from their duties, they would even pay for the privilege of fulfilling them themselves. I am far from taking the common view: I hold enforced labour to be less opposed to liberty than taxes.

The better the constitution of a State is, the more do public affairs encroach on private in the minds of the citizens. Private affairs are even of much less importance, because the aggregate of the common happiness furnishes a greater proportion of that of each individual, so that he has less need to seek it in private interests. In a well-ordered city every man flies to the assemblies: under a bad government no one cares to stir a step to get to them, because no one is interested in what happens there, because it is foreseen that the general will will not prevail, and lastly because domestic cares are all-absorbing. Good laws lead to the making of better ones; bad ones bring about worse. As soon as any man says of the affairs of the State *What does it matter to me?* the State may be given up for lost.

The lukewarmness of patriotism, the activity of private interest, the vastness of States, conquest, and the abuse of government suggested the method of having deputies or representatives of the people in the national assemblies. These are what, in some countries, men have presumed to call the Third Estate. Thus the individual interest of two orders is put first and second; the public interest occupies only the third place.

Sovereignty, for the same reason as makes it inalienable, cannot be represented; it lies essentially in the general will, and will does not admit of representation: it is either the same, or other; there is no intermediate possibility. The deputies of the people, therefore, are not and cannot be its representatives: they are merely its stewards, and can carry through no definitive acts. Every law the people has not ratified in person is null and void – is, in fact, not a law. The people of England regards itself as free; but it is grossly mistaken; it is free only during the election of members of parliament. As soon as they are elected, slavery overtakes it, and it is nothing. The use it makes of the short moments of liberty it enjoys shows indeed that it deserves to lose them.

The idea of representation is modern; it comes to us from feudal government, from that iniquitous and absurd system which degrades humanity and dishonours the name of man. In ancient republics and even in monarchies, the people never had representatives; the word itself was unknown. It is very singular that in Rome, where the tribunes were so sacrosanct, it was never even imagined that they could usurp the functions of the people, and that in the midst of so great a multitude they never attempted to pass on their own authority a single *plebiscitum*. We can, however, form an idea of the difficulties caused sometimes by the people being so numerous, from what happened in the time of the Gracchi, when some of the citizens had to cast their votes from the roofs of buildings.

Where right and liberty are everything, disadvantages count for nothing. Among this wise people everything was given its just value, its lictors were allowed to do what its tribunes would never have dared to attempt; for it had no fear that its lictors would try to represent it.

To explain, however, in what way the tribunes did sometimes represent it, it is enough to conceive how the government represents the Sovereign. Law being purely the declaration of the general will, it is clear that, in the exercise of the legislative power, the people cannot be represented; but in that of the executive power, which is only the force that is applied to give the law effect, it both can and should be represented. We thus see that if we looked closely into the matter we should find that very few nations have any laws. However that may be, it is certain that the tribunes, possessing no executive power, could never represent the Roman people by right of the powers entrusted to them, but only by usurping those of the senate.

In Greece, all that the people had to do, it did for itself; it was constantly assembled in the public square. The Greeks lived in a mild climate; they had no natural greed; slaves did their work for them; their great concern was with liberty. Lacking the same advantages, how can you preserve the same rights? Your severer climates add to your needs;* for half the year your public squares are uninhabitable; the flatness of your languages unfits them for

* To adopt in cold countries the luxury and effeminacy of the East is to desire or submit to its chains; it is indeed to bow to them far more inevitably in our case than in theirs.

being heard in the open air; you sacrifice more for profit than for liberty, and fear slavery less than poverty.

What then? Is liberty maintained only by the help of slavery? It may be so. Extremes meet. Everything that is not in the course of nature has its disadvantages, civil society most of all. There are some unhappy circumstances in which we can only keep our liberty at others' expense, and where the citizen can be perfectly free only when the slave is most a slave. Such was the case with Sparta. As for you, modern peoples, you have no slaves, but you are slaves yourselves; you pay for their liberty with your own. It is in vain that you boast of this preference; I find in it more cowardice than humanity.

I do not mean by all this that it is necessary to have slaves, or that the right of slavery is legitimate: I am merely giving the reasons why modern peoples, believing themselves to be free, have representatives, while ancient peoples had none. In any case, the moment a people allows itself to be represented, it is no longer free: it no longer exists.

All things considered, I do not see that it is possible henceforth for the Sovereign to preserve among us the exercise of its rights, unless the city is very small. But if it is very small, it will be conquered? No. I will show later on how the external strength of a great people* may be combined with the convenient polity and good order of a small State.

---

* I had intended to do this in the sequel to this work, when in dealing with external relations I came to the subject of confederations. The subject is quite new, and its principles have still to be laid down.

CHAPTER 16

That the Institution of Government Is Not a Contract

The legislative power once well established, the next thing is to establish similarly the executive power; for this latter, which operates only by particular acts, not being of the essence of the former, is naturally separate from it. Were it possible for the Sovereign, as such, to possess the executive power, right and fact would be so confounded that no one could tell what was law and what was not; and the body politic, thus disfigured, would soon fall a prey to the violence it was instituted to prevent.

As the citizens, by the social contract, are all equal, all can prescribe what all should do, but no one has a right to demand that another shall do what he does not do himself. It is strictly this right, which is indispensable for giving the body politic life and movement, that the Sovereign, in instituting the government, confers upon the prince.

It has been held that this act of establishment was a contract between the people and the rulers it sets over itself – a contract in which conditions were laid down between the two parties binding the one to command and the other to obey. It will be admitted, I am sure, that this is an odd kind of contract to enter into. But let us see if this view can be upheld.

First, the supreme authority can no more be modified than it can be alienated; to limit it is to destroy it. It is absurd and contradictory for the Sovereign to set a superior over itself; to bind itself to obey a master would be to return to absolute liberty.

Moreover, it is clear that this contract between the people and such and such persons would be a particular act; and from this it follows that it can be neither a law nor an act of Sovereignty, and that consequently it would be illegitimate.

It is plain too that the contracting parties in relation to each other would be under the law of nature alone and wholly without guarantees of their mutual undertakings, a position wholly at variance with the civil state. He who has force at his command being always in a position to control execution, it would come to the same thing if the name 'contract' were given to the act of one man who said to another: 'I give you all my goods, on condition that you give me back as much of them as you please.'

There is only one contract in the State, and that is the act of association, which in itself excludes the existence of a second. It is impossible to conceive of any public contract that would not be a violation of the first.

CHAPTER 17

The Institution of Government

Under what general idea then should the act by which government is instituted be conceived as falling? I will begin by stating that the act is complex, as being composed of two others – the establishment of the law and its execution.

By the former, the Sovereign decrees that there shall be a governing body established in this or that form; this act is clearly a law.

By the latter, the people nominates the rulers who are to be entrusted with the government that has been established. This nomination, being a particular act, is clearly not a second law, but merely a consequence of the first and a function of government.

The difficulty is to understand how there can be a governmental act before government exists, and how the people, which is only Sovereign or subject, can, under certain circumstances, become a prince or magistrate.

It is at this point that there is revealed one of the astonishing properties of the body politic, by means of which it reconciles apparently contradictory operations; for this is accomplished by a sudden conversion of Sovereignty into democracy, so that, without sensible change, and merely by virtue of a new relation of all to all, the citizens become magistrates and pass from general to particular acts, from legislation to the execution of the law.

This changed relation is no speculative subtlety without instances in practice: it happens every day in the English Parliament, where, on certain occasions, the Lower House resolves itself into Grand Committee, for the better discussion of affairs, and thus, from being at one moment a sovereign court, becomes at the next a mere commission; so that subsequently it reports to itself, as House of Commons, the result of its proceedings in Grand Committee, and debates over again under one name what it has already settled under another.

It is, indeed, the peculiar advantage of democratic government that it can be established in actuality by a simple act of the general will. Subsequently, this provisional government remains in power, if this form is adopted, or else establishes in the name of the Sovereign the government that is prescribed by law; and thus the whole proceeding is regular. It is impossible to set up government in any other manner legitimately and in accordance with the principles so far laid down.

CHAPTER 18

How to Check the Usurpations of Government

What we have just said confirms Chapter 16, and makes it clear that the institution of government is not a contract, but a law; that the depositaries of the executive power are not the people's masters, but its officers; that it can set them up and pull them down when it likes; that for them there is no question of contract, but of obedience; and that in taking charge of the functions the

State imposes on them they are doing no more than fulfilling their duty as citizens, without having the remotest right to argue about the conditions.

When therefore the people sets up an hereditary government, whether it be monarchical and confined to one family, or aristocratic and confined to a class, what it enters into is not an undertaking; the administration is given a provisional form, until the people chooses to order it otherwise.

It is true that such changes are always dangerous, and that the established government should never be touched except when it comes to be incompatible with the public good; but the circumspection this involves is a maxim of policy and not a rule of right, and the State is no more bound to leave civil authority in the hands of its rulers than military authority in the hands of its generals.

It is also true that it is impossible to be too careful to observe, in such cases, all the formalities necessary to distinguish a regular and legitimate act from a seditious tumult, and the will of a whole people from the clamour of a faction. Here above all no more weight should be given to invidious cases than that which is demanded by the strictest interpretation of the law. From this obligation the prince derives a great advantage in preserving his power despite the people, without its being possible to say he has usurped it; for, seeming to avail himself only of his rights, he finds it very easy to extend them, and to prevent, under the pretext of keeping the peace, assemblies that are destined to the re-establishment of order; with the result that he takes advantage of a silence he does not allow to be broken, or of irregularities he causes to be committed, to assume that he has the support of those whom fear prevents from speaking, and to punish those who dare to speak. Thus it was that the decemvirs, first elected for one year and then kept on in office for a second, tried to perpetuate their power by forbidding the comitia to assemble, and by this easy method every government in the world, once clothed with the public power, sooner or later usurps the sovereign authority.

The periodical assemblies of which I have already spoken are designed to prevent or postpone this calamity, above all when they need no formal summoning; for in that case, the prince cannot stop them without openly declaring himself a law-breaker and an enemy of the State.

The opening of these assemblies, whose sole object is the maintenance of the social treaty, should always take the form of putting two propositions that may not be suppressed, which should be voted on separately.

The first is: 'Does it please the Sovereign to preserve the present form of government?'

The second is: 'Does it please the people to leave its administration in the hands of those who are actually in charge of it?'

I am here assuming what I think I have shown; that there is in the State no fundamental law that cannot be revoked, not excluding the social compact itself; for if all the citizens assembled of one accord to break the compact, it is impossible to doubt that it would be very legitimately broken. Grotius even thinks that each man can renounce his membership of his own State, and recover his natural liberty and his goods on leaving the country.* It would be indeed absurd if all the citizens in assembly could not do what each can do by himself.

* Provided, of course, he does not leave to escape his obligations and avoid having to serve his country in the hour of need. Flight in such a case would be criminal and punishable, and would be, not withdrawal, but desertion.

Book IV

Chapter 1

That the General Will Is Indestructible

As long as several men in assembly regard themselves as a single body, they have only a single will which is concerned with their common preservation and general well-being. In this case, all the springs of the State are vigorous and simple and its rules clear and luminous; there are no embroilments or conflicts of interests; the common good is everywhere clearly apparent, and only good sense is needed to perceive it. Peace, unity, and equality are the enemies of political subtleties. Men who are upright and simple are difficult to deceive because of their simplicity; lures and ingenious pretexts fail to impose upon them, and they are not even subtle enough to be dupes. When, among the happiest people in the world, bands of peasants are seen regulating affairs of State under an oak, and always acting wisely, can we help scorning the ingenious methods of other nations, which make themselves illustrious and wretched with so much art and mystery?

A State so governed needs very few laws; and, as it becomes necessary to issue new ones, the necessity is universally seen. The first man to propose them merely says what all have already felt, and there is no question of factions or intrigues or eloquence in order to secure the passage into law of what every one has already decided to do, as soon as he is sure that the rest will act with him.

Theorists are led into error because, seeing only States that have been from the beginning wrongly constituted, they are struck by the impossibility of applying such a policy to them. They make great game of all the absurdities a clever rascal or an insinuating speaker might get the people of Paris or London to believe. They do not know that Cromwell would have been put to hard labour by the people of Berne, and the Duc de Beaufort[1] imprisoned by the Genevese.

But when the social bond begins to be relaxed and the State to grow weak, when particular interests begin to make themselves felt and the smaller societies to exercise an influence over the larger, the common interest changes and finds opponents: opinion is no longer unanimous; the general will ceases to be the will of all; contradictory views and debates arise; and the best advice is not taken without question.

Finally, when the State, on the eve of ruin, maintains only a vain, illusory, and formal existence, when in every heart the social bond is broken, and the meanest interest brazenly lays hold of the sacred name of 'public good', the general will becomes mute: all men, guided by secret motives, no more give their views as citizens than if the State had never been; and iniquitous decrees directed solely to private interest get passed under the name of laws.

Does it follow from this that the general will is exterminated or corrupted? Not at all: it is always constant, unalterable, and pure; but it is subordinated to other wills which encroach upon its sphere. Each man, in detaching his interest from the common interest, sees clearly that he cannot entirely separate them; but his share in the public mishaps seems to him negligible beside the exclusive good he aims at making his own. Apart from this particular good, he wills the general good in his own interest, as strongly as any one else. Even in selling his vote for money, he does not extinguish in himself the general will, but only eludes it. The fault he commits is that of changing the state of the question, and answering something different from what he is asked. Instead of saying, by his vote, 'It is to the advantage of the State,' he says, 'It is of advantage to this or that man or party that this or that view should prevail.' Thus the law of public order in assemblies is not so much to maintain in them the general will as to secure that the question be always put to it, and the answer always given by it.

I could here set down many reflections on the simple right of voting in every act of Sovereignty – a right which no one can take from the citizens – and also on the right of stating views, making proposals, dividing and discussing, which the government is always most careful to leave solely to its members; but this important subject would need a treatise to itself, and it is impossible to say everything in a single work.

CHAPTER 2

Voting

It may be seen, from the last chapter, that the way in which general business is managed may give a clear enough indication of the actual state of morals and the health of the body politic. The more concert reigns in the assemblies, that is, the nearer opinion approaches unanimity, the greater is the dominance of the general will. On the other hand, long debates, dissensions, and tumult proclaim the ascendancy of particular interests and the decline of the State.

This seems less clear when two or more orders enter into the constitution as patricians and plebeians did at Rome; for quarrels between these two orders often disturbed the comitia, even in the best days of the Republic. But the exception is rather apparent than real; for then, through the defect that is inherent in the body politic, there were, so to speak, two States in one, and what is not true of the two together is true of either separately. Indeed, even in the most stormy times, the *plebiscita* of the people, when the senate did not interfere with them, always went through quietly and by large majorities. The citizens having but one interest, the people had but a single will.

At the other extremity of the circle, unanimity recurs; this is the case when the citizens, having fallen into servitude, have lost both liberty and will. Fear and flattery then change votes into acclamation; deliberation ceases, and only worship or malediction is left. Such was the vile manner in which the senate expressed its views under the emperors. It did so sometimes with absurd precautions. Tacitus observes that, under Otho, the senators, while they heaped curses on Vitellius, contrived at the same time to make a deafening noise, in order that, should he ever become their master, he might not know what each of them had said.

On these various considerations depend the rules by which the methods of counting votes and comparing opinions should be regulated, according as the general will is more or less easy to discover, and the State more or less in its decline.

There is but one law which, from its nature, needs unanimous consent. This is the social compact; for civil association is the most voluntary of all acts. Every man being born free and his own master, no one, under any pretext whatsoever, can make any man subject without his consent. To decide that the son of a slave is born a slave is to decide that he is not born a man.

If then there are opponents when the social compact is made, their opposition does not invalidate the contract, but merely prevents them from being included in it. They are foreigners among citizens. When the State is instituted, residence constitutes consent; to dwell within its territory is to submit to the Sovereign.*

Apart from this primitive contract, the vote of the majority always binds all the rest. This follows from the contract itself. But it is asked how a man can be both free and forced to conform to wills that are not his own. How are the opponents at once free and subject to laws they have not agreed to?

I retort that the question is wrongly put. The citizen gives his consent to all the laws, including those which are passed in spite of his opposition, and even those which punish him when he dares to break any of them. The constant will of all the members of the

---

* This should of course be understood as applying to a free State; for elsewhere family, goods, lack of a refuge, necessity, or violence may detain a man in a country against his will; and then his dwelling there no longer by itself implies his consent to the contract or to its violation.

State is the general will; by virtue of it they are citizens and free.*
When in the popular assembly a law is proposed, what the people
is asked is not exactly whether it approves or rejects the proposal,
but whether it is in conformity with the general will, which is their
will. Each man, in giving his vote, states his opinion on that point;
and the general will is found by counting votes. When therefore
the opinion that is contrary to my own prevails, this proves
neither more nor less than that I was mistaken, and that what I
thought to be the general will was not so. If my particular opinion
had carried the day I should have achieved the opposite of what
was my will; and it is in that case that I should not have been free.

This presupposes, indeed, that all the qualities of the general
will still reside in the majority: when they cease to do so, whatever
side a man may take, liberty is no longer possible.

In my earlier demonstration of how particular wills are substituted for the general will in public deliberation, I have adequately
pointed out the practicable methods of avoiding this abuse; and I
shall have more to say of them later on. I have also given the
principles for determining the proportional number of votes for
declaring that will. A difference of one vote destroys equality; a
single opponent destroys unanimity; but between equality and
unanimity, there are several grades of unequal division, at each of
which this proportion may be fixed in accordance with the condition and the needs of the body politic.

There are two general rules that may serve to regulate this
relation. First, the more grave and important the questions discussed, the nearer should the opinion that is to prevail approach
unanimity. Secondly, the more the matter in hand calls for speed,
the smaller the prescribed difference in the numbers of votes may
be allowed to become: where an instant decision has to be

---

* At Genoa, the word 'Liberty' may be read over the front of the prisons and on
the chains of the galley-slaves. This application of the device is good and just. It is
indeed only malefactors of all estates who prevent the citizen from being free. In
the country in which all such men were in the galleys, the most perfect liberty
would be enjoyed.

reached, a majority of one vote should be enough. The first of these two rules seems more in harmony with the laws, and the second with practical affairs. In any case, it is the combination of them that gives the best proportions for determining the majority necessary.

CHAPTER 3

Elections

In the elections of the prince and the magistrates, which are, as I have said, complex acts, there are two possible methods of procedure, choice and lot. Both have been employed in various republics, and a highly complicated mixture of the two still survives in the election of the Doge at Venice.

'Election by lot,' says Montesquieu, 'is democratic in nature.' I agree that it is so; but in what sense? 'The lot,' he goes on, 'is a way of making choice that is unfair to nobody; it leaves each citizen a reasonable hope of serving his country.' These are not reasons.

If we bear in mind that the election of rulers is a function of government, and not of Sovereignty, we shall see why the lot is the method more natural to democracy, in which the administration is better in proportion as the number of its acts is small.

In every real democracy, magistracy is not an advantage, but a burdensome charge which cannot justly be imposed on one individual rather than another. The law alone can lay the charge on him on whom the lot falls. For, the conditions being then the same for all, and the choice not depending on any human will, there is no particular application to alter the universality of the law.

In an aristocracy, the prince chooses the prince, the government is preserved by itself, and it is there that voting is most appropriate.

The instance of the election of the Doge of Venice confirms, instead of destroying, this distinction; the mixed form suits a mixed government. For it is an error to take the government of Venice for a real aristocracy. If the people has no share in the government, the nobility is itself the people. A host of poor *Barnabotes*[1] never got near any magistracy, and its nobility consists merely in the empty title of Excellency, and in the right to sit in the Great Council. As this Great Council is as numerous as our General Council at Geneva, its illustrious members have no more privileges than our plain citizens. It is indisputable that, apart from the extreme disparity between the two republics, the *bourgeoisie* of Geneva is exactly equivalent to the *patriciate* of Venice; our *natives* and *inhabitants* correspond to the *townsmen* and the *people* of Venice; our *peasants* correspond to the *subjects* on the mainland; and, however that republic be regarded, if its size be left out of account, its government is no more aristocratic than our own. The whole difference is that, having no life-ruler, we do not, like Venice, need to use the lot.

Election by lot would have few disadvantages in a real democracy, in which, as equality would everywhere exist in morals and talents as well as in principles and fortunes, it would become almost a matter of indifference who was chosen. But I have already said that a real democracy is only an ideal.

When choice and lot are combined, positions that require special talents, such as military posts, should be filled by the former; the latter does for cases, such as judicial offices, in which good sense, justice, and integrity are enough, because in a State that is well constituted, these qualities are common to all the citizens.

Neither lot nor vote has any place in monarchical government. The monarch being by right sole prince and only magistrate, the choice of his lieutenants belongs to none but him. When the Abbé de Saint-Pierre[2] proposed that the Councils of the King of France should be multiplied, and their numbers elected by ballot, he did not see that he was proposing to change the form of government.

I should now speak of the methods of giving and counting opinions in the assembly of the people; but perhaps an account of this aspect of the Roman constitution will more forcibly illustrate all the rules I could lay down. It is worth the while of a judicious reader to follow in some detail the working of public and private affairs in a Council consisting of two hundred thousand men.

Chapter 4

The Roman Comitia

We are without well-certified records of the first period of Rome's existence; it even appears very probable that most of the stories told about it are fables;* indeed, generally speaking, the most instructive part of the history of peoples, that which deals with their foundation, is what we have least of. Experience teaches us every day what causes lead to the revolutions of empires; but, as no new peoples are now formed, we have almost nothing beyond conjecture to go upon it explaining how they were created.

The customs we find established show at least that these customs had an origin. The traditions that go back to those origins, that have the greatest authorities behind them, and that are confirmed by the strongest proofs, should pass for the most certain. These are the rules I have tried to follow in inquiring how the freest and most powerful people on earth exercised its supreme power.

After the foundation of Rome, the new-born republic, that is the army of its founder, composed of Albans, Sabines, and

---

* The name *Rome*, that people claim comes from *Romulus*, is Greek, and means strength: the name *Numa* is Greek too, and means *law*. What likelihood is there that the first two kings of that town should have borne in advance names so well fitted to what they did?

foreigners, was divided into three classes, which, from this division, took the name of *tribes*. Each of these tribes was subdivided into ten *curiae*, and each *curia* into *decuriae*, headed by leaders called *curiones* and *decuriones*.

Besides this, out of each tribe was taken a body of one hundred *Equites* or Knights, called a *century*, which shows that these divisions, being unnecessary in a town, were at first merely military. But an instinct for greatness seems to have led the little township of Rome to provide itself in advance with a political system suitable for the capital of the world.

Out of this original division an awkward situation soon arose. The tribes of the Albans (Ramnenses) and the Sabines (Tatienses) remained always in the same condition, while that of the foreigners (Luceres) continually grew as more and more foreigners came to live at Rome, so that it soon surpassed the others in strength. Servius remedied this dangerous fault by changing the principle of cleavage, and substituting for the racial division, which he abolished, a new one based on the quarter of the town inhabited by each tribe. Instead of three tribes he created four, each occupying and named after one of the hills of Rome. Thus, while redressing the inequality of the moment, he also provided for the future; and in order that the division might be one of persons as well as localities, he forbade the inhabitants of one quarter to migrate to another, and so prevented the mingling of the races.

He also doubled the three old centuries of Knights and added twelve more, still keeping the old names, and by this simple and prudent method, succeeded in making a distinction between the body of Knights and the people, without a murmur from the latter.

To the four urban tribes Servius added fifteen others called rural tribes, because they consisted of those who lived in the country, divided into fifteen cantons. Subsequently, fifteen more were created, and the Roman people finally found itself divided into thirty-five tribes, as it remained down to the end of the Republic.

The distinction between urban and rural tribes had one effect which is worth mention, both because it is without parallel elsewhere, and because to it Rome owed the preservation of her morality and the enlargement of her empire. We should have expected that the urban tribes would soon monopolize power and honours, and lose no time in bringing the rural tribes into disrepute; but what happened was exactly the reverse. The taste of the early Romans for country life is well known. This taste they owed to their wise founder, who made rural and military labours go along with liberty, and, so to speak, relegated to the town arts, crafts, intrigue, fortune, and slavery.

Since therefore all Rome's most illustrious citizens lived in the fields and tilled the earth, men grew used to seeking there alone the mainstays of the republic. This condition, being that of the best patricians, was honoured by all men; the simple and laborious life of the villager was preferred to the slothful and idle life of the *bourgeoisie* of Rome; and he who, in the town, would have been but a wretched proletarian, became, as a labourer in the fields, a respected citizen. Not without reason, says Varro, did our great-souled ancestors establish in the village the nursery of the sturdy and valiant men who defended them in time of war and provided for their sustenance in time of peace. Pliny states positively that the country tribes were honoured because of the men of whom they were composed; while cowards men wished to dishonour were transferred, as a public disgrace, to the town tribes. The Sabine Appius Claudius, when he had come to settle in Rome, was loaded with honours and enrolled in a rural tribe, which subsequently took his family name. Lastly, freedmen always entered the urban, and never the rural, tribes: nor is there a single example, throughout the Republic, of a freedman, though he had become a citizen, reaching any magistracy.

This was an excellent rule; but it was carried so far that in the end it led to a change and certainly to an abuse in the political system.

First the censors, after having for a long time claimed the right of transferring citizens arbitrarily from one tribe to another, allowed most persons to enrol themselves in whatever tribe they pleased. This permission certainly did no good, and further robbed the censorship of one of its greatest resources. Moreover, as the great and powerful all got themselves enrolled in the country tribes, while the freedmen who had become citizens remained with the populace in the town tribes, both soon ceased to have any local or territorial meaning, and all were so confused that the members of one could not be told from those of another except by the registers; so that the idea of the word 'tribe' became personal instead of real, or rather came to be little more than a chimera.

It happened in addition that the town tribes, being more on the spot, were often the stronger in the comitia and sold the State to those who stooped to buy the votes of the rabble composing them.

As the founder had set up ten *curiae* in each tribe, the whole Roman people, which was then contained within the walls, consisted of thirty *curiae*, each with its temples, its gods, its officers, its priests, and its festivals, which were called *compitalia* and corresponded to the *paganalia*, held in later times by the rural tribes.

When Servius made his new division, as the thirty *curiae* could not be shared equally between his four tribes, and as he was unwilling to interfere with them, they became a further division of the inhabitants of Rome, quite independent of the tribes: but in the case of the rural tribes and their members there was no question of *curiae*, as the tribes had then become a purely civil institution, and, a new system of levying troops having been introduced, the military divisions of Romulus were superfluous. Thus, although every citizen was enrolled in a tribe, there were very many who were not members of a *curia*.

Servius made yet a third division, quite distinct from the two we have mentioned, which became, in its effects, the most important of all. He distributed the whole Roman people into six classes, distinguished neither by place nor by person, but by wealth; the first classes included the rich, the last the poor, and those between persons of moderate means. These six classes were subdivided into one hundred and ninety-three other bodies, called centuries, which were so divided that the first class alone comprised more than half of them, while the last comprised only one. Thus the class that had the smallest number of members had the largest number of centuries, and the whole of the last class only counted as a single subdivision, although it alone included more than half the inhabitants of Rome.

In order that the people might have the less insight into the results of this arrangement, Servius tried to give it a military tone: in the second class he inserted two centuries of armourers, and in the fourth two of makers of instruments of war: in each class, except the last, he distinguished young and old, that is, those who were under an obligation to bear arms and those whose age gave them legal exemption. It was this distinction, rather than that of wealth, which required frequent repetition of the census or counting. Lastly, he ordered that the assembly should be held in the Campus Martius, and that all who were of age to serve should come there armed.

The reason for his not making in the last class also the division of young and old was that the populace, of whom it was composed, was not given the right to bear arms for its country: a man had to possess a hearth to acquire the right to defend it, and of all the troops of beggars who today lend lustre to the armies of kings, there is perhaps not one who would not have been driven with scorn out of a Roman cohort, at a time when soldiers were the defenders of liberty.

In this last class, however, *proletarians* were distinguished from *capite censi*. The former, not quite reduced to nothing, at least gave the State citizens, and sometimes, when the need was pressing, even soldiers. Those who had nothing at all, and could be numbered only by counting heads, were regarded as of absolutely no account, and Marius was the first who stooped to enrol them.

Without deciding now whether this third arrangement was good or bad in itself, I think I may assert that it could have been made practicable only by the simple morals, the disinterestedness, the liking for agriculture and the scorn for commerce and for love of gain which characterized the early Romans. Where is the modern people among whom consuming greed, unrest, intrigue, continual removals, and perpetual changes of fortune, could let such a system last for twenty years without turning the State upside down? We must indeed observe that morality and the censorship, being stronger than this institution, corrected its defects at Rome, and that the rich man found himself degraded to the class of the poor for making too much display of his riches.

From all this it is easy to understand why only five classes are almost always mentioned, though there were really six.

The sixth, as it furnished neither soldiers to the army nor votes in the Campus Martius,* and was almost without function in the State, was seldom regarded as of any account.

These were the various ways in which the Roman people was divided. Let us now see the effect on the assemblies. When lawfully summoned, these were called *comitia*: they were usually held in the public square at Rome or in the Campus Martius, and were distinguished as *Comitia Curiata*, *Comitia Centuriata*, and *Comitia Tributa*, according to the form under which they were convoked. The *Comitia Curiata* were founded by Romulus; the *Centuriata* by Servius; and the *Tributa* by the tribunes of the people. No law received its sanction and no magistrate was elected, save in the comitia; and as every citizen was enrolled in a *curia*, a century, or a tribe, it follows that no citizen was excluded from the right of voting, and that the Roman people was truly sovereign both *de jure* and *de facto*.

For the comitia to be lawfully assembled, and for their acts to have the force of law, three conditions were necessary. First, the body or magistrate convoking them had to possess the necessary

---

* I say 'in the Campus Martius' because it was there that the comitia assembled by centuries; in its two other forms the people assembled in the *forum* or elsewhere; and then the *capite censi* had as much influence and authority as the foremost citizens.

authority; secondly, the assembly had to be held on a day allowed by law; and thirdly, the auguries had to be favourable.

The reason for the first regulation needs no explanation; the second is a matter of policy. Thus, the comitia might not be held on festivals or market-days, when the country-folk, coming to Rome on business, had not time to spend the day in the public square. By means of the third, the senate held in check the proud and restive people, and meetly restrained the ardour of seditious tribunes, who, however, found more than one way of escaping this hindrance.

Laws and the election of rulers were not the only questions submitted to the judgment of the comitia: as the Roman people had taken on itself the most important functions of government, it may be said that the lot of Europe was regulated in its assemblies. The variety of their objects gave rise to the various forms these took, according to the matters on which they had to pronounce.

In order to judge of these various forms, it is enough to compare them. Romulus, when he set up *curiae*, had in view the checking of the senate by the people, and of the people by the senate, while maintaining his ascendancy over both alike. He therefore gave the people, by means of this assembly, all the authority of numbers to balance that of power and riches, which he left to the patricians. But, after the spirit of monarchy, he left all the same a greater advantage to the patricians in the influence of their clients on the majority of votes. This excellent institution of patron and client was a masterpiece of statesmanship and humanity without which the patriciate, being flagrantly in contradiction to the republican spirit, could not have survived. Rome alone has the honour of having given to the world this great example, which never led to any abuse, and yet has never been followed.

As the assemblies by *curiae* persisted under the kings till the time of Servius, and the reign of the later Tarquin was not regarded as legitimate, royal laws were called generally *leges curiatae*.

Under the Republic, the *curiae*, still confined to the four urban tribes, and including only the populace of Rome, suited neither the senate, which led the patricians, nor the tribunes, who, though plebeians, were at the head of the well-to-do citizens. They therefore fell into disrepute, and their degradation was such, that thirty lictors used to assemble and do what the *Comitia Curiata* should have done.

The division by centuries was so favourable to the aristocracy that it is hard to see at first how the senate ever failed to carry the day in the comitia bearing their name, by which the consuls, the censors, and the other curule magistrates were elected. Indeed, of the hundred and ninety-three centuries into which the six classes of the whole Roman people were divided, the first class contained ninety-eight; and, as voting went solely by centuries, this class alone had a majority over all the rest. When all these centuries were in agreement, the rest of the votes were not even taken; the decision of the smallest number passed for that of the multitude, and it may be said that, in the *Comitia Centuriata*, decisions were regulated far more by depth of purses than by the number of votes.

But this extreme authority was modified in two ways. First, the tribunes as a rule, and always a great number of plebeians, belonged to the class of the rich, and so counterbalanced the influence of the patricians in the first class.

The second way was this. Instead of causing the centuries to vote throughout in order, which would have meant beginning always with the first, the Romans always chose one by lot which proceeded alone to the election;* after this all the centuries were summoned another day according to their rank, and the same election was repeated, and as a rule confirmed. Thus the authority of example was taken away from rank, and given to the lot on a democratic principle.

From this custom resulted a further advantage. The citizens

* This century, so chosen by lot, was called *praerogativa*, because it was the first to be asked for its vote, and it is from this that the word *prerogative* is derived.

from the country had time, between the two elections, to inform themselves of the merits of the candidate who had been provisionally nominated, and did not have to vote without knowledge of the case. But, under the pretext of hastening matters, the abolition of this custom was achieved, and both elections were held on the same day.

The *Comitia Tributa* were properly the councils of the Roman people. They were convoked by the tribunes alone; at them the tribunes were elected and passed their *plebiscita*. The senate not only had no standing in them, but even no right to be present; and the senators, being forced to obey laws on which they could not vote, were in this respect less free than the meanest citizens. This injustice was altogether ill-conceived, and was alone enough to invalidate the decrees of a body to which all its members were not admitted. Had all the patricians attended the comitia by virtue of the right they had as citizens, they would not, as mere private individuals, have had any considerable influence on a vote reckoned by counting heads, where the meanest proletarian was as good as the *princeps senatus*.

It may be seen, therefore, that besides the order which was achieved by these various ways of distributing so great a people and taking its votes, the various methods were not reducible to forms indifferent in themselves, but the results of each were relative to the objects which caused it to be preferred.

Without going here into further details, we may gather from what has been said above that the *Comitia Tributa* were the most favourable to popular government, and the *Comitia Centuriata* to aristocracy. The *Comitia Curiata*, in which the populace of Rome formed the majority, being fitted only to further tyranny and evil designs, naturally fell into disrepute, and even seditious persons abstained from using a method which too clearly revealed their projects. It is indisputable that the whole majesty of the Roman people lay solely in the *Comitia Centuriata*, which alone included all; for the *Comitia Curiata* excluded the rural tribes, and the *Comitia Tributa* the senate and the patricians.

As for the method of taking the vote, it was among the ancient Romans as simple as their morals, although not so simple as at Sparta. Each man declared his vote aloud, and a clerk duly wrote it down; the majority in each tribe determined the vote of the tribe, the majority of the tribes that of the people, and so with *curiae* and centuries. This custom was good as long as honesty was triumphant among the citizens, and each man was ashamed to vote publicly in favour of an unjust proposal or an unworthy subject; but, when the people grew corrupt and votes were bought, it was fitting that voting should be secret in order that purchasers might be restrained by mistrust, and rogues be given the means of not being traitors.

I know that Cicero attacks this change, and attributes partly to it the ruin of the Republic. But though I feel the weight Cicero's authority must carry on such a point, I cannot agree with him; I hold, on the contrary, that, for want of enough such changes, the destruction of the State was accelerated. Just as the regimen of health does not suit the sick, we should not wish to govern a people that has been corrupted by the laws that a good people requires. There is no better proof of this rule than the long life of the Republic of Venice, of which the shadow still exists, solely because its laws are suitable only for men who are wicked.

The citizens were provided, therefore, with tablets by means of which each man could vote without any one knowing how he voted: new methods were also introduced for collecting the tablets, for counting voices, for comparing numbers, etc.; but all these precautions did not prevent the good faith of the officers charged with these functions* from being often suspect. Finally, to prevent intrigues and trafficking in votes, edicts were issued; but their very number proves how useless they were.

Towards the close of the Republic, it was often necessary to have recourse to extraordinary expedients in order to supplement the inadequacy of the laws. Sometimes miracles were supposed;

Custodes, diribitores, rogatores suffragiorum.

but this method, while it might impose on the people, could not impose on those who governed. Sometimes an assembly was hastily called together, before the candidates had time to form their factions: sometimes a whole sitting was occupied with talk, when it was seen that the people had been won over and was on the point of taking up a wrong position. But in the end ambition eluded all attempts to check it; and the most incredible fact of all is that, in the midst of all these abuses, the vast people, thanks to its ancient regulations, never ceased to elect magistrates, to pass laws, to judge cases, and to carry through business both public and private, almost as easily as the senate itself could have done.

CHAPTER 5
The Tribunate

When an exact proportion cannot be established between the constituent parts of the State, or when causes that cannot be removed continually alter the relation of one part to another, recourse is had to the institution of a peculiar magistracy that enters into no corporate unity with the rest. This restores to each term its right relation to the others, and provides a link or middle term between either prince and people, or prince and Sovereign, or, if necessary, both at once.

This body, which I shall call the *tribunate*, is the preserver of the laws and of the legislative power. It serves sometimes to protect the Sovereign against the government, as the tribunes of the people did at Rome; sometimes to uphold the government against the people, as the Council of Ten now does at Venice; and sometimes to maintain the balance between the two, as the Ephors did at Sparta.

The tribunate is not a constituent part of the city, and should have no share in either legislative or executive power; but this very fact makes its own power the greater: for, while it can do nothing, it can prevent anything from being done. It is more sacred and more revered, as the defender of the laws, than the prince who executes them, or than the Sovereign which ordains them. This was seen very clearly at Rome, when the proud patricians, for all their scorn of the people, were forced to bow before one of its officers, who had neither auspices nor jurisdiction.

The tribunate, wisely tempered, is the strongest support a good constitution can have; but if its strength is ever so little excessive, it upsets the whole State. Weakness on the other hand, is not natural to it: provided it is something, it is never less than it should be.

It degenerates into tyranny when it usurps the executive power, which it should confine itself to restraining, and when it attempts to dispense the laws, which it should confine itself to protecting. The immense power of the Ephors, harmless as long as Sparta preserved its morality, hastened corruption when once it had begun. The blood of Agis, slaughtered by these tyrants, was avenged by his successor; the crime and the punishment of the Ephors alike hastened the destruction of the republic, and after Cleomenes Sparta ceased to be of any account. Rome perished in the same way: the excessive power of the tribunes, which they had usurped by degrees, finally served, with the help of laws made to secure liberty, as a safeguard for the emperors who destroyed it. As for the Venetian Council of Ten, it is a tribunal of blood, an object of horror to patricians and people alike; and, so far from giving a lofty protection to the laws, it does nothing, now they have become degraded, but strike in the darkness blows of which no one dare take note.

The tribunate, like the government, grows weak as the number of its members increases. When the tribunes of the Roman people, who first numbered only two, and then five, wished to double that number, the senate let them do so, in the confidence that it could use one to check another, as indeed it afterwards freely did.

The best method of preventing usurpations by so formidable a body, though no government has yet made use of it, would be not to make it permanent, but to regulate the periods during which it should remain in abeyance. These intervals, which should not be long enough to give abuses time to grow strong, may be so fixed by law that they can easily be shortened at need by extraordinary commissions.

This method seems to me to have no disadvantages, because, as I have said, the tribunate, which forms no part of the constitution, can be removed without the constitution being affected. It seems to be also efficacious, because a newly restored magistrate starts not with the power his predecessor exercised, but with that which the law allows him.

CHAPTER 6

The Dictatorship

The inflexibility of the laws, which prevents them from adapting themselves to circumstances, may, in certain cases, render them disastrous, and make them bring about, at a time of crisis, the ruin of the State. The order and slowness of the forms they enjoin require a space of time which circumstances sometimes withhold. A thousand cases against which the legislator has made no provision may present themselves, and it is a highly necessary part of foresight to be conscious that everything cannot be foreseen.

It is wrong therefore to wish to make political institutions so strong as to render it impossible to suspend their operation. Even Sparta allowed its laws to lapse.

However, none but the greatest dangers can counterbalance that of changing the public order, and the sacred power of the laws should never be arrested save when the existence of the country is at stake. In these rare and obvious cases, provision is made for the public security by a particular act entrusting it to him who is most worthy. This commitment may be carried out in either of two ways, according to the nature of the danger.

If increasing the activity of the government is a sufficient remedy, power is concentrated in the hands of one or two of its members: in this case the change is not in the authority of the laws, but only in the form of administering them. If, on the other hand, the peril is of such a kind that the paraphernalia of the laws are an obstacle to their preservation, the method is to nominate a supreme ruler, who shall silence all the laws and suspend for a moment the sovereign authority. In such a case, there is no doubt about the general will, and it is clear that the people's first intention is that the State shall not perish. Thus the suspension of the legislative authority is in no sense its abolition; the magistrate who silences it cannot make it speak; he dominates it, but cannot represent it. He can do anything, except make laws.

The first method was used by the Roman senate when, in a consecrated formula, it charged the consuls to provide for the safety of the Republic. The second was employed when one of the two consuls nominated a dictator:* a custom Rome borrowed from Alba.

During the first period of the Republic, recourse was very often had to the dictatorship, because the State had not yet a firm enough basis to be able to maintain itself by the strength of its constitution alone. As the state of morality then made superfluous many of the precautions which would have been necessary at other times, there was no fear that a dictator would abuse his authority, or try to keep it beyond his term of office. On the contrary, so much power appeared to be burdensome to him who was clothed with it, and he made all speed to lay it down, as if taking the place of the laws had been too troublesome and too perilous a position to retain.

* The nomination was made secretly by night, as if there were something shameful in setting a man above the laws.

It is therefore the danger not of its abuse, but of its cheapening, that makes me attack the indiscreet use of this supreme magistracy in the earliest times. For as long as it was freely employed at elections, dedications, and purely formal functions, there was danger of its becoming less formidable in time of need, and of men growing accustomed to regarding as empty a title that was used only on occasions of empty ceremonial.

Towards the end of the Republic, the Romans, having grown more circumspect, were as unreasonably sparing in the use of the dictatorship as they had formerly been lavish. It is easy to see that their fears were without foundation, that the weakness of the capital secured it against the magistrates who were in its midst; that a dictator might, in certain cases, defend the public liberty, but could never endanger it; and that the chains of Rome would be forged, not in Rome itself, but in her armies. The weak resistance offered by Marius to Sulla, and by Pompey to Caesar, clearly showed what was to be expected from authority at home against force from abroad.

This misconception led the Romans to make great mistakes; such, for example, as the failure to nominate a dictator in the Catilinarian conspiracy. For, as only the city itself, with at most some province in Italy, was concerned, the unlimited authority the laws gave to the dictator would have enabled him to make short work of the conspiracy, which was, in fact, stifled only by a combination of lucky chances human prudence had no right to expect.

Instead, the senate contented itself with entrusting its whole power to the consuls, so that Cicero, in order to take effective action, was compelled on a capital point to exceed his powers; and if, in the first transports of joy, his conduct was approved, he was justly called, later on, to account for the blood of citizens spilt in violation of the laws. Such a reproach could never have been levelled at a dictator. But the consul's eloquence carried the day; and he himself, Roman though he was, loved his own glory better than his country, and sought, not so much the most lawful and secure means of saving the State, as to get for himself the whole honour of having done so.* He was therefore justly honoured as the liberator of Rome, and also justly punished as a law-breaker. However brilliant his recall may have been, it was undoubtedly an act of pardon.

However this important trust be conferred, it is important that its duration should be fixed at a very brief period, incapable of being ever prolonged. In the crises which lead to its adoption, the State is either soon lost, or soon saved; and, the present need passed, the dictatorship becomes either tyrannical or idle. At Rome, where dictators held office for six months only, most of them abdicated before their time was up. If their term had been longer, they might well have tried to prolong it still further, as the decemvirs did when chosen for a year. The dictator had only time to provide against the need that had caused him to be chosen; he had none to think of further projects.

CHAPTER 7

The Censorship

As the law is the declaration of the general will, the censorship is the declaration of the public judgment: public opinion is the form of law which the censor administers, and, like the prince, only applies to particular cases.

The censorial tribunal, so far from being the arbiter of the people's opinion, only declares it, and, as soon as the two part company, its decisions are null and void.

It is useless to distinguish the morality of a nation from the

---

*That is what he could not be sure of, if he proposed a dictator; for he dared not nominate himself, and could not be certain that his colleague would nominate him.

objects of its esteem; both depend on the same principle and are necessarily indistinguishable. There is no people on earth the choice of whose pleasures is not decided by opinion rather than nature. Right men's opinions, and their morality will purge itself. Men always love what is good or what they find good; it is in judging what is good that they go wrong. This judgment, therefore, is what must be regulated. He who judges of morality judges of honour; and he who judges of honour finds his law in opinion.

The opinions of a people are derived from its constitution; although the law does not regulate morality, it is legislation that gives it birth. When legislation grows weak, morality degenerates; but in such cases the judgment of the censors will not do what the force of the laws has failed to effect.

From this it follows that the censorship may be useful for the preservation of morality, but can never be so for its restoration. Set up censors while the laws are vigorous; as soon as they have lost their vigour, all hope is gone; no legitimate power can retain force when the laws have lost it.

The censorship upholds morality by preventing opinion from growing corrupt, by preserving its rectitude by means of wise applications, and sometimes even by fixing it when it is still uncertain. The employment of seconds in duels, which had been carried to wild extremes in the kingdom of France, was done away with merely by these words in a royal edict: 'As for those who are cowards enough to call upon seconds.' This judgment, in anticipating that of the public, suddenly decided it. But when edicts from the same source tried to pronounce duelling itself an act of cowardice, as indeed it is, then, since common opinion does not regard it as such, the public took no notice of a decision on a point on which its mind was already made up.

I have stated elsewhere* that as public opinion is not subject to any constraint, there need be no trace of it in the tribunal set up to

---

* I merely call attention in this chapter to a subject with which I have dealt at greater length in my *Letter to M. d'Alembert*.

represent it. It is impossible to admire too much the art with which this resource, which we moderns have wholly lost, was employed by the Romans, and still more by the Lacedaemonians.

A man of bad morals having made a good proposal in the Spartan Council, the Ephors neglected it, and caused the same proposal to be made by a virtuous citizen. What an honour for the one, and what a disgrace for the other, without praise or blame of either! Certain drunkards from Samos* polluted the tribunal of the Ephors: the next day, a public edict gave Samians permission to be filthy. An actual punishment would not have been so severe as such an impunity. When Sparta has pronounced on what is or is not right, Greece makes no appeal from her judgments.

CHAPTER 8

Civil Religion

At first men had no kings save the gods, and no government save theocracy. They reasoned like Caligula, and, at that period, reasoned aright. It takes a long time for feeling so to change that men can make up their minds to take their equals as masters, in the hope that they will profit by doing so.

From the mere fact that God was set over every political society, it followed that there were as many gods as peoples. Two peoples that were strangers the one to the other, and almost always enemies, could not long recognize the same master: two armies giving battle could not obey the same leader. National divisions thus led to polytheism, and this in turn gave rise to theological and

* They were from another island, which the delicacy of our language forbids me to name on this occasion. [Added in the edition of 1782 from Rousseau's MS notes.]

civil intolerance, which, as we shall see hereafter, are by nature the same.

The fancy the Greeks had for rediscovering their gods among the barbarians arose from the way they had of regarding themselves as the natural Sovereigns of such peoples. But there is nothing so absurd as the erudition which in our days identifies and confuses gods of different nations. As if Moloch, Saturn, and Chronos could be the same god! As if the Phoenician Baal, the Greek Zeus, and the Latin Jupiter could be the same! As if there could still be anything common to imaginary beings with different names!

If it is asked how in pagan times, where each State had its cult and its gods, there were no wars of religion, I answer that it was precisely because each State, having its own cult as well as its own government, made no distinction between its gods and its laws. Political war was also theological; the provinces of the gods were, so to speak, fixed by the boundaries of nations. The god of one people had no right over another. The gods of the pagans were not jealous gods; they shared among themselves the empire of the world: even Moses and the Hebrews sometimes lent themselves to this view by speaking of the God of Israel. It is true, they regarded as powerless the gods of the Canaanites, a proscribed people condemned to destruction, whose place they were to take; but remember how they spoke of the divisions of the neighbouring peoples they were forbidden to attack! 'Is not the possession of what belongs to your god Chamos lawfully your due?' said Jephthah to the Ammonites. 'We have the same title to the lands our conquering God has made his own.'* Here, I think, there is a recognition that the rights of Chamos and those of the God of Israel are of the same nature.

---

* 'Nonne ea quae possidet Chamos deus tuus, tibi jure debentur?' (Judges xi. 24). Such is the text in the Vulgate. Father de Carrières translates: 'Do you not regard yourselves as having a right to what your god possesses?' I do not know the force of the Hebrew text: but I perceive that, in the Vulgate, Jephthah positively recognizes the right of the god Chamos, and that the French translator weakened this admission by inserting an 'according to you', which is not in the Latin.

But when the Jews, being subject to the kings of Babylon, and, subsequently, to those of Syria, still obstinately refused to recognize any god save their own, their refusal was regarded as rebellion against their conqueror, and drew down on them the persecutions we read of in their history, which are without parallel till the coming of Christianity.*

Every religion, therefore, being attached solely to the laws of the State which prescribed it, there was no way of converting a people except by enslaving it, and there could be no missionaries save conquerors. The obligation to change cults being the law to which the vanquished yielded, it was necessary to be victorious before suggesting such a change. So far from men fighting for the gods, the gods, as in Homer, fought for men; each asked his god for victory, and repaid him with new altars. The Romans, before taking a city, summoned its gods to quit it; and, in leaving the Tarentines their outraged gods, they regarded them as subject to their own and compelled to do them homage. They left the vanquished their gods as they left them their laws. A wreath to the Jupiter of the Capitol was often the only tribute they imposed.

Finally, when, along with their empire, the Romans had spread their cult and their gods, and had themselves often adopted those of the vanquished, by granting to both alike the rights of the city, the peoples of that vast empire insensibly found themselves with multitudes of gods and cults, everywhere almost the same; and thus paganism throughout the known world finally came to be one and the same religion.

It was in these circumstances that Jesus came to set up on earth a spiritual kingdom, which, by separating the theological from the political system, made the State no longer one, and brought about the internal divisions which have never ceased to trouble Christian peoples. As the new idea of a kingdom of the other world could never have occurred to pagans, they always looked

* It is quite clear that the Phocian war, which was called 'the Sacred War', was not a war of religion. Its object was the punishment of acts of sacrilege, and not the conquest of unbelievers.

on the Christians as really rebels, who, while feigning to submit, were only waiting for the chance to make themselves independent and their masters, and to usurp by guile the authority they pretended in their weakness to respect. This was the cause of the persecutions.

What the pagans had feared took place. Then everything changed its aspect: the humble Christians changed their language, and soon this so-called kingdom of the other world turned, under a visible leader, into the most violent of earthly despotisms.

However, as there have always been a prince and civil laws, this double power and conflict of jurisdiction have made all good polity impossible in Christian States; and men have never succeeded in finding out whether they were bound to obey the master or the priest.

Several peoples, however, even in Europe and its neighbourhood, have desired without success to preserve or restore the old system: but the spirit of Christianity has everywhere prevailed. The sacred cult has always remained or again become independent of the Sovereign, and there has been no necessary link between it and the body of the State. Mahomet held very sane views, and linked his political system well together; and, as long as the form of his government continued under the caliphs who succeeded him, that government was indeed one, and so far good. But the Arabs, having grown prosperous, lettered, civilized, slack, and cowardly, were conquered by barbarians: the division between the two powers began again; and, although it is less apparent among the Mahometans than among the Christians, it none the less exists, especially in the sect of Ali, and there are States, such as Persia, where it is continually making itself felt.

Among us, the Kings of England have made themselves heads of the Church, and the Czars have done the same: but this title has made them less its masters than its ministers; they have gained not so much the right to change it, as the power to maintain it: they are not its legislators, but only its princes. Wherever the clergy is a corporate body,* it is master and legislator in its own country. There are thus two powers, two Sovereigns, in England and in Russia, as well as elsewhere.

Of all Christian writers, the philosopher Hobbes alone has seen the evil and how to remedy it, and has dared to propose the reunion of the two heads of the eagle, and the restoration throughout of political unity, without which no State or government will ever be rightly constituted. But he must have seen that the masterful spirit of Christianity was incompatible with his system, and that the priestly interest would always be stronger than that of the State. It is not so much what is false and terrible in his political theory, as what is just and true, that has drawn hatred on it.†

I believe that if the study of history were developed from this point of view, it would be easy to refute the contrary opinions of Bayle and Warburton, one of whom holds that religion can be of no use to the body politic, while the other, on the contrary, maintains that Christianity is its strongest support. We should demonstrate to the former that no State has ever been founded without a religious basis, and to the latter, that the law of Christianity at bottom does more harm by weakening than good by strengthening the constitution of the State. To make myself understood, I have only to make a little more exact the too vague ideas of religion as relating to this subject.

Religion, considered in relation to society, which is either

---

* It should be noted that the clergy find their bond of union not so much in formal assemblies, as in the communion of Churches. Communion and excommunication are the social compact of the clergy, a compact which will always make them masters of peoples and kings. All priests who communicate together are fellow citizens, even if they come from opposite ends of the earth. This invention is a masterpiece of statesmanship: there is nothing like it among pagan priests; who have therefore never formed a clerical corporate body.

† See, for instance, in a letter from Grotius to his brother (April 11, 1643), what that learned man found to praise and to blame in the *De Cive*. It is true that, with a bent for indulgence, he seems to pardon the writer the good for the sake of the bad; but all men are not so forgiving.

general or particular, may also be divided into two kinds: the religion of man, and that of the citizen. The first, which has neither temples, nor altars, nor rites, and is confined to the purely internal cult of the supreme God and the eternal obligations of morality, is the religion of the Gospel pure and simple, the true theism, what may be called natural divine right or law. The other, which is codified in a single country, gives it its gods, its own tutelary patrons; it has its dogmas, its rites and its external cult prescribed by law; outside the single nation that follows it, all the world is in its sight infidel, foreign, and barbarous; the duties and rights of man extend for it only as far as its own altars. Of this kind were all the religions of early peoples, which we may define as civil or positive divine right of law.

There is a third sort of religion of a more singular kind, which gives men two codes of legislation, two rulers, and two countries, renders them subject to contradictory duties, and makes it impossible for them to be faithful both to religion and to citizenship. Such are the religions of the Lamas and of the Japanese, and such is Roman Christianity, which may be called the religion of the priest. It leads to a sort of mixed and anti-social code which has no name.

In their political aspect, all these three kinds of religion have their defects. The third is so clearly bad, that it is waste of time to stop to prove it such. All that destroys social unity is worthless; all institutions that set man in contradiction to himself are worthless.

The second is good in that it unites the divine cult with love of the laws, and, making country the object of the citizens' adoration, teaches them the service done to the State is service done to its tutelary god. It is a form of theocracy, in which there can be no pontiff save the prince, and no priests save the magistrates. To die for one's country then becomes martyrdom; violation of its laws, impiety; and to subject one who is guilty to public execration is to condemn him to the anger of the gods: *Sacer estod.*

On the other hand, it is bad in that, being founded on lies and error, it deceives men, makes them credulous and superstitious, and drowns the true cult of the Divinity in empty ceremonial. It is bad, again, when it becomes tyrannous and exclusive, and makes a people bloodthirsty and intolerant, so that it breathes fire and slaughter, and regards as a sacred act the killing of every one who does not believe in its gods. The result is to place such a people in a natural state of war with all others, so that its security is deeply endangered.

There remains therefore the religion of man or Christianity — not the Christianity of today, but that of the Gospel, which is entirely different. By means of this holy, sublime, and real religion all men, being children of one God, recognize one another as brothers, and the society that unites them is not dissolved even at death.

But this religion, having no particular relation to the body politic, leaves the laws in possession of the force they have in themselves without making any addition to it; and thus one of the great bonds that unite society considered in severalty fails to operate. Nay, more, so far from binding the hearts of the citizens to the State, it has the effect of taking them away from all earthly things. I know of nothing more contrary to the social spirit.

We are told that a people of true Christians would form the most perfect society imaginable. I see in this supposition only one great difficulty: that a society of true Christians would not be a society of men.

I say further that such a society, with all its perfection, would be neither the strongest nor the most lasting: the very fact that it was perfect would rob it of its bond of union; the flaw that would destroy it would lie in its very perfection.

Every one would do his duty; the people would be law-abiding, the rulers just and temperate; the magistrates upright and incorruptible; the soldiers would scorn death; there would be neither vanity nor luxury. So far, so good; but let us hear more.

Christianity as a religion is entirely spiritual, occupied solely with heavenly things; the country of the Christian is not of this world. He does his duty, indeed, but does it with profound indifference to the good or ill success of his cares. Provided he has nothing to reproach himself with, it matters little to him whether things go well or ill here on earth. If the State is prosperous, he hardly dares to share in the public happiness, for fear he may grow proud of his country's glory; if the State is languishing, he blesses the hand of God that is hard upon His people.

For the State to be peaceable and for harmony to be maintained, all the citizens without exception would have to be good Christians; if by ill hap there should be a single self-seeker or hypocrite, a Catiline or a Cromwell, for instance, he would certainly get the better of his pious compatriots. Christian charity does not readily allow a man to think hardly of his neighbours. As soon as, by some trick, he has discovered the art of imposing on them and getting hold of a share in the public authority, you have a man established in dignity; it is the will of God that he be respected: very soon you have a power; it is God's will that it be obeyed: and if the power is abused by him who wields it, it is the scourge wherewith God punishes His children. There would be scruples about driving out the usurper: public tranquillity would have to be disturbed, violence would have to be employed, and blood spilt; all this accords ill with Christian meekness; and after all, in this vale of sorrows, what does it matter whether we are free men or serfs? The essential thing is to get to heaven, and resignation is only an additional means of doing so.

If war breaks out with another State, the citizens march readily out to battle; not one of them thinks of flight; they do their duty, but they have no passion for victory; they know better how to die than how to conquer. What does it matter whether they win or lose? Does not providence know better than they what is meet for them? Only think to what account a proud, impetuous, and passionate enemy could turn their stoicism! Set over against them those generous peoples who were devoured by ardent love of glory and of their country, imagine your Christian republic face to face with Sparta or Rome: the pious Christians will be beaten, crushed, and destroyed, before they know where they are, or will owe their safety only to the contempt their enemy will conceive for them. It was to my mind a fine oath that was taken by the soldiers of Fabius, who swore, not to conquer or die, but to come back victorious – and kept their oath. Christians would never have taken such an oath; they would have looked on it as tempting God.

But I am mistaken in speaking of a Christian republic; the terms are mutually exclusive. Christianity preaches only servitude and dependence. Its spirit is so favourable to tyranny that it always profits by such a regime. True Christians are made to be slaves, and they know it and do not much mind: this short life counts for too little in their eyes.

I shall be told that Christian troops are excellent. I deny it. Show me an instance. For my part, I know of no Christian troops. I shall be told of the Crusades. Without disputing the valour of the Crusaders, I answer that, so far from being Christians, they were the priests' soldiery, citizens of the Church. They fought for their spiritual country, which the Church had, somehow or other, made temporal. Well understood, this goes back to paganism: as the Gospel sets up no national religion, a holy war is impossible among Christians.

Under the pagan emperors, the Christian soldiers were brave; every Christian writer affirms it, and I believe it: it was a case of honourable emulation of the pagan troops. As soon as the emperors were Christian, this emulation no longer existed, and, when the Cross had driven out the eagle, Roman valour wholly disappeared.

But, setting aside political considerations, let us come back to what is right, and settle our principles on this important point. The right which the social compact gives the Sovereign over the subjects does not, we have seen, exceed the limits of public expediency.* The subjects then owe the Sovereign an account of

* 'In the republic', says the Marquis d'Argenson, 'each man is perfectly free in what does not harm others.' This is the invariable limitation, which it is impossible to define more exactly. I have not been able to deny myself the pleasure of

their opinions only to such an extent as they matter to the community. Now, it matters very much to the community that each citizen should have a religion. That will make him love his duty; but the dogmas of that religion concern the State and its members only so far as they have reference to morality and to the duties which he who professes them is bound to do to others. Each man may have, over and above, what opinions he pleases, without its being the Sovereign's business to take cognizance of them; for, as the Sovereign has no authority in the other world, whatever the lot of its subjects may be in the life to come, that is not its business, provided they are good citizens in this life.

There is therefore a purely civil profession of faith of which the Sovereign should fix the articles, not exactly as religious dogmas, but as social sentiments without which a man cannot be a good citizen or a faithful subject. * While it can compel no one to believe them, it can banish from the State whoever does not believe them – it can banish him, not for impiety, but as an anti-social being, incapable of truly loving the laws and justice, and of sacrificing, at need, his life to his duty. If any one, after publicly recognizing these dogmas, behaves as if he does not believe them, let him be punished by death: he has committed the worst of all crimes, that of lying before the law.

The dogmas of civil religion ought to be few, simple, and exactly worded, without explanation or commentary. The existence of a mighty, intelligent, and beneficent Divinity, possessed of foresight and providence, the life to come, the happiness of the just, the punishment of the wicked, the sanctity of the social

occasionally quoting from this manuscript, though it is unknown to the public, in order to do honour to the memory of a good and illustrious man, who had kept even in the Ministry the heart of a good citizen, and views on the government of his country that were sane and right.

* Caesar, pleading for Catiline, tried to establish the dogma that the soul is mortal: Cato and Cicero, in refutation, did not waste time in philosophizing. They were content to show that Caesar spoke like a bad citizen, and brought forward a doctrine that would have a bad effect on the State. This, in fact, and not a problem of theology, was what the Roman senate had to judge.

contract and the laws: these are its positive dogmas. Its negative dogmas I confine to one, intolerance, which is a part of the cults we have rejected.

Those who distinguish civil from theological intolerance are, to my mind, mistaken. The two forms are inseparable. It is impossible to live at peace with those we regard as damned; to love them would be to hate God who punishes them: we positively must either reclaim or torment them. Wherever theological intolerance is admitted, it must inevitably have some civil effect;* and as soon as it has such an effect, the Sovereign is no longer Sovereign even in the temporal sphere: thenceforth priests are the real masters, and kings only their ministers.

Now that there is and can be no longer an exclusive national religion, tolerance should be given to all religions that tolerate others, so long as their dogmas contain nothing contrary to the duties of citizenship. But whoever dares to say: 'Outside the Church is no salvation,' ought to be driven from the State, unless the State is the Church, and the prince the pontiff. Such a dogma is good only in a theocratic government; in any other, it is fatal. The reason for which Henry IV is said to have embraced the Roman religion ought to make every honest man leave it, and still more any prince who knows how to reason.

* Marriage, for instance, being a civil contract, has civil effects without which society cannot even subsist. Suppose a body of clergy should claim the sole right of permitting this act, a right which every intolerant religion must of necessity claim, is it not clear that in establishing the authority of the Church in this respect, it will be destroying that of the prince, who will have thenceforth only as many subjects as the clergy choose to allow him? Being in a position to marry or not to marry people, according to their acceptance of such and such a doctrine, their admission or rejection of such and such a formula, their greater or less piety, the Church alone, by the exercise of prudence and firmness, will dispose of all inheritances, offices, and citizens, and even of the State itself, which could not subsist if it were composed entirely of bastards. But, I shall be told, there will be appeals on the ground of abuse, summonses, and decrees; the temporalities will be seized. How sad! The clergy, however little, I will not say courage, but sense it has, will take no notice and go its way; it will quietly allow appeals, summonses, decrees, and seizures, and, in the end, will remain the master. It is not, I think, a great sacrifice to give up a part, when one is sure of securing all.[1]

CHAPTER 10

Conclusion

Now that I have laid down the true principles of political right, and tried to give the State a basis of its own to rest on, I ought next to strengthen it by its external relations, which would include the law of nations, commerce, the right of war and conquest, public right, leagues, negotiations, treaties, etc. But all this forms a new subject that is far too vast for my narrow scope. I ought throughout to have kept to a more limited sphere.

Table of Geneva MS Sources of the Final Version of the Social Contract

Chapter of S.C.	Geneva MS source (where the source chapter is bracketed, the material has been much reworked in the final version)
Bk. I introduction	I ch. 1
ch. 1	I ch. 3
ch. 2	
ch. 3	(I ch. 5)
ch. 4	
ch. 5	
ch. 6	
ch. 7	I ch. 3
ch. 8	
ch. 9	I ch. 3 and ch. 5 § 2
Bk. II ch. 1	(I ch. 4)
ch. 2	none
ch. 3	none
ch. 4	I ch. 6
ch. 5	none
ch. 6	I ch. 7, II ch. 1 & ch. 4
ch. 7	II ch. 2
ch. 8	
ch. 9	II ch. 3
ch. 10	
ch. 11	II ch. 6
ch. 12	II ch. 5
Bk. III ch. 1	III ch. 1 (MS breaks off)

[Whatever source-material the MS *recto* may have contained for the rest of Bk. III and Bk. IV is lost (except that one paragraph of Bk. III, ch. 6 is in MS Bk. II, ch. 3)]

| Bk. IV ch. 8 | *verso* |

The Geneva Manuscript of the
Social Contract

[A list of the contents of the MS, and an indication of the major variations from the definitive text (referred to as 'S.C.')]

Book I

FIRST NOTIONS OF THE SOCIAL BODY

Ch. 1 *Subject of this work*

So many famous authors have treated of the maxims of Government and of the rules of civil law that there is nothing useful to say on this subject that has not already been said. But perhaps a greater degree of agreement could have been reached and the best relationships within the body politic could have been more clearly established, if its nature had first been determined more clearly. This is what I have tried to do in this book. I am not here discussing the question of the administration of that Body, but the question of its constitution. I am showing how it lives, not how it acts. I am describing its various pieces and springs, putting them in their places, getting the machine ready so that it can work. Wiser men than I will regulate its movements.

Ch. 2 *The General Society of the Human Race*
This chapter is printed as a whole at pp. 169–77 of this volume.

Ch. 3 *The Fundamental Compact*
Earlier version of S.C. Bk. I, chs. 1, 6, 7, 8, 9 (part). The major variations are as follows:
In place of para. 1 of Bk. I, ch. 6:

As soon as man's needs go beyond his faculties and the objects of his

312

desires expand and multiply, he must either remain eternally wretched, or seek to give himself a new being from which he draws the resources he no longer finds in himself. As soon as the obstacles which are harmful to our preservation become stronger, by their resistance, than the forces which each individual can employ to overcome them, the primitive state can no longer exist and the human race would perish if art did not come to the aid of nature.

In S.C. Bk. I, ch. 6, paras. 3, 4 (except the last sentence), 5, 6, 7, 8 and in ch. 7, para. 3 are not in the Geneva MS; in ch. 7, para. 5, the word 'all' and the last two sentences are not in the MS; where S.C. in ch. 7, last para., has the sentence 'This means nothing less than that he will be forced to be free; for this is the condition which, by giving each citizen to his country, secures him against all personal dependence', the MS has the following:

... But it is most important here to remember that the proper and distinctive character of this pact is that the people contracts only with itself; that is to say the people as a body, as sovereign, with the individuals who compose it, as subjects: ...

In S.C. Bk. I, ch. 8, the last para. is not in the MS; in ch. 9, paras. 1 and 5 to 8 are from this chapter of the MS, paras. 3 and 4 are from Bk. I, ch. 5 of the MS (see below), and para. 2 is absent from the MS.

Ch. 4 *What Sovereignty Consists of and What Makes It Inalienable*
(Cf. S.C. Bk. II, chs. 1 and 4, in which the material in this chapter, here given in full, is condensed and reworked.)

There is, therefore, in the State, a common force which sustains it and a general will which directs this force; the application of the one to the other constitutes sovereignty. From this it becomes clear that the sovereign is, by its nature, only a corporate entity, that it has only an abstract and collective existence, and that the idea which is attached to this word cannot be united to that of a single individual. However, as this is one of the most important propositions in the field of political right, we must try to explain it more fully.

I think I can lay down as an incontestable maxim that the general will alone can direct the forces of the State according to the aim for which it was instituted, that is the general good; for if the clashing of particular interests made the establishment of civil societies necessary, the agreement of these very interests made it possible. The common element in these different interests is what forms the social tie; and were there no point of agreement between them all, no society could exist. Now, as the will always tends to the advantage of the being who is doing the willing, as the individual will always has private interest for its object, and the general will common interest, it follows that this latter is, or should be, the only real motive force in the social body.

I agree that one may raise the question of whether some particular will might not be able to agree in all things with the general will, and consequently one may ask, supposing such a particular will *did* exist, whether there would be any drawbacks in entrusting it with complete control of the forces of the community. But, without prejudicing the answers I shall later give to this question, I can say at once that everyone must see that to substitute a particular will for the general will is superfluous when they are in agreement, and harmful when they are in opposition. It is equally clear, moreover, that such a supposition is absurd and impossible by the very nature of things; for the private interest will always tend towards partiality and the public interest towards equality.

Furthermore, if one had found, for a moment, the agreement of these two wills, one could never be sure that the agreement would last the next moment and that opposition would not spring up between them. The order of human affairs is subject to so many revolutions, and ways of thought and ways of being change with such facility that it would be rash to affirm that one would will the same things tomorrow as one does today. If the general will is less subject to this inconstancy, nothing can protect particular wills from it. So, even if the social body could say on one occasion: 'I wish now everything that a certain man wishes', it could never say, in speaking of this same man: 'and what he will wish tomorrow, I shall wish it too'. Now the general will, which must direct the State, is not that of a past time, but that of the present moment; the true character of sovereignty is that there is always agreement of time, place and effect between the direction of the general will and the use of public force; this agreement can no longer be counted on as soon as another will, whatever it may be, disposes of this force. It is true that in a well regulated State one can always infer the duration of an act of the people's will from the fact that it does not destroy it by a contrary act. But it is always in virtue of a present and tacit agreement that the earlier act can continue to have its effect. We shall subsequently see what conditions are necessary to allow us to presume of this agreement.

As in the constitution of man, the action of the soul on the body forms one of the insoluble problems of philosophy, similarly the action of the general will on the public force forms an insoluble political problem in the constitution of the State. It has been the stumbling block for all legislators. I shall explain subsequently the best means that have been used to bridge the gap, and in evaluating them I shall trust reasoning only in so far as it has been confirmed by experience. If willing and doing are the same thing for any free being, and if the will of such a being exactly measures the quantity of his strength which he employs to accomplish it, it is clear that, in everything that does not exceed public power, the State would always faithfully execute what the sovereign wanted in the manner he required, if willing was as simple an act, and action as immediate an effect of this same will in the civil body as in the human body.

But even if the link of which I am speaking could be established as well as possible, all the difficulties would not be resolved. The works of men, always less perfect than those of nature, are never so exactly in harmony with their aims. One cannot avoid in politics, any more than in mechanics, acting more weakly or less quickly and losing force or time. The general will is rarely that of all, and the public force is always smaller than the sum of particular forces; so that there is, in the springs of the State, an equivalent to the friction of machines, which one must know how to reduce to a minimum and which one must at least calculate and subtract in advance from the total force, so as to make the means to be used exactly proportional to the desired effect. But without entering into these painful researches which constitute the science of the Legislator, let us complete the task of fixing the idea of the civil state.

Ch. 5 *False Notions of the Social Bond*
(Cf. S.C. Bk. I, chs. 2, 3, 4, which cover some of the same ground more briefly.)

There are a thousand ways of gathering men together, there is only one way of uniting them. That is why I only give, in this work, one method for the formation of political societies, although in the multitude of aggregations which now exist under this name, there may not even be two which have been formed in the same way, and not even one in precisely the way I describe. But I am looking for the right and reason, and not disputing about facts. Using these guides, let us see how we must judge other paths towards civil association, as most of our writers have imagined them to be.

1. That the natural authority of the father of a family extends over his children when they are no longer weak and in need, and that, by continuing to obey him, they end up by doing from habit and gratitude what they first did by necessity, all this is not difficult to believe. The links which can unite the family are easy to see. But to suppose that when the father dies, one of his children can usurp the power his father had over everyone and exercise it over his brothers, of roughly the same age, and even over strangers, has no reason or justification. For the natural rights of age, of strength, of paternal tenderness, the duties of filial gratitude, all would simultaneously be lacking in this new order. The brothers would be stupid or unnatural to submit their childen to the yoke of a man, who, according to natural law, should give every preference to his own. There are really no ties visible here to unite the chief and the members. Force alone is active and nature is silenced.

There follow five paragraphs largely a verbatim repetition of paras. 2 to 6 of *Political Economy* (pp. 128–31 of this volume).

2. That a rich and powerful man, having acquired immense possessions in lands, should impose laws on those who want to establish themselves there, and that he should only allow them to do so on condition that they accept his supreme authority and obey all his wishes; that, I can still conceive. But how can I conceive that a treaty, which presupposes anterior rights, could be the first foundation of law? Would not this tyrannical act contain a double usurpation: that on the ownership of the land and that oh the liberty of the inhabitants?

There follow para. 3 and the greater part of para. 4 of S.C. Book I, ch. 9.

. . . The rights of a man before the state of society can go no further; and all the rest, being merely violence and usurpation against the right of nature, cannot serve as the foundation for social right.

Now when I have no more land than I need to sustain me, and enough hands to cultivate it, if I hand over any more of it, I shall be left with less than I need. What can I give to others, then, without depriving myself of my own means of subsistence? What agreement can I make with them to give them possession of what does not belong to me? As to the conditions of this agreement, it is quite clear that they are illegitimate and non-existent for those whom they subject without reserve to the will of another. For, apart from the fact that such submission is incompatible with the nature of man and that to deprive his will of all liberty is to deprive his actions of all morality, it is a vain, absurd and impossible agreement to stipulate on one side an absolute authority, and on the other an unlimited obedience. Is it not clear that one cannot commit oneself to anything towards someone of whom one has the right to demand everything? Does not this single condition, incompatible with any other, necessarily involve the nullity of the act? For how could my slave have rights against me, since everything he has belongs to me and since, his right being mine, this right of mine against myself is something totally meaningless?

3. By the laws of war, the victor, instead of killing his captives, reduces them to a state of eternal servitude; no doubt he is acting well from the point of view of his own profit. But since he only acts in this way because of the laws of war, the state of war between the conquered and himself never ends; for it can only end, as it has begun, by a free and voluntary convention. If the conquered are not all killed, this so-called mercy is not really mercy at all, since it has to be paid for by one's liberty, which alone can give value to life. As these captives are more useful to him alive than dead, he allows them to live for his interest and not for theirs. They therefore owe him nothing but obedience, and that only so long as they are forced to obey him. The moment that the enslaved people can throw off the yoke imposed by force and get rid of its master, that is to say, of its enemy, it should do so. In recovering its legitimate freedom it is

merely making use of the laws of war which remain valid so long as the violence which authorizes them continues to exist. Now how could the state of war serve as a basis for a treaty of union whose only objects are justice and peace? Can one conceive of anything more absurd than to say: 'We are united in a single body, given that we are at war with one another'? But the falsity of this so-called right of killing captives has been so fully recognized that no civilized man would now dare to exercise or claim this fantastic and barbarous right. There is not even a hired sophist who would dare to maintain it.

I say, therefore, in the first place, that as the conqueror does not have the right to kill the conquered once they have laid down their arms, he cannot base their slavery on a right which does not exist. In the second place, even if the conqueror had this right, and did not make use of it, the result could never be a civil state, but only a modified state of war.

May I add that by the word *war*, people mean public war and therefore suppose that societies already existed, even though they do not explain their origin. If private war between one man and another were meant, the result could only be a master and slaves and never a hief and citizens. To distinguish this last relationship it is always necessary to postulate some social convention which makes the people into a Body and unites the members among themselves as well as to their chief.

Such is, indeed, the true character of the civil state. A people is a people independently of its chief, and if the prince dies, there still exist, between the subjects, the bonds which maintain it as a nation. You will find nothing of the kind in the principles of tyranny. As soon as the tyrant ceases to exist, everything comes apart and falls into dust, like an oak into a heap of ashes when the fire which has destroyed it goes out.

4. Many learned men have dared to maintain that the passage of time can change a violent usurpation into a legitimate power and that mere prescription can change a usurper into a supreme magistrate and a troop of slaves into a nation. They have every authority behind them save that of reason. Far from it being the case that a long period of violence can, with the passage of time, result in a just government, it is undeniable, on the contrary, that, if a people were

mad enough willingly to grant arbitrary power to its chief, this power could not be transmitted over future generations, and that its continuation is itself able to render it illegitimate. For one cannot presume that children yet unborn will approve the extravagant acts of their fathers, nor can one make them bear the punishment of a fault they have not committed.

I know that we shall be told that, since what has no existence has no qualities, the yet unborn child has no rights, so that the parents can renounce theirs, for themselves and for him, without his having any right to complain. But to destroy such crude sophistry, all that is necessary is to distinguish the rights which the son derives solely from his father (such as the inheritance of property) from the rights which derive from nature and from his human status, such as liberty. There is no doubt that by the law of reason the father can deprive his children of the first, since he is their sole proprietor. But it is not the same with the others, which are the immediate gifts of nature and which consequently no man can despoil them of. Let us suppose that a conqueror, skilful, and jealous of the happiness of his subjects, had persuaded them that without one of their arms they would be both more peaceful and more happy; would this suffice to oblige all the children for ever after to have one of their arms cut off, to fulfil the engagements of their fathers?

As regards the tacit consent by which people try to legitimize tyranny, it is easy to see that this cannot be presumed even from the longest silence. For not merely does fear restrain individuals from protesting against a man who disposes of public force, but the people, which cannot manifest its will other than as a body, has not the power to meet and declare that will. On the contrary, the silence of the citizens provides suffcient grounds for rejecting a chief who has not been recognized; to give him authority, they must speak, and speak in full liberty. Finally, all that is said on this matter by legal experts and others who are paid for the task does not prove that the people has not the right to take back its usurped freedom; it merely shows that it is dangerous to make the attempt. It is also what must never be done when one is aware of greater evils than that of having lost freedom.

The whole of this dispute about the social pact seems to me to reduce itself to one very simple question. What can have persuaded men to unite voluntarily in a social body, unless it be their common utility? Common utility is therefore the foundation of civil society. Given this, how can one distinguish between legitimate States and forced gatherings which nothing authorizes, except by considering the object or the aim of the ones and the others? If the form of the society tends to the common good then it accords with the spirit which governed its institution. If it considers only the interest of its chiefs, then it is illegitimate by the right of reason and humanity. For even if public interest sometimes agreed with that of tyranny, this passing agreement could not suffice to authorize a Government of which it was not the principle. When Grotius denies that all power is established in favour of the governed, what he says is all too true in fact. But it is not facts, but rights that are in question. Th . only proof he gives is a curious one; he derives it from the power of a master over his slave, as if you could legitimize a fact by another fact and as if slavery itself were less iniquitous than tyranny. It was precisely the right of slavery itself that he ought to have established. It is not a question of what *is*, but of what is fitting and just; it is not a question of the power one is forced to obey, but of the power one is obliged to recognize.

Ch. 6   *The Respective Rights of the Sovereign and the Citizen*
This chapter is mostly reproduced as Bk. II, ch. 4 of S.C. with the following exceptions.
The following first paragraph of the MS preceded the first paragraph in the S.C. chapter:

If the common interest is the object of the association, it is clear that the general will must be the rule of the actions of the social Body. This is the fundamental principle which I have tried to establish. Let us see now what the empire of this will over particular wills must be and how it manifests itself to all.

In S.C. II, ch. 4, the second sentence of para. 2 and the whole of para. 3 replaced the following passage of the MS:

Everything consists in making a clear distinction between the rights which the sovereign has over the citizens and those which it must respect in them; and the duties which they have to fulfil in so far as they are subjects from the natural rights they ought to enjoy in so far as they are men. Each man alienates, certainly, by the social compact, only that part of his natural faculties, goods, and liberty whose possession is important to society.

In para. 4 the words after 'useless to the community' replace the following passage of the MS:

But one must not confuse what is fitting with what is necessary, simple duty with strict law, and what can be demanded of us with what we ought to do voluntarily.

In the last para., the words 'What more are they doing than giving back what they have received from it?' are absent from the MS.

Ch. 7 *The Need for Positive Laws*
Of this chapter only the last para. was retained in S.C., to become the last para. of Bk. II, ch. 6. The first two paras. are as follows:

These, it seems to me, are the soundest ideas one can have about the fundamental pact which is at the basis of every true Body politic. It was all the more necessary to develop these ideas because those who have treated this question, having failed to think them out, have always founded civil government on arbitrary principles which do not derive from the nature of this pact. We shall see, in what follows, the ease with which the whole political system can be deduced from those which I have just established, and how natural and luminous the consequences are. But let us complete the task of laying the foundations of our edifice.

As the social union has a determined object, as soon as it is formed one should seek to fulfil this object. So that each one can wish what he needs to do according to the engagement of the Social Contract, it is necessary that each should know what he must wish. What he must wish is the common good; what he must avoid is public harm. But, as the State has only an ideal and conventional existence, its members have no natural and common sensibility by which, through an immediate awareness, they could receive a pleasant impression of what is useful to it and a painful impression as soon as it is offended. Far from foreseeing the ills which attack it, they are rarely in time to provide the remedies when they begin to feel them. If these ills are to be avoided or cured they must be foreseen from afar. How then can particular individuals guarantee the community from ills which they can neither see nor feel till after the event? How can they procure for it benefits which they can only judge to be such from their effects? How can one make sure, moreover, that, since nature is ceaselessly calling them back to their primitive state, they will never neglect this other, artificial condition, the advantage of which is only visible in consequences which are often far distant? Even supposing them always submissive to the general will, how can this will manifest itself in all occasions? Will it always be obvious? Will private interest never obscure it with its illusions? Will the people remain continuously assembled to declare it, or will it resign the task to individuals who will be always ready to substitute their own? Finally, how will all act in agreement, what order will they establish in their affairs, what means will they have to collaborate with one another and how will they share common tasks among themselves?

The third paragraph consists of a verbatim repetition of the words from *Political Economy*: 'This difficulty, which would have seemed insurmountable . . . inconsistently with himself' (pp. 135–6 of this volume), followed by these sentences:

The laws are the unique motive force of the Body Politic; it is only through them that it feels and acts. Without the laws, the State, when it is formed, is only a body without a soul; it exists and cannot act. For it is not enough that each should submit to the general will; to follow it, one must know it. This is why legislation is necessary.

Book II

ESTABLISHMENT OF THE LAWS

Ch. 1 *End of Legislation*
A single paragraph, partly reproduced in the first paragraph of S.C. Bk. II, ch. 6.

Ch. 2 *The Legislator*
Almost the whole of S.C. Bk. II, ch. 7 is derived from this chapter of the MS, but the latter also contains the following passages, later omitted. This paragraph followed the fifth:

> It is not that it has ever been imagined that the will of one man could pass into law without the consent of the people. But how could one refuse this consent to the individual one knows to be the master and who combines within him confidence and the public force? Reasonable people can scarcely make themselves heard; weak people dare not speak: and the enforced silence of the subjects has passed for tacit approval to such an extent that since the Roman emperors, who under the name of Tribunes appropriated to themselves the rights of the people, men have dared to place above the law the will of the Prince who only derives his authority from it. But we are dealing with rights and not with abuses.

The sixth paragraph of the chapter in S.C. was not in the MS. After the seventh, the MS has the following additional four paragraphs:

> To say that once the whole people has willingly, solemnly and unforcedly submitted to a single man, then all the acts of this man's will should, by virtue of this submission, be considered as so many acts of the general will, is to utter a sophism to which I have already replied. I will add that the voluntary and supposed submission of the people is always conditional; that it gives itself not for the Prince's advantage, but for its own; that if each individual promises to obey without reserve, it is for the good of all; that the Prince, in such a case, also undertakes engagements, to which those of the people are

linked; and that even under the most absolute despotism he cannot violate his oath, without, at the same time, relieving his subjects of theirs.

If a people was stupid enough to stipulate nothing in exchange for its obedience, except for the right to command it, even then, this right would be conditional by its very nature. To explain this truth, one must take full note of the fact that those who claim that a gratuitous promise imposes a rigorous obligation on him who gives it, nevertheless distinguish carefully between purely gratuitous promises and those which contain some tacit, but obvious conditions. For in this latter case they all agree that the validity of the promises depends on the execution of the implied condition; as, when a man engages himself in the service of another, he clearly supposes that this other will feed him. Similarly, a people which chooses one or more chiefs and promises to obey them clearly supposes that they will only use the liberty which it is giving up in a manner advantageous to it. Otherwise this people would be insane and its engagements invalid. As for the same surrender extracted by force, I have already shown that it is invalid and that one is obliged to obey force only so long as one is constrained to do so.

It still remains to be discovered, therefore, whether the conditions are fulfilled, and consequently if the will of the Prince really is the general will. Of this question the people is the only judge. So the laws are like pure gold which it is impossible to denature by any operation and which the first test immediately re-establishes in its natural form. Moreover, it is contrary to the nature of the will, which has no control over itself, to engage itself for the future. One can oblige oneself to do something, but not to wish something, and there is a great difference between doing something one has promised because one has promised it and still wishing it even if one had not promised it before. Now the Law of today must not be an act of the general will of yesterday, but of that of today. We have engaged ourselves to do not what all *have* wished, but what all *now* wish. For as the resolutions of the sovereign, as sovereign, regard only itself, it is always free to change them. From which it follows that, when the Law speaks in the name of the people, it is in the name of the people as it is now and not as it used to be. The laws, although received, only have lasting authority so long as the people, being free to revoke them, nevertheless does not do so. This proves its present agreement. There is similarly no doubt that, in the case we are supposing, the public acts of will of the legitimate Prince only oblige individuals so long as the nation, having the power to assemble and freely to oppose them, gives no sign of a desire to disavow them.

These explanations show that, as the general will is the continuous bond of the Body Politic, it is never permissible for the Legislator, whatever previous authorization he may have, to act otherwise than by directing this same will through persuasion, or to prescribe anything to individuals without first having received the sanction of general consent. Otherwise he would risk destroying, by his first action, the essence of the very thing which it is desired to create, and would risk breaking the social bond whilst believing that he was strengthening society.

At the end of the chapter was added the following:

Everyone is sufficiently aware of the utility of political union to render certain opinions permanent and to maintain them through an organization and a body of doctrine. As for the contribution which religion can make to the establishment of civil society, it is also clear that it is no less useful to be able to give to the moral bond an internal force which penetrates to the very soul and is always independent of benefits and misfortunes, indeed of life itself and of all human events.

Ch. 3 *The People to be Set Up*
This chapter is the source for the most part of Bk. II, chs. 8 to 10 of S.C. Before the paragraph that is first in S.C. was this paragraph in the MS:

Although I am concerned here with matters of right and not with practical questions, I cannot avoid casting occasional glances at some practical measures which are indispensable in any good institution.

After the first sentence of para. 4 of ch. 8, the MS adds:

... In general, peoples whose strength has been sapped by a long period of slavery and by the vices which inevitably follow it, lose both the love of their country and the feeling for happiness. They console themselves for their misfortunes by imagining that things could not be better. They live together without any real unity like people assembled on the same piece of land, but separated by precipices. They are unaware of their wretchedness because ambition blinds them; no one sees the place where he really is, but only the one to which he aspires.

A people in this state is no longer capable of finding healthy institutions, because its will is no less corrupted than its constitution. It has nothing left to lose and it can no longer gain anything. Stupefied by slavery, it despises all the benefits of which it knows nothing. Civil strife can destroy it, but revolutions cannot re-establish it; as soon as its chains are broken, it falls in pieces and no longer exists. So, from this point on, it needs a master, never a liberator.

A people which is not yet corrupted can have vices latent in its dimensions which do not exist in its essential substance. May I explain this?

The remainder of para. 4 and para. 5 of ch. 8 are not in the MS, which continues with the whole of what became ch. 9 in S.C. There follows the para. that became para. 9 of Bk. III, ch. 6, and then the following paragraph:

Moreover, a fundamental rule for any society which was well constituted and legitimately governed would be that it should be easily possible to assemble all its members whenever necessary. For we shall later see that assemblies of deputies can neither represent the Body as a whole, nor receive from it sufficient powers to make laws in its name as sovereign. It follows from this that the State should confine itself to a single city at the most. If there are several, the capital will always in fact be sovereign and the others subject, and such a constitution inevitably leads to tyranny and abuses.

Between the fourth and fifth paragraphs of what became ch. 10 in S.C. there occur in the MS the following paragraphs:

At the risk of repeating ourselves occasionally, let us recapitulate the considerations which a Legislator must have in mind before undertaking the institution of a people; these considerations are important if the wasting of time and authority is to be avoided. Firstly, he must not try to change the institutions of a people which is already law-abiding and civilized. Still less should he try to re-establish institutions where people have abolished them, to revive worn-out machinery; for the force of the laws is like the savour of salt. So one can give strength to a people that never had it, but not give it back to one which has lost it. This I regard as a fundamental maxim. Agis tried to revive the discipline of Lycurgus in Sparta: the Maccabees wished to re-establish in Jerusalem the theocracy of Moses; Brutus wished to give its ancient liberty back to Rome; Rienzi later tried to do the same. They were all heroes; even the last of them at one moment in his life. They all perished in their undertakings.

Any large nation is incapable of discipline; a State which is too small lacks consistency; and even mediocrity sometimes does no more than combine the two faults.

It is also important to consider the environment. What allowed the small states of Greece to exist was the fact that they were themselves surrounded by other small states, and that, put together, they were the equivalent of a very large one, when they were united in the common interest. It is a sad position to be between two powerful neighbours which are jealous of each other; it is difficult to avoid being drawn into their quarrels and being crushed with the weaker. Any State which forms an enclave within another can count for nothing. Any State which is too large for its inhabitants, or too populous for its territory, is scarcely in a better position, unless this disproportion is accidental and some natural force can re-establish a better balance.

Finally, one must consider the circumstances; for example there is no point in speaking of rules to a people that is starving, nor of reason to fanatics; war, which silences existing laws, hardly allows new ones to be established. However, famine, fury and war do not last for ever. There is scarcely any individual or any people which does not pass through some happier period and have some time to devote to reason; this is the moment of which one must know how to take advantage.

The last paragraph of ch. 10 is not in the MS; nor are the last three sentences of the first paragraph.

Ch. 4 *The Nature of the Laws, and the Principle of Civil Justice*
This chapter is composed partly of source-material for Bk. II, ch. 6 of S.C., partly of material later omitted. After the material of paras. 2 and 3 of ch. 6 there follows:

> We have said that the Law is a public and solemn act of the general will; and since by the fundamental pact everyone is subject to this will, it is from this pact alone that every law draws its strength. But let us try to give a clearer idea of this word *law*, taken in the proper and limited sense in which it is used in this work.
>
> The matter and the form of the laws are what constitute their nature; the form is in the authority which enacts; the matter is in the thing that is enacted. This part, the only one with which the present chapter deals, seems to have been misunderstood by all those who have dealt with the question.
>
> As the thing that is enacted is necessarily related to the common good, it follows that the object of the law must be general, as is the will which dictates it. It is this double universality which makes the true character of the Law. Indeed, when a particular object has different relations with different individuals, each one having, towards this object, a will of his own, there can never be any perfectly unified general will on this individual object.

After the material of paras. 4 to 8 of ch. 6, there follows:

> The greatest advantage which results from this notion is to show us clearly the true foundations of justice and natural law. Indeed the first law, the only true fundamental law which derives immediately from the social pact, is that each one should prefer, in all things, the greatest good of all.
>
> Now specifying the actions which contribute to this greatest good, by so many particular laws, is what constitutes law in its narrow and positive sense. All that contributes to this greatest good, but which is not specified by the laws, consists of acts of civility and beneficence. The habit which disposes us to practise these acts, even to our own

disadvantage, is what we call force or virtue.

Extend this maxim to the general society of which the State gives us the idea. Protected by this society of which we are members, or by the one in which we live, our natural repugnance towards doing evil is no longer balanced in us by the fear of receiving it. We are therefore led, by nature, by habit and by reason, to treat other men approximately as we do our fellow-citizens. From this disposition, transformed into acts, are born the rules of 'reasoned' natural law, which is different from natural law properly so-called. The latter is merely founded on a true but very vague feeling and is often stifled by our love of ourselves.

It is in this way that the first clear notions of just and unjust are formed within us. For the Law is anterior to justice and not the other way round. And if the Law cannot be unjust, it is not because justice is its basis (which is not necessarily always the case) but because it is against nature for one to wish to harm oneself. To this there are no exceptions.

It is a beautiful and sublime precept to do unto others as we would be done to. But is it not evident that, far from serving as the foundation of justice, it itself needs a foundation? For what clear and solid reason have I for behaving, being myself, according to the will I would have if I were somebody else? It is also clear that this precept is subject to a thousand exceptions which have never been explained except by sophistry. Would not a judge who condemns a criminal wish to be pardoned if he was criminal himself? Where is the man who would ever wish to be refused anything? Does it follow that we should be granted everything we ask? This other axiom, *cuique suum*, on which all right of property is based, what foundation has it other than the right of property itself? And if I do not say, with Hobbes, 'everything is mine', why should I not at least recognize as mine, in the state of nature, everything which is useful to me and of which I can gain possession?

It is, then, in the fundamental and universal law of the greatest good of all, and not in the private relationships of man to man, that one must seek the true principles of the just and the unjust. There is no particular rule of justice which cannot easily be deduced from this first law. This is the case with *cuique suum*, because private property and civil liberty are the foundations of the community. This is the case with *love thy brother as thyself*, because the concern of the individual personality with the whole is the strongest bond of general society, and because the State has the highest possible degree of force and life when all our private passions are united in it. In a word, there are a thousand cases in which it is an act of justice to do harm to one's neighbour, whereas every just action, without exception, necessarily has as its rule the greatest common utility.

Ch. 5　*Division of the Laws*

In addition to the material for Bk. II, ch. 12 of S.C., there occur (between the third and fourth paragraphs of the latter):

> The laws which govern the exercise and the form of the sovereign authority in relation to individuals were called *laws of majesty* in Rome. Such was the one which prohibited appeals to the Senate from the judgments of the people, and such was the one which made the persons of the Tribunes sacred and inviolable.
>
> As for the particular laws which regulate the respective duties and rights of citizens, they are called *civil laws* as far as domestic relations and the ownership of property are concerned, and *police* in all that touches on public order and the safety of people and things.

Ch. 6　*The Various Systems of Legislation*

This is almost identical with Bk. II, ch. 11 of S.C.

Book III

POLITICAL LAWS, OR THE INSTITUTION OF GOVERNMENT

Ch. 1　*What the Government of a State Is*

What remains of this chapter, the last of the surviving part of the *recto* of the MS, is almost identical with the first two paragraphs and the beginning of the third of Bk III, ch. 1 of S.C.

. . .

Civil Religion

The first draft of this chapter (Bk. IV, ch. 8 of S.C.) is scribbled on the back of some pages of the Geneva MS. It differs in many details from the final version, but is not reproduced in this edition.

Émile Book V

Passage containing summary of the *Social Contract*.

For example, going back first of all to the state of nature, we shall examine whether men are born slaves or free, in a society or independent; whether they join together voluntarily or by force; if ever the force which joins them can constitute a permanent right, as a result of which this original force becomes binding even when another has been imposed on it, so that, ever since the power of King Nimrod, who is said to have been the first to subjugate peoples, every other power which has overthrown the original power is unjust and usurping, so that there are no legitimate kings except the descendants of Nimrod or their representatives, or if, when this original power has ended, the power which succeeds it binds us in its turn and destroys our obligation to the former power, so that we are not bound to obey except in so far as we are forced to do so and we are dispensed from obedience as soon as we are capable of resistance. Such a right, it would appear, would not add much to mere force and would be little more than a play on words.

We shall examine whether one cannot say that all illness comes from God and if it would follow from this that to send for the doctor would be a crime.

We shall further examine whether we are in conscience bound to hand over our purse to a bandit when he stops us on the highway and demands it, even if we could hide it from him; for his pistol is also a form of power.

We shall ask whether the word 'power', in this context, means something different from a power which is legitimate and which is consequently subject to the laws from which it derives.

Suppose we reject this view that might is right and admit the right of nature or the authority of the father as the foundation of society. We shall then inquire into the extent of this authority; we shall ask how it is founded in nature and if it has any other justification save the needs of the child, his weakness, and the natural love the father has for him. We shall ask whether, when the child's weakness ceases and his reason develops, he does not become the sole natural judge of what is necessary for his preservation, and consequently his own master, independent of any other

331

man, even his father; for it is even more certain that the son loves himself than that the father loves the son.

We shall ask whether, when the father is dead, the sons are obliged to obey the eldest brother, or some other person who will not have for them the natural affection of a father, and whether, from generation to generation, there will always be a single head to whom the whole family will owe obedience. And we shall ask how, if this were the case, authority could ever have become divided and by what right there could have been more than one head to govern the human race throughout the world.

But if we suppose that peoples have come into existence by their own choice, we shall then distinguish between right and fact; we shall ask whether, being thus subjected to their brothers, uncles and relations, not because they were forced, but because they so chose, this sort of society does not belong in the category of free and voluntary associations.

Turning next to the right of slavery, we shall examine whether a man can legitimately alienate himself to another without restriction, without reserve, without any kind of condition; that is to say whether he can renounce his person, his life, his reason, his very self, all the morality in his actions, and, in a word, cease to exist before his death, in spite of nature which puts him in direct charge of his own preservation and in spite of his conscience and his reason which prescribe to him what he ought to do and what he ought to avoid doing.

If we can perceive any reserve, any restriction in the act of slavery, we shall discuss whether this act does not then become a true contract in which both sides taking part, having in this respect no common superior,* remain their own judges as to the conditions of the contract and consequently remain free in this matter, having the right to break the contract as soon as they consider themselves harmed by it.

If then a slave cannot alienate himself without reserve to his master, how can a people alienate itself without reserve to its head? If a slave has the right to judge whether his master is observing the contract, how could a people not remain judge of the observance of the contract by its head?

Thus we are compelled to retrace our steps, and when we consider the meaning of this collective word 'people' we shall inquire whether some

---

* If they had one, this common superior would be none other than the sovereign; and then the right of slavery, being founded on the right of sovereignty, could not be its principle.

contract, tacit at least, is not required to set up a people, a contract prior to that which we are assuming.

Since the people is a people before it chooses a king, what made it a people, except the social contract? Therefore the social contract is the foundation of all civil society, and it is in the nature of this act that we must seek the nature of the society formed by it.

We shall inquire into the terms of this contract to see if it may not be fairly well expressed in this formula: 'Each of us puts his goods, his person and all his power in common under the supreme direction of the general will, and, in our corporate capacity, we receive each member as an indivisible part of the whole.'

Assuming this, in order to define the terms we require, we shall observe that, in place of the individual personality of each contracting party, this act of association creates a corporate and collective body composed of as many members as the assembly contains votes. This public person generally takes the name of *body politic*; it is called by its members *state* when it is passive, *sovereign* when it is active, and *power* when compared with others like itself. The members themselves take the name of *people* collectively, and severally are called *citizens*, as members of the *city* or sharers in the sovereign authority, and *subjects* as being under the same authority.

We shall note that this act of association comprises a mutual understanding on the part of the public and the individual, and that each individual, in making a contract, as we may say, with himself, is bound in a double capacity; as a member of the sovereign he is bound to the individuals, and as a member of the state to the sovereign.

We shall also note that, since no one is bound by engagements made only with himself, public deliberation, whilst competent to bind all the subjects to the sovereign, because of the two different capacities in which each of them may be regarded, cannot bind the State to itself. And this makes it clear that there neither is nor can be any other fundamental law, properly so-called, except the social contract only. This does not mean that the body politic cannot, in certain respects, enter into undertakings with others; for in relation to the foreigner it becomes a simple being or an individual.

Since the two contracting parties, i.e. each individual and the public, have no common superior to decide their differences, we will inquire if each of the two remains free to break the contract at will, that is to say to repudiate it on his side as soon as he considers himself harmed by it.

To clear up this difficulty, we shall observe that as, according to the social pact, the sovereign is only able to act through common and general resolutions, so its acts must have only general and common objects; from which it follows that an individual cannot be directly harmed by the sovereign unless all are harmed, which is impossible, for that would be to want to hurt oneself. Thus the social contract never needs any other guarantee than the public force, because the injury can only ever be caused by individuals, who are not thereby freed from their engagement, but punished for having broken it.

To decide all such questions rightly, we shall be careful to bear in mind always that the nature of the social pact is special and peculiar to itself in that the people only contracts with itself, that is to say the people as a body, as sovereign, with the individuals as subjects; this condition is essential to the construction and working of the political machine, and it alone makes legitimate, reasonable and safe, engagements which would otherwise be absurd, tyrannical and liable to the grossest abuses.

Individuals having only submitted themselves to the sovereign, and the sovereign authority being nothing other than the general will, we shall see that every man, in obeying the sovereign, only obeys himself, and how one is freer under the social pact than in the state of nature.

Having compared natural liberty with civil liberty with regard to persons, we will compare, with regard to property, the rights of private ownership with those of sovereignty, the private and the common domain. If the sovereign power rests on the rights of private property, these are the rights it must most fully respect; they are inviolable and sacred for it so long as they remain private and individual rights. However, when they are considered as common to all citizens, they are subject to the general will and this will can destroy them. Thus the sovereign has no right to touch the property of one, or several individuals, but it may legitimately take possession of the property of all, as was done in Sparta in the time of Lycurgus; whilst the abolition of debts by Solon was an unlawful deed.

Since nothing is binding on the subjects except the general will, we shall inquire how this will manifests itself, by what signs we can recognize it with certainty, what a law is, and what are the true characteristics of the law. This is a totally new subject; the term law has still to be defined.

The moment a people considers one or more of its members in

particular, this people becomes divided. A relation arises between whole and part which makes them two separate beings, of which the part is one, and the whole minus the part the other. But the whole minus a part cannot be the whole; and while this relation persists, there can be no whole, but only two unequal parts.

But when the whole people decrees for the whole people, it is considering only itself; and if a relation is then formed, it is between two aspects of the entire object, without there being any division of the whole. In that case the matter about which the decree is made is, like the decreeing will, general. We shall examine whether there is any other kind of act which may bear the name of law.

If the sovereign can only speak through laws and if the law can never have any but a general object, equally relevant to all members of the State, it follows that the sovereign never has the power to decree anything with regard to particular cases; and, as it is nevertheless important for the conservation of the State that particular cases should be dealt with, we shall inquire how this can be done.

The acts of the sovereign can only be acts of the general will, that is laws. But these must be followed by determining acts, acts of force or of government, so that these same laws can be put into execution, and these, on the other hand, can only have particular aims. So the act by which the sovereign decides that a chief shall be elected is a law; and the act by which the chief is elected, in pursuance of the law, is only an act of government.

Thus there is a third relation in which the assembled people can be considered, that is as magistrate, or executor of the law which it has made in its capacity as sovereign.*

We will inquire whether it is possible for the people to deprive itself of its right of sovereignty in order to bestow it on one man or several; for the act of election not being a law, and the people, in this act, not being itself sovereign, one cannot see how it can transfer a right which it does not possess.

As the essence of sovereignty consists in the general will, it is equally

---

* These questions and propositions are mostly taken from the *Treatise on the Social Contract*, itself taken from a larger work, undertaken without due consideration of my own powers, and long since abandoned. The short treatise I have extracted from it, and of which this is a summary, will be published separately.

hard to see how one can be sure that an individual will will always be in agreement with the general will. One should rather assume that it will often be opposed to it; for private interest always tends to preferences and public interest to equality, and even if this agreement were possible, no sovereign right could result unless it were also necessary and indestructible.

We shall inquire whether, without violating the social pact, the heads of the people, under whatever name they are chosen, can ever be anything more than officers of the people, ordered by it to execute the laws; whether these heads are not accountable to the people for their administration, and whether they are not themselves subject to the laws which it is their business to see observed.

If the people cannot alienate its supreme right, can it entrust it to others for a time? If it cannot give itself a master, can it give itself representatives? This question is important and merits discussion.

If the people can have neither sovereign nor representatives, we shall inquire how it can pass its own laws; whether it should have many laws; whether it should change them frequently; whether it is easy for a great people to be its own legislator.

Whether the Roman people was not a great people;

Whether it is a good thing that there should be great peoples.

It follows, from the preceding considerations, that there is in the State an intermediate body between subjects and sovereign, and this intermediate body, consisting of one or more members, is entrusted with the public administration, with the execution of the laws, and with the maintenance of civil and political liberty.

The members of this body are called *magistrates* or *kings*, that is to say governors. The whole body, considered in relation to the men who compose it, is called *prince*, and considered in relation to its actions is called *government*.

If we consider the action of the whole body upon itself, that is to say the relation of the whole to the whole, or of the sovereign to the State, we can compare this relation to that between the extreme terms of a continuous proportion which has government as its mean proportional. The magistrate gets from the sovereign the orders it gives the people and, when everything is reckoned in, its product or its power is of the same degree as the product or power of the citizens, who are on the one hand subjects and on the other sovereigns. None of the three terms can be altered without the proportion being instantly destroyed. If the sovereign wishes to govern, or if the prince wishes to give laws, or if the subjects refuse to obey, disorder takes the place of regularity and the State is dissolved and falls into despotism or anarchy.

Suppose the State is composed of ten thousand citizens. The sovereign can only be considered collectively and as a body; but each separate person has, as being a subject, an individual and independent existence. Thus the sovereign is to the subject as ten thousand to one, i.e. each member of the State has as his share a ten-thousandth part of the sovereign authority, although he is wholly under its control. If the people numbers a hundred thousand, the condition of the subject undergoes no change and each equally is under the whole authority of the laws, whilst his vote, being reduced to one hundred-thousandth part, has ten times less influence in drawing them up. The subject therefore remaining always a unit, the relation between him and the sovereign increases with the number of citizens. From this it follows that, the larger the State, the less the liberty.

Now, the less relation the particular wills have to the general will, that is morals and manners to laws, the more should the repressive force be increased. On the other hand, as the growth of the State gives the depositaries of the public authority more temptations and means of abusing it, the more power the government has to contain the people, the more power the sovereign should have in its turn to contain the government.

It follows from this double relation that the continuous proportion between the sovereign, the prince, and the people, is by no means an arbitrary idea but a consequence of the nature of the State. It follows further that, one of the extreme terms, viz. the people, being fixed, whenever the duplicate ratio increases or diminishes, the simple ratio does the same in its turn, which cannot happen without the middle term changing as often. From this we can draw the conclusion that there is not a single unique and absolute form of government, but that there must be as many governments differing in nature as there are States differing in size.

If, the more numerous the people, the less morals correspond to laws, we shall inquire whether, by a fairly obvious analogy, we may not also say that the more numerous the magistrates, the weaker the government.

To make this principle clearer, we will distinguish, in the person of each magistrate, three essentially different wills: first, the private will of the individual, tending only to his personal advantage; secondly, the common will of the magistrates which is relative solely to the profit of the prince and which may be called corporate will, being general in relation to the government, and particular in relation to the State, of which the government forms part; and, in the third place, the will of the people, or the sovereign will, which is both general in relation to the State regarded as a whole, and to the government regarded as a part of the whole. In a perfect act of legislation, the individual or particular will should be at zero; the corporate will belonging to the government should occupy a very subordinate position, and consequently the general and sovereign will is the guide of all the rest. On the other hand, according to the natural order, these different wills become more active in proportion as they are concentrated; the general will is always the weakest, the corporate will second, and the individual will is preferred to all; so that each one is first of all himself, then a magistrate, and then a citizen – in an order exactly the reverse of what the social system requires.

This granted, let us suppose the government is in the hands of one man. Here we have the particular and corporate wills wholly united and consequently the latter is at its highest possible degree of intensity. But as the use to which the force is put depends on this degree, and as the absolute force of the government, being always that of the people, is invariable, it follows that the most active government is that of one man.

Suppose, on the other hand, we unite the government with the legislative authority, and make the sovereign also the prince, and all the citizens so many magistrates; then the corporate will, being completely confounded with the general will, can possess no greater activity than that will, and must leave the particular will as strong as it can possibly be. Thus the government, having always the same absolute force, will be at the lowest point of its activity.

These rules are incontestable and there are other considerations which serve to confirm them. We can see, for instance, that magistrates are more active in the body to which they belong than the citizen in that to which he belongs, and that consequently the particular will has much more influence. For each magistrate is almost always charged with some governmental function, whilst each citizen, taken singly, exercises no function of sovereignty. Furthermore, the bigger the State grows, the more its real force increases, though not in direct proportion to its growth; but, the

State remaining the same, the number of magistrates may increase to any extent without the government gaining any greater real force, because it is the depositary of that of the State, which we are assuming remains constant. Thus this plurality of magistrates decreases the activity of the government, whilst its force cannot increase.

After having proved that the government grows remiss in proportion as the number of magistrates increases, and that, the more numerous the people, the greater should be the repressive force of the government, we shall conclude that the relation of the magistrates to the government should vary inversely to that of the subjects to the sovereign; that is to say, the larger the State, the more should the government be tightened, so that the number of the rulers diminish in proportion to the increase of that of the people.

In order to make this diversity of forms clearer, and to assign them their different names, we shall observe, in the first place, that the sovereign may commit the charge of the government to the whole people or to the majority of the people, so that more citizens are magistrates than are mere private individuals. This form of government is called *democracy*.

Or it may restrict the government to a small number, so that there are more private citizens than magistrates; and this is named *aristocracy*.

Lastly, it may concentrate the whole government in the hands of a single magistrate. This third form is the most usual, and is called *monarchy*, or royal government.

We shall note that all these forms, or at least the first two, admit of degree and even of very wide differences. For democracy may include the whole people or may be restricted to half. Aristocracy, in its turn, may be restricted indefinitely from half the people down to the smallest possible number. Even royalty may sometimes be shared, either between father and son, between two brothers, or in some other fashion. There were always two kings in Sparta, and the Roman Empire saw as many as eight emperors at once, without it being possible to say that the Empire was split up. There is a point at which each form of government passes into the next, and, under three comprehensive denominations, government is really susceptible of as many forms as the State has citizens.

Nor is this all. As each of these governments can, in certain aspects, be subdivided into several parts, one administered in one fashion and one in another, the combination of the three forms may result in a multitude of mixed forms, each of which admits of multiplication by all the simple forms.

There has been at all times much dispute concerning the best form of government, without consideration of the fact that each is in some cases the best, and in others the worst. For our part, if, in the different States, the number of magistrates should be in inverse ratio to the number of citizens, we shall conclude that, generally, democratic government suits small States, aristocratic government those of middle size, and monarchy great ones.

These inquiries furnish us with a clue by which we may discover what are the duties and rights of citizens, and whether they can be separated from one another; what is our country, in what does it really consist, and how can each of us ascertain whether he has a country or not?

Having thus considered every kind of civil society in itself, we shall compare them, so as to note their relations one with another; great and small, strong and weak, attacking one another, insulting one another, destroying one another; and in this perpetual action and reaction causing more misery and loss of life than if men had preserved their original freedom. We shall inquire whether too much or too little has not been accomplished in the matter of social institutions; whether individuals who are subject to law and to men, while societies preserve the independence of nature, are not exposed to the ills of both conditions without the advantages of either, and whether it would not be better to have no civil society in the world rather than to have many such societies. Is it not that mixed condition which partakes of both and secures neither?

'Per quem neutrum licet, nec tanquam in bello paratum esse, nec tanquam in pace securum.' – Seneca, *De Trang: Animi*, cap. 1.

Is it not this partial and imperfect association which gives rise to tyranny and war? And are not tyranny and war the worst scourges of humanity?

Finally we will inquire how men seek to get rid of these difficulties by means of leagues and confederations, which leave each state its own master in internal affairs, while they arm it against any unjust aggression. We will inquire how a good federal association may be established, what can make it lasting, and how far the rights of the federation may be stretched without destroying the right of sovereignty.

The Abbé de Saint-Pierre suggested an association of all the states of Europe to maintain perpetual peace among themselves.* Is this

* Since I wrote this, the reasons *for* have been set out in the extract from this *Project*; the reasons *against*, at least those which seemed to me to be solid, will be found in the collection of my writings, immediately following this same extract.

association practicable, and supposing that it were established, would it be likely to last? These inquiries lead us straight to all the questions of international law which may clear up the remaining difficulties of political law.

Finally we shall lay down the real principles of the laws of war, and we shall see why Grotius and others have only stated false principles.

NOTES

These notes are conceived on a modest scale and are not intended as an alternative to standard works of reference or as a guide to the interpretation of Rousseau's thought. They aim, primarily, at elucidating some of the more obscure references in the text.

DISCOURSE ON THE ARTS AND SCIENCES

p. 4 (1). Rousseau is referring to the thought and language of the Scholastic philosophers, for whom he shows a contempt characteristic of most eighteenth-century thinkers.

p. 6 (1). This emphasis on the hypocrisy of eighteenth-century society may be justified. But one is also tempted to see in it the beginnings of the persecution complex which was to develop in Rousseau's later years.

p. 7 (1). The exception here may well be Diderot – at that time one of Rousseau's closest friends.

p. 8 (1). The mythical Egyptian ruler, Sesostris, was reputed to have conquered the whole of the East. Some eighteenth-century linguists even tried to prove that the Chinese language was an offshoot of the Egyptian.

p. 9 (1). Tacitus gives this title to Petronius.

p. 10 (1). Rousseau is referring to Tacitus, who painted an idyllic portrait of the Germanic tribes.

(2). This is in all probability a reference to the Swiss, with whom Rousseau could identify himself, although his native Geneva was not then part of the Swiss Federation.

p. 11 (1). Lacedaemon was another name for Sparta. Rousseau's admiration for the austere Greek republic owed much to Plutarch, whose *Lives* had been one of his favourite books ever since childhood.

p. 12 (1). This 'quotation' from Socrates comes from Plato's *Apology*.

p. 16 (1). The philosopher who discovered the 'ratios in which attraction acts' was Newton. The relations of spaces traversed in equal times was the subject of Kepler's second law. Diderot and d'Alembert had both investigated the mathematical problems of curves. Malebranche had elaborated the theory of 'vision in God'. Leibniz, among others, had proposed the 'pre-established harmony' of body and mind. Fontenelle had speculated on the existence of other inhabited planets, and Réaumur, among others, had studied reproduction among insects. It was still possible in the eighteenth century, to apply the term 'philosophy' to all these diverse activities, and though one may suspect Rousseau of wishing to denigrate the scientists by coupling them with the more extreme speculative philosophers, he may well have had no such intention.

p. 17 (1). Rousseau names no names in the diatribe that follows. Certainly there had been a corruption of taste and morals in France in the first half of the eighteenth century, as well as a questioning of traditional beliefs. But among the most active questioners was his friend Diderot, and Rousseau himself was to contribute his quota of doubts. Perhaps this explains why his criticism remains so general.

(2). Whether luxury was harmful or beneficial to society was the subject of endless debate in the eighteenth century. One of its more recent and eloquent defenders had been Voltaire in his poem *Le Mondain*.

(3). As he later specifies, Rousseau is referring here, in particular, to the work of the economist, Melon.

p. 18 (1). A further reference to the Swiss fight for independence.

(2). A reference to the Dutch revolt against Spain.

p. 19 (1). Voltaire was then almost universally considered the greatest poet of the age. Rousseau admired him, though they were later to become bitter enemies. But his admiration, as can be seen from this passage, was even at this stage not unqualified.

(2). Charles ('Carle') Vanloo and Jean-Baptiste Pierre were prominent among contemporary painters.

p. 20 (1). Rousseau probably owes this anecdote, and many of those which follow, to Montaigne, of whose *Essays* he was an avid reader.

p. 22 (1). Rousseau's criticism of the educational system prevalent in his day sprang from his own experience as a tutor, and was to find expression in other writings, more particularly in *Émile*. But the things he criticizes here – the emphasis on Latin, for example – are also attacked by many contemporaries such as d'Alembert in his *Encyclopedia* article on 'College'.

(2). Montaigne.

(3). Diderot had written in his *Pensées philosophiques* that 'there are people of whom one should not say that they fear God, but that they are frightened of him'.

p. 24 (1). Louis XIV, at any rate in the early years of his reign, was a distinguished patron of the arts and sciences. The Academies of Science and Inscriptions were both founded during his reign.

p. 26 (1). Rousseau knew Berkeley's work, and is no doubt referring to it here.

(2). The first part of this statement probably refers to La Mettrie, whose outspokenly materialistic *L'homme machine* had been published in 1748. The second part may also refer to earlier views of La Mettrie, though the most famous exponent of this pantheistic view was Spinoza.

(3). Rousseau may be thinking of Diderot here, for the latter's *Lettre sur les aveugles* of 1749 had emphasized the relative nature of all moral concepts. But similar views are to be found in other writers of the time.

p. 28 (1). Cicero.

(2). Francis Bacon.

DISCOURSE ON THE ORIGIN OF INEQUALITY

p. 31 (1). Rousseau largely ignores the second half of this question, probably because he has an ambivalent attitude to the whole idea of 'natural law' itself. He does not deny that there is a natural law, and he can at times appeal to it. Yet for reasons he expresses in the *Preface*, and also in the deleted second chapter of the Social Contract (see p. 169 ff.) he is very sceptical about the attempts of the 'natural law' theorists of the seventeenth and eighteenth centuries to define and codify it. He is even more doubtful whether 'natural law' could be known to man in his 'natural' state.

p. 32 (1). On Rousseau and Geneva, see note (1) to p. 181.

p. 43 (1). The inscription read: 'Know thyself'.

p. 45 (1). The Genevan jurist, Burlamaqui was an influential writer on natural law, to whom Rousseau owed not a little. His *Principles of Natural Law* were published in 1747.

p. 50 (1). The last of these references is clearly to Hobbes. The first two are probably to two of the most influential 'natural law' theorists – Grotius and Pufendorf.

(2). This phrase is frequently quoted, but not easily interpreted. Rousseau has just been speaking of the biblical account of the origin of mankind and society. He clearly rejects this, but equally clearly, given the nature of eighteenth-century censorship, he dare not say so. Moreover, if he is putting on one side the 'facts' of the Bible, he is also going further than this; he is affirming that we do not possess factual knowledge of the nature of primitive man and must therefore use rational hypothesis instead. This indeed is what he largely does. Yet he does not totally neglect 'the facts', for he makes considerable use of travellers' accounts of primitive peoples, especially in some of his footnotes which are not reproduced in this edition (see note (1) to p. 118).

p. 54 (1). Probably a reference to Montesquieu's *Esprit des lois*, Bk. I, ch. 2.

(2). Richard Cumberland, seventeenth-century philosopher and divine.

p. 55 (1). Correal's account of his travels in the West Indies was published in 1722.

p. 60 (1). Moralists, of course, have been much divided on this matter. In his defence of the passions, Rousseau could well have been influenced by Diderot, who had written eloquently in their favour in his *Pensées philosophiques*.

p. 64 (1). Condillac, a friend of Rousseau's, and one of the most influential eighteenth-century French philosophers, had first formulated his views on the origin of language in his *Essai sur l'origine des connaissances humaines of* 1746. He frequently returned to the problem, as did other eighteenth-century thinkers, Rousseau among them.

p. 67 (1). Here, in his discussion of the formation of abstract ideas, Rousseau owes much to Locke's *Essay Concerning Human Understanding*.

p. 71 (1). Since Rousseau is often thought of as idealizing 'natural man' this statement should be underlined. There are, admittedly, other passages in his works which suggest that the state of nature is 'good'. But Rousseau's conception of virtue, when he develops it as he does, for example, in *Émile*, is almost Kantian in its emphasis on the need for the conscious adoption of a moral code which has general applicability. 'Natural' man was happy, but he was not virtuous; and virtue, for Rousseau, is of a higher order than happiness.

p. 73 (1). As he makes clear in his footnote, Rousseau makes a marked distinction between what he calls 'amour-propre' (which is perhaps better left untranslated) and 'amour de soi-même' (which may be translated as love of self): whereas the latter is little more than the instinct of self-preservation, the former (which develops with social intercourse) is the source of pride, vanity, competitiveness and similar vices. The distinction is somewhat arbitrary, since 'amour-propre' did not, and does not, necessarily have any such pejorative meaning in general usage. However, it serves Rousseau's purpose admirably in so far as it allows him to make a verbal distinction between those aspects of concern for one's own well-being which he regards as natural and of which he approves, and those which appertain to society and of which he disapproves.

p. 74 (1). Mandeville's *Fable of the Bees* (1714) set out to show that man was essentially selfish, and indeed vicious, but that the interaction of private vices resulted in public benefit. His work was very influential in the eighteenth century, even though it aroused a good deal of criticism, as it does here from Rousseau.

p. 90 (1). Rousseau is doubtless thinking here primarily of Hobbes, whose *Leviathan* contained the most influential formulation of this viewpoint.

p. 100 (1). It is interesting to note the contrast between this statement and the praise of military 'virtue' to be found in the *Discourse on the Arts and Sciences*.

(2). Among the former, Hobbes was prominent, though by no means unique. Among the latter, d'Alembert, in the Preliminary Discourse of the *Encyclopedia*, had provided a recent example.

p. 103 (1). Robert Filmer's *Patriarcha* contained the classic statement of this view. Rousseau refutes it again, briefly, in Bk. I, ch.2 of the *Social Contract*. See p. 182.

p. 105 (1). Barbeyrac was one of the more influential of the natural law theorists of the early eighteenth century and had translated the work of both Grotius and Pufendorf into French.

p. 118 (1). Strictly speaking, this is not an appendix, but a footnote to p. 60 of the *Discourse* itself. Its length, however, together with the importance of the ideas it contains, merit giving it a more prominent position.

Altogether, there were some twenty footnotes to Rousseau's text, which he indicated by the lower-case letters of the alphabet. This was originally note (i) and is sometimes referred to as such. Two other footnotes of importance for the understanding of Rousseau's thought have been included at the appropriate place in the text. The rest have been omitted, since they contribute relatively little to the understanding of Rousseau's political philosophy. Some, like note (a), which discusses an anecdote related by Herodotus, illustrate Rousseau's desire to reveal his historical erudition. Others contain detailed references to the accounts of travellers (e.g., notes (e), (f) and (j)). Some seek to support the points Rousseau is making about human or animal nature by reference to the work of contemporary scientists – in particular to Buffon's *Natural History*. In one of the longest notes, (c), Rousseau attempts to prove that man must always have been by nature a biped, and cites many cases of humans who have been brought up by wild animals. Much of the content of these notes is of interest to the student of eighteenth-century science and anthropology; but much is not sufficiently relevant to the main theme of this work for them to be reproduced in full here.

(2). The famous author in question is the eighteenth-century scientist Maupertuis, whose *Essai de philosophie morale* of 1749 had attempted to quantify happiness and had proceeded to calculations which led to the pessimistic conclusions indicated by Rousseau.

(3). In fact, the body of the *Discourse* (see note (1) to p. 71), Rousseau has been careful to make no such categorical statement. In this and other ways, the present footnote takes up a more extreme and radical position than the one he normally adopts.

DISCOURSE ON POLITICAL ECONOMY

p. 131 (1). Rousseau is probably referring to Locke's *Two Treatises of Government* and to Sidney's *Discourses Concerning Government*.

(2). The *Encylopedia* gives cross-references to the articles 'Politique' and 'Souveraineté'.

p. 132 (1). The *Encylopedia* gives a cross-reference to the article 'Droit', describing it as 'the source of this great and luminous principle of which this article is the development'. The article 'Droit naturel', by Diderot, has important affinities with the present one.

p. 134 (1). The *Encylopedia* gives, here, a further cross-reference to Droit'.

p. 135 (1). The word 'satires' is significant here. Rousseau does not take the common view of Machiavelli, but regards *The Prince* as a satire. He develops this idea in the *Social Contract*; see p. 244.

p. 150 (1). The *Encylopedia* gives a cross-reference to the article 'Education'.

THE GENERAL SOCIETY OF THE HUMAN RACE

p. 171 (1). This paragraph and the following one contain Rousseau's most explicit rejection of the view, often wrongly attributed to him, that idealizes the 'noble savage'. They do not contradict the main thesis of Part I of the *Discourse in the Origin of Inequality*. (See note (1), p. 71.)

(2). In French, *personne morale*. See note (1), p. 192 (below).

p. 172 (1). In French, *être moral*. See note (1), p. 192 (below).

(2). The sentence italicized is a quotation from Diderot's *Encyc-*

lopedia article *Droit naturel (moral)*, where it is put into the mouth of an imaginary 'violent reasoner' whose arguments Diderot goes on to counter. The word 'stifle' (Fr. *étouffer*) is also taken from the article. In later years, when Rousseau was suffering from persecution mania, he interpreted this word of Diderot's as a serious threat to himself.

p. 174 (1). The italicized passages are further quotations from Diderot's article. Note that Rousseau accepts the definition of 'general will' given by Diderot in the latter passage. It may well reflect Rousseau's own thinking at the time it was written, since he and Diderot were then close associates.

p. 175 (1). Another quotation from Diderot's article.

THE SOCIAL CONTRACT

Foreword, *p.* 180 (1). This foreword is somewhat disingenuous. *The Social Contract* was worked on for two years after the decision to abandon the larger projected *Political Institutions*, and considerably altered as a result (see pp. xlix–lii).

p. 181 (1). Geneva was not wholly a free state in Rousseau's day, being subject to the joint protection of Berne, Zürich, and France. Rousseau had forfeited his citizenship in 1728 on his conversion to Roman Catholicism, and was not readmitted until he made a personal application, including a recantation, in 1754. As a citizen he was a member of the *Conseil Général*, a body which one party among the Genevans chose to regard as sovereign, though real political power rested with the oligarchic *Petit Conseil*.

(2). This is the consecrated translation of one of Rousseau's most famous phrases, though 'man *was* born free' is arguably more accurate. Either translation fits Rousseau's general meaning, which is both historical and moral.

p. 183 (1). There is no good ground for attributing this view to Hobbes, who advocated absolute rule on the ground that it was in the interest of all.

(2). The allusion is to the theory put forward by Robert Filmer in *Patriarcha*, that the right of monarchs to rule is derived from that of Adam.

p. 192 (1). In French '*corps moral et collectif*'. The word *moral* is here used in a technical legal sense. A *corps moral* or *personne morale* is (according to this sense) a body of people, e.g. a corporation or company, that for some legal purposes functions as a single person – it may, for example, own property or be sued in the courts. Since the English word 'moral' is never used in this sense, one must find some other word; and 'corporate' seems the least objectionable despite the pleonasm of 'corporate body'.

p. 195 (1). In French *'personne morale'*. See the last note.

p. 201 (1). Rousseau is referring to those seventeenth-century political theorists, Hobbes and Pufendorf in particular (but not Locke), who had thought of sovereignty as consisting in a number of distinct rights, which must, if they are to be effective, be in the hands of the same person or body (or else, in the view of some others, need not be so). This view in turn reflects the various prerogatives attributed to the monarch under feudal law. See especially Hobbes: *Leviathan*, ch. 18.

p. 204 (1). Lycurgus was the legendary lawgiver of Sparta. Solon was a fully historical person, who drew up the Athenian law code in the early sixth century B.C. Numa and Servius were both early kings of Rome, to whom the Romans attributed many features of their religious and their political institutions respectively. Here the reference is, in the case of Servius, to the voting-groups of the various Roman assemblies, described by Rousseau at length in Bk. IV, ch. 4; in the case of Numa, to his alleged division of the Roman people into groups according to their trades. The references to Lycurgus and Solon are more obscure. Nothing in Plutarch's *Life* of either (from which Rousseau would have derived his information) seems particularly relevant.

(2). What Machiavelli means by *sette* and *partigiani* (here translated 'sections' and 'followers') can only be understood from the context, which Rousseau does not quote. This context shows that the contrast Machiavelli is making is between on the one hand those divisions in the state that arise from public controversy, and on the other hand those that arise from the provision by certain powerful citizens of favours and advantages to their own followers. It is such followers who are called *partigiani* and (collectively) *sette*.

p. 215 (1). The first written Roman law-code was drawn up by two successive boards of ten, the *'decemviri'*, in 451 and 450 B.C. During those years the decemvirs also exercised the authority of the ordinary magistracies, which were left unfilled. The board of 450 attempted to continue in power illegally in 449, and had to be forcibly overthrown.

p. 217 (1). The prophet Mohammed.

(2). William Warburton (1698–1779), Bishop of Gloucester, wrote in 1736 *The Alliance between Church and State*, a defence of the

Anglican establishment in terms of the Social Contract, and many other now forgotten works of scholarly controversy.

(3). A tradition recorded by Diogenes Laertius is that Plato was asked to legislate when the new city of Megalopolis (in Arcadia) was being founded jointly by the *Thebans* (not the Cyreneans) and the Arcadians, but refused when they unwilling to accept an equal distribution of land. The Arcadians were in fact far from rich.

(4). The laws of the various Dorian cities of Crete were similar to those of Sparta, as was already noticed in antiquity (see Plato, *Laws* book I, and Aristotle, *Politics* book II). The vice Rousseau refers to will be either homosexuality (see Aristotle, l.c.), or mendacity (as in a common ancient proverb).

p. 224 (1). The Corsicans had been in rebellion against their rulers, the republic of Genoa since 1734, and their resistance had aroused much admiration throughout Europe. Sovereignty over the island was not taken over by France until 1768, six years after the publication of the *Social Contract*.

p. 226 (1). Montesquieu.

p. 230 (1). A *continuous* (or *continued*) *proportion* is one that has the form $a : b :: b : c$. Where the variables have numbers as their domain, this may be represented as $\frac{a}{b} = \frac{b}{c}$. The *mean proportional* (a now obsolete expression) is the term b, and its value is shown by the equation $b = \sqrt{ac}$.

p. 240 (1). Montesquieu.

p. 256 (1). The Cardinal de Retz.

p. 257 (1). The '*serrar del maggior consiglio*' ('locking of the Greater Council'), the passing of the law which confined membership of the council to a hereditary patriciate, actually took place in 1297. Rousseau has confused it with the institution in 1198 of the Doge's accession oath.

(2). A writing, published in 1612, supporting the claim to suzerainty over Venice of the Holy Roman Emperors.

p. 274 (1). A leading member of the group of noblemen opposed to the government of Cardinal Mazarin in mid seventeenth-century France. Because of his popularity he was known as the 'king of the markets'.

p. 280 (1). A contemptuous term used to describe the impoverished members of the Venetian nobility, many of whom lived in the parish of St Barnabas.

(2). The Abbé de Saint-Pierre (1658–1743) published, among other political tracts, the *Discours sur la Polysynodie*, recommending that the various departments of government should be administered by councils elected from among those qualified by experience. Published in 1718, this work was taken as an attack on the ministers of the recently dead Louis XIV, and it led to the Abbé's expulsion from the Académie Française. Rousseau worked for some years after 1756 on the Abbé's manuscripts, published in 1761 an abridgement of another of his tracts, the *Projet de Paix Perpetuelle*, and prepared a similar abridgement, with comment, of the *Polysynodie*.

p. 308 (1). At the time Rousseau wrote, the Roman Catholic church did in fact use its monopoly of the right to marry in France to prevent the legal marriage of Protestants. In the first draft of this chapter, on the *verso* of the Geneva MS, Rousseau explicitly refers to this. This footnote was suppressed from most of the first edition, on last-minute instructions from Rousseau, after it had already been set up in type; but there are copies of the edition that have it.

INDEX